The Military
and Democracy

The Military and Democracy

*The Future of Civil–Military
Relations in Latin America*

Edited by

Louis W. Goodman
Johanna S.R. Mendelson
Juan Rial

Lexington Books

D.C. Heath and Company/Lexington, Massachusetts/Toronto

Library of Congress Cataloging-in-Publication Data

The Military and democracy : the future of civil-military relations in
  Latin America / edited by Louis W. Goodman, Johanna S.R. Mendelson,
  and Juan Rial.
        p.   cm.
    Includes bibliographical references.
    ISBN 0-669-21126-5 (alk. paper).—ISBN 0-669-21127-3 (alk. paper
  : pbk.)
    1. Latin Americ—Politics and government—1948–   2. Civil
  –military relations—Latin America—History—20th century.
  3. Representative government and representation—Latin America–
  –History–20th century.   4. Latin America—Military policy.
  I. Goodman, Louis Wolf.   II. Mendelson, Johanna.   III. Rial Roade,
  Juan.
  F1414.2.M537   1990   89-36112
  322'.5'098—dc20   CIP

Published simultaneously in Canada
Printed in the United States of America
Casebound International Standard Book Number: 0-669-21126-5
Paperbound International Standard Book Number: 0-669-21127-3
Library of Congress Catalog Card Number: 89-36112

The paper used in this publication meets the minimum requirements of
American National Standard for Information Sciences—Permanence of
Paper for Printed Library Materials, ANSI Z39.48-1984. ∞™

The first and last numbers below indicate year and number of printing.

89 90 91 92 8 7 6 5 4 3 2

Contents

II. The Armed Forces, Civilians, and the Perception of Threat to the Social and Political Order 91

III. Military Professionalism and the Missions of the Armed Forces 141

IV. Civil–Military Relations and the Future of Democracy in Latin America 197

Preface

This volume is the result of a project entitled "Civil-Military Relations and the Challenge of Democracy," jointly sponsored by The School of International Service of The American University in Washington, D.C., and PEITHO, Sociedad de Analisis in Montevideo, Uruguay, since late 1986. This project was initiated because of a view shared by the project directors that social scientists can play a role in creating knowledge useful for understanding the roles of both civilians and military men in Latin American politics.

In early 1987 we invited some twenty experts on civil-military relations to a planning meeting at The American University in Washington, D.C., to identify major issues for examination. The broad framework for the joint project reflected in the four sections of this volume were developed at that meeting. In addition, possible participants and chapter authors were identified and a work plan was set up. Scholars were invited to join the project as essay writers on the condition that each ask a group of civil-military relations practitioners (either military men or civilians involved in national security affairs) for advice on the development of their essays and to critique the final product.

Drafts of essays were initially presented at a meeting held in Panama City, Panama, in December 1987. Following this meeting, in May 1988, a conference including more than 50 Latin American military officers at the rank of colonel or above, including three defense ministers, was held at The American University to further critique these essays and to discuss the themes raised by the project. As of that date this was the largest privately sponsored meeting of high-ranking Latin American military officers held in the United States.

Following this meeting, plans were developed both to revise essays for the preparation of this volume and to extend the network in discussions that had been developed in the collaboration among scholars, military men, and practitioners. The result will be planned regional meetings on civil-military relations in Central America and South America. The first of these meetings was held in June, 1989, in Guatemala City, Guatemala. Through the sponsorship of the Guatemalan Ministry of Defense, its Centro de Estudios Militares and the civilian social science research institute, ASIES (Asociacion de Investigaciones y Estudios Sociales) political leaders and military officers from the region gathered to discuss the theme of civil-military relations. In particular, this conference focused on democratic transitions in several of the Central American nations and the roles civilians and the armed forces play in the process.

Through the publication of this book a wider examination of these themes is possible. While self-consciously social scientific and aiming to create new knowledge, the editors of this volume have a clear value preference for pluralist democracy. We hope that the publication of this volume will strengthen civilian and military support for this form of government in Latin America.

This project could not have been completed without the assistance of many individuals whose names are not listed among the authors of this volume. Genaro Arriagada, Rafael Bañon, Cesar Sereseres, Gabriel Marcella, Charles Moskos, Eliezer Rizzo De Olivera, Yoram Peri, Amos Perlmutter, and Alfred Stepan were among the scholars present at the project's initial planning meeting and have provided valuable assistance throughout the project. Dr. Marcella and General Fred F. Woerner, Commander in Chief of the United States Southern Command, provided valuable assistance for the organization of the December 1987 meeting in Panama City including organizing discussions among project participants and SouthCom staff. Many military men and civilians assisted project authors in development of their essays. Prominent among them were the individuals who attended the May 1988 conference in Washington, D.C.

The project also would not have been possible without the crucial roles played by staff at PEITHO and The American University. Silvana Rubino at PEITHO and Tricia Juhn of The American University served as initial coordinators assisting the project directors. Michael Gold, a doctoral student at The American University, also played a key role throughout serving as rapporteur for its meetings and as the coauthor of this volume's bibliography. Fernando Bosch provided superb translations of essays into English. Harriet Lora, Maria Gil Montero, Patricia del Carmen Loo, Elizabeth Arias, Steven Pierce, Constantine Avanatopolis, and Luis Julia also played key roles assisting the project at The American University. Dr. Norma Parker and Ms. Roma Knee, of the Office of Democratic Initiatives, USAID, Dr. Luigi Einaudi, Terry Kleinhauf, Dr. Michael Fitzpatrick, Bismark Myrick, and Col. Curtis Morris, Jr., USAF of the Office of Policy Planning and Coordination, Bureau of Inter American Affairs, U.S. Department of State provided sage advice and assistance with logistics throughout the project.

The project could neither have been begun or continued without the financial support of a number of generous donors. Primary financial support was provided by the Office of Democratic Initiatives of the United States Information Agency. Special support for the May 1987 conference was provided by the John D. and Catherine T. MacArthur Foundation, and transportation of Latin American officers to that conference was provided by the Secretary of the Army of the United States.

Louis W. Goodman
Washington, D.C.

Johanna S.R. Mendelson
Washington, D.C.

Juan Rial
Montevideo, Uruguay

The Military and Democracy: An Introduction

Louis W. Goodman

A cold war of distrust has marked relations between civilians and military men in Latin America for the past forty years. The result has been an alternation between military and civilian rulers in most countries. Following World War II, military men such as the Peruvian Manuel Odría, the Venezuelan Marcos Pérez Jiménez, the Colombian Gustavo Rojas Pinilla, and the Argentine Juan Domingo Perón held power until the election of civilian presidents. Many civilian regimes gave way to military rule in the 1960s and 1970s. The military governments that took power were often marked by fear of social chaos and Marxist subversion as well as by harsh repression of civil rights.

The 1980s have witnessed a return of civilian rule as well as growing social and economic problems.[1] It has been argued that democratic civilian rule with coherent internationalist economic policies can lead nations in Latin America and Central America toward paths of greater citizen capacity for life, liberty, and the pursuit of happiness. For this to take place, however, a new pattern of civil–military relations must be set in the region.[2]

Throughout Latin American history, military and civilian leaders have not trusted one another. Military leaders have seen civilian politicians as incompetent and self-indulgent. The frequent military ascension to power has often been motivated by a perceived need to save their nations from weak, corrupt, and undisciplined civilian leadership. For the military, the 175 years since independence from Spain has been marked by one crisis of civilian rule after another and continual heroic military salvation of the homeland.[3]

Many Latin American civilians hold a very different view of the history of their civil–military relations. Few civilians dispute that there was great social disorder following the early nineteenth-century wars of independence.[4] There is also consensus that alliances were gradually forged between economic notables and military leaders to establish a semblance of political order.[5] Within this context, rumblings for the interests of the middle and lower social groups in society began with the development of political parties and labor unions in South America in the late nineteenth-century and later in Central America and the Caribbean.[6] Civilian leaders considered that their efforts at making government responsible to the wider population had been thwarted by a self-important military that had forged an unholy alliance with local oligarchies. Although national militaries were defeated by popular uprisings in Mexico (1910–17), Bolivia (1952), and Nicaragua (1978), they were successful in suppressing "disorderly" popular groups elsewhere.

For democracy to take root in Latin America, both military men and civilian leaders must take on new roles. The hurly-burly of pluralist democracy is very different from the controlled military-oligarchy dominance of the Latin American past. Recognition that the military is one of the strongest formal institutions in societies that are in dire need of political and social coherence poses challenges to Latin American civilian leaders that are very different from those confronted by their developed-nation counterparts. In short, if new roles are not learned that permit civil–military trust and cooperation, the future of Latin American politics will continue to be chaotic. Perhaps military men will not hold formal office, but they will hold titular civilian leaders on short leashes, limiting the continued development of their nations. If new roles can be learned by Latin American civilians and military, then the complex arrangements necessary for pluralist democracy, respectful of the variety of political forces in South American and Central American nations (including military interests), may be accomplished.

The four parts of this volume set a framework for understanding how these new roles might be learned. The first part focuses on how transitions from military to civilian rule took place in the late 1970s and early 1980s. There has been a great variety of experience with these transitions, and chapter authors spell out the differences that made for successes and failures. A key to success has been the recognition by civilians that a transition from military to civilian rule is not instantaneous. Successful transitions have utilized a process of incremental rather than immediate civilian control.

In the first part, Juan Rial, in his chapter, "The Armed Forces, Civilians, and the Transition to Democracy," provides an overview and classification scheme for the military histories of the more then twenty nations of Latin America. He then discusses the various ways the region's armed forces relate to both the rest of the political system and to society in each nation. Gabriel Aguilera, in chapter 2, "Armed Forces, Democracy, and Transition in Central America," discusses the variety of national circumstances in that region. He particularly examines the problem of how the military functions in nations involved in civil war. Carina Perelli, in her essay "The Legacies of Transitions to Democracy in Argentina and Uruguay" (chapter 3), attempts to explain why the Uruguayan political system has achieved some stability and how civilians have gained increasing authority, whereas in the case of Argentina, civilian authority is much more problematic. Insights into the problems of transition in Argentina are provided by María Susana Ricci and J. Samuel Fitch in chapter 4, "Ending Military Regimes in Argentina." These authors point out that by the end of military rule in 1983, the Argentine armed forces had developed a partnership with a particular small segment of civilians, which made it difficult for rapid and complete assumption of power by civilian groups with ties to political parties. This picture of a problematic transition can be viewed in comparative context in Alfonso Yurrita's chapter (chapter 5), "The Transition from Military to Civilian Rule in Guatemala." Yurrita traces the long evolution of the Guatemalan military from its brutal engagement in civil conflict to its decision, as an institution, to allow free elections and to permit a civilian to take office. As he shows, neither the Guatemalan nor other militaries can usefully be seen as homogeneous. He concludes that one key to a transition from military to civilian rule is for men who are confident that civilian rule is in both national and institutional interests to take charge of the military institution.

The second part of this volume examines a key issue that has divided military and civilian leaders in Central and South America for the last fifty years: the perception of threat to the social and political order. One of the major problems for the establishment of democracy in the region has been that military and civilian leaders do not always agree on what constitutes a threat to the social and political order. In fact, in the 1970s, a number of military takeovers of civilian governments were prompted by civilians' carrying out what they saw as necessary peaceful politics. In the first chapter in this part (chapter 6), Carina Perelli describes how South American military men have redefined the NATO vision of communism as a threat to social order. She goes on to explain how this has become rooted in much of South American military doctrine, which, in turn, has made NATO-type civil–military relations impossible in South America. Perelli argues that this type of military doctrine is an important obstacle to shared perceptions and objectives among South American civilians and military personnel.

The difficulty of managing perceptions of threats is made particularly clear in Marcial Rubio Correa's chapter, "The Perception of the Subversive Threat in Peru" (chapter 7). Few would contest that Peruvian political and social order is threatened by the actions of the Shining Path (Sendero Luminoso) guerrilla group and that that threat must be met in some measure by physical force. However, Mr. Rubio points out how aspects of Peruvian military and political life have exacerbated this threat, in part, because of overblown perceptions of threat and inappropriate reactions.

Perception of threat and attempts to control the social and political order is also the subject of the next essay. In his chapter "The Limits of Influence" (chapter 8), Richard Millett discusses the history of U.S. involvement in Central America and the Caribbean. He explains that national and international political realities have changed so that U.S. power, exercised both directly and indirectly through local military allies, is now limited. Millett argues that democratic political means are now not only the preferred but perhaps the only effective way to deal with threats to the social and political order of the region.

The third part of this volume addresses the question of future roles for the military. There is no question that despite national institutional diversity, both South and Central American militaries see themselves functioning as professionals. The essays in this part examine the definition of military professionalism that Latin American militaries have developed for themselves and the resulting military missions that derive from those definitions. Jack Child's chapter, "Geopolitical Thinking" (chapter 9), focuses on a conflict that has been most visible in the militaries in the Southern Cone of South America, whose journals have provided a forum for debates on military professionalism for some years. The debate is over how the key role of defending nations' national security can be accomplished. One school of military thought argues that this role can be achieved only by anticipating and preparing for conflict. According to this vision, a number of influential officers argue that Latin American militaries should emphasize preparations for potential armed conflict against regional and other possible enemies. A contrary view, advocated by other influential Latin American officers, argues that a nation's security can best be defended by undertaking cooperative activities, especially with militaries of neighboring nations. Dr. Child examines this debate and suggests that new missions for Latin militaries will emphasize cooperation rather than conflict within the region.

Argentine strategist Virginia Gamba-Stonehouse also examines the evolution of military missions in her chapter, "Missions and Strategy: The Argentine Example" (chapter 10). Ms. Gamba-Stonehouse focuses on the Argentine military and argues that tasks undertaken by the military should increasingly derive from strategic thinking that is long-term and less linked to particular short-term events. Similarly, she suggests that civilian officials should be trained to communicate effectively with military strategists so that national security objectives can be achieved through strong civil–military collaboration. Although both Gamba-Stonehouse's and Child's chapters chronicle the evolution of military thinking in the Southern Cone, neither author would argue that these militaries are completely homogeneous and devoid of conflict. In fact, major cleavages exist within the Argentine military, as evidenced by the mutinies of so-called nationalist officers in 1987 and 1988 and by debates within the Brazilian military about its role in the new republic.[7]

The subject of the role of the Brazilian military in the return to democratic rule is discussed by Alexandre Barros in his chapter, "The Brazilian Military in the Late 1980s and Early 1990s: Is the Risk of Intervention Gone?" (chapter 11). The Brazilian military held power from 1964 to 1985. It created an elaborate institutional structure both for its own rule and for a transition to a civilian president. Like other Latin American militaries, Brazil's has not completely removed itself from the political arena. Dr. Barros argues that the military has played a role in the politics of Brazil's new republic and will continue to do so for the foreseeable future. He points out, however, that this role will be quite different from the intervention of the early 1960s and will likely involve not a military head of state but, rather, military influence at other levels in many areas of Brazilian politics.

The final essay on military roles (chapter 12), by Louis W. Goodman and Johanna S.R. Mendelson, discusses the possibility that the military in Latin America will take on a new mission: drug interdiction. Based on interviews with high-ranking Latin American officers, they report that these officers are concerned that if the military assumes control of narcotics trafficking, this may interfere with their ability to perform their traditional national security mission. The authors argue that this role should be played by a specially trained national gendarmerie, supplied with sufficient resources to address problems on a nation-by-nation level within a context of international cooperation. Furthermore, they argue that expansion of military missions beyond traditional roles is not desired by Latin American militaries and also increases the possibility that the military will be tempted to exercise political roles, which would undermine rather than strengthen pluralist democracy.

The fourth part of the book discusses civil–military relations in the future of democracy in Latin America. In a sense, it parallels the first part by extending the theme of transitions into the future. In his chapter, "Civil–Military Relations in a Democratic Framework" (chapter 13), Augusto Varas provides an overview of civil–military relations in the region and a basis for anticipating future civil–military relations on a country-by-country basis. Dr. Varas concludes his essay by offering an agenda of issues that must be addressed for civil–military relations in Latin America to be strengthened within a domestic context.

Adolfo Aguilar Zinser focuses on the case of Mexico in chapter 14, "Civil–Military Relations in Mexico." Mr. Aguilar points out how Mexican civil–military relations have a history and a focus quite distinct from those of other countries in the region. Mexico's political system was formed by an agreement among victorious revolutionary-military generals early in the twentieth century. Mexican politics have consistently taken into account Mexico's propinquity to the United States. These circumstances have resulted in a military that has refrained from taking power for more than seventy-five years and that has developed a doctrine of national security and a role within national politics that distinguishes Mexico from other nations in Latin America. Mr. Aguilar discusses prospects for continuation or change of these missions for the Mexican military as Mexico enters a decade in which substantial political and economic change is likely.

Constantino Urcuyo's chapter, "Civil–Military Relations in Costa Rica: Militarization or Adaptation to New Circumstances?" (chapter 15), provides a comparative context for other Latin American militaries. Costa Rica is the only Latin American country that has formally abolished its armed forces. Instead, Costa Rica's national defense is provided by a small specialized force, which is, in some part, dependent on the international context for its national security. Dr. Urcuyo examines the extent to which this arrangement is likely to survive through the twentieth century and the type of evolution one would expect. This analysis is particularly germane in light of threats to Costa Rican national security engendered by civil wars in Central America as well as the fact that the Costa Rican situation is often held up as a model for other Latin American nations.

Another model of civil–military relations is described by Felipe Aguero in chapter 16, "The Military and Democracy in Venezuela." Thirty years ago, civil–military relations in Venezuela, between dictator Marcos Pérez Jiménez and national politicians, were as fractious as those of any other Latin American nation. When Pérez Jiménez stepped down, Rómulo Betancourt was elected president and completed a term as democratically elected president, which not only changed the nature of civil–military relations in Venezuela but also laid the groundwork for democratic succession that has now lasted more than thirty years. How this came to be and prospects for other nations to learn from Venezuelan experiences are the subject of this chapter.

The book's final chapter is written by Juan Rial. Together with his chapter in part I, it directly discusses the interests of the Latin American military as an institution for sustaining democratic regimes and refraining from involvement in politics. This chapter conveys the central messages of this book: For democracy to flourish, both the military and civilians in Latin America need to learn new ways to relate to each other; it is in the interest of both civilians and the military, individually and institutionally, to seek those roles aggressively; this will likely be achieved incrementally, not instantaneously; and civil–military relations may vary dramatically— both regionally, between Central and South America, and on a nation-by-nation basis.

Notes

1. National data reported by the Inter-American Development Bank in its annual report *Economic and Social Progress in Latin America* (Washington, D.C., 1987) clearly show that economic growth has slowed dramatically in the 1980s, in some nations rolling back domestic product per capita to pre-1970 levels. This economic slowdown, though brewing during military rule, has forced many civilian governments to launch severe economic austerity measures, disappointing those who had hoped for state action to improve social welfare and to diminish wealth inequality. This problem has been exacerbated by a situation of massive external indebtedness, causing most Latin American nations to remit scarce surpluses to international creditors rather than using them to attend to domestic problems. Richard E. Feinberg and Ricardo Ffrench-Davis's edited volume *Development and External Debt in Latin America* (Notre Dame, Ind.: University of Notre Dame Press, 1988) provides up-to-date discussions of external dimensions of this problem; Hernando de Soto's *El Otro Sendero* (Lima, Peru: Editorial El Barranco, 1986) has provoked wide controversy about how overwhelmed and underfunded domestic agencies might help private citizens improve their situations. In addition, old problems such as rural-to-urban migration and population growth and new problems such as narcotics trafficking have made the challanges confronting Latin American leaders particularly daunting.

2. For a selection of key works on past civil–military relations in the region, see Abraham F. Lowenthal and J. Samuel Fitch, eds., *Armies and Politics in Latin America* (New York: Holmes and Meier, 1986). Outstanding recent works on civil–military relations in the region, all with a focus on South America, include Alfred Stepan, *Rethinking Military Politics* (Princeton, N.J.: Princeton University Press, 1988); Rosendo Fraga, *Ejercito: Del Escarnio al Poder* (Buenos Aires: Planeta, 1988); and Alain Rouquié, *The Military and the State in Latin America* (Berkeley: University of California Press, 1987). A more complete list is contained in the bibliography prepared by Michael Gold and Juan Rial for this volume.

3. The military as national savior is best articulated through military oral histories and ceremonial addresses. In the early 1960s, Edwin Lieuwin, in *Arms and Politics in Latin America* (New York: Praeger, 1964), and John J. Johnson, in *The Military and Society in. Latin America* (Stanford, Calif.: Stanford University Press, 1964), described the historical evolution of Latin American armed forces since independence.

4. A synthetic discussion of conditions in postindependence Latin America can be found in most histories of the region; see, for example, part 6 of Robert Jones Shafer, *A History of Latin America* (Lexington, Mass.: D.C. Heath, 1978), entitled "Political Instability and Minimal Social Change (Independence to the 1880s)." The novel *Life in the Argentine Republic in the Days of the Tyrants: Or Civilization and Barbarism* (New York: Hafner, 1960), by Argentine philosopher-politician Domingo F. Sarmiento, provides a striking fictionalized description of the disorder in the countryside of postindependence Argentina.

5. This is discussed, for example, in Lieuwen, *Arms and Politics in Latin America*, ch. 1, and in Johnson, *The Military and Society in Latin America*, chs. 1–3.

6. See David Collier and Ruth Berins Collier, *Shaping the Political Agenda*

(Berkeley, Calif.: University of California Press, 1989) for a comparative historical perspective on the evolution of national political systems in Latin America and the role of labor unions in shaping their agendas. For a comparative analysis of the evolution of Latin American political systems, see Guillermo O'Donnell, Philippe Schmitter, and Lawrence Whitehead, eds., *Transitions from Authoritarian Rule: Prospects for Democracy* (Baltimore: Johns Hopkins University Press, 1986).

7. The evolution of the split between "professionals" and "nationalists" in the Argentine armed forces is discussed in Fraga, *Ejercito*. The debates within the Brazilian military, particularly differences between the intelligence system and other elements, are examined in Stepan, *Rethinking Military Politics*.

Part I
The Armed Forces, Civilians, and the Transition to Democracy

1

The Armed Forces and the Question of Democracy in Latin America

Juan Rial

The Armed Forces of Latin America or of the Latin Americas?

The term *Latin America* is broadly used in social science literature, in the press, and in everyday discourse. As a result, it is difficult to get beyond very basic and weak generalizations when one refers to the group of countries that fall under that label. A first point to be made when discussing the subject of civil–military relations in Latin America is whether an analysis of that group of countries, taken as a unit, makes sense.

For most U.S. and Western European scholars, for their political groups, and for the members of their armed forces and related agencies, there is a "reality" behind the term *Latin America*. In this reality, Latin America is a region with the same predominant languages (Spanish and Portuguese), the same cultural traditions (for example, Catholicism), the same "nonmodern" cultural norms (for example, *machismo*), and unstable political organization. It is a region in which authoritarian manifestations prevail and personalism is imposed through *caudillismo* and clientelistic relationships.

Although this stereotype of Latin America does not greatly aid the understanding of phenomena occurring in the area, it does have practical consequences. For U.S. academia and society, Latin America exists and can (we might say *must*) be treated as a unit. In fact, many of the decisions made by the U.S. political class involving the region or various countries of the region are based on this vision.

The same treatment of the region as a unit exists on the part of Latin Americans, although here it takes on another nature. It expresses the desire for the existence of unity, even though, in daily life, such unity has not actually materialized.

The effects of considering Latin America as a unit in terms of the military take a broader scope through the idea of pan-Americanism, which includes the United States and Latin America in an asymmetric relationship.¹ The operational consequences of pan-Americanism, at the military level, were the signing of the Rio de Janeiro Inter-American Reciprocal Assistance Treaty in 1942 and the subsequent creation of the Inter-American Defense Board, the Inter-American Defense College and recently, the holding of periodic conferences of the armed services of the Americas.

The myth of Latin America exists, and its unifying effects are so strong that they erase local particularities. A first point to be taken into account in studying civil–military relationships in Latin America is the existence of those differences between the states and the societies that comprise the region.

All Latin American nations have in common the presence of a preeminent state. Historically, the state has tried to mold societies—many of which were created together with the state, while others were only somewhat integrated. Localism and regionalism predominated. The building of the nation was generally undertaken more quickly than the formation of the state. In any event, today, with a few exceptions, this process has peaked.² The results are not the same in all nations of the region, however. In some cases, the process was carried out in empty spaces, with new populations; in others, it was imposed on indigenous populations, without integration. On some occasions, it has been the work of a primarily civilian elite; on others, it has been that of a mixed elite, with the participation of armed caudillos and their men, together with noteworthy urban leaders. Many countries have created their own nation and state. These entities may not be all-encompassing, however, in that they exclude not only territories but also important segments of society.

The peculiarities of the construction of each state and the different traits of each society in which they are inserted must be taken into account for a study of the political role of the armed forces in Latin America. A rapid review of the origins of some of the existing armed forces will illustrate my position.

The Mexican case cannot be compared to any other in Latin America. The Mexican armed forces emerged as part of the triumphant movement following the revolution that began in 1910. The consolidation of the Partido Revolucionario Institucional (PRI) resulted in the military's assuming the capacity of armed forces at the service of a dominating party.

There are two other cases in which the armed forces arose from a postindependence revolutionary movement: Cuba and, more recently, Nicaragua. However, the differences in ideological references, as compared to the Mexican case, indicate that there are two realities requiring specific analyses.

In Cuba and Nicaragua, the subject of civil–military relations maintains a low profile. In each case, the armed forces are dependent on a dominating party, the Cuban Communist party (PCC) in Cuba and the Sandinista National Liberation Front (FSLN) in Nicaragua. At the same time, the military command is part of the political leadership, though under a model very different from that of the Soviets and Eastern Europeans.[3] And, more important for us, they are cases in which liberal democracy is not part of the founding myth of the states. Democratic-liberal forms were specifically rejected in Cuba and qualified and restricted in Nicaragua. In both countries, Marxist ideology (both explicit and implicit) predominates. For the same reason, these two armed forces lack contacts with their counterparts in Latin America and with those of the United States.

Some countries in Central America and the Caribbean had the active presence of U.S. military forces at the beginning of the twentieth century. When U.S. forces departed, they left in their place new bodies created during the period of occupation: armies or national guards constituting the armed forces of Cuba, Haiti, Nicaragua, Panama, and the Dominican Republic. Subsequent history makes it impossible, for our purposes, to deal with these cases as a group. We have already seen that in Cuba and Nicaragua, the forces emerging from the occupation were destroyed by armed revolutionary movements. In the Dominican Republic, the same process was about to take place in 1964. Renewed U.S. military intervention avoided a similar outcome, but the armed forces had to be reestablished.

In Haiti under Duvalier, the armed forces ceded their preeminence to a paramilitary organization, the "Ton-ton Macoutes." The fall of "Baby Doc" in 1986 brought to the foreground an army that is now going through a period of accelerated reconstruction as it attempts to incorporate professional guidelines.

In Panama, the institution designed by the United States continues to exist: the ex-National Guard, which today is the Defense Force.[4] It includes specialized services and professional officers, who increasingly attend professional schools in other American countries. To this end, it has become "politicized"; it has created its own corporative foundations (although still very much shaded by the *caudillismo* of the chiefs) as a national basis. It has also become a support for populist politics, which has led it to cyclical confrontations with its creators.

The military corporations of these Central American and Caribbean countries are not associated with a founding national myth. The patrimonial, predatory nature of these military corps have made them increasingly indefensible from an ideological standpoint. In confrontations with opposing military forces that have strong ideological cohesion, they not only have suffered military defeats but also, in some cases, have been destroyed. In other cases, they had to undertake profound changes, such as in the Dominican Republic in 1965. Another case is that of the ex-National Guard in Panama, which assumed anti–United States leadership under Torrijos and was subsequently continued by General Noriega. In Panama, recovery of the Canal implied a substantially protagonist role for the Defense Force, which identified with its leaders (Torrijos first and later Noriega). This provided a founding myth for the corporation that totally escaped the initial U.S. mold.

In Central America, Guatemala, El Salvador, and Honduras have military forces whose origins are in some way connected to the colonial past.[5] Two of these countries are living in a situation of civil war. The war is apparently entrenched in favor of the armed forces in Guatemala, where a return to a democratic regime is being tried.[6] In El Salvador, the conflict continues without a foreseeable resolution. And Honduras is part of the conflict centered in Nicaragua. Although international alignments would permit a group study of these cases in Central America, the local differences warrant a careful, country-by-country analysis.

In Guatemala, the deep social division based on racial differences has made it possible to better manipulate control of the population than in neighboring El Salvador, where the campesino rebellions, as that in 1932, have historically posed a conflict centered on the opposition of classes.

Finally, also in Central America, is Costa Rica, the famous country that "abolished" the armed forces in 1949, following a civil war, and created a police force under the title Public Security Force, with a nonprofessional, elective command. The "abolition" of the armed forces did not imply the destruction of any professional force,[7] for the simple reason that there never was one.[8] Although the current international conflict in the area has tended to "militarize" Costa Rica again—a prospect resisted by the majority of the elites in that country and by almost all those of their Central American neighbors—it is still an exceptional case whose relevance goes beyond the Latin American sphere.[9]

In South America, the origin of the majority of the armed corps goes back either to the struggle for independence or directly to the colonial force. The Hispanic countries are in the first category, although there are marked differences among them. Brazil is in the second category. Although, in all cases, the current armed forces do not maintain much continuity with their origins, given the professional changes undertaken since the end of the nineteenth century, this past allows them to identify themselves as a part of the process of construction of their states and, therefore, as guardians of the nation.

The Venezuelan armed forces took quite some time to modernize. The process began after the fall of the old patrimonial Andean caudillos. In 1935, the last of the Andeans was deposed by the army. Afterward, the corporation reestablished the military academies; thus, a professional officer corps was created. Its nucleus was composed of the sons of the old Andean caudillos. While this process was taking place, a coup d'etat produced a new dictatorship. The transition from that dictatorship institutionalized what Bigler has termed the oldest case of a civil–military relationship within a classical democratic-liberal framework in Latin America.[10] I might add, however, that for this to happen, the democratic-liberal framework itself had to be given a new, extended meaning: Certain spheres of military autonomy had to be preserved within the framework.

Colombia, where the armed forces accept the supremacy of civil power, has specific problems that derive from a lack of national integration. The constant reproduction of rural violence[11] gives a permanent, central role to the military forces, who are always at the borderline of active intervention in political decisions.[12]

The countries in the heart of Andean America share a lack of national integration, associated primarily with the continuing problem of the indigenous population in Ecuador and Peru and the disintegration between regions in Bolivia. For the armed forces in these territories, these problems were and are relevant. In the three cases, because of the fear of indigenous uprisings, the mestizo and white elites did not lead the independence process during the nineteenth century. This process was ensured by the presence of troops from the northern and southern part of the continent. Subsequent events have posed very different problems for the armed forces of each of these countries, however.

In Peru, indigenous masses that are not fully incorporated as citizens and are under the effect of an agitation movement promoted by intermediary social groups (mestizos) today pose the chief problem of stability under the democratic regime. Peru is the only Latin American example in which the armed forces were a chief protagonist, rather than an opponent, in the modernization process.[13] The Peruvian case could be compared to that of Guatemala, where the armed forces also backed the modernization process and then were confronted by an insurrection of the indigenous base, directed by mestizos (*cholos* or Ladinos).

In Peru, the modernization process at the end of the 1960s was promoted by a state controlled by the military. In Bolivia, the case is the reverse: "Modernization from below" had the armed forces as victim, with their disbanding following the 1952 revolution. Their reconstruction was undertaken on a professional basis, with the support of the United States.[14]

Ecuador is an intermediate case. The armed forces' modernization projects, although important, did not go so far as to reformulate the country's structure.[15] However, neither have they had to confront a revolutionary process based on agitation of an indigenous population that lacks effective status as citizens.

In sum, in the heart of Andean America, the social situations of the three countries establish very different conditions for the relationships between the armed forces and their governments and political regimes, as compared to other zones in the region.

The countries of the Southern Cone (Argentina, Chile, and Uruguay), all with high degrees of modernization, appear to be much more homogeneous in their social makeup. In each country, the urban population predominates, with significant middle classes. In political terms, the differences are marked, thereby changing the framework of political action for each of the armed corps of these countries. In Chile and Uruguay, political parties ensured the stability of democratic regimes through the beginning of the 1970s. At the outset of the 1970s, Chile attempted to undertake a pacific, nonmilitary transition from capitalism to socialism. After three years, the armed corporation, without whose participation it would be difficult to consolidate the process, considered this experience to be a threat to the "good" order and put an end to it.

Since 1930, Argentina has not had a stable political regime. The existence of competitive democracy has not coincided with that of an *estado de derecho* (*Rechtstaat*), except episodically, and the exclusion of political actors, often accompanied by authoritarian forms, has been the prevailing rule. Between 1930 and 1986, there were only six years of the simultaneous existence of a democratic regime and an *estado de derecho*. During the same period, there were six military governments that derived from coups d'etat (1930, 1945, 1955, 1961, 1966, 1976) and, in turn, other coups within each of these processes. Military caudillos (Justo and Perón) were constitutional presidents for fifteen years. Their presidencies coincided with the exclusion of other actors or with limitations on liberal guarantees. This fact makes Argentina one of the countries most cited in connection with the political action of its armed forces, although, paradoxically, this subject is one of the least studied.

The three countries of the Southern Cone have undergone or are still undergoing a process in which the armed forces, as the chief political actor, developed a political-corporative ideological corpus in their attempt to change the "political formula"[16] as a first step in reestablishing the polity in each of the three countries.[17] Only the Chilean military corporation was relatively successful in this venture, at least until October 1988. This process was never completed in Argentina or Uruguay.

Paraguay is the only South American example of the survival of a prebendal regime based on the support of the military;[18] for that reason, it cannot be compared with other nations.

Finally, there is Brazil, which shared with the countries of the Southern Cone the new experience of a refoundational military power.[19] After culmination of the stage of corporative handling of the government by the armed forces, it is moving toward a new model of relationships between the military and the political system that is unlike that of the other countries of the Southern Cone.

If what we are seeking is to understand actual policies, a case-by-case study is essential, even if we start out with general hypotheses for the treatment of the problem.[20] From an academic point of view, however, I will set forth a general framework in order to cover the entire subject while attempting to make the least number of references to specific countries. We will first look at the socioeconomic and political orders that are common to all but two countries of the region (Cuba and Nicaragua).

It is important to note that the idea of the armed forces as an institution, which I address here, should not be confused with the concept of organization. The concept of institution is broader in scope and refers to an organization that shapes mentalities among its members. The members of an institution share values and visions of the world, myths, and rituals, many of them organized and others institutionalized by nonformalized routes and twists. What is essential for the existence of an armed force is a strong ideology, not merely the routine expression of it in the form of condensed doctrines and weak ideologies. Strong ideology is at the heart of the socialization process. It is transmitted to the members of the institution, so that even if there is change according to the circumstances (such as adoption of new organizational or technological guidelines), the institution itself remains unchanged and permanent.

Another important clarification should be made before leaving this point. Throughout this chapter, I will make generic references to the armed forces when, in many cases, the concrete application of the term would appear to cover only the chief service—that is, the army. In all the countries of Latin America, the army is a dominating influence, and in many cases, particularly in the smaller countries, it is the only one that counts. However, in spite of the fact that the other services (the navy and the air force) have myths and rituals of their own, their ideological basis and their dependence on the army is so overwhelming that the points I make about the army cover them as well.

Armed Forces, Capitalism, and the West: The Question of Democracy

Alfred Vagts has correctly sustained that an armed force rests "upon the order in which it takes form";[21] the military forces are thus the guardians of the status quo that is predominant at the time of their origin. It cannot be affirmed that the armed contingents of Latin America were born within a capitalist context. However, at the time of creation of these *caudillista* military forces as part of the independence movement at the beginning of the nineteenth century, the countries of Latin America were linked interdependently with the countries of Western Europe, which were in the process of building capitalism. The initial framework within which the region's armed forces appeared was that of the expansion of capitalism into what is called, today, the Third World. "Order" was geared to protecting the constant expansion of the market, to the detriment of precapitalist forms and "organizational neo-archaism," imposed in the uninhabited zones by the first settlers. The relationship between the new military forces and the social sectors that dominated that growing market was very close.

This was the first reference of a material nature, but there was a second, more important one of an ideological nature, in the weak, doctrinal sense. The national armies of Latin America were formed within a liberal ideological setting. Even those that did not fight a war of independence (as in the case of Brazil) adopted that political formula. Some of these military organizations were associated with oligarchic republics; others sustained monarchical regimes.

Although the armed forces in the countries of Latin America today do not maintain organizational and structural continuity with their nineteenth-century predecessors, the majority of the organizations present themselves as creators of their nation and, in many cases, of their state. This permanence is expressed through the founding myths and the ritualized traditions that affirm them.

Almost all of the professional forces of South America were created only at the end of the nineteenth century. The Central American forces were created in the twentieth century, some quite recently. Nevertheless, the majority of these armed corps trace their official history back to the period in which independence was obtained. There are two exceptional cases: Cuba and Nicaragua. In those states, the founding myth refers to the "second" independence. The ideological framework of the armed corps in these two countries is not democratic-liberal but socialist.

The armies of Latin America, with the exception of those of Cuba and Nicaragua, were created to support the construction of a social order dominated by market relationships. The armies of Cuba and Nicaragua also had the chief mission of supporting a new political system that imposed a revolutionary change in the social structure, implying the end of the capitalist regime.

In the majority of cases, the political framework existing at the time of creation was professedly liberal. Bolivia in 1952 is an example of the opposite. In other countries, a democratic situation did not exist at the time of creation or modernization of the military force (as in Brazil in 1889, the Dominican Republic in 1964, and Uruguay in 1975). Nevertheless, in almost all Latin American countries, the desired political regime was based on liberal doctrine, at least as expressed in discourse. The armies lived with democratic governments, even if the concept of democracy put into practice was restricted and elitist (as in the so-called oligarchic republics). In that framework, problems with the military forces derived from a lack of agreement between the ruling classes and the political class, among which were the heads of the armed groups.

The primary societal reference, the market, has caused constant tensions and maladjustments within the Latin American armed forces. Latin America attained not a triumphant capitalism but, rather, forms that have been classified by some academic trends as dependent. In view of a reality perceived as unsatisfactory, the loyalty of the armed forces with respect to the capitalist socioeconomic system tends to be questioned cyclically. However, socialism, as the alternative system, has been associated with ideological tendencies contrary to the existence of the current armed corporations. As a result, the military have ended up accepting the existence of capitalism. This acceptance has not been without criticism, however.

Both liberalism and socialism have an antimilitaristic doctrinal position, but they accept the military as a necessary evil.[22] Liberals and Marxists tolerate the military corporations, given that it was the solution of a military question that made it possible to impose the doctrine they sustain in the political order. But both seek the application of the ancient maxim of Cicero: "Cedant arma togae," or, as Mao Zedong rephrased it, "The party commands the rifle."

Living with the military apparatus has been a constant concern of the ruling and political classes throughout history. A response tested by both the ruling classes and the political class, and traditionally accepted by the armed forces, has been the armed forces' alienation from society. The armed corps accept the socioeconomic framework in which their activity takes place as a given. They also accept the political order that derives from its existence.

Capitalist development pushes the military forces to strengthen that alienation. Many classical thinkers believe that societal projects that attempt to exclude war convert the military into plunderers. The capitalist system tends, intrinsically, to limit the legitimacy of armed institutions. It reduces them to a sort of security instrument or, in Janowitz's formulation, to constabulary forces.[23] Such forces must look after society by exercising violence or threats, but they lack the means for their own legitimization. In the most important armed force of the region, that of the United States, this is the prevailing model.

The predominant professional approaches of the United States, especially with regard to recruitment of personnel, tend to give the market a leading role.[24] The alienation of the military from civilian and political society is markedly reduced in this type of force. Nevertheless, there are many who doubt the efficacy of a force that is perceived virtually as a business corporation. Moskos has further elaborated his conception to allow for the possibility of a plural model. Such a model includes a military force based on institutional principles for its elite units and on professional principles for the remaining units, with diverse support services.[25] Here, the problem of the legitimacy of a force that seeks to banish itself from its own sphere reappears.

Members of the Latin American officer corps generally tend to consider only the institutional model as valid. They do not accept the idea that they are members of an organization that can be created, changed, and even "closed down." They believe that they are part of a transcendent institution, not of an organization merely with a list of personnel in hierarchical order, material and financial resources, and a job to do. For them, the primary job is the institution itself, not its incidental purpose or its use. Assuming institutional positions implies discussing the political models of all of society. This is normally what is done by the armed corporations of the "underdeveloped" or "developing" world.

Trying to get beyond capitalism has been a constant temptation for the armed forces of various nations of the Third World. For those born within that framework, however, doing so can imply the fall of the military institution and the triumph of those whom the armed forces normally consider their enemies. Keeping in mind that, as armed forces, these corporations can act only in the name of a social order that is accepted in practice, they are faced with a dilemma. They must support the capitalist system or accept the possibility of their own self-destruction. It seems very unlikely that they will be able to find another route. In cases where the armed forces constitute an established part of a state whose desired order or whose prevailing doctrinal-ideological form takes on socialist traits (as is the case in many African countries), there are attempts to get beyond the current order by other routes, which, because our subject is Latin America, will not be included here.

Acceptance varies with regard to the Western framework, if we understand as such the political-cultural references, including democratic-liberal doctrines. The armed forces are enthusiastic defenders of traditional values associated with family, private property, and religious beliefs.[26] In that sense, they affiliate themselves with the West. This affiliation does not extend to the set of political doctrines that are considered progressive.

Adherence to forms of thought derived from the Christian tradition is a constant among the armed forces of Latin America. In many countries, the military position coincides with the official state position, in that Catholicism is acknowledged as the official religion of the country. In other cases, this stand accentuates the divorce between the armed corporation and the state, particularly when there is marked secularization of the state, which is perceived to be associated with a democratic-liberal political regime. In all cases, the democratic-liberal doctrine and its implementation are perceived to favor the dissolution of traditions rooted in a natural order. This is one of the main reasons why such a doctrine is considered to be a threat to the maintenance of life-styles taken as valid pillars of an order that "must exist."

Historical processes have led to an alignment of the idea of democracy with the West, the Christian cultural tradition, and the values associated with it. The "free world" with which the armed forces of Latin America identify themselves defends democratic values. The armed forces cannot repudiate democracy; they must act in its name.

Despite the lack of confidence shown by the officers of a majority of the military forces of Latin America with regard to democracy and liberalism, they have no other alternative than to sustain democratic values, even if attempts are made to deny liberalism and to qualify democracy restrictively. The armed forces need to sustain Western democratic values. The alternative implies the possible defeat and suppression of the existing armed corporations upon denial of those values. In line with the logic (albeit perverse) that suggests that "the enemy of my enemy is my friend," it could be said that almost all of the armed forces of Latin America have a vested interest in preserving democracy as a transcendent myth. This point should be taken into account by the political classes of Latin America when they address the subject of their relations with the armed forces.

Among the members of the military forces there is a much greater questioning of liberalism and the ideas based on individual guarantees for the citizen than there ever could be with regard to the operation of representative institutions in line with the principles of the majority. Individual guarantees have been perceived as instruments utilized by organizations and interest groups that seek to "subvert order," not as guarantees for the good of individual citizens. Thus, political formulas such as "democradura" (to use Schmitter's conceptualization) find supporters within the military corporations.[27] On the other hand, the existence of elections and representative institutions tends to be less controversial. The substantial exception is with regard to the participation in the political game of those who are perceived as enemies of the prevailing system. Furthermore, with regard to institutional functioning, deliberative bodies (such as parliament) are accused of demagoguery and inefficiency.

Some members of the officer corps identify the West with older processes. They believe that today's West is the heir of Greece, Rome, and the Holy Roman Empire—the defender of Catholicism and of the so-called natural order. They believe that the Reformation introduced a deviation of that tradition by opening the door to liberalism and to the "dissolving" values introduced by the North Atlantic revolutions. These versions, which assume an integralist character (at times Catholic, at others secular),[28] do not tend to be the dominating ones, except in some of the more important armed corps—that is, those of the Southern Cone.

The combination of the Western concepts of liberalism and democracy is a complex one. Even the idea of democracy as *consosatio*, based on medieval theories (Altusius), is more acceptable than the formulation aimed at the predominance of an established majority.

In other political contexts, these problems are not linked to the legitimacy of corporations in the North Atlantic world. They are outside the institutional framework. In most of Latin America, the issue of corporative legitimacy is part of the institutional construction itself. As such, it comprises the organization that structures it.

Only rarely have the armed corporations of Latin America proposed alternatives that contest Western models. "Corrective" institutional measures are introduced when the military forces intervene in the management of everyday politics. Such measures are based on the principle of exceptionality—of the commissarial dictatorship they believe the armed forces should exercise as defenders of the nation and the state.

No social revolution has been possible without a change in the armed forces. In the majority of cases, that change implies their destruction. The norm is for the armed forces to defend the old social order, although, on occasion, they do participate, generally as leaders, in a process of reform or creation of a new socioeconomic system. Japan in the nineteenth century and Peru between 1968 and 1975 are examples.

In Latin America today, it seems unlikely that the military forces will be willing to embrace a project of social change that removes their countries from the capitalist system. At most, some armed corporations may adhere to reform projects, but the difficulty of such change is often similar to that of revolutionary change.

If this is true, the armed forces of Latin America, with the exception of Cuba and Nicaragua, will continue to act within a capitalist framework.[29] Thus, the limit of possible conscience for these corporations will lead them to sustain democratic forms[30] and, under favorable circumstances, to tolerate or even support an *estado de derecho* in which liberalism fully prevails. Provided that the military corporations do not perceive that antisystem parties can win the elections, they will respect the rules of the game of democracy. The *estado de derecho* will be supported, provided that social conflict does not reach a level that constitutes a perceivable threat for the state and for the prevailing socioeconomic system. If this were to happen—given that the armed forces act corporately and tend to think within the same paradigm—the military institution might perceive that the enemy was trying to take advantage of the liberal guarantees structured in the *estado de derecho*. Once this situation occurred, it would lead the military to the suppression, or at least the limitation, of the said guarantees.

The Armed Forces as Political Actor: Frameworks for Analysis

Normally, studies of the armed forces as a political actor have one of two visions as points of departure. Either the armed forces are a state instrument of a particular social class or stratum or they are a social or state segment that has a certain relative autonomy and its own interests.

In line with the first position, a study of the armed forces is not substantially relevant for understanding the position and attitudes they adopt as a political actor: They are mere executors. According to this position, study should be focused on their constituents, the social classes or strata. According to one variation of this position, the officers represent the interests of their social sectors of origin. According to a second variation on this theme, they are bound to defend the interests of the ruling or dominating classes. Most Marxist and neo-Marxist literature, as well as diverse functional-positivist approaches and others of a more syncretic nature, adopts this position.[31] Regarding Latin America, one of the best examples of this approach appears in the work of Nun.[32] However, Nun's ideas regarding the armed forces as representatives of the middle classes could lead to other developments (limited to stricter aspects of military and political sociology), without aspiring to constitute, in themselves, a full explanation. Analytically and intellectually, these approaches tend to ignore the importance of the armed forces as an institution. They also tend to put aside the problems stemming from the alienation of the military corporation from both civilian and political society.

The second position admits, in principle, that the armed forces are a segment separate from the body of society. Early socialization mechanisms separate the members of the armed forces (particularly the officer corps) from the rest of the members of society.[33] Specific forms of organization and socialization and, even more important, the values assumed by their members distinguish the armed forces from the rest of civilian and political society.[34] Approaches of an institutional type have markedly improved our understanding of the military forces and their political positions.[35] However, these studies were conceived with the military forces of developed countries as their chief reference. This presupposes the existence of a subordination of the armed forces to the prevailing political order. For this reason, the majority of studies regarding Third World countries—especially Latin America—begin by considering them anomalies, exceptions to the accepted Western model.

An example of this position is seen in the concept of professionaliza-tion sustained by Huntington.[36] However, his argument, does not seem to be in line with certain facts. Moreover, it would appear to be disproved by some historical cases, such as that of the Wehrmacht, in which inter-vention in politics occurred while the military force maintained a high degree of efficacy as a combat machine. It is even more troublesome if we consider that the Wehrmacht shared its activities with a totally politicized corps, the S.S., which had executor combat units (Waffen-S.S.) in addition to police and intelligence units, all of which could be considered highly politicized and with significant levels of autonomy.[37] Even a very cautious writer such as Finer, in sustaining that the armed forces are a "purposive instrument," was granting them a subordinate nature that is not assumed by any of the military forces in recent historical experience.[38]

The question of the political role of the armed forces does not imply a yes or no response. It would be more appropriate to refer to a continuum from less to more. On this point, suffice it to remember Clausewitz's famous definition of war—a very chief occupation of the armed forces of any time and place, no matter how equivocal the concept may be in reducing the political to conflict, in "vulgarizing" its content. Following this argument, the subject is relevant beyond the military forces as a corporative institution; it is important, or should be important, to society and to the political system as a whole.

The analytical frameworks adopted in Latin America tend to have that of the advanced West as their imaginary reference. There are certain paradigms, used for the study of the armed forces of Latin America—"models of thought" that are not necessarily theories in and of them-selves, many with points of contact and reiterations in their propositions.

We start with two ideal types—that of the armed forces of the ad-vanced West and that of the autonomous, professionalized forces of South America (Brazil and the countries of the Southern Cone)—as a way of orienting our work. Other intermediary types could be elaborated, but for our current purposes, we are more interested in pointing out the differ-ences between these two polar types. Table 1–1 makes it possible to visualize these ideal types.

The table summarizes diverse theoretical positions and paradigms for studying the military question. (I refer the reader to the bibliography at the end of this book for further discussion of the concept set forth here.) As can be seen, the difference between the two ideal types is radical. In the dominant model of the armed forces of the Southern Cone, the level of autonomy attained is high and the institutional reference, as well as the ideological aspects (both strong and weak, or doctrinal) tend to shape a semiclosed institution. The last form of political intervention included in

Table 1–1
Ideal Types of Armed Forces

Country	Dependent capitalist	Advanced North Atlantic
Ties to larger society	Autonomous from the state Segmented from society Self-defined as societal and state group	Instrument of social classes or strata Instrument of the state Specialized professional groups Relates to special interest groups
Self-Concept	Perception of institutional superiority Group loyalty No individualism Closed socialization alienated from civil society	Plays administrative role Has formal and informal functions Justifies institution to public Exists in public marketplace Open socialization, in contact with civil society
Professionalization	Ideological orientation Institutional or plural models	Technical orientation Plural models
Ideology	The institution serves the nation and not society	The institution serves society and cannot have its own ideology
World View	Institutionally based Soldier as politician Manichaean	Socially based Pluralist
Foundation Myths of the armed forces	The armed forces creates the nation The military is guardian of national order	The nation requires arms/or security The armed forces are citizens in uniform
Legitimacy	As the guardian of the nation the military will intervene when it is necessary	Provided for by the Constitution Actions ordered and governed by civilian authority
Doctrines	Struggle between good and evil War between the West and Marxism Third World War is being fought	Defends the West and its values Adheres to liberalism Fights small wars: counterrevolutionary, low intensity conflicts, terrorism
Forms of political intervention	Institutionally driven Information and disinformation Repression Policing of society Allied with dominant or leading groups in society Authoritarian reconstitution of society	State or socially controlled Information and disinformation Repression Serves the ruling classes Controls society under direction of State authority

the typology—under corporative control, with allies in civilian and political society—thus far has always failed in real-life situations.

Taking on projects whose ideological basis is found in a historical period predating the Enlightenment makes it difficult to obtain firm allies for a long-term enterprise. International contexts in which there is a predominance of the rationalism deriving from the Enlightenment, superimposed on postmodern cultural developments, are not favorable to such attempts. The outcome of military interventions that are geared to leading the everyday political process has been a return to the preceding order (after a period of commissarial dictatorship in which there is a marked patrolling of society). Of course, restorations are not always complete. Time leaves its mark. New political practices and new actors are incorporated and others are pushed out.

But the bases of the "original" order are restored: the market economy, plus representative democratic forms. Corporate liminality, transmitted to vast social strata, "does not permit" any other alternative. In this framework, in which we move today, the question of the relationship between the armed forces and the rest of the political system and society takes on significant relevance.

Notes

1. See John Child, *Unequal Alliance: The Interamerican Military System, 1938–1978* (Boulder, Colo.: Westview Press, 1980).

2. The national construction of Bolivia has been late in coming, and it is arguable whether it has reached its culmination. National and state formation was aborted or delayed in some of the Central American and Caribbean countries, particularly those that underwent U.S. occupation (Cuba, Haiti, the Dominican Republic, Puerto Rico, Nicaragua, and Panama).

3. See Jorge Domiguez, "The Civic Soldier in Cuba," in Catherine Kelleher, ed., *Political-Military Systems: Comparative Perspectives* (Beverly Hills, Calif.: Sage, 1974) and William M. LeoGrande, "A Bureaucratic Approach to Civil-Military Relations in Communist Political Systems: The Case of Cuba," in Dale R. Hespring and Ivan Vovyes, eds., *Civil-Military Relations in Communist Systems* (Boulder, Co.: Westview, 1978). The Soviet armed forces emerged during the postrevolutionary international civil war. The process that put the Bolsheviks in power was eminently political, not military. The political and military commands did not coincide. In Eastern Europe, the current military forces were created within the framework of the Soviet occupation following World War II. Only one force was created independently—the Yugoslavian force—because of resistance against the Wehrmacht; and it is not by chance that in that country, dissidence with the USSR, in spite of a common Communist ideology, began at an early stage.

4. See Renato Pereira, *Panamá: Fuerzas Armadas y Política* (Panamá: Nueva Universidad, 1979).

5. See Ernesto Chinchilla Aguilar, *Formación y Desarrollo del Ejército de Guatemala* (Guatemala: Editorial del Ejército, 1964).

6. See Eugene K. Keefe, "National Security" in Richard F. Nyrop, ed., *Guatemala: A Country Study* (Washington, D.C.: US Government Printing Office, 1983).

7. The Polytechnic Institute, where military officers were to be trained, was created in 1852 but subsequently disappeared. The "officers" were politicians whose task was to command armed men, not professionals in the exercise of violence.

8. See Constantino Urcuyo, "Les Forces de Securité Publique et la Politique au Costa Rica, 1960–1968" (Ph.D. diss., Université de Paris, 1978).

9. See Chapter 15, "Civil-Military Relations in Costa Rica: Militarization or Adaptation to New Circumstances?" by Constantino Urcuyo.

10. See Gene E. Bigler, "The Armed Forces and Patterns of Civil-Military Relations" in John D. Martz and J.D. Myers, eds., *Venezuela: The Democratic Experience* (New York: Praeger, 1977).

11. See Richard Maullin, *Soldiers, Guerrillas, and Politics in Colombia* (Lexington, Mass.: Lexington Books, 1973).

12. See Mark J. Ruhl, *Colombia: Armed Forces and Society* (Syracuse, N.Y.: Syracuse University Press, 1980).

13. See Alfred Stepan, *The State and Society: Peru in Comparative Perspective* (Princeton, N.J.: Princeton University Press, 1978); Cynthia McClintock and Abraham Lowenthal, eds., *The Peruvian Experiment Reconsidered* (Princeton, N.J.: Princeton University Press, 1983); and Victor Villanueva, *El CAEM y la Revolución de la Fuerza Armada* (Lima: IEP, 1972).

14. See Gary Prado Salmon, *Poder y FFAA, 1949–1982* (La Paz: Los Amigos del Libro, 1984).

15. See J. Samuel Fitch, *The Military Coup d'Etat as a Political Process: Ecuador, 1948–1966* (Baltimore: Johns Hopkins University Press, 1977).

16. This is Mosca's term; see Gaetano Mosca, *The Ruling Class*, trans. H.D. Kahn, ed. and rev. A. Livingston (New York: McGraw-Hill, 1939).

17. See Genaro Arriagada, *El Pensamiento Político de los Militares: Estudios Sobre Chile, Argentina, Brasil y Uruguay* (Santiago: CISEC, 1981); Andres Fontana, *Fuerzas Armadas, Partidos Politicos y Transicion a la Democracia en Argentina* (Buenos Aires: Estudios CEDES, 1984); Hugo Fruhling, Carlos Portales, and Augusto Varas, *Estado y Furzas Armadas* (Santiago: FLACSO, 1982); Carina Perelli, *Someter o Convencer: El Discurso Militar en el Uruguay de la Transición y la Redemocratización* (Montevideo: Ediciones de la Banda Oriental (EBO), 1987); Robert A. Potash, *The Army and Politics in Arqentina, 1928–1945: Yrigoyen to Perón* (Stanford, Calif.: Stanford University Press, 1969); Juan Rial, *Las FFAA: Soldados Políticos Garantes de la Democracia?* (Montevideo: EBO, 1986); Alain Rouquié, *Pouvoir Militaire et Societé Politique dans la Republique Argentine* (Paris: FNSP, 1978); Augusto Varas, ed., *Transicion a la Democracia: America Latina y Chile* (Ainavillo, Chile: ACHIP, 1984).

18. See Carlos Maria Lezcano, "Fuerzas Armadas en Paraguay: Situación Actual y Perspectivas," Paper presented to the Congreso Latinoamericano de Sociología, Rio de Janeiro, March 1986.

19. See Alfred Stepan, *Rethinkinq Military Politics: Brazil and the Southern Cone* (Princeton, N.J.: Princeton University Press, 1987); Edmundo Campos Coelho, *Em Busca de Identidade: O Exercito e a Politica na Sociedade Brasileira* (Rio de Janeiro: Forense Universitaria, 1976); Ana Lagda, *SNI: Como Nasceu, Como Fonciona* (Sao Paulo: Brasiliense, 1983).

20. See Louis W. Goodman, "Civil–Military Relations," *Harvard International Review* 6 (1986): 13–16.

21. See Alfred Vagts, *History of Militarism: Romance and Realities of a Profession* (New York: Norton, 1959).

22. See Sam Sarkesian, *Beyond the Battlefield: The New Military Professionalism* (New York: Pergamon Press, 1981).

23. See Morris Janowitz, *The Professional Soldier: A Social and Political Portrait* (New York: Free Press, 1960) and Morris Janowitz, *Military Institutions and Coercion in Developing Nations* (Chicago: Chicago University Press, 1977).

24. These approaches have led Charles Moskos to develop his model of an armed force governed by occupational rather than institutional criteria. See Charles Moskos, "From Institution to Occupation: Trends In Military Organization," *Armed Forces and Society* 4 (1978): 41–50.

25. See Charles Moskos and Frank Wood, *The Military—More Than Just a Job.* (Elmsford Park, N.Y.: Pergamon, 1987).

26. See Philippe Schmitter, ed., *Military Rule in Latin America* (Beverly Hills, Ca.: Sage, 1973).

27. We understand by *traditional* the perception of values and beliefs taken to be very old, associated with the continuance over time of a sociopolitical order, even if that "tradition" has been constructed as a social reality very recently.

28. See Perelli, *Someter o Convencer.*

29. Here, I do not discuss the possibility of defeat of some of the armed forces at the hands of other, opposing military corps, as may be the case in El Salvador. Even if this should happen, it would not invalidate the application of this argument to the majority of the remaining countries.

30. This is not the place to discuss the subject of the convergence of capitalism with democracy. I merely note that the form in which this subject is perceived by the military tends toward this association. And that perception, regardless of whether it is true (or whether it functions efficiently in our countries) does have practical effects. On the subject of perception, see M.R. Van Gils, ed., *The Perceived Role of the Military* (Rotterdam: Rotterdam University Press, 1971).

31. Summarized under the headings of instrumentalism, professionalism, and teleological functionalism are the diverse proposals that place the armed forces in a subordinate role with respect to agents of external power. See Samuel P. Huntington, *Political Order in Changing Societies* (New Haven, Conn.: Yale University Press, 1968); John J. Johnson, *The Military and Society in Latin America* (Stanford, Calif.: Stanford University Press, 1964); Martin C. Needler, "Political Development and Military Intervention in Latin America," *American Political Science Review*, 60 (1966): 616–26. Guillermo O'Donnell, *El Estado Burocratico-*

Autoritario, 1966–1973: Triunfos, Derrotas y Crísis (Buenos Aires: Editorial de Belgrano, 1982, among others).

32. See José Nun, "The Middle Class Military Coup," in Claudio Veliz, ed., *The Politics of Conformity in Latin America* (Oxford: Oxford University Press, 1967).

33. See Karl Demeter, *The German Officer-Corps in Society and State* (New York: Praeger, 1965); Joseph Ellis and Robert Moore, *School for Soldiers: West Point and the Profession of Arms* (London: London University Press, 1974); Samuel E. Finer, *The Man on Horseback: The Role of the Military in Politics* (London: Pall Mall Press, 1962), Morris Janowitz, *The Professional Soldier: A Social and Political Portrait* (New York: Free Press, 1960).

34. This is called the organizational/psychosocial paradigm, by Samuel Stouffer, et. al., *The American Soldier* (Princeton, N.J.: Princeton University Press, 1949) and Erving Goffman, "On the Characteristics of Total Institution: The Inmate World" in Donald Crassey, ed., *The Prison Studies in Institutional Organization and Change* (New York: Holt, Rinehart & Winston, 1961). To this line of argument, I would add the contribution of Michel Foucault, *Vigilar y Castigar* (Mexico: Siglo XXI, 1983).

35. See Samuel E. Finer, "The Men on Horseback–1974: Military Regimes," *Armed Forces and Society* 1 (1974): 5–28, and Morris Janowitz, *The Professional Soldier*, and *Military Conflict: Essays in the International Analysis of War and Peace* (Beverly Hills, Calif.: Sage, 1975).

36. Samuel P. Huntington, *The Soldier and the State: The Theory and Politics of Civil-Military Relations* (Cambridge, Mass.: Howard University Press, 1957).

37. Huntington used a circular argument: If the military forces intervene in politics, they are not professional. They are qualified as such only if they act as a "neutral instrument" in the political sphere.

38. Finer, "The Men on Horseback–1974: Military Regimes.".

2

The Armed Forces, Democracy, and Transition in Central America

Gabriel Aguilera

T he purpose of this chapter is to discuss the relationship between the military and civilians and the issue of transition toward democracy in some Central American countries. Transition entails political change. If the point of departure is an authoritarian regime, transition is the process of replacing this regime by a different one, and the goal is either a liberal-democratic regime (as conceived in the context of the Western political culture) or a revolutionary one. Some, however, contend that the goal can also be a different form of authoritarianism.[1] Of the three models of transition, the first two are relevant for Central America.

In the democratic transition model, one "departs" from autocratic regimes (illegitimate administrations, controlled by the military, that resort to repressive mechanisms to manage the civilian society) and "arrives" at legitimate, civilian-controlled governments, whose relations with the civilian societies are based on consent. The key step, in this model, is the opening of political space, including free elections, restoration of the rule of law, and conferring of power to the political forces that win the elections. This model can be used to evaluate the Salvadoran and Guatemalan processes.

In the second model, the point of departure is the same, but the new regime's legitimacy is based on a revolutionary reality—not on elections, which initially are not even held. The key aspect is the radical transformations undergone by the economic and social structure. This model applies to the Nicaraguan case.

The transition process begins with the overthrow of the old regime, usually through violent means (coup, revolution, and the like), or possibly

The author wishes to thank General Ricardo Peralta Mendez and Dr. Mario Solorzano Martinez from Guatemala, Colonel Adolfo Majano from El Salvador, and Dr. Jorge Arturo Reina from Honduras for their cooperation.

through peaceful means. Then a consolidation process develops, during which the new regime progressively strengthens its crisis-management capabilities and (in the first model) restructures the relations between civil and military powers and achieves added social consensus for transition.

During the transition period, the armed forces may oppose the process, cooperate with it, or launch it and keep it going. In other words, the existence of a military component in an authoritarian regime does not imply, per se, rejection of a democratic transition on the part of the people in uniform; indeed, there have been cases in which some military sectors have initiated and led the transition. In the revolutionary transition model, social change is often so deep that the armed forces are replaced by others of a different nature.

Once the new regime has consolidated its authority with respect to other political segments and has demonstrated its legitimacy before the political and civil society as a whole, the term *consolidation* can be used; transition would end, and the new regime, and the social model inherent to it, would be the determinant of the next period of the history of the nation where the process has taken place.

Within the scope of this chapter, this consolidation period is of utmost importance for the first of the aforementioned models of democratic transitions. We will focus on the country cases of Guatemala, El Salvador, and Honduras for comparison.

In El Salvador and Guatemala, although transition has been started, the process as such is not finished. An ongoing internal war has frozen the transition, specifically affecting the redefinition of the civil–military relationship. It also has negatively influenced other problem areas, such as human rights. In Honduras, consolidation has yet to be achieved. Though the political regime is not being challenged by any major domestic armed conflict, as in other cases, the lawfulness and legitimacy of the electoral processes are not reflected in a fully democratic operation of the regime, a fact that has also strained civil–military relations.

The Central American situation is being heavily influenced by agents and processes alien to the national dynamics of the Isthmian countries, a reality that affects each of them differently. This influence tends to be decisive in the cases of Honduras and El Salvador, and it probably erodes these countries' sovereignty and international self-determination.

This chapter assumes that the already-mentioned factors of civil war and the influence of extraregional agents and processes affect and undermine the process of transition toward democracy in all three countries. The progress of democratization is contingent on finding a solution to such problems.[2]

The Ouster Crisis: El Salvador, Guatemala, and Honduras

The process of modernization of the armed forces of El Salvador and Guatemala, and their turning into "state structures" rather than tools of regional or personal interests, took place during the last decades of the nineteenth century, in the wake of the so-called liberal revolutions in those countries.[3]

These revolutions engendered dual political regimes. On the one hand, a modern set of democratic institutions, such as the alternation of political parties and elections, was established; on the other hand, to the extent that the old oligarchic sectors transformed themselves and remained dominant, the conservative ideology did not disappear. This accounts for a series of inconsistencies, such as the expansion of agricultural exports based not on heavier use of wage-earner labor but on patterns of control of workers close to servitude.

Consequently, at the political level, the system was liberal only on the outside; electoral tampering and the state's resort to violence as a means for political and social control became a rule. This was reflected in the long-lasting dictatorial regimes of this period. The armies of both countries came into being within the framework of an equally contradictory tradition: On the one hand, they committed themselves explicitly to the liberal ideology and to democracy; on the other hand, they became an instrument and a source of support for the dictators. This set of problems prevented the establishment of democratic relations between the armed forces and the rest of society. Democratic thought, however, continued to influence the ideology of the military.

During the 1940s, a series of socioeconomic factors and changes in the international arena led to the disappearance of the "old regimes" of the liberal era. The so-called revolutions in Guatemala (1944) and El Salvador (1948), both military coups, put an end to long dictatorial periods and inaugurated processes of political and social opening.

The Guatemalan "revolution," with its efforts toward economic and social change, particularly the agrarian reform program launched by the administration of Colonel Jacobo Arbenz Guzmán, were opposed by the local oligarchy and the U.S. Government of that time; in addition, the Army split. The opening came to a tragic end when Arbenz Guzmán was overthrown by a U.S.-supported invasion.[4]

The Salvadoran process was more cautious; its leaders were careful to pursue low-keyed objectives, trying to keep the internal split to a minimum. Consequently, no substantial progress was made toward solving the economic and social problems; social support for the regime ebbed. This became more apparent during the administration of Colonel Jose Maria Lemos, who was eventually deposed in 1960.[5]

After the failure of reform in both countries, the regimes that developed were basically authoritarian. Democratic institutions became a province of military and civil cliques, who regularly used government resources for their personal benefit. As these regimes were illegitimate, they responded to the growing rebellion of segments of the population. Serious human rights violations ensued.

In Honduras, there was no liberal revolution of comparable depth to those of Guatemala and El Salvador. As a result, armed bands serving local caudillos and an endless series of civil wars were rampant well into the twentieth century. Only in the 1940s were the modern armed forces organized; they kept a low profile until 1956, when the young army deposed President Julio Lozano as he was concocting electoral fraud. The next president, Ramon Villeda Morales, put into place a series of political and socioeconomic reforms; but in order to grant civilians stronger control over the army, he created a parallel military corps (the National Guard), a move that prompted another coup in 1963.[6] The officer that overthrew Villeda Morales became the country's leading political character for more than a decade. Colonel Oswaldo Lopez Arellano, who took power through a third coup in 1972, started a process of social reforms, including an agrarian reform program second only in scope to that of Guatemala in 1951.[7]

Salvadoran and Guatemalan societies reacted in different ways to the impact of the kind of political regimes that developed during the 1960s and the 1970s. The type of response that proved most disquieting was the armed uprising of a part of the population, which gave birth to a state of internal war that still prevails in both countries. Underlying these uprisings were increasing social and economic demands, which the government did nothing to remedy. The lack of political democracy, and thus of the institutional channel for those demands to be submitted and processed, as well as increasing state repression of actual or potential opponents, led to rebellions. These were repeatedly suffocated. By the end of the 1970s, these uprisings had grown substantially.[8]

Originally, the forces represented by the Faraburdo Martí National Liberation Front/Democratic Revolutionary Front (FMLN/FDR) alliance in El Salvador and the Revolutionary National Union of Guatemala (URNG) in Guatemala professed different ideological creeds, but they finally endorsed a joint program of revolutionary suppression of the existing order on the basis of a socialist paradigm. From a sociological point of view, these forces rely on strong peasant and (in the case of Guatemala) indigenous support. On the other hand, some social segments reacted in a nonarmed way, demanding the end of dictatorship and the establishment of a democratic, Western-style regime. These forces voiced their dissent basically through political parties and other pressure groups, such as business unions, religious or professional associations, and the like. Their aims were democracy and social reform. From an ideological standpoint, the democratic opposition was rather heterogeneous, but in both countries the Christian Democrats became a central factor. Though this type of opposition was not as threatening as the guerrilla opposition for the authoritarian regimes, they succeeded in stressing the illegitimate nature of the guerrillas and in widening the gap between themselves and the society as a whole. Within the armed forces, the reaction was twofold. On the one hand, the internal war was the most serious threat to national security. Since the guerrillas were competing with the army, victory would mean defeat. Hence, fighting and defeating the guerrillas is the main goal.

On the other hand, certain strong segments of the armed forces believed that the illegitimacy of the incumbent rulers, growing corruption, and excessive governmental repression, which tended to become indiscriminate, posed another type of threat to national security. As political polarization became more acute, no solution to the social issues could be sought. The war effort itself was being impaired. Within the armed forces, a division became apparent between those concerned with only one aspect of the crisis (the threat of the guerrillas) and those who contended that both components of the crisis fed one another.

The complexity of the political-military situation was compounded by the end of the 1970s by an economic crisis that reflected, in part, the Central American and global crisis. In addition, the management of the economy by the authoritarian regimes was very inadequate, and corruption was on the increase, leading almost to the bankruptcy of these governments. Furthermore, in June 1979, the victory of the revolutionaries in Nicaragua put an end to a situation similar to those of El Salvador and Guatemala, thus giving basis to the concern of the officers who feared the same outcome unless changes were effected.

Finally, the external picture became most unfavorable for El Salvador and Guatemala as a result of claims of human rights violations and electoral fraud. This led to a sharp reduction of international support for both governments in the political, economic, and military spheres, a fact that some groups of officers perceived as eroding the war effort.

In El Salvador, the 1977 presidential elections brought to power Colonel Carlos Humberto Romero. The electoral process was deemed fraudulent by the Union Nacional Opositora (UNO), a coalition of three antigovernment parties: the Christian Democratic party, the Social Democrats of the Movimiento Nacional Revolucionario (MNR), and the Marxist Union Democratica Nacionalista (UDN). The UNO claimed that its candidate, Colonel Castillo Claramont, had been the winner.[9] By mid-

1979, it had become apparent that the ruling groups were concocting new fraud schemes. The internal insurrection climate tended to worsen, fed as it was by disaffection to the regime.

On October 15, 1979, the coup of the group known as Military Youth was supported throughout the armed forces, except for the security units. The coup manifesto justified the move as an attempt to defend people's right to take arms against the anarchy, violence, and corruption prevailing in the country. Restoration of democracy, respect for human rights, and a solution to social problems were promised.[10] A military junta, including two military officers (Colonels Majano and Gutierrez) and three civilians (Dr. Ungo and engineers Mayorga and Andino), was appointed. This coup was the first step in a transition process. Obviously, the military tried to conclude an alliance with the democratic opponents of the regime in order to broaden their socioeconomic and political basis. This effort failed because of two types of problems. First, there was a problem in defining the nature and scope of the changes to be effected by the armed forces and the democratic opponents of the regime. One group emphasized political-socioeconomic reform. Another group felt that socioeconomic reform was as important as political reform and supported more radical and accelerated changes, recognizing the inevitability of a social split. Other contentious issues included the possibility of investigating and punishing past military violations of human rights.

Both sectors were unable to reach an understanding. In January 1980, the junta was dissolved, as several government members resigned.[11] The democratic opposition divided, and the Social Democratic party, as well as a Christian Democratic group, decided to form a political coalition with the rebels, the Democratic Revolutionary Front (DRF), which issued an alternative government program, the "Programatic Platform for a Democratic Revolutionary Government."[12] Coincidentally, this crisis led to the ouster of several leaders of the October 1979 uprising.

After the crisis, the government reorganized itself according to a pact between the armed forces and the Christian Democratic party. The junta was restructured several times during the internal conflict. Several socioeconomic reform measures were implemented, such as the Acts of Agrarian Reform (March 6, 1980) and the Banking System Nationalization (March 8, 1980).[13]

Internal warfare continued and was given fresh impetus. In spite of the transition, the rebels, far from laying down their arms, increased the war effort. They were strengthened and given additional legitimacy by the crisis of the first transition administration and the subsequent creation of the DRF, an ally of the FMLN. The transition did not put an end to the conflict; rather, the military capabilities of the rebels tended to increase in the years that followed.

The continuation of the war prevented a solution to the human rights issue. Extremely serious violations occurred, including the murder of the archbishop of El Salvador, Msgr. Arturo Romero, and four American nuns of the Maryknoll Order; and the "death squads" continued to operate.[14]

In retrospect, transition in El Salvador would have accelerated at a lower cost to society if all the democratic opposition groups and the armed forces had remained united, as they were when the first transition government was installed. Unity was destroyed by conflicting views about the ways and means and the nature of achieving democratic social changes. The transition forces split into two groups—the "pragmatists" and the "idealists". In historic terms, this division brought tragic consequences for El Salvador. In spite of a move toward elections for a constitutional assembly, approval of a new constitution, and presidential elections (Napoleon Duarte was sworn in as the first democratic president in several decades), the transition process is yet to reach the stage of consolidation.

Transition in Guatemala was similar, although it occurred later. By 1981, the era of President General Romeo Lucas Garcia, who had taken over in 1978 through allegedly fraudulent elections, was approaching its end. During his administration, the negative aspects of the political regime were exacerbated; violations of human rights and corruption reached unprecedented levels. In addition, the military capabilities of the guerrillas reached their peak. In March 1982, national elections of questionable legality were held. The candidate of the ruling group, General Alfredo Guevara, was proclaimed the winner amid widespread protests from the other participating parties and the media.

On March 23, 1982, a successful coup was staged by midlevel and junior military officers. Their manifesto[15] pointed to alleged electoral fraud and corruption and promised to restore democracy and continue the war against the guerrillas, who were depicted as Communists. After the uprising, the first transition government was installed; it included General Rios Montt, General Horacio Maldonado, and Colonel Francisco Luis Gordillo. In June of the same year, the government was restructured. It was left in the sole hands of General Rios Montt.

This first transition administration was assailed by three problems. The coup itself and the installation of the government had been decided unilaterally by the military. The civilians who were appointed to hold public office served in their capacity as individuals only. Once the government was installed, an advisory body—the State Board, on which the unions were represented—was created. The only field of convergence was a forum at which the government and political parties discussed the terms and conditions, and the means, of political "opening." Although the coup was enthusiastically supported by the democratic opposition groups, they did not perceive themselves as participating in the preparation of government plans. The major political parties opposed the process.

President Efrain Rios Montt developed a style of government that was regarded as authoritarian and personalistic. Some of his attitudes, particularly his Christian fundamentalism, created hostile reactions from several sectors. These discrepancies came to an end with a second coup, which took place on August 8, 1983. Rios Montt was ousted, and General Oscar Mejia Victores was appointed head of state by the commanders-in-chief.[16]

The Mejia Victores administration succeeded in establishing adequate communication links with the democratic opposition in order to reach consensus with several social protagonists about political opening.

Neither the first nor the second transition government was able to solve the internal war and human rights problems. Though Rios Montt issued an amnesty decree and urged the insurgents to lay down their arms, the URNG, which had made public a plan for a "revolutionary, patriotic, popular and democratic government" in January 1982, rejected the offer. The military administrations applied a new strategic and tactical approach, which allowed them, in two years' time, to inflict serious blows to the rebels and to recover initiative in the military field, though at a very high human cost.[17]

The Honduran political regime exhibited different traits. Although the Lopez Arellano coup in 1972 was the first of a series of military dictatorial regimes that lasted almost a decade, the structure of the relationship between the state and civilian society was not one of illegitimacy and repression. Between 1972 and 1975, Lopez Arellano implemented social policies, including an agrarian reform program that was compared at that time with the "military reformist" measures being implemented in Peru and Panama. However, like Peru and unlike Panama, no attempt was made to conclude an alliance with civilian sectors, particularly the political parties. The government was the sole executor of those programs.[18]

The social dynamics in Honduras were less conflictive. No major revolutionary alternatives to the project were ever designed. Starting in 1978, old rebel organizations made efforts to regroup and new ones were organized. Their size and the scope of their operations remain limited, which suggests that these groups have been unable to attract popular support.

In April 1975, Lopez Arellano was ousted through an internal army coup based on alleged bribery by a transnational banana company. Overall, resistance to reform plans was not a key factor in this coup. The decisive force was the armed forces. General Juan Alberto Melgar Castro took power.

Gradually, the reform program lost momentum and virtually stagnated. Since implementing reforms had been the leading aim of the military regime, the abandonment of this goal made the regime unjustifiable. This, in turn, gave added strength to the democratic opposition's demand for constitutional structures. The administration of Melgar Castro, however, was reluctant to return power to the civilians; in addition, new claims of governmental corruption and narcotics trafficking activities were asserted. A new coup brought about the removal from office of Melgar Castro in August 1978.[19] A military junta was appointed, chaired by General Policarpo Paz Garcia. Elections for a constitutional assembly were held. Later, through presidential elections, the civilians recovered the power.

Consolidation Agenda

In all three countries, the transition sequence was identical: (1) coups or major nonconsensual changes in the armed forces, which affected the membership of the government; (2) installation of one or more transition governments, which organized political opening; and (3) elections of constitutional assemblies and the executive and legislative branches of government.

Although the installation of civilian, freely elected regimes has been a major step in the transition process, it has been accompanied by a series of problems that, in essence, have to do with a redefinition of the role of the armed forces within both the political society and the society as a whole. The agenda includes several issues.

The Pact of Transference of Power

The armed forces do not implement a political opening and the transference of power unconditionally. They establish a series of rules governing the relationships between themselves and the civil administration. These negotiations are not institutional; they have not been provided for in each nation's laws. Negotiation of such a pact belongs to a different realm—that of realpolitik—where the social players holding power negotiate such possession.

A "pact of Transference"[20] normally consists of understandings following informal discussions; it is based on the good faith of the participants. No explicit penalties are set for whoever fails to fulfill his obligations. Each segment of the pact can be negotiated separately: Usually, the first part consists of an agreement between the armed forces and the political parties about certain constitutional provisions regarding the army or its interests; next, the names of the presidential candidates can be negotiated in a similar manner; finally, negotiations can be held with the elected candidates.

During the negotiations, the players try to find areas of convergence. The military tend to be interested in (1) the civil government's refraining from intervening in the internal affairs of the armed forces—in other words, a warranty that the internal operation of the army will not be manipulated by the civilians, particularly in matters concerning authority; (2) the army's formally or informally retaining "power provinces" on grounds of national security; (3) ideological assurances that the civil administration will not modify the political system in ways inconsistent with the Western democratic model; and (4) no reprisals against members of the armed forces for past actions connected with domestic security.

The civilians are often interested in (1) transfer of power to the legitimately elected political forces; (2) military noninterference in the thrust of government affairs; and (3) the armed forces' role being confined to the boundaries specified in the Law.

The conclusion of the pact creates two sets of problems: how to interpret the pact and how to fulfill it. Given the nonstatutory nature of its clauses, each player can construe them in a different way, particularly if their representatives do not remain the same. Similarly, the existence of a pact does not mean that the participants will completely fulfill their respective obligations. As pacts are about the limits of power, the players may attempt to extend these limits, even through noncompliance.

Human Rights

The military often think that charges of human rights must not result in formal judicial proceedings. Amnesty often has been decreed prior to the transferral of power; likewise, the alleged offenses would be justifiable under the logic of civil war, as they were committed under circumstances in which the rules of ordinary warfare do not apply. The issue is simultaneously legal and political. In the legal sphere, a number of proceedings can be carried out (abrogation of the amnesty statutes, indictments, and, eventually, sentences) in order to assign liability for criminal violations of human rights. Usually, in the absence of evidence, no charges can be pressed. In the political sphere, the civil government must decide whether to challenge the armed institutions on this issue, as the Argentine government did, and take steps to accumulate the evidence needed for the trials.[21]

This aspect can seriously impair consolidation. For the sake of realpolitik, civil governments often choose to shun confrontation with the military. This does not solve the problem, because the civilian protagonists may continue to press their demands and may try to stir the conscience of the population about them. Though a democratic government might be prepared to refrain from solving this problem, it would be unacceptable for the problem to continue to recur. In this area, the quality of the armed forces–civil authorities' understanding on restoration of human rights becomes crucial.

Reserved Areas

During the transition period, military predominance in government must gradually ebb, until the people wearing uniforms fill the space assigned to them according to the needs of national defense, as stated in the constitution and the legislation in force. This target may also be attained gradually. Setting precise limits on military jurisdiction in the political (and perhaps civil) society can become a source of dissent. The armed forces could feel it necessary, for the sake of national security, to be present or to exercise influence in certain areas, particularly if they do not trust the civilians as capable managers in those realms. The Central American case features a number of ambiguous situations in which the same area falls into several jurisdictions.

In this regard, the issue of resource allocation has become very important. The socioeconomic and administrative needs of the armed forces cannot be deemed as important as those of other sectors. Usually, the armed forces are assigned a larger percentage of resources. However, there is no margin for gradually reducing armament costs if civil war persists; on the contrary, these costs tend to increase. But even if the army is not directly involved in a major domestic war effort, it can be argued that embryonic conflicts, or the regional situation, may require larger defense spending.

On the other hand, the military may distrust the civilians as resource managers. Instances of corruption or waste by civilian administrations in the sphere of investment policies tend to weaken the civilian position in negotiations with the military regarding the budget.

War Effort Management

In a civil war scenario, the civilian government can choose to seek military victory over the rebels or to strive for peace through negotiated political agreements. This involves a threat for the transition if, in the arena of realpolitik, the armed forces prove scarcely flexible in their negotiations with the rebels; perhaps they are prepared to accept conditional surrender

Negotiations btwn. Mil & Army — & civilian govt in a difficult position.

but not to agree, in part, to the demands of the rebels—not to mention power-sharing. Indeed, as limited negotiations for surrender are not acceptable to highly sophisticated rebel forces, civil governments are in no position to approach a political solution realistically. A complicated situation ensues: As no military solutions to Central American-type civil wars seem to be in the offing, and political solutions are not feasible, war is likely to continue. To a large extent, however, this distorts the process of consolidation and even threatens to freeze its development.

Socioeconomic Reforms

Transition has been a means for fulfilling the demands of political democracy—underscoring the inception of the crisis but not the demands for socioeconomic reform. The armed forces view this problem from the perspective of the war effort. Timely reform programs, for example, can help switch the loyalties of the poor peasant masses, which make up a substantial part of the rebel social base. However, the military feel that the civilians are solely responsible in this area.

Civil administrations face pressures in addition to those exerted by the military. They maintain an uneasy relationship with the ruling classes, particularly those that endorse an oligarchic ideology, which sometimes are represented in the government. Often, a strategy of reaching consensus among the power factors of a society may prevent the implementation of the swift and profound reforms some sectors of the armed forces might deem desirable. The pace of transition slackens as a result.

External Factors

No realistic solution to the political situation in Central America can be designed that ignores the foreign players' behavior, influence patterns, and motivating interests. The governments and armed forces of the countries reviewed here believe that the rebel movements operating in their territories are supported by foreign forces.[22] The U.S. government projects geopolitically on the Central American region—most intensely in two of the countries dealt with in this survey, El Salvador and Honduras. The U.S. economic and military assistance is crucial for the Salvadoran war effort and is a major factor in the process of accelerated militarization in Honduras; in addition, the U.S. military presence in Honduras is the largest on the Isthmus outside Panama. The degree of dependence on U.S. military aid, exacerbated by the Nicaraguan conflict, reduces the international self-determination of the countries involved.

Conclusions

Finding a solution to regional conflicts is crucial for the consolidation of the transition process. The most acute of these problems is probably civil war, which is at the root of other problems. Certainly, war has facilitated the modernization of the armed forces. In all three countries, modern war devices (in some cases, latest-generation ones) are available to the air and ground forces; the officers and the troops are combat-trained or, as in Honduras, undergo continuous training. The need for counterinsurgency has widened the scope of military training. However, war makes the armed forces a preponderant factor relative to other social players. Besides bearing the direct and indirect human and physical costs of the conflict, the Central American countries have to assign a substantial percentage of their budgetary resources to military spending, at the expense of other development programs. The issue of internal war, however, is linked to the activities of the foreign players, who are outside the control of the regional countries. Internal warfare and the activities of external protagonists are the two sides of the main issue for Central American democratization. Therefore, the various peace plans being advanced to put an end to the different types of conflict (within each country, among the regional countries, or between these countries and foreign powers) constitute the most promising road toward democratization in the area.

Other issues must also be taken into account. Building a democratic regime is not contingent only on the influence and the ideology of the military. The political parties and, overall, the civilian players are also a factor. When civil governments do not further the interests of the nation—defending national sovereignty and international self-determination—the physical fact that the government is being taken care of by civilians is not a sign of democratization. Honduras is a case in point: In this country, violation of human rights and the implementation of foreign policies whose net result has been a severe limitation of the country's self-determination occurred after the withdrawal of the military and the installation of a civil government. In Honduras, the civil authorities attempted to monitor the internal developments in the armed forces, but to no avail.[23]

It is also important to identify the type of democratic model that is to be built. The armed forces believe that it is the Western democratic prototype. They also recognize that there is a need for socioeconomic change. They would not accept any other models, such as that of Nicaragua, where emphasis is given simultaneously to what the country calls a democracy of participation and a democracy of distribution. Nor would they accept views different from their own regarding the role of the armed forces. Therefore, it is inconceivable that a historic process such as that in

Costa Rica, a country that abolished its army precisely during the period of consolidation of its democratic system, in 1948, can be reproduced.

It is equally relevant to define the policies of national security. These policies typically cover the defense of the territory and sovereignty of the nation or, according to other definitions, also include a solution to the country's social problems. Reviewing these concepts must be the responsibility of the military, government, and civilian players without foreign interference. The ongoing Central American conflict, for example, has originated for the benefit of nonregional forces. The conflict creates national security views inconsistent with the interests of the countries of the region.

Finally, both civilians and the military must strive to establish modern and realistic mutual relations and must put aside the set of stereotypes that often contaminate such relations. Civilians tend to perceive the military as monolithic, failing to perceive the diversity of tendencies and opinions within the armed forces. The military are thought of as one-dimensional, the one dimension being armed struggle. Civilians tend to build a relationship with the military based on accepting the military's exercise of an amount of power greater than that required for the performance of their functions. Consequently, civilians seek the support of the military through flattery and furtherance of matters in which the army is specifically interested. Civilians also seek to manipulate and divide the armed forces, irrespective of their nature and functions.

In turn, the military image of the civilians is that of "politicians"—characters using public office to attain personal privileges at the expense of national interests. Another misperception is that of popular leaders as rebels who bring forward demands for change. Finally, the armed forces have yet to perceive themselves as a state institution that must be open to public monitoring, despite the fact that they perform distinct functions.

Central American countries have not yet solved a set of fundamental problems. Not only must they learn how to build democratic regimes and update relations between the armed forces and the rest of the society, they also must learn to manage the issues of people's access to food, health services, employment, and education. This situation, in itself the source of conflict, is compounded by nonregional forces. Ultimately, the task of consolidating democracy involves both opening political space and solving the problems of modernization.

Notes

1. See Guillermo O'Donnell and Philippe Schmitter, *Transition from Authoritarian Rule: Tentative Conclusions about Uncertain Democracies* (Baltimore: Johns Hopkins University Press, 1986).

2. Our research deals with recent events. This approach is based on the well-known fact that the 1979 crisis gave birth to a succession of separate stages. The methodology used consists of interviews on the issues with civilian and military participants of the countries involved and tapping ancillary sources.

3. See Edelberto Torres-Rivas, *Interpretaciones del Desarrollo Social Centroamericano* (San Jose, Costa Rica: EDUCA, 1973).

4. See Stephen Schlesinger and Stephen Kinzer, *Bitter Fruit* (Garden City, N.Y.: Doubleday, 1982).

5. See Jorge Caceres, "El Partido Revolucionario de Unificacion Democratica: Un Estudio de las Ideologias Radicales en la Formacion Social Salvadorena," Ph.D. dissertation, Essex University, 1978.

6. See Leticia Salomon, *Militarismo y Reformismo en Honduras* (Tegucigalpa: Editorial Guaymuras, 1982).

7. Under the Guatemalan agrarian reform program, between January 1953 and June 1954, 603,615 hectares of land were expropriated and distributed. For figures, see Guillermo Paz, *Guatemala: Reforma Agraria* (San Jose, Costa Rica: EDUCA/FLACSO, 1986); and Jorge Arturo Reina, *Analisis de los Conflictos en America Central* (San Jose, Costa Rica: CEDAL, 1987).

8. See Gabriel Aguilera, "Las Fases del Conflicto Bélico en Guatemala," Unpublished manuscript, 1961–85.

9. Five years earlier, in 1972, the candidate of this very coalition, Napoleon Duarte, had presumably won the elections; but on that occasion, also, the electoral results had been manipulated. This led to an uprising of democratic military groups in which Duarte was involved; it was crushed.

10. See Napoleon Duarte, *My History* (New York: Putnam's, 1986).

11. For the text, see "Proclama de la Fuerza Armada de El Salvador," *Revista ECA*, no. 372/373 (October 15, 1979).

12. For the disputation between the two sectors, see the following documents: "El Gabinete de Gobierno, los Magistrados de la Corte Suprema de Justicia y Funcionarios de Instituciones Autonomas, se dirigen a las Fuerzas Armadas por intermedio del COPEFA"; "El COPEFA responde al Gabinete, Magistrados y otros Funcionarios del Gobierno"; "Y Renuncias de los Miembros Civiles de la Junta Revolucionaria de Gobierno, Gabinete, Magistrados de la Corte Suprema de Justicia y Funcionarios de las Instituciones Autonomas," *Revista ECA*, no. 375/376 (January–February 1980).

13. See Rafael Menjivar, *El Salvador: El Eslabón Mas Pequeño* (San Jose, Costa Rica: EDUCA, 1980).

14. Only in a gradual and incomplete manner has the following transition administration made progress toward preventing the participation of the state security bodies in this action. See Gabriel Aguilera and Edelberto Torres-Rivas, *Centroamerica: Los Hechos que Formaron la Crisis* (San Jose, Costa Rica: ICADIS, 1986).

15. See Duarte, *My History*.

16. See "Proclama del Ejército de Guatemala al Pueblo," *Politica y Sociedad* 15 (July–December 1984).

17. Also, the issue of human rights violations remained extremely serious during both administrations.

18. See "Proclama del Alto Mando y del Consejo de Comandantes Militares en que se Releva a Rios Montt," *Politica y Sociedad* 15 (July–December, 1984).

19. Between 1980 and 1984, up to 75,000 civilians lost their lives as a result of the war. For details, see Chris Krueger and Kjell Enge, *Security and Development Conditions in the Guatemalan Highlands* (Washington, D.C.: WOLA, 1985).

20. See Reina, *Analisis de los Conflictos*; and Richard Millet, "Historical Setting," in James D. Rudolph, ed., *Honduras: A Country Study* (Washington, D.C.: American University, 1984). The Pact of Withdrawal of the Guatemala military government (1966) was embodied in an affidavit specifying the terms and conditions of the army commanders and the acceptance thereof by the candidates elected as president and vice-president of Guatemala. This document was secret, but a facsimile was published later. See "El Pacto Secreto de 1966," *Polemica* 14 (1984).

21. An example of investigations that succeeded (because the political will to carry them out was in place) is Argentina after the transition period. For a description, see National Committee on Disappearance of Persons, *Nunca Más* (Buenos Aires: EUDEBA, 1985).

22. Nicaragua, Cuba, and other socialist countries are accused of giving support to the rebels. See Duarte, *My History*; and Edgardo Paz Barnica, *La Politica Exterior de Honduras (1982–1986)* (Madrid: Editorial Iberoamericana, 1986).

23. See Reina, *Analisis de los Conflictos*; and Marc Rosenberg, *Can Democracy Survive the Democrats? From Transition to Consolidation in Honduras* (Miami: Florida International University, Latin American and Caribbean Center, October 24, 1986).

3

The Legacies of Transitions to Democracy in Argentina and Uruguay

Carina Perelli

On December 1, 1983, Raul Alfonsín took office as president of Argentina. On March 1, 1985, Julio Maria Sanguinetti was sworn in as president of Uruguay. Both owed their offices to the success of their parties in elections perceived as free and competitive—that is, democratic.

After long years of military government, the inhabitants of the River Plate countries renewed contact with liberal democracy and with an *estado de derecho*,[1] which had been attacked in rhetoric and in practice by the left and greatly neglected by average citizens and their representatives throughout the 1960s and the beginning of the 1970s. Vast sectors of young people, totally or partially socialized under the dictatorship, readied themselves, full of hope, to experience for the first time everyday life under that political blessing so often mentioned by their elders: a democratic regime.

Many of the former harsh critics of the so-called "bourgeois political formalisms that mask the basic relationships of exploitation"—survivors of the generation of 1968 that had wanted to transform utopian ideals into realistic goals—emerged from exile, inxile,[2] prison, and clandestine detention centers to write blank checks of political confidence for the bourgeois regime that the dictatorship had taught them to revalue.

Generations socialized under a democratic-liberal regime (Uruguay) or in the shadow of this ideal (Argentina), who had witnessed the struggle for hegemony between two conceptions of the violence upon which law is built,[3] breathed a sigh of relief, ready to return to a democratic system, be it real or imagined.

Whatever their doctrinal or experiential point of origin and whatever their long-term goals, most citizens had achieved a fragile consensus in those days: Democracy, however formal, was preferable to any other regime. It seemed that the impossible was approaching reality; once and for all, the debate over the legitimacy of the democratic regime in the River Plate area had finally been settled.

In the euphoria of refound dialogue, few seemed to notice the problems still remaining. For the great majority, the transition had ended with the swearing in of the president. Items on the agenda that were still to be addressed were forgotten, silenced, or overlooked. Critical was the fact that the heavily politicized armed forces were inserted into the framework of a regime whose doctrinal limitations could not recognize them as a political actor. The democratic-liberal doctrine, following the original European formulation, does not in any way accept the existence of nonrepresentative actors.

Some of the problems that urgently needed to be addressed were the symbolic break with the past, represented basically, though not exclusively, by the prosecution of human rights violations under the military government; and the generation gaps, particularly evident in the difficulties of the political class in finding a discourse capable of unifying a highly heterogeneous population. In addition, there were the legacy of fear and the loss of the sense of security that permits a full and responsible exercise of rights and obligations in a democratic-liberal framework; the feelings of guilt (and the possible compensatory overreaction that those feelings could lead to) of a population that had not resisted military authoritarianism;[4] and the external limits on change, both economic and political.

While citizens celebrated the recovery of a paradise lost, the political class—aware that the problems of transition were far from over—preferred to defer taking up a bitter and tough agenda. After all, in a democratic and representative regime, the pessimists who promise only blood, sweat, and tears run the risk of being severely penalized by the popular vote. Tragic altruism, as politicians well know, works only in periods of great crisis.

Moreover, upon recovering an arena by right its own, the political elite also rediscovered its old reflexes—those mechanisms for operating the political system that, in the past, had yielded good dividends: elite negotiations, appeals to political realism and to the *raison d'état*, and justification of political actions with exclusively political arguments. Probably no sector of society minimized to as great an extent the changes that had taken place in civil society, on the one hand, and in the military, on the other, during the de facto regime.

Even the most lucid sectors of the political class perceived the final legacies of the transition as negotiable. Human rights violations and the multiple traumatic aftermaths of repression would be resolved with exclusively political criteria. The reinsertion of the armed forces—perceived as the reincorporation in the democratic tradition of a diffuse and lax group of individuals generically called "the military"—would occur on its own once the functioning of the political system had been normalized and spirits had been calmed. The application of individual actions in a mixture of strict regulation and generous incentives would make it possible to co-opt the various military personalities.

The military corporation itself had also engaged in wishful thinking, at least with regard to three crucial aspects of the situation it was to face after the inauguration of the new regime. First, it had minimized the cost of its mishandling of the government (both economically and repressively) in terms of discredit to its image in the eyes of the civilian population. If slight resentment and scorn had always shaded the relations of civil society with the military in these countries, by the end of the last period of military rule, those shades had become insurmountable barriers. The military came to be called "murdering and thieving *milicos*,"[5] with whom no interrelation was possible.

Second, the military cadres felt that they had fulfilled their duty—in the words of Admiral Emilio Massera, saving the nation from a fate worse than death, from possession of its soul by Marxist subversion.[6] To do so, it had been necessary to subdue such subversion without the benefit of negotiation, given the nature of the enemy. With surprise and pain, they discovered that the suppressed civilian population had come to cordially hate the military, rather than appreciate their political "salvation."

Third, the military did not correctly evaluate the internal costs of its transformation into a political actor. It did perceive the danger to the institution represented by the day-to-day administrative wear on its cadres and structures, with the concomitant risk of an increasingly civilian and political outlook among its members.[7] It did not, however, foresee the internal fractures that the transformation would bring with it. As we will see later, the division between the "pragmatists" and the "fundamentalists" within the military is simply a parallel to that produced within civilian society, between the "politicians" and the "ethicists." Such division is singularly important, in that it transforms political problems into problems of principle—by definition not negotiable. The potential for compromise is thus limited.

The return to an *estado de derecho* would stimulate and exacerbate these tensions by bringing into operation a rationality that is neither ethical nor political, but legal. It is the march of justice that provokes a series of chain reactions that ends up undermining, to a large extent, the credibility and legitimacy of the democratic regime so enthusiastically inaugurated.

An Initial Legacy of the Past: A New Civil Vision of the World?

The last de facto military regime in Argentina and the only military dictatorship of the 20th century in Uruguay left a deeper mark on their respective societies than would have been supposed at first sight, as a result of both the quantity and the quality of the control they exercised over citizens.

The repression implemented as a means for controlling the population in the two cases operated with different parameters. In Uruguay, the emphasis was on subduing the entire population at all times; whereas in Argentina, the emphasis was on paralyzing, via terror, clearly delineated social sectors that were considered dangerous.

Both systems gave rise to the emergence of a "culture of fear." This culture was characterized by, among other traits, the use of the "oblique voice"; the dissociation between person and persona; the romanticization of the past; the draining and subsequent privatization of the public sphere, accompanied by the invasion of public control in the private sphere; a break in the continuity of societal memory; and hostile resentment toward all overly manifest or open exercises of power.[8]

The culture of fear affected identities as well as social practices. Some of its manifestations were rapidly perceived, interpreted, and even used by the political class to take better advantage of the stability of the political system. Thus, part of the discipline acquired by the population during the de facto period, together with the fear of falling back into a destabilizing situation, greatly moderated the tenor of the strictly material demands of workers.

Fear inspired the prudence needed to modify the ideological spectrum of the political system to a series of moderate shades. This process reduced excessively pronounced left and right profiles. At the same time, it excluded all unreasonable actors who were incapable of attenuating the radicalism of their positions. Fear constituted the very foundation of the hyperstability of the political system.[9]

Other legacies of this culture of fear were less easily perceivable, given that this peculiar vision of the world was superimposed on another more universal and official one. The official vision was of a world ordered by the *estado de derecho*, with equality as its measure, law as its rule, and justice as its guide.

Nevertheless, the underground legacy of the years of terror did not cease to be essential because of its invisibility. Three salient features should be pointed out, because they will have a direct bearing on the political sphere.

The first feature was the prioritization of symbolic goods over material goods. This feature climaxed with the reintroduction in the political arena of the founding principles. But because of their own hierarchy and their isotopic value, founding principles depoliticize the political arena, in that, by definition, they are nonnegotiable. There can be only agreement or disagreement on them. In essence, this quality is similar to the incontestability of mathematical axioms or the basic truths of logic.

A second feature consisted of a double movement: On the one hand, personal identity came to be perceived as political; on the other hand, the political became a personal matter for large sectors of the population. For years under the influence of total repression, members of the civilian population had to split themselves into person and persona, playing the role of the good citizen, making sure that the length of their hair, the look of their clothes, the expression on their faces, and the tone of their voices were in line with officially defined parameters. This care in the presentation of the self extended also to the type, quality, and frequency of interpersonal relations. High degrees of self-censure were developed as a defense strategy against the possibility of repression. For civilians, surviving implied being capable of blending and maintaining anonymity. This, in turn, implied a rigorous self-control of the personal; self-assault in order not to be assaulted; and the eradication of every difference, every shade, that makes a person a recognizable self. Thus, inxile took place in the individual's own body. The body became political, to the extent that it became a sphere in which a struggle for power was taking place. Members of the military went through a similar process of rigorous self-control. Soldiers, perhaps more than civilians, effaced their distinctive traits and fused with the mass. The mass in this case, however, was no longer anonymous; it was a heavily structured and disciplined body with its own history and traditions, to which one belonged voluntarily and with pride. The body was not, in this case, a locus of the struggle for power but, rather, an offering sacrificed for the good of a greater corpus, the military corporation.

A third feature of this legacy was manifested in the way in which identities were established during the authoritarian period. If, as social psychologists adduce, there is no possible self-identification outside the identification made by others, the identities of the interlocutors were heavily demarcated. On the one hand, the military held the reins of a power perceived as absolute and unlimited; on the other, a subdued civilian population developed a negative sense of identity under the oppressive rule of the elite. In spite of apparent external similarities, the experience of the members of the military corporation was different. Within the military institution, the situation was structured not on the axis of subduer versus subdued but, rather, on the relationship of commander versus subordinate.

The person exercising command represented the potential future reward for current loyalty and sacrifices. This explains why the armed forces were not capable of correctly evaluating the extent of hate and level of resentment of a civilian population "subjected to discipline."

This new world vision has had different impacts in Argentina and Uruguay, however. In Uruguay, this legacy is inserted within a society that is socially homogeneous and heavily integrated in terms of its political culture. From the turn of the century through the military coup in 1973, the country had consolidated a hegemonic vision of the world. This view was translated into a universal political mythology and an official history, which even the most opposing political groups considered unquestionable. The hegemonic version of Uruguayan history yielded a shared past that flowed without ruptures toward an oncoming future.

Argentina, on the other hand (for reasons not relevant here), has always struggled with the contradictions born of the heterogeneity of its political culture. There are as many versions of Argentine history as there are political and social trends, as many memories as there are political actors.[10]

In view of these factors, Uruguay's new vision of the world represents a marked rupture of the former hegemonic political culture framework. This rupture brings with it a double consequence.

On the one hand, as we will see later, it causes problems at the level of the representation of interests on the part of the political class, which continues operating with the former political culture references. It continues to establish a strong distinction between ethics and politics and to seek political solutions to problems diagnosed as political under that scheme.

On the other hand, Uruguayan society had always employed a hegemonic referential scheme, which allowed it to interpret reality with common parameters. The new vision of the world (as represented by the ethicist version of reality) would tend toward hegemony. In this way, the cognitive dissonance produced by living in a permanent conflict of interpretations would be reduced. This tendency would be facilitated by the equalization of experiences in the authoritarian period, generated by the type of repression and control exercised in the country during the de facto regime.

In Argentina, the ethicist vision of the world is added to the multiple preexisting interpretations of reality. This facilitates its politicization and, consequently, the attenuation of its impact at the level of the civilian population.[11]

Paradoxically, and as we will see later, these tendencies are inverted at the other pole of the relationship: the military. It is in Argentina that the ethicist tendency would have greater weight within the armed forces;

whereas within the Uruguayan military, predominant control of the force would be on the side of the political current.

A Second Legacy of the Past: Internal Changes in the Military Institution

In both Argentina and Uruguay, a military career is not just another job in which the individual can get ahead and have a more or less secure economic horizon. Instead, the military corporation is an institution in the broadest sense of the term.[12] This implies the establishment of a particular vision of the world and an identity different from those prevailing in a nonmilitary environment. This organic ideology is structured on the basis of values that, in essence, have remained unchanged since the Middle Ages: honor, dignity, loyalty, abnegation, and the mystique of duty. Organic ideology, internalized through the process of military socialization and made current in every gesture of the daily lives of the members of the institution, translates into a strong esprit de corps, a feeling of the "we" self-perceived as superior to the "other"—the civilian.[13]

Organic ideology and military identity with it do not, in themselves, contain anything to threaten the stability of the democratic regime. Nevertheless, those ingredients become highly explosive when they are mixed with another component: the daily exercise of political power.

In effect, if we consider the evolution of the armed forces in the two countries, despite the evident differences between the two cases, there is a common trajectory, whose point of departure is the military coup—effected by certain sectors of the corporation in support of civilian sectors—and which would be synthesized in the notion of the armed forces as instrument,[14] guided by a more or less global project for society as a whole. This is summed up in the concept of the armed forces as a quasi-autonomous political actor. The Argentine armed forces increasingly assumed this role of detaching themselves from civilian allies and recruiting technocrats as isolated decision makers.[15]

The internal changes taking place in the military institution along this trajectory are open to debate, to the extent that the subject has not been sufficiently studied.[16] I believe that prolonged contact with power (either directly, through its daily exercise resulting from the assault on the state represented by a military coup, or indirectly, as an undesired but omnipresent political actor who exerts pressure on the civilian trustees of representative power) triggers a process similar to that described by Lechner for the Latin American left of the 1960s. He called this the process of ideological inflation.[17]

That inflation is marked by the search for a totalizing vision that is capable of unifying the direction of the social process. The process of ideological inflation is characterized by the sanctification of political principles, by the utopia, and by the establishment of a specific source of power for the notion of totality as fully realized identity. The sanctification of political principles translates into the establishment of strong collective identities, characteristic of religious communities, and into the search for "purity." The corollary of this process, which leads to a greater ideological consistency of the group, is the development of a tendency toward the demonization of the "other," perceived as adversary.

The process tends to be accompanied by an ongoing questioning of the spaces established and by the extension of a particular rationality. This is characteristic of the extension of one space—in this case, the military space—to all of social life. The religious charge contained in this manner of doing politics, according to Lechner, attempts to counteract the feeling of uncertainty. It will be manifested in the attempt to find ethical redemption, in the existence of a political mystique of revolutionary bent (without the term *revolutionary* necessarily having the connotation of common sense, which associates it with the left), and in salvation crusades, which converge in the construction of the new man.[18]

The other side of this process, ideological deflation, is characterized by the revaluation of secularization and a call for realism, which discharges ethical-religious commitments from politics, disassembles the search for redemption and plenitude, and visualizes politics as the art of the possible via a call for a collective construction of order.

The exercise of political power by the military seems to have contributed to stretching the armed forces' conscience. In other words, the limits of what is considered possible and desirable, both for society and for the institution, make it possible for the military corporation *in totum*, as well as for its individual members, to perceive the military institution as a political actor, without cognitive dissonances at the level of the system of beliefs—the organic ideology.

The existence in the international market of military doctrines (such as the French doctrine of revolutionary war, which justifies this self-perception) contributes to the consolidation and deepening of a politicized military mentality. The military's prolonged contact with the exercise of political power operated like the hand of Pandora, opening a box that potentially contained the ill of Messianism. This ill was not directed only against civilian society. Once the armed forces become a political actor, and as they continue exercising political power over a sufficiently prolonged period, the corporation tends to lose its monolithic character. Within the military organization, a form of political system, with factions and "parties," begins to develop. This tendency puts the very existence of the institution in danger. At the same time, it causes a continuous pendular movement in the official (the high command) military position.

The rupture in the monolithic character of the military institution and the emergence of more or less visible factions and currents of opinion inside the military corporation gives rise to varied political, doctrinal, and ethical tendencies. Different cleavages divide the officer corps and can even reach the noncommissioned officers. However, these many factions tend to regroup according to their peculiar characteristics and to conform to two currents: the processes of ideological inflation and ideological deflation. This is what observers outside the corporation perceive in black and white as the tension between fundamentalists and pragmatists.[19]

The essence of the military group journalists call fundamentalist is, in many senses, similar (though of a different stamp) to the ethicist current present in civilian society. At the height of the process of ideological inflation, it advocates an ecclesiastic vision of the world, whose central nucleus is formed by the sanctification of the principles that guide its actions—principles that can be synthesized in the struggle between Good (incarnated in the Christian West) and Evil (embodied in the international Communist movement).

What is known as the military pragmatist tendency is characterized by a call for realism. The epitome in Argentina was General Dante Caridi and his failed attempt to "repair discipline and the chain of command." In Uruguay, it is Lieutenant General Hugo Medina, with his project to get the army and the armed forces through the democratic transition in "the best possible way." Another characteristic of this trend is a conception of politics as the art of the possible through negotiation, dialogue, and pressure, but also through the limitation of redeeming aspirations and a commitment to civilians.

In this overview, it does not seem daring to say that there are greater possibilities for dialogue between the so-called military pragmatists and the members of the political class. There exists a greater probability of antagonistic empathy between military fundamentalists and civilian ethicists than of understanding between the military currents in the process of ideological inflation and the military sectors secularized by ideological deflation.

This is particularly serious, to the extent that it polarizes the military force, provoking a fracture in the sense of "we." If this fracture does occur, the very foundation of the esprit de corps that serves as the basis for the legitimacy of verticality is destroyed. This, in turn, casts serious doubts on the legitimacy of the chain of command. The quality of the commander–subordinate relationship, manifested in the discipline–due obedience axis, deteriorates and tends to become a subduer–subdued relationship.

The comparison between Argentina and Uruguay is particularly illustrative of this situation. In broad terms, both countries have covered the same trajectory: from a military coup by military factions in support of certain civilian groups, followed by the relative hegemony and control of the military institution by one of the groups or military parties.[20] The recognition of the armed forces as a political actor by the rest of society is included in the process, finally reaching a new internal division of the corporation into highly politicized sectors that confront one another. It is marked by a perpetual struggle for control of the institution and for the imposition of a particular conception of what the good order is.

In Argentina, this process began in 1930; in Uruguay, the process has been much more compact. We could even say that the first stage did not exist. What began at the outset of the 1970s implies significant differences in the political urgencies deriving from the internal situation of the armed forces. The process is much more acute in Argentina.

Talk of the "Lebanization" of the military corporation in Argentina is not irrelevant.[21] In Uruguay, on the other hand, the possibility of an internal struggle inside the armed forces, though latent, has not yet made its public appearance. For the time being, the Uruguayan corporation retains its unity. This would allow the political class, should it seek to do so, to enter into negotiations that would facilitate a more peaceful internal transition.[22]

If there is a breakdown in the military sense of "we," the generals and, more particularly, the chiefs of each branch who tend to embody the most pragmatic current will lose their characteristics not only as chiefs but also as legitimate representatives of the entire corps. If the corporation is split, with whom can the politicians negotiate? If they negotiate with each chief of each current, how can the deepening of the internal fracture be prevented?[23]

A Third Legacy of the Past: A Political Class with Difficulties in Adapting to the New Situation

Dealing with the tension and conflicts produced by the two legacies already discussed would have been an arduous task even for the best of political classes. The group that assumed representation of the citizens in both countries at the end of the authoritarian period was far from "human." The problems in the two countries are quite different, however.

The Argentine case involves political novices, with no experience in direct management of government. It is one of the tragedies of this country that a political class can never constitute itself and gain enough experience in the management of the *res publica*, as the series of military coups and the brief interregnums of democratic governments conspire against its development.

In Uruguay, a political class does exist, although the present incumbents lack, for the most part, experience in political management. Contrary to what happens in Argentina, this political class uses as its point of reference the old vision of the world that Uruguayans once shared. Twelve years of military rule are thus erased. This contributes to the hyperstability that impedes the use of absolute values. The absence of definitions in transcendent problems is compensated by an abusive use of language. This generates a degradation of political rethoric: Discourse becomes noise and, in some cases, the speaker becomes a charlatan.[24]

The other side of the coin is the reification of instrumental values: Political engineering is transmuted into democratic liturgy.[25] The use of a sclerotic reference has a particularly grave consequence. There is a sort of perceptive blindness of the political class with regard to the new phenomena: The facts are not seen or, worse yet, they are defined and pigeonholed as old practices, as a way of reducing cognitive dissonance.[26] This generates error in the handling of problems, in the substance of the solutions proposed, in their timing, and in the register of the discourse selected.[27]

These errors are especially virulent at the most profound points of tension: civilian–military relations, the symbolic end of the de facto regime, the new demands of a society severely traumatized by the authoritarian experience, and the profound changes within the military institution. The extreme treatment of such issues leads to partial solutions, which neither fully satisfy any of the parties involved nor attack the basic problem.[28] Decisions are perceived to be wrenched from politicians by force or threat, with the politicians appearing to have lost all power of initiative in connection with certain issues.[29]

This is only one step away from discrediting the political class—a process that eats away at the institutions and, ultimately, attacks the sources of legitimacy of the regime. The squandering of the wealth of confidence in the institutions and the political class, besides increasing the sense of disenchantment with democracy, weakens the power of convocation that the politicians may have. Perversely, this reinforces the ethicist movement.

Such a situation ends up weakening the position of the military pragmatists inside the military institution. The lack of control over different crises by the politicians only helps reinforce some of the strongest military prejudices. Democracy begins to be equated to a lack of efficiency and a lack of seriousness in the management of the *rex publica*. As time passes and the mistakes made by the military in government are forgotten, this conjecture strengthens the fundamentalist posture within the military institution, leaving the cultivators of a more pragmatic line less room to maneuver.

In intrinsically perverse dynamics, the political class, upon losing its capacity for articulating various demands, has become a potentiating element of the same crisis it fears provoking. For a deterioration to reach such a degree, however, a crisis that would polarize the different postures is necessary.

Such a crisis took place at the moment when a symbolic end was given to the past. It was catalyzed by an extrapolitical factor—the cold logic of law and its concomitant practice, the inexorable march of procedures in justice.

The Catalyst: The Cold Logic of Law

With the advent of democracy, there was a rebirth of the *estado de derecho* whose basis lies in the separation of powers. Consolidation of the *estado de derecho* in a democratic-liberal framework implies not violating or perverting the law. Nevertheless, in the problem at hand, the symbolic end to the past via a definitive pronouncement on the violations of what doctrine and jurisprudence consecrate as essential rights of the persona, following the cold logic of law, implies colliding with the possibility of a negotiated political solution to a conflict not provided for in the pure theory of law.

Relying on the pure theory of law implies that the metajuridical problems have already been resolved. In other words, it presupposes the existence of an agreement on fundamental (acting as founding) metajuridical isotopic terms of the pyramid of norms.[30]

In both Argentina and Uruguay, the problem arising from the application of the logic of law to the cases of violation of human rights by the military forces during their management of government was rooted in the fact that such an agreement on fundamentals does not exist in this instance. The restoration of the constitution of 1967 in Uruguay or that of 1853 in Argentina presupposes the fiction of a presumed basic consensus regarding the nonexistence of an armed corporation as a political actor. It also implies a second fiction: the acceptance by everyone involved in a single definition of the limits that are to prevail in societal life. In other words, underlying such isotopic norms is the idea of a consensus regarding the liberal framework and its liminalities.

To the extent that one of the parties involved, the armed forces, does not participate in this founding framework and has the real power to sustain its position, the logic of law—considered neutral when there is a consensus on its pure theory—comes to be visualized as political and to affect the situation politically.

Moreover, in this perverse "game," the political actor par excellence within the framework of the democratic-liberal agreement on fundamentals—the political class—cannot attempt to manipulate the law so as to deactivate its potential political effect without putting the very foundation of the state of law in danger.

Similarly, for the population, the naturalization of the democratic-liberal scheme implies a series of myths, strongly rooted in the collective social imagination: equality of all citizens before the law, separation of powers, and the right of all citizens to be protected by justice and to make claims before a court of law. To accept that such myths no longer exist implies tacit acceptance that the agreement on fundamentals has changed. This is precisely the nonnegotiable point in the present context.

Notes

1. I prefer to use the Spanish expression, as there is no precise English equivalent for this concept, which is synonymous with the German concept of *Rechtstaat* and the French concept of *état de droit*. The English expression "rule of law" is inadequate to express the Spanish concept.

2. *Inxile* is a term used to refer to the phenomenon of withdrawal and self-isolation adopted by a large number of Uruguayan citizens who stayed in the country during the dictatorship. It is a sort of exile within one's own walls, as a form of protection against the state's control apparatus. See Carina Perelli and Juan Rial, *De Mitos y Memorias Politicas: La Represion, el Exilio y Despues* . . . (Montevideo: EBO, 1986).

3. In both countries, given the existence of a guerrilla movement, there was violence upon which law is built on the part of the radicalized leftist sectors. In their fight, they confronted the armed forces, which are theoretically in charge of the violence upon which law is preserved. In the cases in question here, however, military violence attempted to found a new order. This last process cannot be considered closed as yet. An illustration of it can be seen in the videocassette "Operativo Dignidad" ("Operation Dignity"), made in Argentina in September 1987 by the army sector that followed Lieutenant Colonel Aldo Rico. Both concepts of violence are taken from Walter Benjamin, *Para una Critica de la Violencia* (Mexico: Premia, 1982).

4. See Guillermo O'Donnell, *Y a Mi que Me Importa* . . . (Buenos Aires: Centro de Estudios Sobre Estado y Sociedad, 1985).

5. *Milicos* is a term used in military jargon to refer to the lowest-rank troop personnel; within the military organization, it has a paternalistic connotation. For civilians, however, it is a generic, pejorative, and at times insulting term for all members of the armed forces and the security police.

6. Massera's speech was set forth in his own defense at the trial brought against him in Buenos Aires in 1985. The speech was reproduced in abridged form in *El Diario del Juicio* (Buenos Aires: Abril, 1985) and in the Uruguayan military magazine *El Soldado*.

7. We see the epitome of this in Admiral Emilio Massera, in his negotiations with Peronists and Montoneros in Argentina. See Miguel Bonasso, *Recuerdo de la Muerte* (Buenos Aires: Bruguera, 1984). In Uruguay, the parallel could be General Gregorio Alvarez and his presidential ambitions, fulfilled between 1981 and 1984.

8. "Culture of fear" is a concept coined by Juan Corradi. See Juan Corradi, "The Monster of Destruction: Terror in Argentina," *Telos*, no. 54 (Winter 1982), and Corradi et al., eds., *The Culture of Fear in the Southern Cone* (Berkeley: University of California Press, forthcoming). "Oblique voice" is an expression developed in Guillermo O'Donnell, "On the Fruitful Convergences of Hirschman's Exit, Voice and Loyalty, and Shifting Involvements: Reflections from the Recent Argentine Experience," in A. Foxley, G. O'Donnell, and M. McPherson, eds., *Development, Democracy and the Art of Trespassing: Essays* (Notre Dame, Ind.: University of Notre Dame Press, 1986). About the repression in general in Argentina and Uruguay, see O'Donnell, *Y a Mi que Me Importa . . .*, and Perelli and Rial, *De Mitos y Memorias Politicas*.

9. The concept of hyperstability implies maximum guarantees for all political actors, impeding all types of change that alter the status quo. It also implies, as indicated, a growing centripetal process, which causes, at a certain point, conflicts that work in the opposite direction: the beginning of centrifugal, polarizing processes and also entropy. Hyperstability can lead to a blowup, as it fails to take into account the need for change, even though change is necessary to maintain the status quo. The lack of change, in a minimum hypothesis, leads to the discrediting of the regime and to disbelief, which are translated into delegitimization and disloyalty.

10. See Oscar Landi, *El Discurso Sobre lo Posible: La Democracia y el Realismo Politico* (Buenos Aires: CEDES, 1985).

11. The "ethical" as a new form of politics represents a new pattern that is emerging in Latin America after the defeats of the extreme left, as the left tries to recover its political space. The extreme right, which inaugurated this form of political struggle in the past by appealing to transcendent values to win, is now suffering the consequences of this problem: the politization of ethics and the ethicization of politics.

12. The idea of an occupational model for the armed forces, instead of an institutional one, was developed in Charles Moskos, "From Institution to Occupation: Trends in Military Organization," *Armed Forces and Society* 4, no. 1 (1977) and "Institution/Occupational Trends: An Update," *Armed Forces and Society* 12, no. 3 (1986). The concept of institution is taken from Hans Blumenberg, *Work on Myth* (Cambridge, Mass.: MIT Press, 1985).

13. The concept of organic ideology of the armed forces is developed in Morris Janowitz and Jacques van Doorn, *On Military Ideology* (Rotterdam: Rotterdam University Press, 1971); and in Amos Perlmutter, *The Military and Politics in Modern Times* (New Haven, Conn.: Yale University Press, 1977). About the

values inside the military institutions, the best source is Alfred Vagts, *History of Militarism: Romance and Realities of a Profession* (New York: Norton, 1959).

14. The best elaboration of this argument in Latin America was made in Jose Nun, "The Middle Class in Military Coup," in Abraham F. Lowenthal and J. Samuel Fitch, eds., *Arms and Politics in Latin America* (New York: Holmes and Meier, 1986). A sophisticated development applied to Argentina was presented in G. O'Donnell, "Modernizacion y Golpes Militares: Teoria, Comparacion y el Caso Argentino," *Desarrollo Economico*, no. 64 (January–March 1973).

15. The Onganía administration is a good example of this trend. See Robert Roth, *Los Años de Onganía: Relato de un Testigo* (Buenos Aires: La Campana); Lt. Gen. Alejandro A. Lanusse, *Mi Testimonio* (Buenos Aires: Laserre, 1977); and María Susana Ricci and J. Samuel Fitch, "Ending Military Regimes in Argentina: 1966–73 and 1976–83," chapter 4 in this volume.

16. The best works on the subject are Alain Rouquié, *Poder Militar y Sociedad Politica en la Republica Argentina*, 2 vols. (Buenos Aires: Emecé, 1979), which covers the period that ended in 1973; Robert A. Potash, *The Army and Politics in Argentina, 1928–1962* (Stanford, Calif.: Stanford University Press, 1962), which ends its analysis in 1962; and the most recent and best study, Rosendo Fraga, *El Ejército, del Escarnio al Poder, 1973–1976* (Buenos Aires: Sudamericana, 1987).

17. Norbet Lechner, "El Problema de la Democratization en el Contexto de una Cultura Postmoderna," in *Los Patios Interiores de la Democracia* (Santiago: FLACSO, 1988).

18. See Raoul Girarder, *Mythes et Mythologies Politiques* (Paris: Du Seuil, 1986).

19. In the Uruguayan case, the institutionalization of a joint system of command made possible a resolution of the problem.

20. This concept is taken from Juan Rial, "Las Fuerzas Armadas como Partido Sustituto," *Nueva Sociedad*, no. 81 (1986); and Alain Rouquié, *La Politique de Mars: Les Processus Politiques dans les Partis Militaires* (Paris: La Sycomore, 1981).

21. The military question, centered in the past, and the consequences of a failed symbolic closure of the past led the armed forces, and especially the army, to a situation of real chaos. At the time of this writing, Argentina has suffered three military rebellions, two led by Lieutenant Colonel Rico and one by Colonel Seineldin. About the rebellion, see the following accounts by journalists or partisans: H. Verbitsky, *Civiles y Militares* (Buenos Aires: Contrapunto, 1987); and Ernesto López, *El Último Levantamiento* (Buenos Aires: Legasa, 1988).

22. A law passed in 1986—Ley de Caducidad de la Pretensión Punitiva del Estado, a type of amnesty—closed the possibilities of revising the past and the possible abuses committed by members of the armed forces. This pragmatic measure was taken by the majority of the political class, under pressure from pragmatists of the armed forces. But the ethicists in the civil society promoted a referendum to reject the law. As a movement, it achieved the number of signatures required by the constitution, thus opening the possibility of a popular vote on the

matter. This occurred in April 1989, and the referendum was rejected by 58 percent of those who voted.

23. In Argentina, fifty of the eighty generals who retired during the Alfonsín administration did so for political reasons. ¡The army has had four chiefs that were forced to resign by unrest inside the corporation linked to the legacies of the past. In Uruguay, only three generals retired for political reasons during the Sanguinetti administration. The chiefs were able to control discipline inside the services, and there were no rebellions.

24. There is a striking abuse of rhetoric on the part of Latin American politicians, who often trap themselves with their own words. This generates expectations or interpretations that, in reality, are unfulfillable or do not jibe with the perception of reality. For example, after the Seineldin rebellion in December 1988, Alfonsín chose to deliver a formal speech to the Congress. He told the congressmen that he would not accept a negotiation with the insurgents in the army. Facts have again proved him wrong.

25. The best example of this is the insistence on constitutional or electoral reforms as the main route for resolving the problems affecting the republic. See Carlos Nino et al., *Primer y Segundo Dictamen del Consejo para la Consolidación de la Democracia*, 2 vols. (Buenos Aires: Eudeba, 1986–87); and J. Rial, "Gobernabilidad, Partidos Políticos y Reforma Política," in *Revista de Ciencias Sociales*, No. 3 (Montevideo: FCU, 1988).

26. In Argentina, the military rebellions of April 1987 and December 1988 were perceived as attempted traditional coups d'etat, when they were really corporatist protests led by ultrarightist ethicists. In Uruguay, the police demands in November 1987 were considered an uprising, when in fact they were a sui generis social movement.

27. Thus, the Uruguayan police were dealt with as *milicos*, when one of their claims was demilitarization. In Argentina, Rico and Seineldin's *carapintadas* ("painted faces," a derogatory term for their followers) were accused of launching a traditional coup when they strongly condemned the political ineptitude of the previous political commanders, claiming the dignity of their condition as professional soldiers.

28. The Ley de Caducidad of December 1986 in Uruguay and the two laws in Argentina—Punto Final in December 1986 and the Obediencia Debida in May 1987—constitute good examples of this.

29. There is a manifest lack of coherent military politics on the part of the democratic governments and parliaments in Argentina and Uruguay. Neither the mission nor the role of the armed forces has been defined, except rhetorically (for example, in the defense law approved by the Argentine Congress). This subject remains in the hands of the military institution.

30. See Hans Kelsen, *Teoría Pura del Derecho* (Buenos Aires: Eudeba, 1962).

4

Ending Military Regimes in Argentina: 1966–73 and 1976–83

María Susana Ricci
J. Samuel Fitch

The overthrow of a civilian government by military intervention raises a fundamental question: What will the armed forces do with the power they have seized? Despite the inevitable post-coup manifestos that promise to restore order, stability, and effective government, military regimes typically fail to fulfill those promises. In this chapter, we will argue that these failures are not a result of bad faith or poor leadership but, rather, a direct consequence of the lack of governing capacity of the armed forces. Drawing on the experience of two recent episodes of military rule in Argentina, we argue that these military regimes demonstrate the inherent inability of the military to constitute an effective governing elite, either by itself or with its civilian allies. Although other military regimes in the region may have lasted longer or achieved greater economic success, we believe the Argentine military's political deficiencies are characteristic, rather than exceptional.

Recent military regimes in South America differ from their historical predecessors in two critical respects. First, "modern" military regimes claim to represent the armed forces, rather than the personal rule of a particular officer. Therefore, their organizational structure is and must be different from personalist military regimes, like those of Batista or Somoza, in which the armed forces are subordinated to the military ruler, rather than vice versa. Second, these institutional military regimes assumed power with the intention of making significant political and socioeconomic changes in their societies. Regardless of their ideological orientation, the leaders of these regimes clearly declared that they did not intend to serve merely as an interregnum between civilian governments. The

The first draft of this chapter was written by María Susana Ricci and draws heavily on her doctoral dissertation, "Elite Gubernamental y Regímenes Militares en la Argentina: 1966–73 y 1976–83," University of Belgrano, 1987. A promising scholarly career was tragically ended by her unexpected death in January 1988. Samuel Fitch served as the discussant for Dr. Ricci's paper at the Panama City conference and subsequently translated, edited, and revised this chapter. The original data and much of the analysis belong to Dr. Ricci; any errors of fact or interpretation are the responsibility of the second author.

substantially greater duration of military rule implied in those aspirations requires a correspondingly greater capacity to govern.[1]

Thus, institutional military rule requires the armed forces to create a new "governing elite."[2] The success or failure of this elite depends on many factors: the substantive ideological and policy directions chosen, the resources available, the social forces supporting and opposing the regime, and other aspects of the domestic and international context. However, the outcomes of military rule also depend, in part, on certain qualities of the governing elite itself:

1. *Structure*: An effective governing elite requires a recognized and accepted structure that defines roles and relationships among members of the elite. In military regimes, the critical question is the relation between those officers that hold governmental office and the rest of the armed forces.

2. *Political experience and expertise*: Particularly those members who hold top governmental posts need prior experience in policymaking and political leadership. Technical expertise can normally be obtained from advisors and staff; political expertise in managing technical experts, integrating technical and political criteria, and generating support from public constituencies is rarely available except through prior apprenticeship in government positions.

3. *Political linkages*: An effective political elite requires linkages to the rest of the population. These linkages provide critical feedback about the consequences of government policy decisions as well as input from social groups whose cooperation is essential to the success of those policies. These linkages also provide citizens with the symbolic and institutional mechanisms to interpret and respond to the policy offers and ideological positions of different factions within the political elite.[3]

In the sections that follow, we consider each of these characteristics of the governing elites constituted by the 1966–73 and 1976–83 military regimes in Argentina.

The Structure of Power

In 1966, the "Argentine revolution" led by General Juan Carlos Onganía pledged to carry out a program of economic and social transformation. In principle, the Argentine revolution would have led to a major realignment of political forces, eliminating the Peronist–anti-Peronist cleavage that had dominated Argentine politics since 1955. In 1976, the Process of National Reconstruction (known as the Proceso), headed by General Jorge Videla promised even more sweeping changes in Argentine society, including "modernization" of the economy and the state, "moralization" of public life, and restoration of public confidence in government. Both regimes immediately abolished what they saw as the "political impediments" to the necessary policy changes—dissolving the congress, intervening in provincial governments and dissolving provincial legislatures, replacing members of the supreme court, and suspending partisan political activity. Unlike previous military regimes in Argentina, both regimes effectively abolished the federal structure, directly subordinating provincial and local authorities to central government authority. Both assumed a self-proclaimed "constituent power," declaring that the new regimes were not bound by existing constitutional or juridical norms except insofar as they did not conflict with the objectives and decrees of the "revolutionary government."[4]

Having dismantled the institutional structures of the previous civilian regimes, both Onganía and Videla faced the question of defining a different structure of power for the new regime. Onganía's response was to create a regime with only limited participation by active-duty officers and no formal mechanisms of accountability to the military institution. Fearing the reemergence of factional strife within the armed forces,[5] Onganía attempted to avoid the politicization of the "military as institution" by minimizing its involvement in the "military as government."[6] At his insistence, the powers of the military junta were limited to considering future amendments to the Statute of the Argentine Revolution and designating a successor if the presidency were vacated. As commanders of the three armed forces, the members of the junta were subordinate to General Onganía as president and commander-in-chief.

As president, Onganía exercised the legislative powers of the congress, dictating "laws" published with the same numeration and format as those of previous civilian governments. In the official view, the Argentine revolution had fixed objectives but no fixed term in office. Thus, the military regime was explicitly not provisional or transitory but, rather, a presidentialist regime of indefinite duration. Early in his term, Onganía reorganized the executive branch, expanding the Executive Office of the Presidency and reducing the number of ministries, but simultaneously increasing the number of secretaries of state charged with implementation of the "national policies and strategies" formulated by the ministers.[7] The General Secretariat of the Presidency became the nexus for study, approval, rejection, or modification of proposals sent to the president by ministers, secretaries of state, and governors.[8] The structure of power was thus unipersonal, autocratic, and highly centralized, modeled in key respects on the ideal type of a military hierarchy.

The armed forces accepted this relationship and remained "apolitical" for more than three years. Many officers shared Onganía's belief that active military participation in the government would result in politicization, fragmentation, and decreased professionalization. Nevertheless, for the armed forces, the Onganía model amounted to a military government in which the military did not govern. After an initial honeymoon, the officer corps began to resent being ultimately responsible for the performance of a government that was perceived as following its own political objectives, rather than those of the armed forces. Although Onganía repeatedly denied having corporatist intentions, the armed forces and various sectors of civilian opinion interpreted ideas such as "community participation" as having corporatist overtones. Army documents began to circulate that stressed the desirability of returning to constitutional democracy, explicitly rejecting "obsolete corporatist formulas." The liberal internationalist economic policies of the Onganía administration likewise clashed with the economic views of most of the officer corps.[9] Amid increasing signs of economic failure, the explosion of popular opposition in the Cordobazo riots sealed the fate of Onganía, who was overthrown in a palace coup thirteen months later.

With the installation of General Marcelo Levingston as president in 1970, the armed forces took a more forceful institutional role in the new government. Legislative faculties were endowed in the president, but an amendment to the Statute of the Revolution required that all major decisions be approved by the junta of commanders-in-chief, thus inserting the commanders—especially the army commander General Alejandro Lanusse—directly in the decision-making process. In principle, the president and the junta would share authority over decisions of major import, so that both would be committed to and responsible for the decisions that were made. In practice, this arrangement also proved unstable. As General Levingston appeared to waver in his commitment to a transition to civilian government, the junta deposed Levingston and assumed power itself in March 1971. General Lanusse was named president of the nation and was assigned legislative and executive powers *in representation of the junta*, which retained the right to approve or disapprove major decisions by a majority vote.[10]

After two years of negotiation and maneuver, elections were held in 1973, and power transferred first to Héctor Cámpora and then to former president Juan Perón. After Perón's death a year later, a crumbling economy, spiraling polarization, and political violence led to a new military takeover in March 1976. Once again, the armed forces searched for a political formula to define the relationship between the military government and the military institution. This time they chose the inverse of the

Onganía model, insisting on a government *of* the armed forces, rather than one merely installed and supported by the military.

During the Proceso, the military junta, composed of the commanders of the army, navy, and air force, constituted the "supreme organ of the State." The junta reserved the right to name the president and members of the supreme court and to exercise all executive powers as well as final legislative authority. The Legislative Advisory Council, consisting of three officers from each service, was created to act as legislative advisors to interpret "military thought" with respect to major issues. The council had the power to refer projects of law, including those proposed by the president, to the junta for a final decision or to approve lesser, undisputed decrees. In an effort to avoid interservice rivalries, certain ministries were assigned to each service—Foreign Relations and Welfare to the navy; Interior and Labor to the army; and Defense and Justice to the air force. Despite the formal commitment to an equal sharing of power—government by thirds—the army also had significant influence in the Ministries of Economics and Education and a 50 percent share of the provincial governorships, compared to 25 percent for the other services.

The tripartite division of the government between the services was both unwieldy and unstable. Governing by thirds created not only inertia but reciprocal veto powers that made decision making extraordinarily difficult and inefficient. This structure also led most officials to be more loyal to their respective services than to the military government. The result was an extraordinary fragmentation of the state apparatus and the general subordination of government decision making to the corporate interests, internal conflicts, and chain of command of each service.[11]

By authority of the Statute of the Process of National Reconstruction, the junta appointed the army commander, General Videla, president of the nation for a three-year term. Under the threat of a serious guerrilla challenge, the military government initially managed to maintain its internal unity. However, as the guerrilla threat was exterminated through extensive repression, internal splits reemerged over economic policy, political strategy, and the power and autonomy of the repressive apparatus. In 1979, a hard-line general revolted against Videla's successor as army commander, General Roberto Viola. In 1980, after substantial delay caused by the inability of the junta to reach consensus on a new president within the mandated period, Viola was finally named to the top post, with the navy abstaining and the army supporting but internally divided. Eight months later, Viola was ousted by army commander General Leopoldo Galtieri. Galtieri assumed the presidency while retaining his position as commander-in-chief of the army, thus violating the interservice accord that (after Videla's first term) the president would be a "fourth man" subject to the junta of commanders. The Argentine defeat in the Malvinas led, in turn, to the overthrow of Galtieri.

In the end, both Argentine military regimes failed to forge a stable relationship between the military government and the military institutions. Having worked diligently to overcome the factional conflicts in the army in the early 1960s, Onganía could not avoid the repoliticization and splintering of the military under the military government, even with only minimal military participation in that government. The Proceso could not avoid interservice rivalry and factional splits, despite its elaborate and cumbersome attempts to devise a scheme that would guarantee long-term military support for the military regime. Substantive divisions within the armed forces over policy directions further complicated the process of policy formation and presidential stability.

Both the minimum participation and the maximum participation formulas for defining the relationship of the military institution to the military government ultimately failed. These failures cannot be attributed simply to poor leadership or to the deficiencies of the organizational formula. The Argentine experience suggests that this is a fundamental contradiction that cannot be resolved by manipulating the organizational chart of the military regime.

Political Experience and Expertise

Little attention has been paid to the civilian component of military governments. Yet given the limited numbers of top-ranking officers, the armed forces cannot govern by themselves.[12] During the first military regime, the presence of civilians was especially marked. In the Onganía administration, the governing elite of top office-holders consisted of 5 officers and 125 civilians.[13] (In the Levingston interregnum, there were 15 officers and 75 civilians; under Lanusse, 16 officers and 100 civilians.) During the Proceso, the military presence was substantially higher. Each service had its "feudal domains," and active-duty officers were appointed to a much wider range of subordinate posts—as commanders of the federal police, intervenors of the central labor federation and key unions, and heads of the major state enterprises. Nevertheless, in terms of composition, both were effectively civil–military regimes.[14] Even at the high point of military dominance, civilians held two-thirds of the top government posts.[15] Overall, combining both military regimes, only about a third of the ministerial positions and a quarter of the top government posts were held by military officers.

The key question is the political capacity of this mixed civil–military elite. Most professionalized militaries deliberately attempt to restrict outside influences and to reinforce internal mechanisms of socialization. Professional training and political-ideological instruction serve as mechanisms for the formation of cadres that meet the desired professional profile. In Argentina, the objective has been to create military personnel with a high degree of technical capacity and a strong "apolitical" orientation.[16] The military educational system is organized completely independently from the national system of education; internally, the system of promotion by merit is the backbone of the military's bureaucratic structure. The armed forces are by design substantially isolated from civil society. In order to maintain their cohesion and prestige, officers withdraw into the institution. As a result, neither the armed forces nor their officers are prepared to deal with societal conflicts or to recognize the need for political mediation of those conflicts.

The armed forces have as their raison d'être the use of legitimate violence. From this mission, the armed forces derive their own norms and system of organization. The most important organizational values derive from their pyramidal structure and centralization of command. The armed forces are not structures organized to accommodate conflict and political bargaining. Rather, they are bureaucratic structures, in which verticality, hierarchy, and subordination are ensured through strict military discipline. In such institutions, there are no formal mechanisms of counterpower, no checks and balances, and no limitation of central authority. Within the institution, there are no provisions for factional divisions or internal deliberation. Hence, the armed forces are not capable of regulating or accommodating conflicts that arise from civil society, even though such conflicts inevitably infiltrate the military and erode command authority when the military assumes political power.

Civilian officials in Argentine military governments tended not to compensate for the political deficiencies of their military colleagues. In a sample of civilians and officers holding government posts during these two military regimes, 62 percent of the civilians reported no affiliation with any political party.[17] (Those who were affiliated were predominantly associated with parties of the center-right.) In most cases, these civilians were political "notables" and spokespersons for sectoral demands, rather than political leaders. In modern societies, the trend has been toward professional politicians, who use political parties as collective structures to resolve conflicts among competing interests according to the formal and informal rules of the political game. In the Argentine case, both military regimes tended to select civilian officials who had spent most of their lives *outside* strictly political organizations or individuals who had had, at best, part-time political careers.

In order to assess the prior political experience of this governing elite, the previous posts held by this sample of civilian office-holders were examined. Nearly 40 percent of this prior experience was at the administrator or advisor level, 30 percent at the subsecretary level, and 30 percent at the secretary or minister level. Most of this prior government experience was in either the economics ministry or the education ministry. Moreover, roughly 80 percent of all the positions held—including all of the higher-level positions—were held during previous *military* governments! Looking at the data somewhat differently, the interruptions in the public service of these civilian functionaries correspond to the civilian governments that preceded each military regime. Thus, we conclude that these civilian officials generally had prior government experience, but that this prior experience tended to be *administrative* experience during military governments, rather than *political* experience in office-holding during periods of open political activity.

With respect to the military office-holders, only 10 percent had held any prior political post within the military, although 27 percent had served as service liaisons to the executive or legislative branch. All had held general staff posts, and over half had served abroad, but nearly 60 percent had never held a prior governmental post. (The remaining 40 percent had held posts in the military government following the overthrow of Perón or in the Videla administration.) The military members of this elite shared with the civilians a general lack of prior political experience.

Reflecting the bureaucratic nature of the professional military career in modern societies, the Argentine military's approach to governing was bureaucratic, rather than political. Instead of seeing the task of governing as generating policies with public support and resolving conflicting conceptions of what policies would serve the common good, the military tended to rely on expert judgment of what policies were needed, assuming no need for consultation or popular participation in the formulation of those policies. This bureaucratic bias is evident in the structuring of the policy process, especially during the Onganía administration.

One prominent example was the institution of the National System for Planning and Action for Development, charged with responsibility for formulating policies and strategies for development and preparing regional and sectorial medium- and long-term plans, budget proposals, and related program proposals. Elaboration of these plans was entrusted to the National Development Council on the basis of policy objectives specified by the government. The National Development Council, in turn, was supposed to coordinate its policies with the National Security Council in order to harmonize development with security. These two bodies were to elaborate a national plan for security and development that would establish medium-range plans and provide the basis for specification of annual programs and the corresponding budgetary allocations. Once approved by the president and the cabinet, these policy documents would be binding on the public sector and would "guide" the private sector as well. In both cases, detailed attention was given to which bureaucratic agencies would be represented in each council, but no attention was given to representation of or consultation with the public or groups outside the government.

In the Proceso, the military likewise assumed that the Council of Legislative Advisors would interpret collective military opinion with respect to major policy issues and, with the assistance of the appropriate technical experts, translate that opinion into laws that would effect major socioeconomic and political changes. Apart from the erroneous assumption that Argentine officers shared a single common vision of the preferred alternative to the status quo, this structure assumes a normative model for policymaking, modeled on the military general staff, in which the staff analyzes issues and formulates alternatives for the commander to decide. In this model, it would obviously be illogical to ask the opinion of soldiers or noncommissioned officers or to seek input from those whom the decisions are designed to affect.

Implicit in the Argentine military's approach to governing is a bureaucratic-professional mentality that assumes that good policy is the result of expert judgment and devotion to the common good. In this view, poor policy results from poor leadership, deficient organization, or an excess of external pressures that prevent good leaders from acting in the common interest of the nation. Hence, the characteristic military assumption is that good government is largely a matter of bringing in honest, well-intentioned leaders—that is, themselves and like-minded civilian "experts"; redrawing the organizational chart; and reducing the capacity of civil society to interfere with "rational" decision making by the new governing elite. In Argentina, both military regimes accordingly drafted a group of apolitical—that is, nonpartisan—civilian allies into the top levels of government. The result was that both the civilian and military components of the governing elite shared a basic lack of political experience and expertise that left them singularly ill-equipped to deal with a highly conflicted, politically mobilized society.

Societal Linkages

As noted earlier, the Argentine military has generally maintained a substantial degree of isolation from civil society. Given the desire to promote a professional military identity and the desire to avoid the threats to internal discipline inherent in contact with a conflictive society, the armed forces have deliberately minimized societal contacts, particularly at the lower ranks of the officer corps. This does not imply that the armed forces are a closed institution. In practice, contacts with civil society occur in the everyday life of most officers—in social gatherings with civilian relatives, in exposure to the national media, and at the upper levels, in extraofficial social-political contacts with civilians seeking to influence the armed forces.[18] Nevertheless, the armed forces, by design, are not structured to facilitate linkage and communication with civil society, except as necessary to carry out their military missions.[19]

Based on our sample of civilian and military officials in the 1966–73 and 1976–83 military regimes, the civilian component of the governing elite seems to share many of military's deficiencies in terms of political linkages to the rest of society. Indeed, in some respects, the civilian component of this governing elite may be narrower than the military component.

In terms of social backgrounds, both the civilian and military officeholders in these two regimes were middle- to upper-middle-class or above. Among the fathers' occupations listed, merchants, professionals, and other middle-class professions dominated, with only a small minority of landowning families and almost no representation of working-class backgrounds. Of the civilians interviewed, 90 percent were born in the federal capital or the province of Buenos Aires. In contrast, nearly two-thirds of the military officers were born in other provinces. In both primary and secondary education, the civilians were more likely to have attended private schools, with the military having a higher proportion attending religious schools. (Over 40 percent of the civilians attended one of the three top elite secondary schools in the country.[20]) In a country where roughly 1 percent of the population had some university education,[21] all but two of the civilians had university degrees; slightly more than half had done graduate work abroad. All but one were professionals, predominantly lawyers (52 percent) and economists (24 percent). All of the officers interviewed were graduates of their respective general staff schools, and nearly all claimed knowledge of at least one foreign language.[22]

Despite the limitations of the data,[23] this civil–military elite appears to be distinguished by the absence of representatives of the popular classes[24] and by its high level of education. Asked to explain how they came to be named to positions in a military government, the civilians stressed their personal achievements (30 percent), professional experience (20 percent), or expertise (13 percent) and the fact that they knew the person who named them to the office (45 percent).[25] Although the details varied, the general pattern was that military leaders had a general profile of the kind of civilian desired, which was used to screen the pool of potential nominees. In both military regimes, professional experience and expertise figured prominently, along with guarantees that the individual would act in accordance with the objectives fixed by the regime, rather than partisan or sectorial interests. This conception of office-holding in terms of expertise in serving fixed national objectives is consistent with the military's view of governance as administration and reinforces the conclusion that civilian members of these regimes were not chosen for their capacity to represent the social classes to which they belonged or to link the regime to those classes.[26]

Another indication of the narrowness of this governing elite lies in its political-ideological makeup. When asked to identify the most important political problems facing Argentina,[27] both the civilians and officers, by wide margins, stressed deficiencies in political leadership and cultural or educational factors. The civilians listed lack of productivity and educational factors as the most important economic problems; the military listed productivity and statism. Although declining standards of living was the third most frequently mentioned economic problem, maldistribution was mentioned by only 12 percent of the civilians and 16 percent of the officers. With regard to the role of the armed forces, a majority of both civilians and officers agreed on the necessity of a military role in internal security as well as external defense.[28]

In the absence of equivalent survey data for other civilian elites or for the Argentine public, the significance of the viewpoints expressed by this civil–military elite are a matter of interpretation. Nevertheless, the generally conservative tone of both the civilian and military responses is evident, as is the absence of attitudes associated with the Peronist party or the Radical party. Together, these two parties have dominated electoral politics in Argentina for decades, representing a large majority of the population. Among the office-holders from these two military regimes who were interviewed, no one identified with the Peronist party or had a family member so identified. (On the contrary, many of the civilians interviewed reported that their earliest political activities were in anti-Peronist organizations.) None identified with the Radical party, and only 21 percent had families who identified with that party. Although the evidence is not conclusive, it suggests that the overall viewpoint represented in this governing elite is substantially more conservative than that of the society at large. In essence, the leaders of military governments surround themselves with like-minded civilians, rather than seeking to incorporate a diversity of viewpoints.

This is not to say that either military regime managed to achieve ideological agreement within the governing elite. Despite the points of agreement discussed earlier, the civilians interviewed were more likely to emphasize the lack of belief in democracy as a political problem; the military were more likely to emphasize the failure of the political parties. The civilians were more likely to consider inflation a critical economic problem; military officers were more likely to see speculation as the problem. Civilian office-holders were far more likely to define the role of the state as "subsidiary" or "minimal," promoting private initiative; military officers were more likely to favor a stronger "guiding" or "controlling" state. Both military regimes suffered from serious conflicts between the antiliberal economic orientations of the bulk of the officer corps and the liberal internationalists who controlled economic policy. Ideological differences and policy disagreements occur in any regime. These military regimes were notable only for their lack of structural ability to accommodate and express constructively the inevitable conflicts over the general premises and specific items of state policy.[29]

Some Comparisons

A comprehensive comparison of the military regimes in Argentina with those of other South American countries is beyond the scope of this chapter. Nevertheless, the political deficiencies of military governments in Argentina appear to be common to institutional military rule elsewhere in the region. Difficulties in defining a stable structure of power between military rulers and the armed forces are almost universal.

In Peru, the 1975 overthrow of the "revolutionary government of the armed forces" resulted from a variety of substantive policy failures, but also from internal military splits over the direction of government policy. The position of the government was weakened by charges that General Velasco was defying institutional norms and ruling in his own right, rather than as the institutional representative of the armed forces.[30]

In Uruguay, the "council of generals" became the ultimate decision-making body within the military regime, in which the military never formally took over the executive.[31]

In Brazil, the armed forces designated a succession of military presidents. Once appointed, they were subject to the standard rules of the Brazilian presidency—that is, relative independence, subject to the need to negotiate with "the military power" and maintain military support to stay in office. Conflicts between military factions were common, but the strict rotation of the presidency and intramilitary negotiations prevented any serious threats to the stability of the regime.[32]

In Chile, the supreme authority was initially the military junta, rather than General Pinochet, who was a relatively late convert to the plot to overthrow Allende. Within a year, however, Pinochet became president of the republic (instead of president of the junta). Following the forced dismissal of the air force commander from the military junta in 1978, Pinochet became the *generalissimo* of the armed forces as well as president and commander of the army. In sharp contrast to the Argentine Proceso, officers serving in government posts in Chile do so as appointees of the president, not the military services—from which they are, in effect, granted temporary leave. Despite conflicts with the air force and navy commanders, Pinochet resolved the tension between the military as government and the military as institution by subordinating the latter to the former in a highly personalized regime, which is not, in fact, accountable to the armed forces.[33]

In all of these cases, internal military disagreements over government policy impeded the effectiveness of the policymaking process and weakened military support for the military government. In those cases where suppression of "subversion" was an important regime objective, the hardliners in control of the antisubversive apparatus eventually threatened to take control of the government and/or the army. Succession crises were common, as military regimes lack the normal constitutional mechanisms for nomination, election, and succession of government leaders. Typically, these military regimes rapidly lost their initial base of public support, in part because the liberal economic policies favored by most of these governments resulted in substantial economic sacrifices by the majority of the population. At the same time, these regimes lost support because they were structured not to provide political linkages to civil society (or to enforce such linkages through formal mechanisms of accountability) but, rather, to impose the "bitter medicine" deemed necessary by a narrow civil–military elite that presumed to have remedies for society's economic and political ills. All of these regimes—including Peru's reformist military regime—proved impossible to legitimate, resulting in systematic recourse to repression, political weakening, liberalization, and an eventual military withdrawal of support for continued military rule.

Some of these regimes lasted considerably longer than their Argentine counterparts—twenty-one years in Brazil and, thus far, fifteen years in Chile. In the Brazilian case, military governments—like their civilian predecessors—managed to achieve a substantial degree of economic success, due in large part to the special attractions of Brazil to foreign investors and to the relative weakness of civil society in resisting government-imposed sacrifices. In Chile, the extraordinary degree of threat to the existing social order during the Allende regime, divisions in the political opposition, Pinochet's skill in playing on middle-class and elite fears, and a strong tradition of military subordination have sustained the Pinochet regime, despite its policy failures and the rebirth of civil opposition.[34] The economic fortunes of military regimes may vary, and the civilian alternatives may be more or less threatening to key elites. Nevertheless, the political flaws of institutional military rule appear to be a constant.

Conclusions

The contradictions between military government and the military institution are fundamental and inescapable. The officers selected to head the initial and subsequent military governments are not elected by the officer corps; hence, there can be no assurance that their views and policy preferences will represent those of the armed forces. As there is, in fact, no single military view on national issues, factional divisions inevitably arise within the military government and between the government and the rest of the officer corps. As long as the essence of military institutions in Latin America remains the hierarchical relations of discipline and obedience between superiors and subordinates, the military president as commander-in-chief cannot be made subordinate to less-senior officers. Thus, he also cannot be held accountable to the armed forces without violating the principle of hierarchy. If the president is not the commander-in-chief, then the armed forces become a hierarchy headed by a committee. Although the junta form of government is often adopted, it is rarely stable, except in the short term. It is almost never successful in avoiding personal or service rivalries. Despite the formal equality of the military services, the army and its commanders are invariably the dominant political forces in military regimes. Over time, disagreements over policy matters and power struggles within the military government spill over into the military institution. Opposition civilians attempt to penetrate the military's institutional boundaries in the search for disgruntled officers who share their complaints about the military government. Because promotions, assignments, and retirements influence the factional balance between supporters and opponents of the incumbent military faction, political criteria replace professional merit in institutional decision making. Professional norms become subordinate to personal and political loyalties. In the end, military government is a contradiction in terms; the armed forces cannot govern without subverting their own essence.

The other flaws of the governing elite of military regimes likewise seem inescapable. Given the professionalized military's distaste for partisan politics and its bureaucratic preference for order and efficiency, most officers have a negative view of politicians. This negative image is reinforced by a natural tendency to blame civilian political leaders for the political and economic crises that led to the military decision to install a military regime. Nevertheless, those who have the responsibility for constituting the new military government face a dilemma. Most, if not all, of the potential civilians who might be called to join the new government are either relatively inexperienced or—in the military's eyes—compromised by their prior participation in the old regime, just overthrown. As a result, military governments are typically populated by relatively unknown civilians who meet the test of technical competence and conformity with the ideological direction of the government. Most, however, lack political skills and experience in constructing alliances, building public support, resolving conflicts, or maintaining legitimacy. As in the Argentine case, the military officers who hold posts in these governments are typically competent administrators, but they have no political experience other than in the internal personal and bureaucratic politics within the armed forces, except perhaps for a minority who held minor posts in previous military governments.

A similar dilemma exists with respect to the political linkages of the governing elite during military regimes. Selecting officers or civilian notables with recognized political ties to political and/or economic constituencies would contradict the military view that the armed forces embody national values and represent the national interest. In this view—common to most bureaucratic institutions but exaggerated in the military—the policy preferences of representatives of civil and/or political society are suspect, because they represent a part of the nation, rather than the interests of the whole nation. Moreover, they represent short-term, rather than permanent, interests. The military's preference for governments without political linkages to society derives from this institutional self-image as being located "above" society—above classes, above partisan interests, and above base economic motives. This preference for a government suspended above society is reinforced by antidemocratic and technocratic elements of military thought that stress the inability of the people (soldiers) to know or act in the public good—hence the need for a strong government (officers) to make decisions in the best interests of the population, even when those decisions are contrary to the wishes of those involved. This conception of the relationship of state authorities and society overlooks the impossibility of any purely objective identification of "national interests" or "the common good". Thus, military governments, by closing off linkages to the rest of society, become captive to the corporate interests of the state apparatus (including the armed forces) and the interests and values implicit in the ideological viewpoints predominant within the upper ranks of the officer corps. The result is not, in practice, a government that is any more disinterested, objective, or honest than the average civilian government. Indeed, by their nature and structure, modern military regimes in South America typically serve a narrower set of interests and values than that of their civilian counterparts. However, military governments cannot resolve that deficiency by selecting civilians with strong societal linkages without introducing conflicting interests, demands, and values into regimes with no formal structures for conflict resolution and mediation. The result of doing so may be a government with a stronger base of civilian support, but also a government more vulnerable to internal factionalization, fragmentation, and threats to military discipline. Opening the military regime to civilian linkages is likely to reduce the autonomy of the governing elite. The resulting loss of autonomy may be the necessary condition for civilian support and political stability, but the political virtues of power-sharing are rarely appreciated by those whose careers are spent climbing an elaborate ladder of hierarchical authority.

The central thesis of this chapter is that the essence of government is politics, rather than administration. From this perspective, the governing elites created by recent military regimes in Argentina have suffered from inherent weaknesses that cannot be remedied by tinkering with organizational charts or substituting one set of leaders for another. This chapter is thoroughly pessimistic in regard to the hopes of those Argentines and others in the hemisphere who have looked to military governments as the solution to the conflict, disorder, and instability that often characterize civilian regimes. Civilian regimes, especially those based on limited participation and only conditional loyalty to the rules of constitutional democracy, have also failed in the basic tasks of governing. Only in rare cases in Latin America have civilian regimes been able to construct a stable and democratic relationship with the armed forces. If, however, the political weaknesses of military regimes are such that—sooner or later—they will fail, the civilian and military leaders of Latin America must turn to the task of redefining civil–military relations in democratic regimes with a renewed sense of dedication and urgency.

Notes

1. Paul Cammack and Philip O'Brien, "Conclusion: The Retreat of the Generals," in P. Cammack and P. O'Brien, eds., *Generals in Retreat: The Crisis of Military Rule in Latin America* (Manchester, England: University of Manchester Press, 1985), pp. 190–97.

2. As used in this chapter, the term *governing elite* refers to those who wield the power to govern others in any society—specifically, in this case, the holders of top offices in the state apparatus. The *political elite*, defined as those who wield the greatest political power, including power and influence over government office-holders, is a distinct (though potentially overlapping) social category.

3. Waldino Suárez, "Congreso y Clase Política en la Argentina," in *La Reforma Parlamentaria: Propuestas para el Fortalecimiento del Poder Legislativo* (Buenos Aires: El Cid, 1983), pp. 85–86.

4. See Mario Justo López, *Introducción a los Estudios Políticos*, Vol. 2 (Buenos Aires: Kapelusz, 1975); and Andrés Fink, *Los Gobiernos de Facto ante el Derecho y ante la Circunstancia Política* (Buenos Aires: Depalma, 1984).

5. Felix Luna, *De Perón a Lanusse*, 2nd ed. (Buenos Aires: Planeta, 1972), p. 187.

6. See Alfred Stepan, *The Military in Politics: Changing Patterns in Brazil* (Princeton, N.J.: Princeton University Press, 1971), pp. 253–66, and *Rethinking Military Politics: Brazil and the Southern Cone* (Princeton, N.J.: Princeton University Press, 1988).

7. "Ley 16.956 del 23 de Septiembre de 1966, Reorganización de los Ministerios y Secretarías de Estado Nacionales," in *Leyes Nacionales 1966* (Buenos Aires: Publicaciones de los Organismos Técnicos del Disuelto Congreso de la Nación, 1967), p. 100.

8. See Roberto Roth, *Los Años de Onganía* (Buenos Aires: La Campana, 1980).

9. See Guillermo O'Donnell, *El Estado Burocrático-Autoritario 1966–1973: Triunfos, Derrotas y Crisis* (Buenos Aires: Belgrano, 1982), pp. 95–103, 121–65.

10. See Alejandro Lanusse, *Mi Testimonio* (Buenos Aires: Laserre, 1977); and Rubén Perina, *Los Militares en la Política Argentina* (Buenos Aires: Belgrano, 1983).

11. For a detailed and sobering account of the deficiencies of the decision-making process during the Proceso, see Andrés Fontana, "Political Decision Making by a Military Corporation: Argentina 1976–1983," Ph.D. dissertation, University of Texas at Austin, May 1987.

12. In 1968, the Argentine officer corps consisted of roughly 4,000 men. Of these, 11 percent, or 440, were colonels or generals, with probably an equal number of lieutenant colonels. See Alain Rouquié, *Poder Militar y Sociedad Política en la Argentina: 1943–1973*, Vol. 2 (Buenos Aires: Emecé, 1982), pp. 312–13.

13. For the purposes of this study, top office-holders were defined as ministers, secretaries of state, and subsecretaries of state.

14. Cf. Amos Perlmutter, "The Comparative Analysis of Military Regimes: Formations, Aspirations, and Achievements," *World Politics* 33, no. 1 (1980): 97.

15. In Chile from 1973 to 1985, slightly less than half of the ministers were military officers; in Brazil from 1964 to 1983, 30 percent were military officers and the rest civilians. See Carlos Huneeus M., "La Política de la Apertura y Sus Implicancias para la Inauguración de la Democracia en Chile," *Revista de Ciencia Política* (Pontificia Universidad Católica de Chile), 7, no. 1 (1986): 40–41.

16. Carlos Moneta, "Fuerzas Armadas y Gobierno Constitucional Después de Malvinas: Hacia una Nueva Relación Civico-Militar," in C.J. Moneta, E. López, and A. Romero, *La Reforma Militar* (Buenos Aires: Legasa, 1985), pp. 83–84. In practice, the desired orientation is more properly characterized as "nonpartisan" than as "apolitical."

17. The sample consisted of thirty-three civilians and twenty-seven officers, including two former presidents, nineteen former ministers, twenty-one secretaries of state, and eleven subsecretaries. Although the sample was not random, we believe that it is generally representative of the officers and civilians serving in these governments.

18. Even these contacts are often deliberately selective in ways that protect the military from the intrusion of societal conflicts. For example, by tacit agreement, certain topics may be placed off limits in discussions with relatives who do not share political viewpoints considered acceptable within the armed forces. Officers are typically selective in the media viewpoints to which they expose themselves, and peer pressures most likely reinforce that selectivity. Even political contacts with disgruntled civilians, as occurred prior to both the 1966 and 1976 coups, appear to be subject to implicit rules designed to emphasize the corporate nature of the contact and to diminish the possibility that individual officers will become incorporated into the clientele of civilian leaders. More research is needed on the mechanisms through which military institutions insulate themselves from civil society.

19. In Argentina, those military missions require significant contact in the process of recruiting draftees and volunteers, in the operation of military bases throughout the country, and in the procurement of the financial and material resources necessary to sustain the institution. The military's contact with draftees from diverse parts of the country is sometimes alleged to be the source of a superior military knowledge of the needs of "the nation," but these contacts are not structured for communication about the needs of the populations in question. To the contrary, these are top-down contacts structured around the satisfaction of the functional requirements of the armed forces. At the most, these contacts expose officers to other social strata, about whom some officers may *infer* certain needs and/or desires. Obviously, in these kinds of situations, an officer's interpretation of the information gathered from such contacts depends more on the officer's political-ideological perspective than on the felt needs or desires of the civilians with whom he comes into contact in the fulfillment of his professional duties.

20. These were the Colegio Nacional Buenos Aires, the Escuela de Comercio Carlos Pellegrini, and the Escuela Argentina Modelo.

21. This is based on the 1947 census, which is the closest to the period in which this cohort of leaders was receiving its university training.

22. Of the officers interviewed, nearly half claimed a knowledge of two languages. English was the most common foreign language (83 percent), followed by French (55 percent).

23. Data such as these do not permit a comprehensive investigation of the class ties of this elite. It is not known, for example, to what extent these individuals owned various forms of capital. Although a majority of the civilian professionals described themselves as in independent practice rather than working in business enterprises, this does not adequately identify the possible relationships to domestic or international capital. A much more detailed investigation of family backgrounds would be required to establish the class backgrounds and current ties of these individuals. See Maurice Zeitlin and Richard Ratcliff, "Research Methods for the Analysis of the Internal Structure of Dominant Classes: Landlords and Capitalists in Chile," *Latin American Research Review* 10, no. 3 (1975): 5–61. Within the limits of this analysis, the picture that emerges of the governing elite during these military regimes is similar to that of contemporary European soci-

eties. Cf. Robert Putnam, *The Comparative Study of Political Elites* (Englewood Cliffs, N.J.: Prentice-Hall, 1976); Lewis Edinger, *Political Leadership in Industrialized Society* (New York: Wiley, 1967); and Donald Matthews, *The Social Background of Political Decision-Makers* (New York: Random House, 1954).

24. Within the Argentine military, the proportions of officers entering the military academy from lower- middle-class and working-class backgrounds have been increasing. Recall, however, that this cohort of officers entered the military academies in the late 1940s and early 1950s. A significant number of officers from working-class Peronist families entered the military during this period, but these officers were less likely to rise to the top military ranks during a period in which the armed forces were generally anti-Peronist.

25. Military office-holders also stressed their personal reputation (45 percent) and prior professional experience (69 percent) but placed more emphasis than the civilians on personal connections (69 percent) and ideological agreement (48 percent) with the government (includes multiple responses). The top-level civilians—that is, ministers—typically were named directly by the president or the junta, and they, in turn, generally named the lower-ranking civilians in their ministries.

26. In the case of the selection of Martínez de Hoz as the finance and treasury minister in the Videla administration, an informed source reported that one of the selection criteria was his connections to the international banking community, because the military leadership saw that it would be necessary for Argentina to borrow money to deal with the economic crisis inherited from the preceding civilian administration.

27. The interviews were conducted during 1985 and 1986, and the frame of reference of the question was contemporary problems, not those in the periods of military government.

28. The majority opinion in the sample in favor of an internal security role is directly contrary to the provisions of the new national defense law, which reserves that role exclusively to security forces under the Ministry of the Interior. A sizable minority of the civilian appointees and officers felt that the armed forces should participate in state leadership, without, however, assuming a "directive" function.

29. For example, Fontana, "Political Decision Making," p. 154, notes that military notions of hierarchy and obedience affected the internal interactions of the military governments. In meetings of high-ranking officers that dealt with government policy, often the presiding officer would present a policy statement or position, which might then be subject to clarifying questions, but not to real debate or discussion.

30. See Alfred Stepan, *State and Society: Peru in Comparative Perspective* (Princeton, N.J.: Princeton University Press, 1980); Cynthia McClintock and Abraham Lowenthal, eds., *The Peruvian Experiment Revisited* (Princeton, N.J.: Princeton University Press, 1980); and George Philip, *The Rise and Fall of the Peruvian Military Radicals* (London: Aldene Press, 1978).

31. Juan Rial, *Las FFAA: Soldados Políticos Garantes de la Democracia?* (Montevideo: Ediciones de la Banda Oriental, 1986), and "Las FFAA como Partido Sustituto" *Nueva Sociedad*, no. 81 (1986).

32. Alfred Stepan, *Rethinking Military Politics: Brazil and the Southern Cone* (Princeton, N.J.: Princeton University Press, 1987), pp. 2–5.

33. Genaro Arriagada Herrera, "The Legal and Institutional Framework of the Armed Forces of Chile," in J. Samuel Valenzuela and Arturo Valenzuela, eds., *Military Rule in Chile: Dictatorship and Oppositions* (Baltimore: Johns Hopkins University Press, 1986), pp. 117–43.

34. Karen Remmer, "State Change in Chile, 1973–1987," Paper presented to the Conference on State Change, Institute of Behavioral Sciences, University of Colorado, May 25–27, 1988; Manuel Antonio Garretón, "Political Processes in an Authoritarian Regime: The Dynamics of Institutionalization and Opposition in Chile, 1973–1980," in Valenzuela and Valenzuela, eds., *Military Rule in Chile*, pp. 144–83.

5

The Transition from Military to Civilian Rule in Guatemala

Alfonso Yurrita

A n understanding of the Guatemalan transition to democracy cannot be confined to a period as brief as that of 1984–88, when a formal transition from military to civilian rule took place. The democratic process and the civil–military relationship issue must be more specifically assessed, taking 1944 as the starting point. It was in that year that a series of components converged to make the army share the civilian goals of liberal democracy. Historically, there have been some other similar instances, such as the 1871 liberal revolution, when the army became professionally structured. This chapter attempts to analyze the arduous path Guatemala's social institutions, particularly the military ones, have had to follow since 1944.

A better comprehension of this process requires studying the military institution as such, separate from ideological or personal connotations—that is, in the context of its whole set of problems, just like any other social institution. Some premises have to be taken into account, including the fact that the Republic; the military values of subordination, obedience, honor, and nationalism; Christian and Western principles; principles of liberal democracy; and identification with Maya-Quiche ethnic roots are the backbone of the Guatemalan armed forces' thought and activities.

[margin annotation: Backbone of mil's thought + activities]

Such references are very often evoked by civilian political leaders to arouse an army reaction that is favorable to their causes. This is particularly true in the case of the "traditionalist" leaders, who are despised by the Marxist "revolutionaries," for whom the army is an obstacle to be overcome in order to gain power. The army, however, is esteemed by the civilians—particularly the peasants, who in one way or another have been in touch with the military and have borne the brunt of conscription.

I was granted valuable, unselfish help by the Ministry of Defense of Guatemala, particularly Defense Minister Division General Hector Alejandro Gramajo, as well as the specially appointed consultants, Colonel Jose Luis Quilo, Colonel Luis Rios, Colonel Mario Terraza, and Colonel Gonzalo Yurrita Nova—a member of the 1957 military junta, who has always shared with me the arduous experiences of military life. Dr. Cesar Sereseres, a professor at the University of California, Irvine, contributed his valuable advice and assistance.

The October 1944 Revolution: A Basis for the Politicization of Guatemala's Army

The October 1944 revolution changed the military's status from an institution of the president's personal power to a structure that set in place a liberal-bourgeois revolution. Until 1944, the country was literally militarized: Militarization embraced the public education institutions and the government entities; political authorities were monitored by military officers in the political-administrative jurisdictions called *Departamentos*; and above all, a militaristic approach pervaded every aspect of the social life. Thus, the army commands—including the position of war minister—were assigned to generals who were "fully trusted by the President."[1]

The 1944 revolutionary process, however, inserted the army into a legal framework that, instead of solving the problem of military control, transformed it into a political issue. The creation, by the constitution, of the Defense Board set out a conflict between the armed forces commander, Colonel Francisco Javier Arana—a line officer—and the defense minister, Colonel Jacobo Arbenz—an academy officer. This deepened an old problem within the armed forces between line and academy officers. The Defense Board corralled the army by granting it limited autonomy. The head of the armed forces was elected by the politicians through the congress, where the president could not legally intervene. The independence of the military structure gave those politicians the opportunity to consider running for the presidency. The military thus became a pawn on the politicians' chessboard. As a result, a growing number of well-known military men were appointed to high-ranking governmental positions.

The 1954 U.S. intervention and overthrow of Colonel Jacobo Arbenz involved the army in yet another conflict: the north–south confrontation. It also aggravated the already existing institutional crisis within the armed forces.[2] It created frustration regarding military values such as defense of national sovereignty; subordination, obedience and nondeliberation; and support for the constitution. Loyal, but inept, commanders, lacking training and adequate equipment, could not militarily resist the "invasion" or, to a larger extent, U.S. military pressure.

Under the circumstances, military values were set in a crisis. The military academy itself was affected. It wanted to avenge the affront to Guatemala's military heritage. The army rebelled, and on August 2, 1954—parting from the sacred military values of subordination and obedience, it attacked the "liberation forces" quartered at the capital on the occasion of the August 1, 1954, victory parade, in which the army was made to participate along with the "liberators." The coup had inflicted a great wound to military honor—although, in reality, the coup had been set up by the army's internal forces.

Many analysts—mainly in North America—have failed to understand the origins of this issue. They have given more importance to the negative aspects of Guatemala's "democratization," brought about by the local authorities' intervention. The same applies to the Left—particularly the Marxists, who have striven to develop such perceptions for their own sake, to damage the reputation of the system. After Colonel Arbenz was overthrown, the military crisis was basically associated with the search for the discipline of Ubico's times: military values and an Arévalo-style democratic process. The latter was supported by the U.S. government.

In 1957, the murder of Colonel Carlos Castillo Armas, the president of the Republic (a military caudillo of the right wing who staged the overthrow of Colonel Arbenz with U.S. support), and the ensuing political crisis led to the formation of a military junta. A "democratic" process inside the armed forces gave several military men the chance to embrace the goals of democracy and restructure and seek out its fundamentalism. They succeeded in part, but they failed in the long run.

When General Miguel Ydígoras, a former political boss during General Jorge Ubico's era, was elected president, the fears of many officers were temporarily calmed. However, things changed very little. Corruption and social and political crisis were compounded by the 1959 setup of an anti-Castro base, manned by Cuban exiles and supported by the United States. The goal of assisting the United States with an invasion of Cuba (a project that ended in the Bay of Pigs fiasco) was an affront to the armed forces' sovereignty. The recent wounds of the north–south conflict were opened anew.

This situation eroded the perception of the military as defenders of national sovereignty. In addition, the military felt humiliated, because not even the general staff was consulted about this presidential decision by an active-duty general from whom restoration of the military principles was an expectation. Amid a new conflict with the high command, and a new debate about the qualities of the midlevel commanders, uneasy feelings grew deeper, resulting in the early insurrection of a group of junior officers on November 13, 1960. They belonged to one of the factions that were struggling for army order and honor.

The coup attempt failed. Frustration created by desertion of some of the coup leaders led others to accept manipulation by Marxist-Castroist groups. The deserters took refuge in the mountains, forming a revolutionary movement. In Guatemala, this marked the beginning of the guerrilla movements that have left a trail of social and political violence.

Amid serious social conflicts, several coup attempts were staged. For the first time in the army's and Guatemala's history, the high command itself staged a coup (1963), frightened by the ghost of "renewed Communism" and manipulated by rightist groups.

The psychological impact on the armed forces of the recent developments in Cuba must be borne in mind when considering the military's
perspective of events in Guatemala. The dismantling of the Cuban professional army by a triumphant guerrilla force, as well as the early guerilla
uprisings in Guatemala, gave the military leaders strong incentive to stay
in power. Although the high command attempted to end manipulation of
the army by taking control, when it withdrew from power in 1966, an
"affidavit of understanding" was signed with president-elect Julio César
Méndez Montenegro. The president had to commit himself to "maintaining the present structure of the Government [the army],"[3] in which civilian power remained subordinated to the military. This entente between
the high command and the politicians resulted in a distinct role for each
group in the promotions of military graduates of a given year. The influence of the Adolfo Hall Vocational Military Institute, established during
the Castillo Armas rule to integrate the civilians into the military realm,
established an important future link between military men and civilians. In
this manner, the high commanders consolidated their power (given the
civilian authorities' mistrust of counterinsurgency), particularly in General
Carlos Arana's presidential period, in 1970.

What emerged from this arrangement was a caste of politicians and
interest groups that sought protection from the high commands. It also
created a feeling of overconfidence that resulted in the government's leading the state and the army to a serious crisis, which began in early 1980.
Until the March 23, 1982, coup, the institutional stability of the armed
forces had been eroding. General Ricardo Peralta, cofounder of the Centro
de Estudios Militares (CEM), has stated:

> If the Army is at all guilty, its guilt is not institutional. The blame must
> fall on those leaders who at a certain point forgot the moral values
> taught to its sons by the Politechnical School [the military academy].
> [They have] impaired the prestige of the institution, choosing to serve
> their personal interests instead of national good.[4]

The Military Development Concept as Challenged by Political, Social, and Economic Crisis

A number of factors led to the change of attitude by the armed forces of
Guatemala that resulted in the pivotal 1982 coup. The 1976 earthquake—
and the aid activities performed by the army—put the army in close
contact with Guatemala's poorest citizens. The army relied on two key
institutions to project itself in the rural areas: the National Emergency
Committee and, later, the National Reconstruction Committee (CRN). In
the beginning, the CRN was led by Peruvian-trained officers (such as

General Peralta Méndez) or officers trained in other South American countries, who would eventually become influential in the political-military ideological processes. The military created its own doctrines, and a "military developmental" philosophy emerged with Social-Christian currents.

Another factor was the impact on the military of the counterinsurgency efforts of the 1960s and the Alliance for Progress–fostered civic action program. The armed forces were forced out of their barracks and confronted social reality. The Alliance for Progress fostered the national security doctrine: "No nation can develop without security, and conversely, no security can exist without development."[5] In Latin America, this doctrine severely impaired political-military leadership in the face of the revolutionary crisis created by Castroite insurgencies as well as the processes of democratization themselves. The distorted notion of national security merits consideration, as it became an issue for the army of Guatemala at the time of the national crisis.

A second generation of insurgents also led to consolidation of the development doctrines. This group made a deeper impact than the first one, in that they attempted to influence the highlands indigenous people. Insurgents infiltrated the indigenous groups in order to accelerate the revolutionary process. They were mostly led by Marxist intellectuals or college students, survivors of the 1962–70 insurrections. Unlike the 1960s insurgencies, however, on this occasion a number of Catholic priests— mostly foreigners and rediscoverers of the "noble savage" of Father Las Casas—involved themselves. These priests converted themselves and the indigenous populations into "good revolutionaries."

Impressed by the underdevelopment of the indigenous areas, such priests drew inspiration mostly from the ideas of the "theology of liberation." They, in turn, organized the indigenous communities, using community power structures such as the Catequistas, who later were absorbed by a "peasant union." This sparked the struggle of indigenous groups against the Ladinos; it also set various indigenous groups in conflict among themselves.

This new revolutionary conflict—the so-called low-intensity war— developed within the so-called sector covering the Departamentos of Huehuetenango, Quiche, San Marcos, Quetzaltenango, Totonicapan, Retalhuleu y Solola. At its height, the struggle also affected the Departamento of Chimaltena.

Between May 25 and June 30, 1980, a group of officers of the CEM command and staff course studied the nation's political, social, and economic processes and the crisis generated at the presidential palace, which had become a source of concern for some military men. This study, named "Strategic Assessment of the Guatemalan State, 1980" (revised in

1981 and 1982), was submitted to the highest governmental levels.[6] No attention was paid to this study until the army took power on March 23, 1982. At that time, the "Strategic Assessment" was amended and turned into a government plan and afterward into so-called campaign plans.

A Nonpolitical, Nonpartisan Army?

In most of the countries where the institutions of government are unstable, political parties are divided. Where local selfishness emerges and corruption flourishes, the army represents the only stable, organized, and efficient force. The expansion of military activities into other spheres reveals the existence of a weak, sick social system.

Why, in 1982, was this behavioral change in the Guatemalan army taking place? Since October 20, 1944, not only had the army been involved in a series of crises, but it was also engaged in a twenty-seven-year war against its own indigenous population. Cesar Sereseres has pointed out that between 1980 and 1982:

> [Many] hundreds of officers had fallen in the battlefield. Decisions by the High Command engaged in party politics made the officers believe that such decisions had failed to solve the problems. . . . They [the army] despised development plans such as the so-called "Plan Ixil", prepared by the Economic Planning Secretariat—SEGEPLAN—for the highland region rejected by the Cabinet of then President Romeo Lucas. The Government fell prey to growing corruption; fraudulent elections were celebrated, and Captains started to complain before their trainers that their power was being "eroded".[7]

The army felt that the society had merely assumed a role of spectator-critic. The military institution was being manipulated by the politicians, which made the military commanders who took power after the 1982 coup exclaim: "No more opportunistic politicians! . . . We do not want to see the same faces again!"[8] This allusion to such political manipulation of the army ultimately became the leitmotiv of the early 1980 political-military crisis.

Previous studies of the armed institution—such as the 1974 work by Jenkins, Sereseres, and Einaudi—had already predicted a potential crisis of the country's military and political crisis:

> We see Guatemala's future as the stage of a complex internal balance of political manipulations associated with national elections, in addition to the various viewpoints about the appropriate rôle of the armed forces, and the factions and coalitions within them and the civilian field, and among military groups.[9]

Another issue with which the Guatemalan army had to deal was the Central American crisis, which became regional and international as the Nicaraguan issue attracted East–West confrontation. El Salvador was depicted by the U.S. administration as the country that "'drew the line' against Soviet expansionism." The army perceived all these conflicts as closely linked to its own issues of defense of the national sovereignty and territorial integrity of Guatemala and the freedom of the Guatemalan people. The Nicaraguan experience—the army said—showed them that military counterinsurgency efforts can be made "with or without U.S. support." They, however, had to face the following:

> Less than one fourth of their 18,000 soldiers could move and stay in the mountains; . . . 5,000 reservists and former soldiers were mobilized and sent to battle with poor equipment and were ill-trained, against well-armed and experienced guerrilla men. There was a need for more officers, parts, equipments, and weapons. The Air Force provided limited transport resources for the few operations forces and insufficient troop supply for air-based civic action and medical evacuation activities. While the Air Force was incapable of providing air support to the Army the few available aircraft had to remain on land periodically for maintenance. To meet the existing needs, the Air Force had to rely on the private airplanes of the Guatemalan Air Club.[10]

The Stability Thesis versus National Security

The army decided to launch a plan to defend the state. It began by defining "political" strategies for consolidating the state and the armed forces themselves, as a sine qua non for withdrawal from power—the so-called military abdication.

In search of a fundamentalism of its own, the Army designed a campaign strategic plan in five stages:

1. *Victory 82*: "To achieve reconciliation within the Guatemalan family for the sake of peace and national concord. To restore constitutional order, so as to guarantee respect for political participation and prevent frustrations through real democracy." The military actions taken included reinsertion of the population groups that had cooperated with the "terrorist criminals" and "use of all available means to fight the terrorist groups existing in military units."

2. *Consolidation 83*: "The main target was the civilian population, whereby the focus was that of meeting their needs . . . achieving most effective military presence at all affected areas, integrating the public serv-

ice organizations in the anti-terrorist struggle, so that the effort and the process of pacification of the country gained momentum."

3. *Institutional Restoration 84*: "Restoration of the constitutional order. Reconstruction of the facilities destroyed by the subversion and return of the people removed from their original places of abode."

4. *National Stability 85*: "Intensification of military operations so that the Government institutions could orient their support to social and economic programs, including motivation for massive electoral participation of the country's active political groups, so as to return the Guatemalan people their exclusive sovereign right of choosing the Fatherland's destiny."

5. *Consolidation 86 and Strength 87*: "These two stages were designed to strengthen the Guatemalan Army through professional leadership at all levels . . . in order to support free use of power by the Government."[11]

The original campaign plans were based on principles taken from the traditional national security and development doctrine. However, the notion of national security was examined in the light of the subsequent revision by the army. The term *security* itself began to be boldly questioned—because of possible ideological confrontations within the army and certain political groups, based on past experience. The army, like other armies in Latin America, felt that they were being "used." They decided to challenge the political powers in the context of the principles introduced by the Alliance for Progress, which ended up being one of the factors in the fall of the civilian governments.

In 1986, apparently trying to be a part of the solution, not of the problem, the army redesigned its strategy, focusing on the "thesis of national stability."[12] The national security doctrine was the target of criticism as a U.S. notion—hence, not valid for the region; military security could be attained only through alliances, rather than locally, without the geopolitical context. Hence, *security* is construed as a synonym for *welfare*—that is, as a minimum level of satisfaction of the needs of the majority of the population, rather than those of a small minority. The target would be to reach such stability, conceived as the balance of the political, economic, psychosocial, and military powers.

Military Fundamentalism and Democracy

After the March 23, 1982, coup, the army tried to redefine itself as an institution, because the coup itself created risks for its very existence. On August 8, 1983, the military commanders in charge of governmental affairs were "relieved"—that is, switched. This resulted from an attempt to manipulate the army—this time by fundamentalist religious groups, who took advantage of the appointment as president of the Republic and general commander of the army of a retired general and religious minister, Efraín Ríos Montt, and the appointment of other well-known religious ministers to key government positions. The image of the Catholic Church had been eroded during the subversive period by a series of dead and "disappeared" people and the elimination of its lay catechism cadres, as well as open participation in the previous political process. Religious groups brought to the conflict areas clashed with the military officers and Catholic groups. The latter challenged the government's protective attitude toward the former. In this regard, military history is linked to resistance to anything clerical—an effect of the liberal Revolution.

Some other interesting aspects of military thought during this process are, to a significant extent, linked with the "Strategic Assessment"—namely, the "permission" to form political parties of socialist leaning, including, though not explicitly, Marxist parties. Some change of attitude relative to the positions held within the institution itself reflected the convergence of the high command with radical right-wing groups.

As to those who considered themselves insurgents within the military, it is very clear that the struggle is military in nature; and as an army's function is winning wars, the resulting attitude is strictly professional. According to General Héctor Gramajo Morales: "We must defeat the adversaries." The evaluation by the other side—the rebels—is identical to that of the Army: "The process of war is much more complex. It includes very important qualitative factors impacting its development and consolidation."[13]

The Basic Government Statute of 1982 included an issue that is closely associated with the "Strategic Assessment" but, stemming from the army, can be described as a series of military commands: the issue of human rights in Article 23 ("Individual Guarantees"), identified as "the essential basis of the Nation's internal organization." The human rights crisis institutionally involved the army, which became exposed to high-level foreign affairs policies, creating a conflict with U.S. policies.

A series of statements against Guatemala's governments were also made by the UN Human Rights Committee (Geneva Subcommittee for Prevention of Discrimination and Minority Protection). The first was issued on March 14, 1979, followed by statements on March 7, 1980; March 11, 1981; March 11, 1982; March 8, 1984; and August 1984. In addition, the UN General Assembly issued Resolutions 37/184 (December 1982) and 1983/12 (September 1983), and the Subcommittee released Resolutions 19827 (September 17, 1982) and 1983/12 (September 5, 1983).

This all lent itself to developing stereotypes about the Guatemalan issue as a conflict exclusively between the indigenous people and the army. This image was apparent in many groups and works, particularly abroad (for example, the publication of Jean-Marie Simon, *Guatemala: The Country of the Eternal Spring and the Eternal Tyranny*, and the arduous work of the indigenous Guatemalan woman Rigoberta Menchú, who calls the Guatemalan army "the army of the rich").

The human rights issue is also associated with violence and the Guatemalan culture. In historical perspective, this can be summarized as a process of 'technological development' from the machete to firearms. This issue deserves in-depth discussion, given its complexity, including the element of the lack of credibility of the Judiciary and the security organizations in the Guatemalan society, which the Army had already analyzed. The army, in order to channel the struggle, sees itself as preventing the kind of indiscriminate political or ordinary criminal violence that could propitiate a state of social anarchy.

Abdication or Transition to Democracy

The Army defined itself in the Basic Government Statute of 1982 as "nonpolitical, based on non-deliberative obedience." The commanders made use of lobbies as advisory organs until a constituent assembly was established. Attempts were made to reorganize political structures shattered by the coup, and also by intellectual and physical repression resulting from the war and the doctrine of national security.

This led to the creation of an instrument to further the process of transition: the State Board, on which the major social pressure groups were represented, along with the legal political parties—that is, those that had not cooperated with the previous regime. For the first time, the major indigenous ethnic groups of the country were represented. In addition, the army relied on a system that had been beneficial to it in the past (during the 1963–66 rule and during the 1976 earthquake): the formation of technocratic-bureaucratic cadres to design and implement its development strategic policies, freeing the army to take care of purely military affairs.

A governmental structure was to be designed by civilians in the framework of the National Reconstruction Committee and based on the local powers as the developmental tool. In other words, the decision making was to be shifted to the village or municipal levels. Thus, the Interinstitutional Coordinating Boards were born. Though coordinated by the military, they were created to enable the state organizations to solve municipal problems efficiently, based on the "philosophy of turning the citizens into active factors in their own development."[14] Thus, the traditional "civil action" of the army became the new function of "civil affairs." The difference between the two programs was that the former's goal was "improving the image of the Army," whereas the latter's goal was "promoting a better standard of living for the population."[15] Another reason for the change was suspicion of a connection between civil action and the security doctrine developed under the Alliance for Progress.

Under this umbrella, the political groups were permitted to develop and design the constitution and the future political participation system according to their own criteria. Initially, the burgeoning of political parties led to the creation of twenty parties to participate in the establishment of the constituent assembly. Most of them tended to be conservative, rather than reformist, although some reformist individuals did participate. The Electoral Court's structure was changed to make it a credible organization (78 percent of the respondents affirmed that the elections were "fair," and 67 percent affirmed that the presidential elections would be free). Only twelve parties campaigned in the presidential election of 1985. They remained as structurally and ideologically inconsistent as ever, although by then, the European Social-Christian, Social-Democratic, and socialist movements had started to prepare their cadres. On that occasion, civic participation amounted to 69 percent of the registered citizens, the largest participation level since 1958.

The change of these political processes can also be partly explained by the interest of the world hegemonic blocks in Central America. They helped design political systems akin to their own, be they those of Western Europe, Eastern Europe, or the United States. Their branches started to cover Central America, a fact that will greatly influence the political scene in this region.

Civil–Military Relations during the Transition

On January 14, 1986, a civilian-led administration, elected according to democratic-liberal premises, was inaugurated. The army returned to its barracks. For the first time since 1944, no military men—on active duty or retired—were holding key positions in the government's civil institutional spheres. This retrenchment started six months before the delivery of power by the military to the civilians, following a general regulation issued by the army. The new policy of the military reflected, in part, the pursuit of "military fundamentalism" and, above all, the interest of the army in strengthening itself after the erosion it experienced during the previous processes (1944–85).

Dropping the security doctrine was a bold decision in the context of the traditional military thought of recent years. However, it reflects the military's perception of being manipulated by the high command and its allies, the politicians—the "petty politicians" of the notorious constitutional Defense Board, set up in 1944. This board limited the armed forces to performance of police functions—as the "state watchman"—or used its infrastructure to serve its own purposes (those of the "petty politicians"), thus impairing the professional capabilities of the military and the development of all of the other state institutions.

Another factor will influence the process toward democracy: the regional Central American conflict. From this upheaval, doctrines and methods emerge, mostly reflecting external motivations and the interests of the hegemonic powers to solve this conflict in accordance with their geopolitical views.

Conclusions

An attempt has been made toward democratic development and civilian control over the armed forces within the Guatemalan transitional framework. For this attempt to succeed, however, some requisites have to be met. Setting out the rules and describing the process is not enough. First, a party system has to be established that is representative and ideologically strong enough to be able to consolidate the process. In this regard, another institution that needs internal strengthening is the army. Although the army was not impaired by the previous processes to the same extent as the South American armies were, the magnitude of the interests created along the extended and traumatic path to its present condition did leave its imprint. Nonetheless, the army is institutionalized to a larger extent than the other institutions and can still be easily manipulated, because of the pronounced weakness of the society and the existence of serious economic, political, social, and anthropological problems. This is called political, economic, psychosocial, and military power—in sum, national power—by the new national stability doctrine of the army.

Second, both the army's "military power" and the "civil power"— economic, political, and psychosocial powers—will have to manage identical problems stemming from past factors. Even though the crisis is now less acute, domestic Central American and international political-economic problems remain. This is compounded by a factor with which there is little experience—namely, constitutional-ideological opening. All of these components have to be taken into account in considering the potential confrontation of ideologically motivated groups on the issue of state management.

Several questions can be posed, of which the following are the most important: Will the armed forces continue to be an ad hoc tool available to the groups that have traditionally seen it as an institution that could be used to solve their economic, political, and social problems? Will it continue to be regarded as a barrier by those who wish to effect "structural change" through violence, even though a mass movement be involved (the conspiratorial way)? Will civilian institutions and the military be able to implement their ideological design of self-legitimation and organization, targeted to respond to the processes included in the constitutional spirit (the electoral way)? If these were not feasible, the military institution would remain the most stable of all institutions; and attempts would be made to use it, as the most readily available tool, when the civilian tools seem inadequate.

For civilian institutions to prevail, civilian cadres must be trained and motivated to develop ideologically firm political designs that give the populace clear, specific, and honest answers. Moreover, the civil system must be strengthened so that it can coexist in harmony with the military structures.

Although not a necessity in terms of democratic consolidation, the issue of the integration of the Guatemalan population is yet to be resolved. Also unresolved is the issue of the inflow of assistance this population needs in order to reach a level of full development. Various economic and ideological models are being reviewed throughout the world, and it all depends on the Guatemalan and Central American societies' finding appropriate models and avoiding violent formulas, such as those applied so far. If this fails, the national stability model that the army strove to put into place will also fail. The unforeseeable consequences of a new polarization process—such as those of the past forty-four years—will make themselves felt. In such circumstances, no chance will remain for the civilian institutions to formalize themselves. The military institution itself will also be in serious trouble.

Notes

1. Colonel Ruiz assessed the military of the Ubico period (1930–44) as follows:

> The military stood out exclusively by being bold and brave. Education did not matter, whereby even in 1944 a great number of illiterate Generals commanded our Army, since the politicians manipulated the Army at whim. . . . General Ubico, . . . who put Cabrerista officers in important positions . . . the progressive-minded Commanders and petty Officers . . . countered by the retrograde Cabrerista commanders, who used fear to enforce discipline.

Colonel Enrique Ruiz Garcia, "El Poder Militar" *Revista Militar de Guatemala* (August–December 1954).

2. Certain leftist groups—above all, the insurgent Marxist groups—have created the myth that the end occurred in 1954, with the U.S. military intervention in Guatemala's politics. According to Sereseres:

> The roots of the insurgency of the 1980's can be traced to that of 1944–1954, the "Decade of the Revolution". Today's guerrilla leaders claim to maintain special links with the "unfinished revolution" of President Arbenz . . . which leftist intellectuals idealize and depict in romantic traits as the "Decade of the Revolution", and the radical leaders who make such presentation have supplied the guerrillas a mythology and a sense of their own identity.

Caesar Sereseres, "Guatemalan Insurgency and Counterinsurgency: The Highlands War, 1978–1982," (Irvine: University of California, School of Social Sciences, 1984). The guerrillas justify their struggle as follows: "Armed revolution became necessary in Guatemala because an oppressive regime has been in place for 34 years—since the 1954 U.S. violent armed intervention."

3. See "El Pacto Secreto de 1966," *Polemica*, no. 14–15 (1984).

4. General Ricardo Peralta M., El Ejército y la Paz, Texto de la Lección Magistral, con Motivo del XVII Aniversario del Centro de Estudios Militares de Guatemala" *Revista Cultural del Ejército*, No. 9 (1987). The Centro de Estudios Militares is a very important army officer training center—one that has helped change the army's attitudes regarding national issues in recent years.

5. *Seguridad y Desarrollo*, a strategic paper (Guatemala: Centro de Estudios Militares de Guatemala n.d.).

6. "Apreciación Estratégica del Estado de Guatemala," a part of the CEM command and staff officer course, May 25–June 27, 1980 (Guatemala: unpublished).

7. Sereseres, "Guatemalan Insurgency and Counterinsurgency."

8. General Efraín Rios Montt stated this to the press, as quoted in "The Coup That Got Away," *Time* (April 5, 1982).

9. B. Jenkins, C. Sereseres, and L. Einaudi, "U.S. Military and Guatemalan Politics." Paper presented at the Arms Control and Foreign Policy Seminar, Santa Monica, California, 1974.

10. Sereseres, "Guatemalan Insurgency and Counterinsurgency."

11. Juan Bolaños, "27 Años de Lucho por la Libertad," *Revista del Ejército de Guatemala* (1987). Among the other publications in which this plan is outlined: See also General Hector Alejandro Gramajo, "Contrainsurgercia en Guatemala: Un Casode Estudio." *Military Review*, Edición Hispanoamericana, 66, no. 11 (November 1986).

12. The army expounded its stability thesis for the first time in "Tesis de la Estabilidad Nacional" *Revista Militar* (May/August 1986).

13. Guerrilla commander Gaspar Ilom (Rodrigo Asturias), in *ORPA Boletin Informativo*, Guatemala, September 18, 1983.

14. General Héctor Gramajo Morales, *Gobierno Militar: Informe General* (Guatemala: Ejército de Guatemala August 8, 1983–January 14, 1986).

15. Ibid.

Part II
The Armed Forces, Civilians, and the Perception of Threat to the Social and Political Order

6

The Military's Perception of Threat in the Southern Cone of South America

Carina Perelli

Threat and Threat Perception

The subject of the military's perception of threat in the Southern Cone of South America has long been relegated to a second plane. The military corporation has been viewed more as an instrument than as a political actor, with its own perceptions and motivations. Explanations for the actions of the armed forces leaned more toward a structural vein.

In this context, it was not the military institution that defined the threat against which it was to act; rather, it was the group or class whose interests were defended by the armed forces in their capacity as *brazo armado*.[1] The military corporation was seen by political analysts as a mere executor, which could be mechanically activated by the threat perceptions of other social sectors to which it was subordinated.[2] To the extent that the armed forces are seen as a political actor with a great degree of autonomy, the study of this topic becomes essential for understanding the motivations behind the political actions of the military.

In their capacity as professionals of legalized violence within the state, military institutions throughout the world monitor threats to society on a constant basis. For the armed forces of the West, the main threat has a single name: communism. Nevertheless, the way in which the enemy is perceived varies considerably, in spite of the fact that this variation tends not to be taken into account by analysts, by politicians, or, in many cases, by the military corporations themselves.

For the countries of the NATO pact, the enemy has a perfectly demarcated locus: the Soviet Union and its satellites. The threat is managed in conventional terms. At this point in the twentieth century, this basically implies a defense policy based on deterrence. On the other hand, the perception of the threat (and the vision of the "good order" put in check by the threat) is shared, in different degrees, by both political and civil society. This is reflected in the decision-making process in times of crisis. Decision making involves the participation of members of the political society, exercising their governmental functions, as well as that of the chiefs of the military institution. The final decision rests in the hands of the political elite. Although this is not the policy generally applied in their zones of immediate influence (the back or front yards, as in Central America, the Mediterranean Basin zones in the Near East and Asia), in none of these NATO countries do the armed forces perceive a serious internal threat. Moreover, in none of these countries does the military corporation look suspiciously upon the functioning of democracy, with a fear that the democratic regime may become the ground of choice for "international Communist subversion." Despite recurrent episodes of terrorism, the enemy is always defined as the "other"—certainly a dangerous rival, but a controllable and identifiable one. In none of these countries has the military institution ceased to be subordinated to civil power, in spite of the existence of the enemy and of the threat the enemy is perceived to represent. In sum, in none of the countries of the developed West has the threat come to be perceived as intrinsic to the democratic regime itself and to the free functioning of an "easily subvertible" society.

On the contrary, the definition of the threat set forth by the armed forces of the Southern Cone is more diffuse and, at the same time, stricter than that of their allies in the First World. Although their enemy is apparently the same (international communism), their definition of this enemy varies significantly from that of the NATO countries. In the first place, the threat is not spatially circumscribed but, instead, is potentially present in all spheres of human action, at all levels, and in all forms. The world is perceived as the ground for continuous struggle between the enemy (the international Communist movement) and the forces of order (the military). But the privileged form of this struggle is not necessarily armed insurrection or any other form of open warfare (sedition, in this doctrinal context) but, rather, the subversion of the established order.

"All those who oppose the true order are subversives. . . . Where there is error, there is subversion," stated a commander-in-chief of the Uruguayan army, paraphrasing Saint Ciprian.[3] This opinion was reaffirmed by the official posture of the Uruguayan army, set forth during the Fourteenth Conference of American Armies in 1981 in a definition of subversion as:

> . . . action geared to undermining the military, economic, psychological, moral, or political force of a regime. The Uruguayan Army defines subversion as actions, violent or not, with ultimate purposes of a political nature, in all fields of human activity within the internal sphere of a state and whose aims are perceived as not convenient for the overall political system.[4]

It is in light of this conception of subversion that it is possible to construe a perception of threat that is intrinsically different from the one supporting the actions of the armed forces of the West, as well as the justification and the legitimization of the appropriate means and instruments to combat it.[5]

According to this view, to speak of a subversive war is to speak of a war in which the ultimate objective of the enemy is the conquest of the population, taking the mind of the adversary and the will of its commanders. It no longer involves an "amplified single combat, represented by two fighters, in which each one, by employing physical force, attempts to submit the other to its will." The means of this new type of war are, in essence, political and psychosocial: Military action will be resorted to only in the final instance.[6] The ultimate material employed by the enemy is human nature itself, which is weak, malleable, "bad." The battlefield is, then, the everyday existence of mankind, with its vices and passions. Thus, an Argentine rear-admiral would come to state:

> In effect, we are at war. But to say that it is a war against communism, for example, is an oversimplification. We are at war against an historical circumstance, against the negative aspects of the human condition, against our very selves. This war [against subversion] must be waged, more than ever, in the soul. The fight is to convince, more than it is to overcome. . . . The crux of the matter is an immaterial question: it is a question of the will, of the stupidity, the badness and the perfectibility of human beings.[7]

In the second place, an affirmation of this sort implies that the enemy is everywhere, particularly within one's own borders:

> The enemy is undefined, it uses mimesis, it adapts to any environment and uses every means, both licit and illicit, to achieve its aims. It disguises itself as a priest, a student or a campesino, as a defender of democracy or an advanced intellectual, as a pious soul or as an extremist protestor; it goes into the fields and the schools, the factories and the churches, the universities and the magistracy; if necessary, it will wear either a uniform or civil garb; in sum, it will take on any role that it considers appropriate to deceive, to lie and to take in the good faith of Western peoples.[8]

This kind of statement leads to two logical consequences. On the one hand, the armed forces as the essence of the nation should include and prioritize, within the definition of their mission, the functions of control and maintenance of internal order. This notion of order is framed by traditional parameters that refer to an idealized vision of the Christian West. This Christian West is a construction removed from time and space: a good order represented by institutions such as the family at its most patriarchal and by values such as loyalty, honor, respect, and duty. On the other hand, within this framework, everything and everyone become suspicious, given their potential subvertibility by international communism. The apparent Messianism of the region's armed forces finds its root here: Only a closed and total institution that resocializes and permanently controls its members and that embodies the values of the pure, uncontaminated Western tradition is in itself pure enough to lead a fight of this sort. In a perverse sense, it is the tradition of the *preux chevalier* revisited. The rest of the social and political actors, even those who constitute temporary allies, are susceptible to subversive contamination.[9] They frequently are not even aware of their own susceptibility,[10] as they bathe in the enemy's favorite culture broth: liberal democracy and the open society that a pluralist regime implies.

Moreover, to affirm that "[international Marxism's] revolutionary war is subversive and not merely seditious, insofar as its objective is not simply the overthrow of democratic institutions, but that its attack is directed at the spiritual assets of the nation, with a view to imposing a new order of values,"[11] implies moving the conflict from the conventional plane to the ideological plane. The armed forces, which are in charge of that fight, must become politicized in order to stop the enemy. Given that the armed forces' basis for legitimacy lies in their role as bulwark of the nation's spiritual assets, attacked by Marxist subversion, this politicization leads them to set the standard of measurement for the degrees of Marxist deviation in various spheres. They also become the judge of such deviations and the executive arm of the repression of the individuals, environments, and activities contaminated by the subversives' sapping. The magnitude and urgency of the threat to the "national being," as perceived and evaluated by the military corporation, will determine the modes and tempos of the political participation of the military actor.

Thus, as a reflection of the perception of threat on the basis of the distinction between subversion and sedition, the armed forces come to identify themselves as guardians and guarantors of a "good order," which they themselves have defined as such and which can differ widely from that prevailing among the rest of society. It is precisely the notion of subversion that makes it possible for that discrepancy to exist without producing a serious cognitive dissonance.

Furthermore, the fight against subversion is a permanent fight in two senses. On the one hand, there is no room in this sort of struggle for a distinction between periods of peace and periods of war. On the other hand, communism is a permanent aggressor and subversion a "timeless strategy."[12] The enemy lies in wait, ready to take advantage of the tiniest breach in the armor of the forces of the West. Because of this, the political mission of the armed forces is also permanent, and its continued interference in the nation's political life (directly, through the exercise of government, or indirectly, through pressure on the other political actor, as a "gray eminence" behind the throne) is thus justified and legitimate.

Moreover, the subversive war is a total war. This implies that it is a kind of conflict in which there is no room for negotiation or reconciliation of interests. It is the supreme "all or nothing"—a war that is resolved by the annihilation of the enemy or by one's own extermination, because what is at stake is the very essence of humanity. As announced—literally, not figuratively—by Lieutenant General Jorge Rafael Videla in 1976:

> Today, like yesterday, the Argentine army will win the fight, annihilating the very last vestige of those who ignominiously attempt to affront the majesty of the Republic and the dignity of its children.[13]

Argentine General Díaz Bessone quoted Friedrich Hayek to support the necessity of preserving the credo to win the great ideological battle of the epoch, saying "moral war par excellence (and for that very reason, a mortal one as well) which must be fought by crusaders. A war that leaves no room for moderates, for indifferents, for the lukewarm."[14] To a great extent, this explains the animadversion of the military involved in the struggle toward the political center and toward the liberal right.

Moreover, the very nature of the silent conflagration in which they are involved lends legitimacy to two important postures of the armed forces: their nonsubordination to the civil power, on the one hand, and their politicization, on the other. The military of this region firmly believes that it is living a total war, a situation in which wars are life-or-death struggles.[15] This would be the case of the antisubversive struggle, in which the forces of Good confront the forces of Evil and what is at stake is the very soul of the nation.

There is no place for the lukewarm in this battle. The indifference shown by liberal politicians regarding the fate of the West, the lightness with which they perceive the magnitude and the imminence of the threat, and the liminality of the permissive doctrine on which such perceptions are founded disqualify them from leading the fight and from making the ultimate decisions. Those decisions can remain in the hands of only one institution: the armed forces—the "safeguard of the permanent."[16] Thus, a Uruguayan military periodical defined the mission of the armed forces as follows:

> The carnal, concrete, living expression of the Fatherland in sovereignty is the armed forces, whose mission is the defense of unity, of integrity and of honor, as well as of everything essential and permanent in the country: the supreme interests of the Nation.[17]

Affirmations such as "Our country will be strong and honorable through its army, and its army will be so through the force of its spirit"[18] may seem Messianic. Perhaps it should be remembered, before making hasty and simplistic judgments, that Messianism would seem to be the only possible alternative within Manichaean and apocalyptic ideological parameters. Here, we are a long way from definitions of threat such as those that prevail within NATO. In the Southern Cone, however, the armed forces—in a state of permanent alert—perceive a threat that is all the more alarming in that it is less defined: subversion lying in wait, ready to contaminate, corrupt, and destroy the very values of the West.

This perception of the threat, shared and reelaborated by the armed forces of the Southern Cone, is disseminated throughout the rest of the subcontinent through numerous technical missions,[19] military publications, and the very prestige of the military institutions that nourish it. A perception of threat of this kind has a particularly solid, and even prestigious, doctrinal support, which makes it all the more impenetrable to the onslaughts coming from civilian trenches.

The Doctrinal Framework of the Antisubversive War

The thought processes of the officer corps in Southern Cone armies were always tinted with a more or less marked anticommunism. In their capacity as trustees of the legitimate violence of the state and, consequently, as defenders of the good order prevailing in a society, the armed forces of the region always sought to prevent all antisystem movement—anarchism and socialism, first, and later, after the Bolshevik revolution, communism. Nevertheless, never before had the anticommunism of the region's armed forces been expressed in the form of a military theory consisting of the analysis of a specific war.[20]

In effect, during the 1950s, the collaboration between Latin American armies and the U.S. military rested on a perception of threat founded on the possibility of Soviet aggression through conventional war operations. This is, in fact, the hypothesis of conflict that underlies the Inter-American Reciprocal Assistance Treaty of 1947 as well as certain joint military exercises (Operation Unitas) that endure to this day.

However, as of 1960, the idea of conventional wars in South America (in the form of either direct aggression by an extracontinental power or a possible conflict among countries in the area) began to be perceived as highly improbable. This does not imply that the region's armed forces, particularly those of the Southern Cone, flatly rejected the possibility of Communist aggression in South America but, rather, that such aggression began to be considered on the basis of different parameters. Those parameters, theoretically formulated in the light of a major turn in the strategic thinking of the West, seem to have been adopted by the region's military corporations at the time when an important potential crisis first began to emerge. This potential crisis consisted of a certain draining of the sense of mission of the armed forces: what could be called an existential crisis of the armed forces. Until then, this mission had, by definition, been the defense of the respective states against foreign aggression. With the disappearance of such a possibility, the military institution faced a lack of a sense of its very existence. In view of the increasing remoteness of the possibility of their being called to action in conventional warfare, the armed forces faced an existential crisis that could be solved only by redefining their role and mission.

The perception of the Communist threat as a variant of internal war (the revolutionary or subversive war) is substantially identical in all the armies of the Southern Cone. Although that conception does have roots in the indirect approach ideas of Liddel Hart, in the indirect strategic action of General Beaufré,[21] and in the U.S. conception of flexible response, it is the French countersubversive doctrine, developed by a group of prestigious officers of the French army during the war in Indochina (1945–54) and the war in Algeria (1954–62)[22] that gives theoretical consistency, structure, and homogeneity to the approach to the problem adopted by the military institutions in the area.[23]

Moreover, given its high degree of structure and simplification, the doctrine of revolutionary war—also known as _guerre dans la foule_ (war among the crowd) and _guerre d'action psychologique_ (psychological action war)—has the quality of providing a simple and all-inclusive "explanation" for everything that is new and different in society, without questioning the basis for validity of the official discourse supporting the good order. This ability to make intelligible any manifestation with the potential to disrupt reality is based on two mechanisms intrinsic to the doctrine: Manichaeanism, on the one hand, and a conspirative vision of history, on the other. The dangerous combination of these two mechanisms is further enhanced by a series of "recipes for action"—techniques for the total battle between Good and Evil. Thus, this view ends up by modifying even the military's own perception of its role in history.

Among the basic principles guiding action at the core of this doctrine, there are two of extreme importance for the redefinition of the political role of the armed forces of the region: first, the willingness to learn from the enemy and to copy its strategy and tactics, methods, and techniques; and second, the extreme valuation of psychological warfare. Following these lines of thought implies admitting and legitimating the politicization of the army, to the extent that in the conflict between subversion and countersubversion, it is impossible to draw the line between politics and war. Furthermore, the form taken by this doctrine is that of a self-fulfilling prophecy, in that even the most minimal deviation from the good order will automatically be considered a verification of the fundamental principles of the theoretical corpus.

In effect, if reality is never what it seems to be, given the work of Marxist infiltration, if the world is divided into two camps that no longer dispute the territory but, rather, the soul of humanity, then there is no place for third positions, as the enemy lies in wait for such weaknesses. A strike, a demonstration, even a rock concert can be perceived as an enemy threat to the good order, an order defined with rigidity and precision, in normative terms.

As the key for reading reality, which receives the feedback of self-verification over the course of time, the doctrine of revolutionary war extends the military institution's perception of threat to unthinkable limits, both in time and in space. At the same time, it provides an inextinguishable justification for the military's political action in terms of what Sun Tzu would call the sense of rectitude[24] of the armies involved in the fight against Communist Evil and what, since Weber,[25] we generally call legitimacy of action.

An Uncomfortable Conclusion

Thus far, we have seen how the armed forces of the Southern Cone of South America have a perception of threat that is substantially different from that prevailing among their colleagues in NATO and very similar to that existing (if not prevailing) among the other forces of South and Central America.[26]

In the view of the region's military corporations, the common threat to the West, communism, does not undertake frontal or open attacks in conventional theaters of operations. Instead, Communist aggression takes place within a variant of internal war: revolutionary or subversive warfare, which is defined by current doctrine as a form of conflict that has the following characteristics:

1. It is a total war, whose objective is the annihilation of the adversary, not merely the taking of the adversary by force.

2. Its goal is to control the population—its values and way of life.

3. It is a permanent war, in which there is no distinction between periods of peace and periods of war and no formal declaration of the start or end of hostilities.

4. It is a global war, in which there is no distinction between the civil front and the military front or between war and politics.

5. It is a moral war, involving two antithetical visions of the world—the two struggling for their survival—in which, consequently, there is no room for third positions.

6. It is a nonconventional war, in which the enemy employs dirty tactics, techniques, and methods, infiltrating the societies it seeks to dominate, taking advantage of the weaknesses of human nature to win positions, using the tools of psychological action more than those of armed conflict of the conventional type or the irregular type (guerrilla warfare, both rural or urban), called sedition in some doctrinal elaborations.[27]

The doctrine legitimates the political action of the military to the extent that it views the armed forces as the last hope of the West—the bulwark, support, and repository of the good order attacked by international Communist subversion.

We have also seen that this doctrine constitutes an adaptation to the southern latitudes of the French doctrine of countersubversive war, formulated during the wars in Indochina and Algeria by French army officers, many of whom would later constitute the central nucleus of the Organisation de l'Armeé Secrete.[28] The French doctrine of revolutionary war is a simple, rigorous, and heavily structured doctrine. It provides a key for reading reality that makes intelligible a complex and changing reality and enables the armed forces, an institution that sinks its roots in medieval values, to cope with social complexity and change.

With its Manichaean and conspirative vision of history, this doctrine has certain internal structuring mechanisms that make disconfirmation by empirical contrast impossible. The French doctrine of revolutionary war, taken to its maximum power by the local experience of the armed forces of the region, operates like self-fulfilling prophecy, insofar as the more recent, though less far-reaching, doctrines and social phenomena provide feedback for the military's vision of the conflict. Moreover, the threat perceived through these lenses does not openly conflict with the more global strategic conceptions prevailing in the West, for which reason external observers, both civil and military, can think that there is an apparent consensus. However, this doctrine ultimately discredits some of the most important assumptions understood to govern relations between civil power and the military institution in the West.

A doctrine of this sort, with its rigorous structuring and deceiving simplicity, is ideologically imperialistic. It tends to incorporate into its own corpus—reshaping and frequently discrediting for this purpose—all doctrine or theories of lesser scope, which thus become simply more grist for the same mill. In this sense, a doctrine like the prevailing one could be superseded only by another of equal level, rigor, and importance, capable of making reality intelligible with the same degree of simplicity and plausibility. Thus far, there seems to be no military or civilian doctrine on the ideological market that meets these requirements.

Notes

1. Literally "armed arm," *brazo armado* is a Spanish expression commonly used to denote a nonthinking instrument at the service of another entity.

2. One of the best-known and more elegant explanations was elaborated by José Nun, "The Middle Class Military Coup," in Claudio Véliz, ed., *The Politics of Conformity in Latin America* (Oxford: Oxford University Press, 1967), reprinted in Abraham Lowenthal and J. Samuel Fitch, *Arms and Politics in Latin America* (New York: Holmes and Meier, 1986).

3. Lieutenant General Luis V. Queirolo, quoted in *El Soldado*, No. 64 (August 1980). *El Soldado* is a monthly review published by the Centro Militar in Montevideo; it is an unofficial voice of the officer corps, especially composed by members of the army. Ciprian was one of the fathers of the Catholic Church in the second century.

4. Lieutenant General L.V. Queirolo, Speech delivered at the 19th Conferencia de los Ejércitos Americanos, Washington, D.C., November 1981, quoted in *El Soldado*, No. 80 (December, 1981).

5. An anonymous article appeared in *El Soldado*, No. 56 (December 1979), sustaining in this regard:

> Defense against violence is not possible without resorting to force. Organized force is always preferable to chaos. . . . We have reason and truth on our side; but reason and truth need force in order to survive the violence unleashed by those who want to "bury" us with our institutions.

This argument was developed in full by General Ramón J. Camps, who was chief of police of the province of Buenos Aires, in his books *Caso Timmerman: Punto Final* (Buenos Aires: Tribuna Abierta, 1982) and *El Poder de la Sombra: El Affaire Graiver* (Buenos Aires: Roca, 1983).

6. Quoted from General Alberto Marini, *De Clausewitz a Mao Tse-tung: La Guerra Subversiva y Revolucionaria* (Buenos Aires: Círculo Militar, Biblioteca del Oficial, 1968). The same argumentation is made in Julio Carreto, *La Ideologia y la Nueva Guerra* (Buenos Aires: Círculo Militar, 1987) (published three years after Raul Alfonsín took office); and Ramón Genaro Diaz Bessone, *Guerra Revolucionaria en la Argentina* (Buenos Aires: Fraterna, 1986; reprinted by Circulo Militar, Biblioteca del Oficial, 1988). In Uruguay, the first expression of this kind of thinking was made in Buenaventura Caviglia Campora, *Ps.P. Psico-Politica: Verdadera Dimensión de la Guerra Subversiva* (Montevideo: Ediciones Azules,

1974), and followed officially by the Junta de Comandantes en Jefe, *La Subversión: Las Fuerzas Armadas al Pueblo Oriental* (Montevideo: JCJ, 1977). In the same vein, see, also, the arguments set forth by Brazilian General Adolpho Joao De Paula Couto, *Seguranca Interna: Guerra Revolucionaria* (Brasilia: Asociacao de Diplomados da Escola Superior de Guerra, 1971). Chilean Colonel Elio Bacigalupo stated that the ideology is the principal source of subversive war, in his article "El Estado y la Seguridad Nacional," *Revista de Seguridad Nacional* (Santiago de Chile) (July–August 1976). This publication was made by the High Academy of National Security. The chief of state, General Augusto Pinochet, said that Marxism is a doctrine perverse per se, in a speech delivered on September 11, 1976 ("Discurso en el Tercer Aniversario del Gobierno," Santiago, Presidencia, 1976).

7. Carlos Marino Mazzoni, "El Ser Nacional," *Boletín de la Escuela de Guerra Naval* (Buenos Aires), Año VII, No. 7 (1975).

8. General Breno Borges Forte made these declarations at the Tenth Conference of Commanders in Chief of American Armies, as chief of staff of his army. I quote from *Estrategia* (Buenos Aires) 24 (September–October 1973).

9. Even the Catholic Church is under suspicion. The Brazilian hierarchy is seen as an ally of the subversive movements. On the contrary, in Argentina the close collaboration of the Church and the armed forces was clear. See Emilio F. Mignone, *Iglesia y Dictadura: El Papel de la Iglesia a la Luz de Sus Relaciones con el Régimen Militar* (Buenos Aires: Pensamiento Nacional, 1986). In Chile, the Catholic hierarchy, especially during the reign of Archbishop Silva Enriquez, was against the Pinochet regime. But at the same time, the military Catholic chaplains supported the dictatorship. This was also the case of other Christian churches, the Evangelics being the most important. See Humberto Lagos and Arturo Chacón, *La Religión en las Fuerzas Armadas y de Orden*, 2nd ed. (Santiago: Presor-Lar, 1987).

10. The military writings on the subject abound in expressions such as "useful cretins" and "traveling companions," taken from the enemy's revolutionary jargon. Furthermore, it is almost impossible to find references to professional politicians in which the terms *demagogy*, *politicking* or *party politics* are absent. Nevertheless, the same writings do admit the possibility of honest error among Marxists (especially young ones). In those cases, it is stated, attempts should be made to reeducate and reconvert the persons, "saving" them from their errors. Following the Inquisition's tradition, the fight is against the sin—Marxist doctrine—not against the sinner.

11. Major José C. Araujo, "Honor Militar y Marxismo en un Estado Liberal: El por qué del Anatema," *El Soldado*, No. 103 (July–August 1985).

12. General Alberto Marini, *Estrategia sin Tiempo* (Buenos Aires: Circulo Militar, 1971).

13. Lieutenant General Jorge Rafael Videla, in *La Nación* (Buenos Aires) (May 25, 1976).

14. General Ramón Genaro Díaz Bessone, *Guerra Revolucionaria en la Argentina, 1959–1978*, 2nd ed. (Buenos Aires: Circulo Militar, Biblioteca del Oficial, 1988). Díaz Bessone was chief of intelligence and later minister of planning during the Videla administration.

15. Erick Ludendorf, *La Guerra Total* (Buenos Aires: Pleamar, 1964). The first edition, in German (*Der totale Krieg*) was printed in 1921. A first approximation of this position was made in Carl von Clausewitz, *On War*, ed. and trans. Michael Howard and Peter Paret (Princeton, N.J.: Princeton University Press, 1976), originally published 1832–34.

16. Lieutenant General L.V. Queirolo in *El Soldado*, No. 74 (August 1980).

17. "El Ser Militar," *El Soldado*, No. 94 (January–February 1984).

18. *El Soldado*, No. 56 (December 1979).

19. Official and unofficial missions to Panama, Honduras, and El Salvador— in addition to numerous unofficial Uruguayan and Chilean technical missions to Central America—were complemented by technical exchanges of experiences and documentation. The most notorious was the presence of Colonel Mohammed Ali Seineldín in Panama between 1986 and 1988. Seineldín was the leader of the military revolt in Argentina in December 1988.

20. Genaro Arriagada, *El Pensamiento Político de los Militares* (Santiago: CISEC, 1981).

21. Basil Liddel Hart, *Strategy: The Indirect Approach* (New York: Knopf, 1953; (first Argentine ed. Buenos Aires: Círculo Militar, Biblioteca del Oficial, 1960). André Beaufré, *Strategie de l'Action* (Paris: Armand Colin, 1966; first Argentine ed. Buenos Aires: Pleamar, 1966).

22. The best-known books on the subject are two by Roger Trinquier, *La Guerra Moderna* (Buenos Aires: Rioplatense, 1973), and *Guerra, Subversión, Revolución* (Buenos Aires: Reioplatense, 1975). See, also, Gabriel Bonnet, *Las Guerras Insurreccionales y Revolucionarias* (Madrid: Ediciones Cid, 1967). But the most effective dissemination of the doctrine was by way of the novels of Jean Larteguy, *Los Centuriones* (Barcelona: GP, 1960), and *Los Pretorianos* (Barcelona: GP, 1960). In Argentina, a French military mission was active between 1958 and 1962. This mission helped disseminate the doctrine. Among other tasks, the French officers published articles in the most prestigious military reviews. The following is but a short list of the articles printed at the time: R. Bentresque, "Un Método de Razonamiento en Guerra Subversiva," *Revista de la Escuela Superior de Guerra (RESG)* (Buenos Aires), No. 335 (October–December 1959); H. Grand d'Esnon, "Guerra Subversiva," *RESG*, No. 338 (July–September 1960); M. Mom, "Guerra Revolucionaria," *RESG*, No. 331 (October–December 1958) and No. 334 (July–September 1959); Patrice de Nourois, "Una Teoría para la Guerra Subversiva," *RESG*, No. 329 (April–June 1958), and "Guerra Subversiva y Guerra Revolucionaria," *RESG*, No. 331 (October–December 1958); J. Nougues, "Radioscopía Subversiva de la Argentina," *RESG*, No. 334 (January–March 1962). As a result of this influence, Argentine officers also collaborated in the task and wrote articles on the subject; for example, two were written by officers who became important chiefs of the Argentine army in the late 1960s: General Alcides López Aufranc, "Guerra Revolucionaria en Argelia," *RESG*, No. 335 (October–December 1959); T. Sanchez de Bustamante, "La Guerra Revolucionaria," *RESG*, No. 339 (October–December 1960). In Brazil, there were articles by Claude Delmas and J. Hogard, published in *Mensario de Cultura Militar* (July–August 1959 and September–October 1960). In Uruguay, the first chief of the Estado

Mayor Conjunto, (ESMACO)—the structure in charge of intelligence and coordination of repression, created in the late 1960s—was Colonel Gregorio Alvarez, who studied in Argentina at the Intelligence College. Later, Alvarez became general and president of Uruguay.

23. General Ramón Camps made the following statement in 1981:

> In Argentina we first received the influence of the French and afterwards that of the Americans, and we used each one separately. Later we joined them and took concepts of both. . . The point of view of the French was more correct than the American one. The first shows the global conception, the second one the military aspect, exclusively. . . But finally we came of age and put into practice our own doctrine, that gave us victory over the armed subversion in Argentina.

La Prensa (Buenos Aires) (January 4, 1981).

24. Sun Tzu, *The Art of War* (Oxford: Oxford University Press, 1963).

25. Max Weber, *Estado y Sociedad*, Vol. 1 (Mexico: FCE, 1944).

26. For instance, the Peruvian manual *Pensamiento Doctrinario Metodológico de la Defensa Nacional* (Lima: CAEM, 1985) shows a similar version, even in its last edition of 1985, published under the Alan Garcia administration. In Guatemala, the articles written by Colonel Jesus Girón Sanchez, "Poder y Justicia," *Revista Militar* (January–April 1983), and Captain H. Cifuentes, "Operación Ixil," *Revista Militar* (September–December 1982), followed the same pattern as that of their Southern Cone colleagues.

27. The U.S. army considered guerrilla warfare similar to insurgent war and never considered the possibility of revolutionary war as a specific form of conflict. See L.E. Cable, *Conflict of Myths: The Development of American Counterinsurgency Doctrine and the Vietnam War* (New York: New York University Press, 1986). According to Douglas Blaufarb, *The Counterinsurqency Era: U.S. Doctrine and Performance* (New York: Free Press, 1977), the Americans considered that the political vision of the French was not useful from a military point of view.

28. [Raoul Salan], *El Proceso del General Salan* (Barcelona: Acervo, 1962). See, also, John S. Ambler, *The French Army in Politics, 1945–1962* (Athens: Ohio University Press, 1966).

7

The Perception of the Subversive Threat in Peru

Marcial Rubio Correa

Democracy in the Peruvian Context

Throughout most of Peru's history, the government has been in the hands of the military. Peru has no political, economic, or social-democratic tradition. In 1980, however, Peru reentered the democratic-constitutional current circulating around Latin America. Ironically, the formal initiation of the terrorist phenomenon in Peru (May 17, 1980), and the challenge it poses to civil–military relations, took place within the process of redefinition of the democratic terms of the political system.

This chapter examines civil–military relations within the framework of the subversion presently challenging Peru, the democratic nature of the government, and the role of the armed forces within the structure of the state. It also presents ideas about the subversive organization known as Shining Path (Sendero Luminoso).

In the past, it was the military that systematically interfered with democracy. It was also the military that launched the most important process of political transformation in this century (the 1968–75 administration). Under the political leadership of General Juan Velasco Alvarado, the social order was radically changed, and the armed forces and their relationship with the community were redesigned. This phenomenon, whose nature is essentially political, suggests at least two issues: how to understand democracy in Peru and the role of the armed forces in the framework of the rule of law.

The Meaning of Democracy in Peru

The evolution of the democratic debate in Peru does not coincide with that in other Latin American countries (particularly in the Southern Cone). Widespread poverty in the face of strongly rightist groups minimizes the need for transformations. Given the electoral results in recent polls, it could be affirmed that for the average Peruvian, democracy should also mean social change. During the past four years, at least 75 percent of the citizens have voted consistently for the candidates proposing change.[1]

The issue of democracy and how to develop it has been discussed in Peru both during constitutional periods and during the long period of military rule, particularly during the administration of General Juan Velasco Alvarado. Although his administration furthered a notion of democracy in which the popular origin of power was disregarded, social and economic democracy was emphasized and greater awareness of such aspects was fostered.[2] On the other hand, the military government did not succeed in developing a new structure of civil society, because attempts were made to manipulate it from above. However, the government promoted an organic approach to civil society, a principle that had been vilified during the previous, oligarchic era.

Throughout the past two decades, a growing awareness of human rights has developed in Peru. Though the society as a whole does not know much about these rights (and their meaning), one can argue that they have become a point of departure for political debate that no one wants to disregard. The issue of human rights, particularly the rights to life and bodily integrity, are very important in the framework of civil–military relations in today's Peru, as traditionally underprivileged social sectors stand between crossfires: the cruelty of the subversives and the equally cruel strategy of counterinsurgency. Even though, in the past two years, the counterinsurgency methods have been less dramatic, they have not yet fully lost this characteristic.

In Peru, the debate on democracy necessarily includes the aspects connected with political rights, socioeconomic transformations, and the practice of human rights. Obviously, the Left, the Center and the Right show significantly different opinions in this regard, but no political group disagrees outright with protection of human rights. In turn, the armed forces appear to have incorporated some ideas on these issues.

The Political Role of the Armed Forces

For many decades, the armed forces performed the role of supporters of the entrenched oligarchic order in Peru. In modern times, this was particularly clear between 1930 and 1960, a thirty-year period during which a series of military dictatorial regimes engaged in violent struggle against the popular political movements represented, in different ways, by the American Popular Revolutionary Alliance (APRA) and the Peruvian Communist party.

This attitude began to change with the 1962 military junta that ruled the country during a twelve-month period. During that period, planning was institutionalized, agrarian reform was instituted, and the first policies on minimum wages were adopted, among other similar measures of considerable importance for so short a period. It was not until the administration of General Juan Velasco Alvarado that the relations between the oligarchy and the armed forces experienced the biggest shock of the century.

Velasco's political process was not socialist, nor had it laid the groundwork for a socialist system. In the long run, what Velasco did was simply to modernize a country that was largely backward (even by South American standards). In an attempt to create a national bourgeoisie, he reversed the wealth flow toward the working segments of the population; through agrarian reform, he definitively neutralized the landowners' oligarchy.

This process included an openly anti-imperialistic stand. Although it did not mean radical hostility to the United States, it did entail some important changes with respect to the previous attitudes of Peru: The International Petroleum Company and some other American mining concerns were expropriated, and the American military mission was terminated. Soviet equipment was chosen for the army and the other military organizations, and external policies emphasized Third World themes and nonalignment.

All this was done within an institutional approach, taking as a foundation the doctrines developed by the Centro de Altos Estudios Militares (CAEM), which had been established formally in 1957 (its predecessor—Centro de Altos Estudios del Ejército, or CAEE—had been formed in 1950).

The relations between the dominant groups in Peruvian society and the military institutions, particularly the army, became poisoned. The experience of the Velasco administration and its institutional setting, as well as the reliance on the CAEM doctrine as the regime's ideological base, made the Peruvian rightists sharply distrustful of the political attitudes articulated by the military in its relations with the rest of the community. Although the generation of radical officers that had ruled under Velasco had withdrawn from active service by the end of 1976, the political groups could not help feeling that the Peruvian military upheld reformist ideas that may have became deeply embedded. Hence, the old practice of relying on the military to keep the status quo became a very risky affair.

On the other hand, the armed forces institutionalized and strengthened themselves significantly within the structure of the state and the political system, not only during the Velasco era but also during the additional five-year term of his successor, General Francisco Morales Bermudez. The existence of a military institutional power that remains in a state of latency after democratic institutions have been established, and that can press its own claims, has always been an intriguing factor for political analysts.

Recent democratic governments have taken Article 278 of the Peruvian constitution as a point of departure for civil–military relations: The armed and police forces have no political role to play. They are subjected to the constitutional powers. This principle has traditionally been construed, within the rule of law, as meaning that the armed forces may not have any political opinion whatsoever.

It has become apparent that a military coup is not the only tool available to the military. Some believe that it is not the most convenient method nowadays to attain specific targets. The scenario of a military administration amid terrorism and crisis does not seem to be attractive, even for the most stubborn hard-liners in the military. Pressure can be exerted efficiently through means other than a coup. Since 1980, successive constitutional governments have made the armed forces responsible for counterinsurgency. The strategic notion of fighting terrorism has assumed an important role for the identification of civil–military relations in the framework of today's democratic-constitutional regimes.[3]

In reality, things are significantly different. Even though the state's institutional structure has been redesigned, and a unified Defense Ministry has been created (which, at least in theory, allows larger political monitoring of the military apparatus), the military, through the political-military commands, retains an important role in the political rule of the regions affected by terrorism. The performance of this function by the military has been a source of numerous clashes with the civil government, whereby the subversive challenge is, again, an important factor for defining the rules of the game within the democratic-constitutional context.

Shining Path

Shining Path[4] is a political party that claims to have an ideological stand of its own, different from those of the other components of the Marxist spectrum. It recognizes the contributions of Lenin, Mao, and Shining Path's founder, Abimael Guzmán, the "fourth sword" of the ideological current to which the party belongs. Shining Path's goal is to take over power in Peru after a long struggle, whose timeframe is estimated to be 50 to 100 years, according to party spokesmen.[5] To accomplish this goal, Shining Path has chosen terrorist subversion as its political tool. Its strategy is based on controlling the Sierra (Andean) area, where it focuses its recruiting and organizational activities. It hopes to "liberate" government forces in as many zones as possible. In spite of the counterinsurgency struggle of the 1980s, Shining Path has expanded its sphere of influence and has grown. Lacking any known external support, and showing rejection for any potential sources, the movement develops its own operative forms and is capable of finding the means necessary to put them into practice. In 1987, it became apparent that Shining Path was engaged in operational activities connected with narcotics trafficking in the jungle zone as a likely source of financing and miscellaneous supplies.

Shining Path is not an "indigenous" movement.[6] Its main (but not exclusive) source of personnel consists of those populations that are in the process of social transformation through emigration from the interior to the cities. Its original center was Huamanga University, attended by children of peasants virtually without any professional future. This is still a major breeding ground for recruits; however, in recent years, the group seems to have decided to project itself toward the society as a whole, with the unofficial help of certain media and by circulating a number of documents among select groups.

The social backgrounds of its recruits helps the group maintain contact with the indigenous populations of the Peruvian Sierra, but this does not make the group an indigenous-based one. Peasant organizations and Shining Path have had quite a few clashes. The dialectics are very complex: Some peasant bases support Shining Path; others fight it.

Shining Path itself disavows the thesis that it is an indigenous movement. Since the second half of 1987, the organization has made its views public with the unofficial help of *El Diario*, a daily paper with an estimated circulation of 20,000 copies.[7]

One key feature of Shining Path is the movement's claim to be the organization that will carry out the revolution in Peru. There are some other, smaller subversive groups, such as Movimiento Revolucionario Tupac Amaru (MRTA), but no form of cooperation exists with Shining Path, which competes with them for hegemony. In other words, Shining Path does not accept any allies or fellow travelers.[8]

In terms of subversive capabilities, Shining Path is, indeed, the most important political group in Peru.[9] Compared with the subversion in Colombia, where there are scattered, separate subversive groups, often at the same operational level, Shining Path can rely on an ideology and a strategy of its own, based on the group's knowledge of Peruvian history (whereby it decided to control the Sierra area). This fact is not relevant in the case of Colombian subversives. On the other hand, the Colombian political system (locked for several decades by the pact between the two major political forces) has often led to the creation of subversive groups that, as a result, would be more flexible to a potential compromise or at least a truce with the system. [10] In the case of Shining Path, none of these options (not even simple dialogue) seems feasible. Whenever Shining Path has entered into negotiations, its attitude has been to demand, not to discuss. This applies even to the situation generated by the June 1986 riots at Lima jails, which ended with a notorious massacre.

Finally, in Colombia, there does not seem to be a relationship between the subversive organization and the social class or group from which the party's cadres are recruited. In Colombia, some guerrilla groups are multibased, whereas Shining Path tends to draw on the sector of people emigrating to the urban areas. As a result, the guerrilla groups combine both rural and urban features. Such a combination profoundly affects and complicates a number of aspects, such as the subversives' own security measures and the cultural standpoints that influence their ideology and their struggle.

The existence of Shining Path creates several issues with regard to civil–military relations within the Peruvian political system, including the following:

Should Shining Path be considered a political party or a "criminal gang"?

Should the strategy applied to fighting Shining Path be of a predominantly military or political nature? (Some compromise solutions are also conceivable. One key aspect of this issue is how to design a structure for governmental management of the conflict, which involves the subject of political-military commands.)

Under counterinsurgency strategy, what treatment should be applied to Sierran populations? Most of those people live amid the crossfire of subversive and countersubversive forces.

What approach to human rights is possible when there is an environment in which rights are violated by both the subversives and the counterinsurgency forces?

Civil–Military Relation Issues

Civilians[11] know little, if anything, about such issues, as this type of analysis has remained the exclusive domain of the military. Although initial steps are being taken to correct this inequality, the problem significantly reduces the possibilities of an adequate dialogue between civilians and the military.

The National Defense System

From 1968 to 1980, military rule left an institutionally strengthened armed forces holding a position of power within the state. Military institutions not only held a measure of power, but also were entitled to use various participation and decision-making instruments that were unconstitutional. The following were the essential features of this organization, legitimated by the military administration through a number of decree-laws:

1. The National Defense Board was in existence, chaired by the president of the Republic. Its other permanent members were the ministers of war, the navy, the air force, foreign relations, the interior, and economy and finance and the chairman of the Armed Forces Joint Command. To these, a number of nonpermanent numbers was added: the general commanders of the three armed forces, the head of the National Planning Institute, and the head of the National Intelligence Service. Under the law creating the system (Decree-Law No. 23653), this board was to participate in the development of national objectives and to set the objectives, policies, and plans for national defense. The board was assigned other important functions by the Law of Mobilization (Decree-Law No. 23118), mainly those of approving the guidelines, plans, and all other policies regarding this issue.

2. Within the National Defense System, there is a Joint Command of the Armed Forces, formed by the three commander-generals of the armed forces, who rotate on an annual basis as chairmen of this organ (while retaining their respective general commands). Because the Joint Command embraces the three armed forces, it cannot be subordinated to any of the three existing Defense Ministries; it is directly responsible to the president of the Republic.

During peacetime, the Joint Command fulfills plans and coordinates the activities of the various military services; in cases of the suspension of constitutional rights it assumes control of internal security. Obviously, this institutional framework had been designed by the armed forces, as it was put into place by a number of decree-laws dating from the last years of military rule.

Civilians criticized these activities on several grounds: The armed forces were granted "deliberative" capabilities, as the National Defense Board necessarily busied itself with political matters, and a substantial proportion of its members were military. Moreover, some felt that this board should have only consultative powers and the role of advising the president of the Republic.

Another objection to the defense board was that it was substituted for the Board of Ministers when extremely important decisions had to be made. The military responded that the board limited itself to developing draft decisions that had to be approved by the president of the Republic, along with his ministers. This has been countered by the fact that final decisions are often identical to the drafts.

The Armed Forces Joint Command, particularly when assuming control of internal security, is assigned responsibilities tantamount to political rule of the areas where constitutional rights are suspended. This is inconsistent with the general principles of the rule of law, as the chairman of the Joint Command is not politically accountable (he can be subjected only to administrative or criminal sanctions), and the president of the Republic is constitutionally exempt from political responsibility. Hence, the decisions made in this area were outside the sphere of political responsibility, as the ministers were not an official link in the decision chain.

In 1987, discussion focused on the creation of a Ministry of Defense. The Ministry of Defense was conceived as a substitute for the three ministries then in existence. It would be responsible to the executive branch. By March 31, 1987, the congress passed Act 24654, establishing such a ministry and delegating to the executive branch the powers to approve the ministerial organic law.

The government argued that the creation of the Ministry of Defense would turn defense management into a more rational process. By concentrating the fiscal aspects of defense in only one ministry, instead of three, significant budgetary savings could result. The ruling party made only cursory mention of the issue of the political irresponsibility of the Joint Command. Izquierda Unida, the main opposition force, tried to focus the discussion on the principle that the creation of the ministry should be orientated toward establishing a democratic framework in this sensitive area of the state's structure.[12]

The second argument was that the creation of the ministry would not entail amending the military organic laws or the National Defense System Law. The government (both the executive and the legislative branches) recognized that this initiative did not mean any modification of the internal structure of the armed institutions. However, the March 1987 act provided for changes in the present structure of the national defense system, particularly with respect to the Joint Command of the Armed Forces, which, as seen before, was the most sensitive aspect of the whole issue.

The legislation creating the Defense Ministry finally became law on September 27, 1987. Despite the initial opposition of the retired officers, and the threat of an air force rebellion, a Defense Ministry was established, and the three armed services abided by the law. A remarkable fact is that during the process of approval of the ministry, the army had repeatedly made known its support for the initiative, which is consistent with its historical position. The army's high commanders had publicly proposed the creation of the ministry for four decades.

In general terms, the law seems to grant the minister of defense the administrative tools necessary to supervise the whole area of defense. The National Defense Board has been replaced by the Board of Ministers, which, in special meetings, has become the highest authority in defense matters. The parallelism between the Board of Ministers and the National Defense Board has thus been corrected. The Joint Command of the Armed Forces is to be supervised by the minister of defense, a highly important political decision in the circumstances.

The development of a defense doctrine has become the responsibility of the defense minister and, as far as its general guidelines are concerned, of the Board of Ministers. Formally, this is also a very important decision, though the extent to which this set of rules is finally implemented and enforced remains to be seen.

All of the foregoing are positive aspects of the new legislation. However, one of the crucial aspects of the development of the ministry was whether the minister would be a member of the armed forces or a civilian. The president of the Republic offered the position to Senator Armando Villanueva, who was the presidential candidate of the Peruvian Aprista party in 1980. However, the senator responded with an open letter excusing himself on the grounds that the person selected should be a general officer of the armed forces. As a result, the person who was holding the position of army general commander at that time became the first minister of defense of Peru. This was further evidence of the institutional power of the armed forces and of the extreme cautiousness of the constitutional government.

The episode of the Defense Ministry showed that the government was able to lead the armed forces even when important decisions were involved. It also demonstrated that defense management still cannot be taken away from the military and assigned to a civilian.

The Armed Forces' Role of Monitoring Internal Security during a State of Emergency

In 1985, a few weeks before the end of the term of the constitutional government, Act 24150 was passed. It institutionalized the political-military commands where a state of emergency had been decreed—that is, in regions experiencing subversive violence.[13] These commands, headed by a general officer of the armed forces, reported to the Armed Forces Joint

Command. Although, in theory, they are supposed to coordinate the activities of the executive power in the area for which they are responsible, in fact, all state power is concentrated exclusively in the hands of one person. The commander is often able to permit or prohibit the operation of the judiciary or the local attorney simply by granting or depriving them of the means to perform their duties or of protection for risky activities.

The military insists that this is the best possible type of organization, given that the state is being challenged by subversive organizations. Some civilian groups contend that this arrangement means that the military has invaded the political sphere and that this must be corrected.[14]

The political-military commands are likely to be replaced or modified in the near future. Various opposition groups, and even some members of the APRA administration, feel uneasy about this public security arrangement. The defense minister himself has used eloquent terms in a press interview, affirming that political-military commands are only nominally political and that they might be modified.[15]

Political Participation of the Armed Forces

Under the Peruvian constitution, the armed forces must not perform any political role and are supervised by the constitutional powers. While a member of the 1987 constituent assembly, President Alan García Pérez interpreted this provision to mean the armed forces' absolute withdrawal from political activities.[16]

The construction of the principle of the army's withdrawal from politics is inconsistent with Peruvian reality and history. It also entails the complete rejection of the view that the armed institutions can adequately—and through democratic, institutional channels—expound their opinion in matters of public concern connected with their technical activities.

The military's viewpoint is completely different.[17] The military have learned politics, and continue to do so in the framework of their institutional activities. For many years, this has been one of tasks of the CAEM, an official organization of the Peruvian state. It is the civilians who do not know much about military affairs. It is their ideas in this regard that need clarifying. The views of the army on issues of public concern regarding the constitutional responsibilities of the military need a forum. This job has yet to be done by the constitutional law experts in our times, in Peru and in many other Latin American countries. This might be the way toward a healthy balance between civilians and the military, enhancing the democratic concept and practices of these nations within existing social and political conditions.

How Shining Path Is Perceived:
The Counterinsurgency Strategy

Another crucial aspect of civil-military relations is the military's perception of Shining Path.[18] Some distinctions have to be made. Civil, political, and social groups are widely split in this regard. Some of them (to a large extent reflecting the 1980–85 administration's views) believe that Shining Path is, in essence, a terrorist-criminal organization that must be eradicated. Others, whose opinions are perhaps most aptly expounded by Izquierda Unida, believe that Shining Path is what I suggested in the second section of this chapter—a political party that struggles in the political arena and, to a lesser extent, in the military arena. It is also perceived as a group that must be countered by political means, without, of course, disregarding repression as a legitimate part of the overall counterinsurgency strategy.

To those who perceive Shining Path as a terrorist-criminal organization, the problem of human rights in the context of repression may be a source of concern but, in any case, one of a definitively secondary nature. What matters is fighting it relentlessly until it is completely annihilated, and this necessarily entails the determination to repress not only the Shining Path cadres proper but also anything that looks like Shining Path.

For those who view Shining Path as basically a political force, repression is necessarily conceived within a more comprehensive political attitude. Such an attitude could be defined as an attempt to approach the community (particularly those segments on which Shining Path relies heavily for support and membership) in order to isolate the movement from the society. This could help defeat it in the political arena, which is perceived as a crucial part of this strategy. In this scenario, respect for human rights must necessarily be a part of the political approach of the problem.

The armed forces' concept of Shining Path does not necessarily conform to one of the two aforementioned models. On the one hand, they perceive repression as essential; on the other hand, however, they are aware (for they have been trained in counterinsurgency) that success could be forfeited if no efforts are made in the political sphere as well. It seems accurate to define the military's stand by saying that this political supplement consists of the adoption of economic development programs for those populations most affected by terrorism, in the context of overall repression.

The military has chosen a mainly repressive option but does not insert it clearly (the way other Latin American armed forces do) within the East–West confrontation scenario. This might reflect the officer corps' mostly popular social origins (the economic and social needs of their own families often helps them "live" and better understand the nation's domestic problems) and the fact that a large proportion of them have participated as public officers in the past decade's social transformation process. Their approach to the issue is, then, basically nationalistic.

Three broad concepts can be noted. In this regard, no smooth civil–military dialogue is conceivable, as no definite point of convergence can be found. It is safe to say that the prevailing feeling in the armed forces' high levels of command is that civilian powers are forcing the armed forces to wage an essentially repressive war against Shining Path without the adoption of the aforementioned supplementary political measures.

The civilians' ideas about dealing with Shining Path are not much clearer. Lack of consensus (except on the goal of repressing the enemy) has led to the impossibility of designing a proper overall political counterinsurgency strategy, despite the fact that such a strategy is being demanded from many political and social quarters. One major point of disagreement is whether political leadership in areas where a state of emergency has been declared must be assigned to the political-military commands mentioned earlier or to civilian authorities.

An especially sensitive question within this context is that of the defense of human rights or, to be more precise, the right to life of a significant proportion of the inhabitants of those areas. These individuals are killed without any basic guarantees. Shining Path does not make a secret of its role in the killings, and the discovery of numerous clandestine graves containing bodies with bullets in the back of the neck bears eloquent witness to the violence coming from the state's side. On the basis of journalistic information available, as well as data from organizations connected with this issue,[19] it can be affirmed that in recent years, the right to life and other human rights have been most seriously violated.

President Alan García took some vigorous initial steps toward correcting these abuses, but the net result appears to have been the prohibition of armed forces operations in the areas where a state of emergency had been declared. Later, the regrettable events in the jails of Lima in June 1986 seriously weakened the president's original stand in this regard. It must be stressed that absolute confusion prevails regarding the specific decisions made by all players, be they the government or the security forces, and regarding what is happening on those levels.

Until a political and antisubversive strategy is adopted, the issue of human rights will remain secondary. The social problems it engenders (deaths, disappearances, orphans, emigration from the emergency areas to safer places, and so on) will be aggravated. And, of course, so long as the policies regarding terrorism and human rights are not clear and precisely defined, civil–military relations concerning these issues will, of necessity, be seriously strained.

The constitutional authorities ruling the country during the past seven years have not developed a consistent counterinsurgency doctrine separate from the one known and applied by the military. Some people believe that in Peru, it is feasible to fight subversion successfully without transgressing the principles of democracy. This requires an effort toward organizing the population (in the short and medium term), which no one has been willing to make in a coherent manner.

Shining Path has been gaining ground since its inception; and even though it has not taken over, it will remain a difficult challenge for those who try to pacify Peru. Shining Path is obviously a wedge between civilians and the military, and its physical means and social support are already sufficient to strain seriously the relations between the other two players.

In short, the Shining Path strategy has succeeded in the medium run, and the Peruvian state has lost ground. The military and the government are being weakened by an internal confrontation. No player has been able to win so far. The armed forces believe that no major political decisions (particularly to meet the need for resource distribution to areas affected by terrorism) are being as aptly and quickly adopted as required by the circumstances. Mutual reproach among government bodies is also a Shining Path target, as a means of undermining morale and making further progress.

Conclusion

An attempt to summarize the major traits of civil–military relations in the context of the subversive challenge in Peru includes the following observations: Democracy has not been structured in such a manner that the armed forces are assigned adequate space. Under the constitution, the armed forces have nothing to say on the nation's issues. This does not seem to be consistent with a reality in which the military is an important part of the state or with the real power the armed forces have accumulated.

From an institutional viewpoint, recent modifications to the state's defense structure enable the government to monitor defense policies effectively and assume the corresponding consequences. The responsibility for what is done in this area lies in the political sphere. This is an improvement relative to the previous state of affairs, in which the Armed Forces Joint Command's decisions were, in a fully undemocratic manner, exempt from political control within the institutional framework.

The government was unable to find a minister of defense other than the army's general commandant. This shows that the military holds a significant share of power and that civil–military relations are not, strictly speaking, those between supervisors and subordinates.

In today's Peruvian politics, a basic aspect of the definition of civil–military relations is the perception of Shining Path and the need for a new counterinsurgency strategy. In the civilian sector, different initiatives have been advanced, none of which identifies fully with the military's counterinsurgency doctrine.

Decisions on the rule of emergency zones (political-military commands versus some other type of structure) and on the human rights issue are crucial. Another basic question is whether the counterinsurgency strategy must be mainly political or repressive in nature. Developing a consistent option as soon as possible will be very important in terms of defining civil–military relations.

In Peru, within the broad model of civil–military relations, there is no absolute separation between the two sides; they overlap intricately, not only in day-to-day political life but also within the legal design of the state. Consequently, existing relations and mutual links have to be redefined. The civilian and military sectors are differentiated, but they do not clash openly. The problem is merely that of a difficult coexistence within the same political system.

Notes

1. Fernando Tuesta Soldevilla, *Peru 1985: El Derrotero de una Nueva Eleccion* (Lima: Centro de Investigacion de la Universidad del Pacifico and Friedrich Ebert Foundation, 1986).

2. See Francisco Moncloa, *Peru, Que Paso? (1968–1976)* (Lima: Editorial Horizonte, 1977), chs. 6–8, 16, 21; and *El Peru de Velasco* (Lima: CEDEP, 1986).

3. "The Army, the Civil Guard and the Police, the Navy and the Air Force are democratic institutions and the guarantee of the existence of the nation, and must be based on estrangement from all types of political activities." Dr. Alan García Pérez, "Peru," *DDAC* 7 (1978): 479.

4. Many studies have been conducted on Shining Path. The most updated studies include Raul Gonzalez, "Violencia e Insurreccion en el Peru," in *Siete Ensayos Sobre la Violencia en el Peru* (Lima: Friedrich Ebert Foundation and Peruvian Association of Studies and Research for Peace, 1985); Carlos Ivan Degregori, " 'Sendero Luminoso': Los Hondos y Mortales Desencuentros," in *Movimientos Sociales y Crisis: El Caso Peruano* (Lima: DESCO, 1986); Marcial Rubio Correa, "Militares y Sendero Luminoso Frente al Sistema Democratico Peruano," *Revista de Estudios Politicos* (Madrid), No. 53 (September–October 1986): 161; Manuel Jesus Granados, "El PCP Sendero Luminoso: Aproximaciones a Su Ideologia," *Socialismo Y Participacion* (Lima, CEDEP), No. 37 (March 1987): 15. It is

also important to read recent years' issues of *Quehacer* magazine, which is published every two months by DESCO.

5. Jose Maria Salcedo, "Con Sendero en Lurigancho," *Quehacer* (Lima), No. 39 (February–March 1986).

6. Some writers, particularly during the first three years of this decade, endorsed the opposite theory, arguing that Shining Path uses and develops the Andean social origin of its cadres and the means it finds to organize itself in the Sierra region.

7. The *El Diario* editorial on Saturday, February 13, 1988 (p. 10), took issue with Henri Favre's article, "Perou: Sentier Lumineux et Horizons Obscurs: La Documentation Francaise 1984." The editorial writer, Eleuterio Rojas, criticized Favre for conveying the impression that Shining Path is a peasant-inspired rather than a proletarian-inspired group and bases its arguments on the document, "Let us start guerrilla warfare!" which he attributes to Shining Path. The critique read:

> Thesis No. 6 in Dr. Favre's document reads: The social basis of the revolution in Peru . . . will be an alliance between workers and peasants; in this alliance, however, peasants will be the main sparking force until the proletariat comes out and develops itself as a leading class.

Little margin remains to consider Shining Path an indigenous movement. In addition, in mid-1986, Henri Favre specifically stated:

> I have never thought Sendero's insurrection had a regional, peasant-based nature, . . . and despite the arguments of the Senderista ideology, I cannot possibly see Sendero as the organized struggle of the downtrodden peasants against a nonexistent latifundium.

Quehacer No. 42 (August–September 1986): 44.

8. See Raul Gonzalez, "Sendero vs. MRTA," *Quehacer*, No. 46 (April–May 1987).

9. The main difference between Shining Path and the MRTA is that the latter is a guerrilla movement, recruiting in universities and trade unions, with a structure comparable to the group operating in Latin America at the end of the 1960s and early 1970s. The MRTA is considered the armed branch of a legal political organization, seeking media coverage through spectacular actions, avoiding bloodshed as a means of terrorizing those who disagree with it, and trying to attract public support. The MRTA believes that Shining Path's radical stance hinders the revolutionary struggle, for it strengthens the armed forces and discredits the cause of social reforms through unnecessary cruelty. Shining Path believes that the MRTA is but one of the counterrevolutionary forces existing within the establishment.

10. See, for example, Patricia Pinzon de Lewin, comp., *La Oposicion en Colombia: Algunas Bases para Su Discusion* (Bogota: Center for International Studies and Friedrich Ebert Foundation of Colombia, 1986), particularly Fernando Cepeda Ulloa, "De la Subversion a la Oposicion" (p. 68), and ch. 8 (p. 235).

11. The term *civilian*, as used in this chapter, refers to those citizens who have not undergone professional military training.

12. Rolando Ames Cobian, "Qué Esta en Debate con el Ministerio de Defensa?" *Quehacer*, No. 46 (April–May 1987).

13. The armed forces' assumption of control of internal order is lawful under Article 231 of the constitution; but this power is available only in exceptional circumstances.

14. According to Rolando Ames Cobian, "Qué Esta en Debate," p. 16, this was the third issue being discussed.

15. Only the right-wing opposition parties—Accion Popular (which ruled the country in 1980–85) and the Christian Popular party—refrained from participating in this controversy. After all, they started the process of approval of Act 24150.

16. Jose Pareja Paz Soldán, *Derecho Constitucional Peruano* (Lima: n.p., 1980), p. 804.

17. It has been adequately summarized by General Mercado Jarrin with the term *participating professionalism*. See Edgardo Mercado Jarrin, "Rol de la Fuerza Armada," *Socialismo y Participación*, No. 13 (March 1981).

18. Two studies included in a recent issue of the magazine of the Centro de Altos Estudios Militares deal with this issue: Jaime Castro, "Los Gobiernos y la Subversion" and "Proyecto de Gobierno," *Defensa Nacional* (publication of the Centro de Altos Estudios Militares), No. 6 (October 1986). As this source is military and is designed to circulate in military circles, both articles become particularly relevant.

19. Americas Watch, *Derechos Humanos en el Peru: Primer Año del Presidente Garcia* (Lima: Comision Andina de Juristas, 1986).

8

The Limits of Influence: The United States and the Military in Central America and the Caribbean

Richard L. Millett

A lthough they share numerous characteristics with the military in Latin America's larger nations, the armed forces in Central America and the Latin Caribbean differ in numerous, important ways. Many of these differences reflect the small size, limited resources, and relative underdevelopment of nations in the region, factors that contribute to high levels of interactions with and dependency on nations from outside the region—notably, the United States.

Among the nations of the Caribbean Basin, the military has been and largely remains overwhelmingly dominated by the army. Only in the Dominican Republic, Cuba, and Honduras do other services have autonomous status. In addition, military establishments in these nations often assume police as well as military functions. Initially promoted by the United States, this close linkage has created numerous problems for U.S. policy.

The United States is not the only external power that has helped shape these forces. Chilean, Spanish, and German officers all played a role in the late nineteenth and early twentieth centuries.[1] In more recent years, numerous nations—including Israel, Argentina, Venezuela, the USSR, South Korea, and Taiwan—have been involved with regional militaries. With the exception of Soviet-bloc influences on post-1959 Cuba and post-1979 Nicaragua, however, these interactions have had limited significance.

Between 1898 and 1934, the United States created new military establishments in Cuba, Haiti, the Dominican Republic, Nicaragua, and Panama. In every case, police and military functions were combined in a single, unified force.[2] According to Dr. Dana G. Munro, who served as the U.S. chargé d'affaires in Nicaragua and the minister to Haiti during this period:

> The establishment of non-partisan constabularies in the Caribbean states was one of the chief objectives of our policy from the time when it

became clear that customs collectorships wouldn't assure stability by themselves. The old armies were or seemed to be one of the principal causes of disorder and financial disorganization. They consumed most of the government's revenue, chiefly in graft, and they gave nothing but oppression and disorder in return. We thought that a disciplined force, trained by Americans, would do away with petty local oppression that was responsible for much of the disorder that occurred and would be an important step toward better financial administration and economic progress generally.[3]

The situation was tailor-made for the ambitions of such political strongmen as Anastasio Somoza García in Nicaragua, Rafael Leonidas Trujillo in the Dominican Republic, Fulgencio Batista in Cuba, José Antonio Remón in Panama and Paul Magloire in Haiti. That this would be the end result of such policies was obvious to some observers even before the dictators took power.[4]

United States efforts to influence the armed forces were not confined to training. In 1923, the State Department pressured five Central American nations into signing the Convention for the Limitation of Armaments. This fixed the size of each nation's military establishment, with limits ranging from 5,200 men in Guatemala to 2,000 in Costa Rica. These nations also signed the General Treaty of Peace and Amity, which pledged them to peaceful settlement of disputes and to the nonrecognition of any government in the region that took power by revolution or other extra-constitutional means.[5]

By 1940, the focus of U.S. security concerns had shifted to the threats posed by the Axis powers. At times, this meant encouraging rather than discouraging a greater military role in politics. The clearest example was in Panama in 1941, where U.S. officials promoted the military's removal of President Arnulfo Arias after he refused U.S. requests to arm Panamanian-flagged merchant vessels.[6]

World War II brought a major renewal of U.S. involvement. American military bases were established and/or expanded in many nations. Lend-lease programs accelerated the development of air force capabilities. American instructors improved training and were frequently assigned directly to national military academies. Officers were sent to the United States for training. In areas of traditional U.S. domination, such as Nicaragua and the Dominican Republic, these programs strengthened the power of existing dictatorships. But in El Salvador and Guatemala, where U.S. influence on the military had been much less, the result was to encourage democratic tendencies within the armed forces. In 1944, young officers in both nations helped topple long-term military dictatorships.

The U.S. involvement declined briefly after World War II but revived with the onset of the cold war. The Inter-American Treaty of Reciprocal

Assistance (the Rio Pact) was signed by all regional nations in 1947. The Mutual Security Act of 1951 provided military grant assistance on a bilateral basis for governments in Latin America. Military agreements were signed with Cuba in 1952, with the Dominican Republic in 1953, with Nicaragua and Honduras in 1954, and with Guatemala and Haiti in 1955.[7] In each case, the dispatch of a U.S. military mission followed. American military aid to Latin America, only $200,000 in 1952, reached a total value of $34.5 million in 1954.[8]

By the early 1950s, U.S. security concerns had begun to focus on the perceived threat of Communist influence in Guatemala. In 1954, large quantities of arms were supplied to Honduras and Nicaragua, while assistance was withheld from Guatemala. This tactic helped ensure that Guatemala's army did not effectively resist the 1954 CIA-sponsored exile invasion and reluctantly acquiesced to U.S. insistence that Colonel Castillo Armas become president.[9] The U.S. operation in Guatemala produced an unwanted side effect, whereby Nicaragua used the arms it had received to support an effort to topple Costa Rica's democratic government. The United States supplied Costa Rica with four F-51 fighter aircraft and helped pressure Nicaragua into withdrawing its support, an act that ended the uprising.[10] This incident underlined the limited control that the United States exercised over arms once they were delivered, but there is no evidence that future policies were influenced by this episode.

By 1956, U.S. attention had shifted to Cuba, where Fidel Castro was waging a successful struggle against the Batista dictatorship. Early in 1958, the United States suspended arms shipments to Batista, hoping to pressure him out of office and forestall a Castro victory. This effort failed, and as Batista's fortunes declined, the CIA began urging dissident officers to gain control. The U.S. efforts, however, were divided and uncoordinated, and the pace of Batista's collapse outran U.S. efforts to respond.[11] In January 1959, Castro took power.

Castro's victory precipitated a war of regional insurgencies. This, in turn, led to a shift in the focus of U.S. military assistance. In the late 1950s, in order to counter rising congressional criticism, requests for military assistance emphasized the role of Latin American armed forces in defending the hemisphere against external attacks. American officials also argued that U.S. training would give Latin Americans "an understanding of the role of the military as an obedient force under the authority of a civilian government."[12] After 1959, the focus shifted rapidly to internal security, with an emphasis on counterinsurgency and civic action.

When Castro took power, there were U.S. Army missions in every Central American nation and U.S. Air Force missions in every nation except Costa Rica. Marines were assigned to training duty in Haiti; but in the Dominican Republic, rising tensions with the Trujillo dictatorship led to a curtailment of the U.S. military presence.[13] In the early 1960s, there was some expansion in the size of these missions. In addition, training opportunities in the United States increased, and the curriculum in the U.S. Army School of the Americas (USARSA), located in the Canal Zone, was changed. Known until 1963 as the U.S. Army Caribbean School, it provided technical training, in English, until 1959, when Spanish became the school's official language. Four years later the institution was given its present name.[14] After 1959, the curriculum expanded to include classes in counterinsurgency, programs for cadets from Latin American military academies, a command and general staff course, and offerings in intelligence and civic action.

Developments in Cuba gave special urgency to U.S. involvement with regional armed forces. By the end of 1961, that nation was well on its way to becoming a full-fledged Soviet satellite. Soviet officers were training Cuban troops, the Soviet bloc was providing the bulk of Cuba's military equipment, and Soviet military personnel were stationed on the island. Young officers, with support from the Left, seized power in El Salvador in 1960 and promised to inaugurate a program of basic reforms. Some of the new leaders expressed admiration for Castro and criticized U.S. policies. As a result, the United States encouraged a January 1961 coup, which installed a moderate, pro–United States junta, headed by Colonel Julio Rivera.[15] In the Dominican Republic, the Trujillo dictatorship had become an obstacle to efforts to isolate Castro. In May 1961, Trujillo was assassinated in a plot that had links to the CIA. Pressures from the United States then forced his family out of power, prevented the military from taking power, and ensured the installation of an elected civilian government at the start of 1963.[16]

The Kennedy administration gave Central America and the Caribbean greater attention than any administration since Woodrow Wilson had. Much of this, of course, focused on Castro's activities and on efforts to control or eliminate his influence. But Kennedy's efforts went beyond crisis management and attempted to promote a strategy that would undercut the appeal of radical groups and contribute to long-range stability. The results were mixed, at best.

The programs were designed to combine improved internal security capabilities with efforts to promote political democracy and economic development. Under the rubric of the Alliance for Progress, the administration stepped up efforts to professionalize the region's armed forces, improve their counterinsurgency capabilities, involve them in civil action, and persuade them to support political and economic reforms and accept the necessity of elected civilian rule. The technical side of this program proved the easiest to accomplish. Counterinsurgency capabilities did improve, and Castro's efforts to promote Marxist revolutions made little progress during the 1960s. In most nations, the officer corps became more professionalized and institutionalized, a trend most notable in Honduras, which finally established a military academy. Civic action programs expanded, notably in Guatemala, where they were directly linked to counter-insurgency, and in El Salvador, where the Rivera government appeared to be taking a reformist course.[17] Efforts to influence civil–military relations and the political behavior of the armed forces, however, proved notably less successful.

Problems began in Guatemala, where the military had been wrecked by internal conflicts since an unsuccessful young officers' revolt in 1960.[18] In March 1963, the military ousted the incumbent government and postponed elections. In October, despite strenuous U.S. efforts to dissuade them, the Honduran military took similar action. Responding to a warning that a coup would lead to a suspension of U.S. military assistance, Colonel Oswaldo López Arellano replied that within a few months, he would find some insurgents carrying Communist propaganda, and the United States would then resume its aid.[19]

Even less successful were U.S. efforts to influence events on the island of Hispaniola. In Haiti, President François Duvalier responded to pressures to liberalize his regime by expelling the U.S. Marine advisors and declaring the U.S. ambassador persona non grata.[20] Efforts to get the Dominican Republic's armed forces involved in efforts to oust Duvalier only succeeded in undermining that nation's elected civilian government. When the military overthrew President Juan Bosch in September 1963, rumors were rife that U.S. military attachés had encouraged such action.[21]

These events forced some rethinking of administration policies. In October 1963, Assistant Secretary of State Edwin A. Martin, writing in the *New York Herald Tribune,* declared that military coups "thwart the will of the people, destroy political stability and . . . nurture communist opposition to their tyranny." But in the same article, Martin seemed to abandon hopes that U.S. pressures could prevent coups and appeared to be moving toward a position where policy would attempt to modify the behavior of and encourage democratic opposition to such governments but would not cut off all assistance or refuse to work with them.[22]

An indication of changed attitudes was U.S. support for the creation of the Central American Defense Council (CONDECA), a loose military alliance of Central American states. It was created in 1963 with three members—Guatemala, Honduras, and Nicaragua—all of which had military governments. El Salvador, Costa Rica, and Panama had observer status, although El Salvador soon became a formal member. By 1966, CONDECA forces, with the participation of U.S. units, conducted joint military maneuvers.[23]

The assassination of President Kennedy, the preoccupation with the war in Vietnam, and the 1965 crisis in the Dominican Republic undermined U.S. efforts to change the political behavior of regional militaries. The situation in the Dominican Republic, especially, should have raised serious doubts about the efficacy of such efforts. Having ousted the elected government, the military began to break up into feuding factions. In 1965, an effort to return Bosch to power split the military, resulting in civil conflict and, ultimately, U.S. intervention. Although this intervention was designed initially to support the military's conservative elements, the United States soon discovered that it had little ability to control any of the factions involved. To justify its intervention, the United States brought Latin American military units into the Dominican Republic, acting under the rubric of the Organization of American States (OAS). With the exception of a group of Costa Rican police, all of these units came from military governments, including Honduras and Nicaragua. Ultimately, with the help of generous bribes, military leaders on both sides were sent into exile, elections were held, and order was restored.[24] The entire episode raised serious questions about the compatibility of U.S. efforts to promote stability and political reform.

Preoccupation with Vietnam diverted U.S. attention away from the Caribbean Basin during the late 1960s and early 1970s. Decisions involving the area rarely rose above the assistant secretary level. The military downgraded the U.S. Southern Command in Panama from a four-star to a three-star post, and the size of military groups assigned to the area slowly declined. In 1970, there were ninety U.S. military personnel assigned to training missions in Central America and Panama. By 1980, this had declined to twenty-five. Only Panama, where the Military Assistance Group had increased from six to seven, escaped these reductions.[25]

Training, especially at USARSA, continued. By May 1975, the school had graduated 1,913 Costa Ricans, 997 Dominicans, 984 Salvadorans, 1,504 Guatemalans, 50 Haitians (reflecting a language barrier as well as political difficulties with the Duvalier regime), 1,976 Honduras, 2,922 Panamanians, and 4,228 Nicaraguans.[26] With the exception of Haiti, which was virtually cut off after 1963, military assistance continued at a substantial level into the 1970s, but the tendency was to substitute credits for outright grants.[27] Although the United States continued to express a preference for civilian rule, pressures on the military to move in that direction declined, contributing to electoral manipulation by the armed forces in Guatemala, El Salvador, and Nicaragua and the ousting of civilian governments in Honduras and Panama.

The lower level of U.S. involvement with Central America's armed forces in the 1970s reflected a decreased level of threat perception. The death of Che Guevara in Bolivia, the collapse of insurgencies in Venezuela and Peru, and defeats administered to insurgencies in Nicaragua and Guatemala contributed to a growing belief that the threat from Cuba and the

Soviet Union had been contained, if not eliminated. The Guatemalan case had the greatest impact. There, from 1966 through 1970, a major insurgent threat had been defeated. American aid and advisors played a large role in this campaign, but the Guatemalan military's success was at least equally due to its use of terror and indiscriminate force.[28]

The decline in involvement with Central America's armed forces was further accelerated by the 1969 war between Honduras and El Salvador. The United States had large military missions in both nations.[29] Shortly before the war, the U.S. mission in El Salvador provided that nation's armed forces with a copy of the order of battle of the Honduran military. When the Hondurans discovered this, they were predictably enraged, believing that the United States favored their enemies. At the same time, pressures to force the withdrawal of Salvadoran troops from Honduran territory angered the Salvadorans. Both nation were upset by the U.S. embargo of arms and ammunition during the war and by the U.S. refusal to provide either nation with new weapons systems until they reached a peace accord.[30] When peace negotiations remained paralyzed throughout the 1970s, they began seeking other sources of armaments. Honduras acquired Super Mysteres from Israel, while El Salvador acquired artillery from Yugoslavia. The war disrupted CONDECA, making joint maneuvers impossible and reducing that organization to little more than a paper bureaucracy.

The U.S. failure in Vietnam and rising congressional pressures in the area of human rights contributed to further declines in U.S. involvement in Central America. In the mid-1970s, grant aid of military equipment was eliminated. All that remained of former programs were small loans to finance purchases of American equipment and military training (IMET) grants. In 1977, the loans had a total value of $10 million, half of which went to Costa Rica; and IMET grants totaled $2.2 million, none of which went to Costa Rica.[31] The value of IMET funds was further reduced by new cost accounting procedures that increased the costs of instruction at U.S. military bases. By the late 1970s, the cost of sending a Latin American officer to the command and general staff course at Fort Leavenworth, even using IMET funds, was considerably greater than having the same officer spend the year at Harvard. If IMET funds were not available, the cost through foreign military sales (FMS) was over three times as great. Even at USARSA, where costs were lower, it took over $3,000 in IMET funds to pay for the command and general staff course in the late 1970s.[32]

The advent of the Carter administration, with its emphasis on human rights, seemed to promise an acceleration in the trend toward reduced involvement. Besides tying military assistance and credits to human rights performance, the new administration pledged to reduce the role of the United States as an arms supplier to the Third World. Guatemala and El

Salvador responded to human rights pressures by abrogating military assistance agreements with the United States, perhaps anticipating that the Carter administration was about to take such action. Neither had much to lose. El Salvador had been forced to seek other sources of equipment since 1969, and in the mid-1970s, U.S. concern over Guatemala's dispute with Belize led to the denial of requests to purchase M-16 rifles. As a result, Guatemala had purchased Arava aircraft, automatic rifles, armored cars, and ammunition from Israel; helicopters from France; and an assortment of other weapons and equipment from France and from Spain, Taiwan, Yugoslavia, and Portugal.[33] Nicaragua made some concessions to U.S. pressures, but the outbreak of civil conflict in that nation in 1978 led to a virtual U.S. embargo on arms sales and, in early 1979, a total cutoff of all military supplies and the forced withdrawal of Nicaraguan students from U.S. military schools. By 1979, in Central America and the Caribbean, only Honduras, Panama, and the Dominican Republic were still receiving FMS credits and sending students to U.S. military schools.

A number of nations moved to fill the vacuum created by the reduction in U.S. programs. Taiwan provided training and some sales. So did South Africa. Central American officers began attending military schools in Argentina, Chile, Peru, and Brazil. Of greatest impact was the expanded role of Israel. Israeli sales of military equipment to Central America began in the 1950s but remained minor until the 1970s. Israel became a major supplier for both El Salvador and Honduras in the aftermath of the war between those nations. Israel also became a major source of weapons for Guatemala. Following the break in military relations with the United States, its role expanded notably. In December 1977, a military assistance agreement was concluded, providing for the training of Guatemalan officers in Israel, the introduction of Israeli advisors into Guatemala, and an expanded program of arms sales. In 1979, Guatemala attempted to purchase Kfir aircraft, but the agreement was vetoed by the United States. In Guatemala, Israeli advisors worked with police and intelligence services as well as with the army, helped build a munitions plant to provide small-arms ammunition, developed the Guatemalan Army School of Transmission and Electronics, and installed a radar system to help detect efforts to smuggle arms to insurgent groups. This assistance is frequently credited with having played a major role in reducing the level of insurgent activity.[34] In Guatemala in the 1980s, Israel's assistance also helped the governments of General Romeo Lucas García and Efraín Rios Montt resist pressures to return power to civilians and to improve human rights conditions.

American pressures did have a positive effect in the Dominican Republic. In 1978, when the military attempted to annul election results, the Carter administration, with support from Venezuela, threatened to impose sanctions. The military caved in, allowing Antonio Guzman to be inaugurated as president.[35] The ability to influence events in that nation reflected several factors, including the absence of an armed insurgency, a high level of economic dependence on the United States, and strong internal opposition to the military's action. The Carter administration also persuaded Panama's strongman, General Omar Torrijos, to begin lessening military control over that nation's politics. These concessions were partial, with the military giving up little real power, and were made in large part to improve prospects for ratification of the Panama Canal Treaties, but they did represent a reversal of political trends in Panama since 1968.

Events in Nicaragua proved much less satisfactory. When civil conflict broke out in 1978, the United States was unable to influence the behavior of that nation's military, the National Guard. This was surprising, as the Guard was a U.S. creation, and more Nicaraguans had been trained at the School of the Americas and other U.S. schools than personnel from any other Latin American nation. Most of the opposition, a large segment of the government, and much of the outside world believed that no government in that nation could survive without U.S. support.

The inability of the United States to influence the National Guard in Nicaragua reflected both an astonishing degree of ignorance in Washington concerning the nature and leadership of that body and the Guard's own total identification with the Somozas. In the words of a former U.S. military attaché: "The military in Nicaragua considered Somoza and the nation as one, inseparable entity."[36] When a few officers attempted to oust Somoza in September 1978, the Carter administration seemed to have no sense of who these officers were, what motivated them, and what alternatives they had in mind. Until the dictator's last weeks in power, the United States failed to establish independent contacts with Guard officers. The U.S. military attaché explained this failure by noting that such efforts "would have upset Somoza"—adding that he had been warned that he might have an "accident" if he tried to initiate such contacts. When such an effort was finally made, it was hindered by high levels of mutual suspicion, by a lack of trust between the ambassador and the military attaché, and by the chaotic situation that prevailed.[37] The final result was exactly what the administration had hoped to avoid: a civil war, which destroyed the National Guard and brought to power the Marxist-dominated Sandinista National Liberation Front (FSLN).

The Sandinista triumph in Nicaragua had varying impacts on the other Central American military establishments. Hondurans sought closer ties with the United States and began moving toward a restoration of civilian rule. In El Salvador, a group of young officers had been plotting to overthrow the dictatorship of General Carlos Humberto Romero since December 1978. More senior officers now joined them and, on October

15, 1979, seized power, installing a civil-military junta. The Carter administration quickly began to provide aid. In 1980, the administration reprogrammed funds to increase military assistance to Central America. A token amount was offered to, but not utilized by the Sandinistas, but the bulk was designated for Honduras and El Salvador. Ultimately, $3.5 million in FMS credits and $400,000 in IMET funds were made available to Honduras and $5.7 million in FMS credits and $20,000 in IMET funds were provided for El Salvador. Part of the credits extended to El Salvador were approved for riot-control equipment, but a general ban on sales of lethal weapons was maintained. The administration also loaned Honduras ten UH-lH helicopters. In making the requests, the administration argued that both nations were "on the right track" and that the aid would be "a key symbol of U.S. support for the political, social and economic reforms the government are making."[38]

In Guatemala, the military's response was quite different. Throughout the last year of the Carter administration, that nation moved steadily to the right, unleashing a wave of repression, rejecting Carter's nominee for ambassador, and even threatening to sever relations. President Romeo Lucas García publicly attacked Carter and vowed that "the gringos are not going to teach us what democracy is."[39] When Ronald Reagan was elected, the Guatemalan military and right-wing politicians celebrated with murders of suspected opponents.

During 1980, Honduras continued to move toward civilian rule. Events in El Salvador were less satisfactory. Conflicts within the officer corps; an unwillingness and/or inability to curb the activities of right-wing death squads; and the murders of Archbishop Romero, of the political leadership of the left-wing Democratic Revolutionary Front (FDR), and, finally, of four American churchwomen kept the nation in turmoil. Efforts at USARSA to teach Salvadoran officers human rights had no discernible effect on the military's conduct. But fearing a repetition of events in Nicaragua and lacking any viable alternative, the Carter administration continued its support, even though two sets of civilians quit the ruling junta in total frustration. When left-wing insurgents, with Nicaraguan support, launched a "final offensive" in January 1981, the Carter administration dropped its ban against lethal aid and rushed arms and munitions to the beleaguered regime.[40]

The Reagan administration took office determined to halt the spread of communism and to repair relations with the region's armed forces. Concern with human rights and democracy, though officially part of U.S. policy, was given lower priority. Assistance to the armed forces in El Salvador and Honduras increased rapidly. Even the Dominican Republic and Haiti saw increases in military assistance. Guatemala proved a special problem. A mission headed by Ambassador Frank Ortiz and by General

Vernon Walters tried to persuade General Lucas to ease up on human rights violations and open up the political system in return for U.S. support. But the effort failed. A 1982 junior officers' coup that ousted Lucas and brought General Rios Montt to power restored some contacts, but continued human rights violations helped block congressional approval of military assistance. Only in 1985, when President Vinicio Cerezo took office, did Congress allow full resumption of military assistance.

Lack of progress in prosecuting those responsible for the murders of the American churchwomen and the killings of two U.S. AID employees and continued human rights violations made aid for El Salvador a subject of controversy between the administration and the Congress. This led to congressional reductions in administration aid requests and kept the prospect of a cutoff of funding constantly alive from 1981 until 1984.[41] By 1984, the Reagan administration had begun to exert effective pressure on El Salvador's military. Several enlisted men were convicted of murdering the churchwomen, death squad activity declined, and Christian Democrat José Napoleon Duarte won the 1984 elections. The military highcommand was reshuffled, and some officers connected with the death squads were discharged, retired, or were sent into diplomatic exile. This reduced congressional opposition and made possible increased funding, beginning with fiscal year 1984.

By 1986, the administration appeared to have made significant progress in restoring stability and promoting democracy in Central America. Guerrilla fortunes in El Salvador and Guatemala appeared to be on the decline. Elected civilian presidents were in office in those nations, as well as in Costa Rica, Honduras, Panama, and the Dominican Republic. Even Haiti showed signs of progress when mass uprisings toppled President Jean-Claude Duvalier. Nicaragua remained a major problem. Soviet and Cuban influence in that nation steadily increased, and the United States administration–supported armed opposition, the contras, seemed incapable of winning strong support in either Nicaragua or the United States.

By the end of 1988, whatever progress the United States had made in the region seemed in danger of unraveling. In El Salvador, a series of scandals discredited the Duarte administration. Death squad activity increased, and the guerrillas managed to reverse the decline in their military fortunes. The Iran–contra scandals, followed by the signing of the Esquipulas II Agreement (the Arias Plan) jeopardized the contras' prospects for additional U.S. funding. In Panama and Haiti, conflicts between the military and the populace reversed whatever progress had been made toward democratization in those two nations. While criticizing the military leadership in both nations and suspending U.S. assistance, the administration seemed unable to influence the course of events effectively. Again, a U.S. administration had discovered the limits of its influence over regional military institutions. The influence of the United States and other nations over the internal political role played by the armed forces in Central America and the Caribbean remains as great an issue today as it was when Woodrow Wilson was dispatching American troops to the region to "teach them to elect good men."

Four observations can easily be drawn from ninety years of close U.S. involvement with the armed forces of Central America and the Caribbean. The first is that U.S. assistance, U.S. policies, U.S. pressures, and the ubiquitous reality of the U.S. presence have been and will continue to be major factors in the development and comportment of these militaries. The second is that the ways in which these armies are influenced by the aforementioned factors often bears little or no relationship to the goals of U.S. policymakers. The third is that the United States has rarely learned from past experiences but, instead, has repeated policies that a previous generation tried and found wanting.[42] Central Americans, on the other hand, have acted with a strong, if often distorted memory of past dealings with the United States. The final observation is that the ability of the United States to shape events in the region has eroded in recent years, as competing institutions, ideologies, and external forces have grown stronger.

These observations undercut arguments that U.S. policies deserve the bulk of the credit for whatever progress has been made toward the development of democratic institutions or, conversely, that these policies are responsible for creating and sustaining military dominations of the political system.[43] But several basic questions remain unanswered. What limiting factors must be taken into account when analyzing the impact of external influences on civil–military relations in the region? To what extent can and/or should there be a common perception of threats, of goals, and of acceptable means to counter threats and achieve goals? Finally, how and to what extent can external influences contribute to desired outcomes in this area?

One constant limiting factor is the wide variety of contrasting and often conflicting views regarding what can and should be the goals of U.S. policy. Dealings between the United States and the armed forces in the region can easily generate five or more distinct sets of perceptions as to desired outcomes. For example, a U.S. administration may favor a military training program as a means of countering the influence of other nations, the Congress may approve it as an avenue for inculcating regional officers with U.S. values, the U.S. military may promote it for its improvement of technical capacities and the opportunities it provides for military-to-military contacts, the regional military may see the program as a way of rewarding or, conversely, sending into golden exile selected officers and of strengthening the power and prestige of the institution within the national context, while that nation's civilian government may believe that the value of such programs lies in their capacity to reduce the military's demands on the national budget. Related to this is the tendency of advocates of military assistance programs to claim that such programs can produce results that those who are directly involved know are quite unlikely. Conflicting goals and exaggerated expectations reduce the likelihood that any policy will have a predictable influence on shaping military behavior.

Related to conflicts over goals are problems created by divergent threat perceptions. American officials and regional military officers may agree on the need to combat communism and oppose Soviet-Cuban influences, but they may define these terms in quite different ways. The officers may see "communism" as anything that threatens the power and privileges of the military, especially if it is accompanied by the threat of holding officers responsible for actions against civilians. With this perception, U.S. suggestions that one way to combat the Communist threat is to reduce the military's role in politics makes little sense. Instead, one encounters attitudes such as those of Honduran cadets, who felt that the best way to combat communism was to burn suspected subversives in public plazas.[44]

Arms sales or the refusal to permit such sales are frequently cited as a means of exerting influence over Latin American armed forces.[45] Proponents of such sales argue that they strengthen U.S. abilities to pressure the armed forces to allow greater democratization, while critics allege that providing military equipment actually makes military domination of politics more likely. Most analytical studies fail to support either conclusion.[46] Providing arms to Nicaragua did nothing to make the National Guard more responsive to U.S. pressures; neither, however, did the Carter administration's arms embargo. In Guatemala, the cutoff of military assistance solidified the alliance between the extreme right and the armed forces. The hope of U.S. assistance helped convince the Honduran military to allow a return to civilian rule; but during the early 1980s, that same aid helped General Gustavo Alvarez exert growing political influence.

This is not to say that providing or denying military assistance has no impact, but rather that the impact is conditioned by other factors, such as the availability of alternative sources of supply, the credibility of U.S. promises and threats, the internal dynamics of each nation's civil–military relations, and the nature of perceived threats to military institutions. Efforts to use arms sales and grants to exert influence often underestimate the sensitivity of nationalist sentiments within the armed forces.

Evaluating the effects of training on military behavior and on civil–military relations is even more difficult. Critics of U.S. training have argued that it makes officers more likely to oppose reforms and insert themselves into politics.[47] In a 1977 study, Dr. John Fitch found that such training could strengthen or modify attitudes; he found no evidence that it was likely to produce sudden or radical alterations.[48] Such observations seem borne out by experiences in the Caribbean Basin. American training has strengthened perceptions of the military's role as a bulwark against communism and, at times, has exacerbated existing perceptions that political ideas from the Left constitute threats to the military and the nation. At times, as in Honduras in the late 1970s and in El Salvador in the mid-1980s, it helped convince the officer corps to accept a broader range of political opinions and give up the exercise of political power in certain, limited areas. But there is no evidence that it led them to transfer their loyalties from the military institution to the civilian government, to recognize the right of civilians to judge the military for its use of power, or to give up limiting and shaping the ways in which civilians are allowed to exercise power. Whenever the military has perceived a threat to its institutional autonomy, it has rejected U.S. pressures and has increased its domination of the political process. This was the case in Nicaragua in 1978–79, Guatemala in 1979–82, Panama in 1986–88, Haiti in 1987–88, and the Dominican Republic in 1963–65.

There remains, of course, the possibility that intensive training of junior officers may, over time, alter institutional attitudes. In theory, this is possible; but in practice, it is problematical. Increasingly, U.S. training is supplemented with training at home or in other nations, thus diluting the impact of any single point of view. Soviet training in Cuba has certainly influenced attitudes in that nation's armed forces and Soviet-Cuban training is exerting similar influences in Nicaragua. But in both cases, old military structures had been destroyed in a revolution, and the new military was both the creation and the instrument of a Marxist political movement that rejected Western distinctions between civil and military powers and actively sought to promote the ideological orientation provided by the foreign instructors.

American influences are also hampered and diluted by the divisions and lack of consistency that characterize U.S. politics. This undermines U.S. credibility. President Carter's human rights policies were constantly subjected to this limitation, especially when officers began to believe that these policies would not endure beyond the 1980 elections. The Somozas were masterful at manipulating internal U.S. divisions and outwaiting administrations.[49] Conflicts between Congress and the executive have sent confused and contradictory messages to the region, further diluting U.S. influence.

None of this is to suggest that the external forces have not influenced civil–military relations in the region or that such influences will not be important in the future. On the contrary, the importance of external influences is more likely to grow than to decrease, in part because the number and variety of such influences will increase. Sensitivity to international pressures will work against a return to open military rule in Central America. Changes will remain incremental and tenuous. Regional militaries will seek to play external actors against each other and will be guided by institutional self-interests. But external influences will influence the perceptions of these interests and of the options available to advance them. A U.S. officer recently observed that although the United States may not prevent the military from interfering in politics, its influence can limit that intervention and make the military more discriminate in the ways in which it uses power.[50]

It will always be easier to exacerbate negative trends in civil–military relations than to promote positive ones, and there will be a constant temptation to seek a quick, cheap fix where none exists. But patience and, to the extent possible, greater consistency can mean that, over time, U.S. influence will promote democracy in the region and lower the level of conflict in civil–military relations.

Notes

1. Frederick M. Nunn, *Yesterday's Soldiers* (Lincoln: University of Nebraska Press, 1983), pp. 110–11.

2. For accounts of these efforts, see Louis A. Perez, Jr., "Supervision of a Protectorate: The United States and the Cuban Army, 1898, 1908," *Hispanic American Historical Review* 52 (May 1972): 250–71; Richard Millett, *Guardians of the Dynasty* (Maryknoll, N.Y.: Orbis, 1977); Marvin Goldwert, *The Constabulary in the Dominican Republic and Nicaragua: Progeny and Legacy of United States Intervention* (Gainesville: University of Florida Press, 1962); James H. McCrocklin, *Garde d'Haiti, 1915–1934* (Annapolis, Md.: United States Naval Institute, 1956).

3. Letter from Dr. Dana G. Munro to Richard Millett, February 14, 1965.

4. Arthur Bliss Lane, the U.S. minister to Nicaragua, wrote in 1935:

The people who created the G.N. [Guardia Nacional] had no adequate understanding of the psychology of the people here. Otherwise they would not have bequeathed Nicaragua with an instrument to blast constitutional procedure off the map. Did it never occur to the eminent statesmen who created the G.N. that personal ambition lurks in the human breast, even in Nicaragua? In my opinion, it is one of the sorriest examples on our part of inability to understand that we should not meddle in other people's affairs.

Arthur Bliss Lane to Willard Beaulacx, July 27, 1935, Arthur Bliss Lane Papers, Yale University Library, New Haven, Connecticut.

5. Thomas M. Leonear. *U.S. Policy and Arms Limitation in Central America: The Washington Conference of 1923* (Los Angeles: California State University, 1982).

6. Steve C. Ropp. *Panamanian Politics: From Guarded Nation to National Guard* (New York: Praeger, 1982), p. 26.

7. The 1954 Agreement between the United States and Honduras, a typical example of these agreements, is reprinted in Edwin Lieuwen, *Arms and Politics in Latin America* (New York: Praeger, 1960) pp. 272–77.

8. Willard F. Barber and C. Neale Ronning, *Internal Security and Military Power* (Columbus: Ohio State University Press, 1966), p. 237.

9. For details, see Stephen Schlesinger and Stephen Kinzer, *Bitter Fruit* (Garden City, N.Y.: Doubleday, 1982), pp. 205–14.

10. Charles Ameringer, *Don Pepe* (Albuquerque: University of New Mexico Press, 1978), pp. 120–24.

11. For details on this period, see Hugh Thomas, *Cuba* (New York: Harper & Row, 1971), pp. 985–1030.

12. Michael J. Francis, "Military Aid to Latin America and the U.S. Congress," *Journal of Inter-American Studies* (July 1964): 397.

13. Colonel James M. Hanson, "The Influence of U.S. Military Polices Toward Latin America," Unpublished M.S. thesis, Southern Illinois University at Edwardsville, 1975, p. 30.

14. Escuela de las Americas, *Catalogo de Cursos* (Panama: USARSA, September 1980), p. 10.

15. Thomas Anderson, *The War of the Dispossessed* (Lincoln: University of Nebraska Press, 1981), pp. 28–29.

16. For an inside account of U.S. policy, see John Barlow Martin, *Overtaken by Events* (Garden City, N.Y.: Doubleday, 1966).

17. Barber and Ronning, *Internal Security*, pp. 127–31; Edwin Lieuwen, *Generals versus Presidents* (New York: Praeger, 1964), pp. 91–94.

18. This revolt was generated, in part, by resentment of the U.S. use of Guatemalan territory to train Cuban exiles for the Bay of Pigs invasion. Some officers involved in this uprising later became leaders of insurgent movements in Guatemala.

19. I was told this story by a U.S. military officer in Central America a few weeks after the coup, and I have subsequently heard similar accounts from Honduran officers.

20. Robert I. Rothberg, *Haiti: The Politics of Squalor* (Boston: Houghton Mifflin, 1971), pp. 238–39.

21. Martin, *Overtaken by Events*, pp. 416–47, 547–90; Jerome Levinson and Juan de Onis, *The Alliance that Lost Its Way* (Chicago: Quadrangle Books, 1970), p. 86.

22. Levinson and Onis, *The Alliance*, pp. 86–87.

23. Gabriel Aguilera Peralta, *La Integracion Militar en Centroamerica* (n.p.: INCEP, n.d.), pp. 53–59.

24. For an account of events during this period, see Abraham Loenthal, *The Dominican Intervention* (Cambridge, Mass.: Harvard University Press, 1961).

25. Aguilera Peralta, *La Integracion Militar*, p. 39; (U.S.) Southern Com-

mand, "Roster of U.S. Military Group Personnel and Ambassadors in Latin America," (Panama: SOUTHCOM, September 30, 1980).

26. Hanson, "The Influence of U.S. Military Policies," pp. 22–23.

27. U.S. Department of Defense, *Military Assistance and Foreign Military Sales Facts* (Washington, D.C.: U.S. Government Printing Office, April 1972), pp. 7, 10, 17.

28. Kenneth F. Johnson, *Guatemala: From Terrorism to Terror*, Conflict Studies No. 23 (London: Institute for Conflict Studies, May 1972), pp. 6–13.

29. In the March 15, 1980, issue of the *Washington Post*, former U.S. ambassador to El Salvador Murat Williams observed that when he arrived there in 1961, "there were more men in the Air Force Mission than El Salvador had either pilots or planes."

30. For accounts of the conflict and its aftermath, see Anderson, *The War of the Dispossessed*, and Maria Virgilio Carias and Daniel Slutsky, *La Guerra Inutil* (San Jose, Costa Rica: EDUCA, 1971).

31. Agency for International Development, *U.S. Overseas Loans and Grants and Assistance from International Organizations: Obligations and Loan Authorizations, July 1, 1945–September 30, 1980* (Washington, D.C.: U.S. Government Printing Office, 1981).

32. Data furnished during interviews at USARSA and in Washington, September–November, 1980.

33. David Ronfeldt and Caesar Sereseres, *U.S. Arms Transfers, Diplomacy and Security in Latin America and Beyond.* (Santa Monica, Calif.: Rand, 1977), pp. 34–35.

34. Bishara Bahban with Linda Butler, *Israel and Latin America: The Military Connections* (New York: St. Martin's Press, 1986), pp. 79–81, 146–48, 160–66.

35. Howard J. Wiarda and Michael J. Dryzanek, *The Dominican Republic: A Caribbean Crucible* (Boulder, Colo.: Westview Press, 1982) pp. 49–50.

36. Lieutenant Colonel Edward N. Meserve, "Arms Transfers, Military Assistance and Military Governments in Central America," Unpublished paper presented at the State Department conference, "Central America: U.S. Interests and Concerns," Washington, D.C., March 19–20, 1979.

37. Robert A. Pastor, *Condemned to Repetition: The United States and Nicaragua* (Princeton, N.J.: Princeton University Press, 1987), pp. 176–77. This volume provides the best available account of the Carter administration's dealings with Nicaragua.

38. Deputy Assistant Secretary of State for Inter-American Affairs John A. Bushnell, "Statement before the Subcommittee on Foreign Operations, House Committee on Appropriations, March 25, 1980"; Cynthia Arnson, *Background Information on El Salvador and United States Military Assistance to Central America: Update No. 2* (Washington, D.C.: Institute for Policy Studies, November 1980), p. 2.

39. *Diario de las Americas* (Miami) (September 8, 1980): 6; (September 13, 1980): 6.

40. A fascinating, if biased, account of U.S. efforts to respond to events in El

Salvador can be found in Raymond Bonner, *Weakness and Deceit: U.S. Policy and El Salvador* (New York: Times Books, 1984).

41. K. Larry Storrs, *El Salvador Air: Congressional Action, 1981–1986, on President Reagan's Requests for Economic and Military Assistance for El Salvador* (Washington, D.C.: Congressional Research Service, March 18, 1987).

42. This is a major theme of Pastor, *Condemned to Repetition*, which notes that U.S. policymakers throughout the 1978–79 Nicaraguan crisis were determined not to repeat the errors of U.S. dealings with Castro, but the policies pursued and the results achieved proved distressingly similar. In my essay "Central America," in Robert S. Litwak and Samuel F. Wells, eds., *Superpower Competition and Security in the Third World* (Cambridge, Mass.: Ballinger, 1987), I identified at least ten strategies that the U.S. used in an attempt to stabilize Central America during the first third of this century, and I found examples of similar policy options that have been pursued within the past decade.

43. For an example of the latter argument, see Tom Barry, Beth Wood, and Deb Preusch, *Dollars and Dictators: A Guide to Central America* (Albuquerque, N.M.: The Resource Center, 1982).

44. Stephen C. Ropp, "In Search of the New Soldier: Junior Officers and the Prospect of Social Reform in Panama, Honduras and Nicaragua," Unpublished Ph.D. dissertation, University of California at Riverside, 1971.

45. For examples of the debate on this issue, see *U.S. Arms Transfer Policy in Latin America.*, Hearing before the Subcommittees on International Security and Scientific Affairs of the Committee on Foreign Affairs, House of Representatives, 97th Cong., 1st sess., October 22, 1981; and *The Sale of F-5E/F Aircraft to Honduras*, Hearing and Markup before the Committee on Foreign Affairs and its Subcommittees on Arms Control, International Security and Science, and on Western Hemisphere Affairs, House of Representatives, 100th Cong., 1st sess., May 19 and June 4, 1987.

46. Charles Wolf, "The Political Effects of Military Programs: Some Indications from Latin America," *Orbis*, 8 (Winter 1969): 889–90; Philippe Schmitter, "Foreign Military Assistance, National Military Spending and Military Rule in Latin America," in *Military Rule in Latin America: Function, Consequences and Perspectives* (Beverly Hills, Calif.: Sage, 1973), p. 148.

47. This attitude is not confined to the far left. During a January 1986 McNeil-Lehrer television program, Roberto Eisenmann, editor of Panama's leading opposition newspaper, *La Prensa*, referred to USARSA as a "school for dictators" and suggested that U.S. training had contributed to the military's dominance in his nation.

48. John S. Fitch, *The Political Consequences of US Military Assistance to Latin America* (Carlisle Barracks, Pa.: U.S. Army War College, Strategic Studies Institute, 1977), pp. 5–12.

49. As late as 1979, the last ruling Somoza could still observe: "Carter said the Shah would stay and I would go, but the Shah has gone and I'm still here."

50. Confidential interview, December 1987.

Part III
Military Professionalism and the Missions of the Armed Forces

9
Geopolitical Thinking

Jack Child

T his chapter examines geopolitical thinking in the Southern Cone of South America over the past two decades, emphasizing the relationships among geopolitical thinking, the military, and democracy. South American geopolitical thinking is little known or understood outside the region. In the past few years, however, there has been an increasing awareness that associating this form of strategic thought with the Latin American military might shed some light on the way the military perceives its role in internal and international affairs. In particular, there have been numerous suggestions that geopolitical thinking was linked to the national security doctrine and the national security states that has characterized much of the Southern Cone of South America over the past quarter-century.[1]

geopolitical thinking linked to nat. sec. doct + the nat. sec. states.

As a result, analysts of South American civil–military affairs have begun to pay some attention to this geopolitical thinking.[2] However, this attention has usually taken the form of very general statements, supported by occasional references to scattered items in the literature. This chapter attempts to analyze this geopolitical thinking systematically, by examining the principal journals and tracking a series of themes that have appeared over the years.

Geopolitical Thinking: Roots, Characteristics, and Significance

The fundamental root of much of the Southern Cone's early geopolitical literature is the organic concept of the nation-state. This perception holds that nation-states are analogous to living organisms that are born, grow, seek living space and resources in order to increase their power, and then eventually decline and perish. The organic state concept was strongly influenced by nineteenth-century European geopolitical ideas, especially those of the Germanic school. A current of this Germanic school was used by Adolf Hitler and the National Socialists to provide a pseudointellectual justification for some of their plans by which Germany would expand its

organic concept of the nation state.

Lebensraum (living space) at the expense of its neighbors. As a result, European geopolitical thinking fell into disrepute after World War II, although it was kept alive by a small number of military and civilian adherents in the Southern Cone of South America.[3]

Proponents of the organic vision of the nation-state tend to take a pessimistic and Darwinian view of international relations, in which the strong states grow stronger and the weak submit or perish. The organic state, especially in its early stages, is seen as vulnerable to the depredations of other organic states that are competing for limited space and resources. The threats—both internal and external—abound. The military tends to identify closely with this organic nation-state and finds its basic mission in the firm defense of the organic state from these domestic and outside enemies.

Using the biological metaphor, the internal enemies of the organic state are envisioned as malignant cells that have gone bad and are attacking their host. The military attempts, first, to contain these cancerous cells through therapy and repressive means. If this should fail, then the ultimate draconian step of surgical removal (extirpation) may be necessary. This type of mind-set leads to a perception that the state is above the replaceable individual cell, and it was used by some within the military to justify the abuses committed by the national security states when faced with Marxist-inspired subversion in the 1960s and 1970s.[4]

The external adversaries of the organic state are both the immediate neighbors and the more distant allies of the perceived subversive elements. Southern Cone geopolitical thinking in the past two decades has stressed the projection of state power as a way to increase the nation's own space and resources. Because of logistical limitations faced by most of the South American military establishments, the principal focus has been the immediate neighbors. A number of deep-rooted border disputes have attracted the attention of much of the Southern Cone's geopolitical literature in this period. One's own nation is frequently portrayed as having been the victim of geopolitical aggression in the past and the possible victim of further territorial mutilations unless one is strong and aggressive.[5] The advocates of geopolitical thinking and the organic state frequently rely on exalted patriotism, jingoism, and chauvinism to stir up popular support for their causes and have attempted to popularize geopolitical ideas by inserting them in the media and educational systems whenever possible.

However, this popularization has been something of a one-way street, as it has not opened up fundamental geopolitical thinking of the military to outside civilian currents. Most geopolitical writers in the Southern Cone are military officers (both retired and on active duty), and the few civilians involved are usually linked to the military in one way or another.

The general features of early Southern Cone geopolitical thinking sketched out in the preceding paragraphs suggest that there was a strong link between geopolitical thinking and the national security states in the 1960s and 1970s in South America, to the point that it could be said that geopolitics was the geography of the national security state and made a significant contribution to the ideological foundations of the national security doctrine. The Brazilian case is particularly striking in this regard. Early Brazilian geopolitical writers such as Marshal Mario Travassos and Everardo Backheuser had considerable influence on the generation of leaders who shaped the Brazilian military revolution of 1964–85, and the impact of later geopolitical thinkers and advisors such as General Golbery do Cuoto e Silva was also significant in this period.[6]

There were also important national variants and other currents that ran counter to this association of geopolitical thinking with the national security state. In particular, there has always been a strain of geopolitical writings that ignore the more aggressive and hostile aspects of the organic state adherents and emphasize, instead, the rational development of national resources and cooperative approaches toward neighboring states. Internally, this "developmental geopolitics" has focused on the relationships among geography, resources, and national growth and has emphasized ways in which the distant areas of the nation could be effectively brought into the mainstream of the country's economic, cultural, and political life. Examples of this tendency are the attempts to develop river systems and move national capitals inland. Internationally, this cooperative approach has focused on South American integration and ways in which the region's economic and political problems could be jointly addressed. Examples are international hydroelectric projects and coordinated policies toward the sector of Antarctica that faces South America.

As will be suggested in the data and tables presented in this chapter, there are strong indications of an important shift in geopolitical thinking in South America shortly after the 1982 Malvinas/Falklands conflict. The shift is away from the earlier, more aggressive and nationalistic forms of geopolitical thinking and toward more cooperative and integrative currents. Although the South Atlantic conflict (and resentment of U.S. support for Great Britain) might have been a catalyst in this process, it appears that a number of other factors may have contributed to this shift, including a decline in U.S. influence in the region, the resolution of Argentine–Chilean differences over the Beagle Channel Islands, the Argentine–Brazilian rapprochement, and joint approaches toward the problem of external debt.

Thus, the significance of Southern Cone geopolitical thinking can be summarized in terms of the links it had to the national security states of the 1960s and 1970s as well as to movements toward South American integration and cooperation in the 1980s. Both of these components show up in the contemporary literature, and there is a danger that the more aggressive side of earlier geopolitical thinking, which still remains, could become prevalent once again. The relationship between geopolitical thinking and democracy can be developed as a corollary: The negative aspects of geopolitical thinking are a threat to South American democracy, especially those currents that sustain the national security state and view neighbors with hostility. The positive side, stressing South American integration and cooperative approaches to common problems, can serve to buttress the delicate process of redemocratization in the Southern Cone by strengthening the region's economic base and diminishing the likelihood of interstate conflict.

Aspects of geopolitical thinking which sustain nat'l Sec. State, t view neighbors w/ hostility threaten democracy.

Positive side

One final facet of geopolitics that underscores its significance is the way it affords an insight into Southern Cone military thinking, which is frequently closed to the outside observer. South American geopolitical thinking is important, in the final analysis, because the South American military officer thinks geopolitically and tends to see his role and the neighboring states in geopolitical terms. In the military educational institutions that give officers their professional formation, geopolitics is taken seriously as the discipline that strongly influences strategy, international relations, and national development. Geopolitical literature, carefully read, can also foreshadow important events. For example, several Argentine geopolitical and military journals in 1981 carried implicit and sometimes explicit predictions of what eventually happened on the April 2, 1982.[7]

Geopolitics important framework in Mil. education

A Survey of the Geopolitical Journal Literature

The Data Base and Methodology

The data base used in this analysis is a body of approximately 2,200 bibliographic items dealing with geopolitical thinking, the Latin American military, the inter-American military system, various South American conflict situations, and Antarctica. The bibliographic items were entered into a computer data base program that permitted sorting by year of publication, country, author, title, and publishing information.

This initial data base was then scanned for items with indigenous geopolitical content. This process resulted in the identification of 568 items from a number of Latin American countries, with a heavy concentration on the Southern Cone. Possible biases generated by my prior work on Southern Cone international relations and Antarctica were recognized, and an attempt was made to search for geopolitical literature in countries outside the Southern Cone.[8] However, as had been suspected, the vast majority of the geopolitical literature of Latin America originates in the Southern Cone, especially in Argentina, Brazil, and Chile.[9]

The items selected generally concentrated on the international aspects of geopolitics—that is, the relationship between geography and the projection of power beyond the borders of the nation-state. This choice tends to ignore internal geopolitics, which focuses on the rational development of national space and resources. It also pays little attention to those aspects of geopolitics that, going back to the common root of the organic theory of the state, are associated with repression and counterinsurgency. These choices were made, in part, because the bulk of the literature deals with external aspects and, in part, because it is hard to draw a line between those aspects of counterinsurgency that are geopolitical in nature and those that are purely tactical.

Once the 568 geopolitical bibliographic items had been identified, each item was coded according to major and minor geopolitical themes. The sorting capabilities of the computer data base program permitted arrangement according to these themes as well other categories of information, as shown in the following analysis.

The Geopolitical Journals

Table 9–1 lists the principal geopolitical journals of the Southern Cone. The first part of the table lists the six journals that are devoted principally to geopolitical topics. A seventh journal, the Uruguayan *Geopolítica* (Instituto Uruguayo de Estudios Geopolíticos), was published sporadically in the late 1970s and early 1980s but is no longer active. As was the case with books, the most significant journals are Argentine. *Estrategia*, published by retired General Juan E. Guglialmelli from 1969 until his death in 1983, is by far the most influential, especially if one considers that the *Revista Argentina de Estudios Estratégicos* is essentially a continuation of *Estrategia*, with many of the same writers and editorial board members. *Geosur* has been the principal vehicle for the Uruguayan "integrationist" geopolitical school led by Bernardo Quagliotti de Bellis, and the *Revista Chilena de Geopolítica* is the organ of the Instituto Geopolítico de Chile, created by the Pinochet regime as a part of the geopolitical school quite deliberately established by the regime. The Peruvian *Estudios Geopolíticos y Estratégicos* is the creation of General Edgardo Mercado Jarrin and is the standard-bearer of the integrationist and Third World current of Peruvian geopolitics.

It is curious that Brazil has no explicitly geopolitical journal. However, several of its military journals carry substantial amounts of this material, especially the two associated with the Escola Superior de Guerra

Table 9–1
Principal Geopolitical and Strategic Journals

Argentina
Estrategia (Instituto Argentino de Estudios Estratégicos y de las Relaciones Internacionales). Published from 1969 to 1983; 73 issues (many double issues).

Geopolítica (Instituto de Estudios Geopolíticos). Published from 1984 to present; 8 issues (as of December 1987).

Revista Argentina de Estudios Estratégicos (Centro Argentino de Estudios Estratégicos). Published from 1984 to present; 8 issues (as of December 1986).

Chile
Revista Chilena de Geopolítica (Instituto Geopolítico de Chile). Published from 1984 to present; 6 issues (as of August 86).

Peru
Estudios Geopolíticos y Estratégicos (Instituto Peruano de Estudios Geopolíticos y Estratégicos [IPEGE]). Published from 1979 to 1983(?); 9 issues (as of December 1983).

Uruguay
Geosur (Asociación Sudamericana de Estudios Geopolíticos e Internacionales). Published from 1979 to present(?); 60 issues (as of April 1985).

Military Journals with Geopolitical Content

Argentina
Revista de la Escuela de Defensa Nacional
Revista de la Escuela Superior de Guerra
Revista de la Escuela de Guerra Naval
Revista Militar
Revista de Temas Militares

Brazil
A Defesa Nacional
Mar (Boletim do Clube Naval)
Revista da Escola Superior de Guerra (ESG)
Revista Maritima Brasileira
Seguranca e Desemvolvimento (ESG Alumni Organization)

Chile
Memorial del Ejército
Revista Geográfica de Chile
Revista de Marina de Chile
Seguridad Nacional

Ecuador
Revista Geográfica (Instituto Geográfico Militar)

Peru
Defensa Nacional (Centro de Altos Estudios Militares)

(*Revista da Escola Superior de Guerra* and *Seguranca e Desenvolvimento*, which is published by the association of ESG graduates).

Identification of Themes in the Journals

A total of 568 journal articles and other miscellaneous items (monographs, pamphlets) was used to identify the major themes in Southern

Cone geopolitical literature. The items were coded by theme and tabulated. The results of this process are shown in tables 9–2 and 9–3.

Table 9–2 shows the fifteen themes tabulated by country of publication. Table 9–3 shows the same themes tabulated by five-year intervals, working back from 1982–86. Two major related themes were not coded separately because they show up so consistently in almost all of the literature: the national search for "greatness" and the belief that one's own country has been the victim of past geopolitical aggressions and must somehow recover from these historic losses.

The major observations from tables 9–2 and 9–3 confirm that production of geopolitical literature in the Southern Cone is principally Argentine (followed by Chile, and then Brazil, Uruguay, and Peru). Further, production of this literature closely tracks with the establishment of the national security state, as very little was produced prior to the 1960s and it reached a peak in the 1977–81 period.

As might be expected, the principal themes tended to peak when a political-military crisis involving that theme became prominent. One can trace the waxing and waning of those crises over the past two decades by a careful analysis of the emergence and disappearance of these themes in the literature. Moreover, there were occasions when the geopolitical literature foreshadowed the crisis and may, in fact, have stimulated it. An example of the foreshadowing phenomenon was mentioned earlier in relation to the 1982 Argentine "recovery" of the Malvinas/Falklands; the actual scenario for the invasion was laid out, and several articles called for military action against Britain if negotiations failed before the 150th anni-

Table 9–2
Geopolitical Themes in Journal Articles, by Country

Theme	Arg.	Braz.	Chile	Urug.	Peru	Ecua.	Bol.	Other	Total
1. South Atlantic	42	12	7	5	1			2	69
2. Antarctica	25	15	15	3	8	1		1	68
3. Malvinas/Falklands	48		5	3	2				59
4. Beagles	24	1	13	3	2			1	43
5. South Pacific	1		26		3			1	31
6. Argentina–Brazil	28	2							30
7. Integration	5			10	7			1	23
8. Southern Andes	10		8						18
9. Bolivian Sea	5		5	2					13
10. Amazon Basin	6	2		3	2				13
11. Hydrographic	8	1							9
12. Nuclear	9								9
13. Critical	1	1	2		1				5
14. Ecuador–Peru					4				4
15. River Plate	3								3
16. General & Misc.	68	27	20	15	22	11	1	7	171
Total	283	61	101	44	52	12	2	13	568

Table 9-3
Geopolitical Themes in Journal Articles, by (Five-Year) Intervals

Theme	Before 1947	1947–51	1952–56	1957–61	1962–66	1967–71	1972–76	1977–81	1982–86	Total
1. South Atlantic						3	6	22	37	69
2. Antarctica	1		5	1		1	13	16	31	68
3. Malvinas/Falklands						1		13	45	59
4. Beagles						1	5	25	12	43
5. South Pacific		5	4	1		1	2	3	15	31
6. Argentina–Brazil						3	16	9	2	30
7. Integration					1	1	3	9	9	23
8. Southern Andes			3	1	1	3	3	7	2	18
9. Bolivian Sea							5	6	2	13
10. Amazon Basin							3	10		13
11. Hydrographic						1	1	5	2	9
12. Nuclear							5	1	3	9
13. Critical								2	3	5
14. Ecuador–Peru								4		4
15. River Plate						2		1		3
16. General & Misc.	1	1	1	1	2	14	39	67	45	171
Total	1	7	14	3	3	31	101	200	208	568

versary of the 1833 British "usurpation."[10] A prime example of the stimulating function of geopolitical writing was the Beagle Channel crisis of 1977–78, when many of the writings in Argentina and Chile included highly aggressive statements regarding the opponent, and threats of military action were common in the geopolitical literature.[11]

The prevailing geopolitical themes today are three interlinked ones: South Atlantic, Falkland/Malvinas, and Antarctica. The salience of these three themes is underscored by the declining attention paid to a number of older tensions that have seen their relevance decreased: sovereignty of the Beagle Channel Islands, Brazilian–Argentine rivalry, strains in the River Plate Basin over hydrographic projects, and concern over one or more Southern Cone nations producing a nuclear weapon.

Themes in the Geopolitical Literature

The principal features of the fifteen major themes in Southern Cone geopolitical literature, presented in rank-order of frequency, are as follows.

The South Atlantic

This geopolitical region is composed of the Atlantic Ocean from the Equator to the northern limit of the Antarctic Treaty region (the 60 degree south parallel) and from the eastern coast of South America to Africa. Included in this area are the Falklands/Malvinas and the islands of the "Arc of the Southern Antilles": South Georgia, South Sandwich, South Orkney, and South Shetlands. In the eyes of the most geopolitical analysts, these islands create a continuity between mainland South America and Antarctica. For Argentina, the chief issue here is the sovereignty of the Malvinas Islands, which led to war with Great Britain in 1982. However, Argentine geopoliticians also emphasize the Mar Argentino, which corresponds to the portion of the South Atlantic that faces Argentina and extends from the River Plate to Antarctica. For South American countries other than Argentina, the South Atlantic is a more significant geopolitical theme than the Falklands/Malvinas Islands themselves. As tables 9–2 and 9–3 indicate, the interest began well before the 1982 crisis. It also shows up consistently in the geopolitical literature of Brazil, Uruguay, and Chile.

In the case of Brazil, geopolitical interest in the South Atlantic can be traced back to its earliest writers, who frequently noted that although Brazil has major continental geopolitical concerns (filling the Amazon Basin heartland and moving its capital), it should also value the Atlantic Narrows (from Dakar to Brazil's northeast salient), and the South Atlantic generally as a theater into which it can project power as it moves to *grandeza* (greatness). In the early 1980s, Brazil's growing interest in Ant-

[margin note top right: Brazil took responsibility of defending South Atlantic b/c Argentina failed.]

[margin note left: Brazil's interest in Antarctica led geopolitical to study South Atlantic as route]

arctica caused its geopolitical writers to study the South Atlantic as the logical route to that continent. After the 1982 South Atlantic war, there was increased interest in Brazil's Rio Treaty responsibilities to defend the area.[12] This point was occasionally made rather bitingly in terms of it now being clear that other South American nations (that is, Argentina) were not capable of defending it.

Uruguay's South Atlantic geopolitical interests stem from a long maritime history in the region and the fact that Uruguay has better natural ports than Argentina. Many of the Colonial Spanish expeditions to the South Atlantic sailed from Montevideo, and this has geopolitical implications today for Uruguay's South Atlantic and Antarctic interests.

[margin note left: Chile as guardian of 3 major passages btwn Atlantic + Pacific. Pushing as far as possible into the South Atlantic]

The Atlantic interests of Chile might seem surprising, but they are related to Chile's perceived geopolitical role as guardian of the three major passages between the Atlantic and the Pacific (Strait of Magellan, Beagle Channel, and Drake Passage). A constant in Chilean geopolitical thinking has been to push as far as possible into the South Atlantic and to move the accepted dividing line between the Atlantic and the Pacific as far to the east as possible.[13] In this connection, Chilean geopoliticians have consistently stressed the idea that the natural dividing line is not the meridian of Cape Horn (as Argentine geopoliticians would have it) but the Arc of the Southern Antilles. This would severely undermine the treasured Argentine concept of Mar Argentino and the continuity between continental, insular, and Antarctic Argentina.

Antarctica

The theme of Antarctica has been a consistent one in South American geopolitical literature. In the past fifteen years, there has been a steady rise in interest, to the point that it is now a major theme and gives all indications of becoming even more significant in the near future, as many nations (with several South American ones in the forefront) prepare for a possible review of the Antarctic Treaty in 1991 or after. Antarctica is the last land surface on earth that is not under effective national sovereignty, and it presents many attractive features for geopoliticians seeking available space and resources in this "frozen *Lebensraum*." Older Antarctic geopolitical literature tended to be highly nationalistic, stressing the Antarctic rights and activities of the writer's nation and downplaying those of other contenders. The recent geopolitical literature on Antarctica is qualitatively different from that in the pre-1982 period,[14] and it has begun to suggest cooperative South American (or Latin American) approaches to the area as a way of countering the extrahemispheric presence in the region. The two South American nations with the longest history of Antarctic interest and presence are Argentina and Chile, and this is reflected in the geopolit-

[margin note left: Since 1982 change from selfish view to cooperative view of Antarctica]

ical literature. However, Brazil and Uruguay now have permanent Antarctic bases and are full (consultative) members of the Antarctic Treaty System. Peru and Cuba are also members of the Treaty System and have a presence in Antarctica through extended visits at the Antarctic bases of other countries. Ecuador's geopolitical writers have also spoken of its potential Antarctic interests. In all of these countries, the geopolitical literature focusing on Antarctica has served to heighten the national consciousness regarding Antarctica specifically and southern regions generally. The post-1982 shift from highly nationalistic Antarctic geopolitical literature to more cooperative South American Antarctic approaches may be an important foreshadowing of coordinated Latin American positions in the region. This is especially significant given Antarctic uncertainties in the post-1991 period.[15]

Malvinas/Falklands

As one might expect, most of the writing on the Malvinas/Falklands is Argentine and supports the Argentine view that the islands are unquestionably Argentina's and must return to its control. Geopolitical analysis of the islands tends to stress their value as a base from which to control the Drake Passage (a key naval choke point), the resources in the area (oil, fish, krill), and their significance in terms of the competing Antarctic claims of Argentina and Great Britain.[16]

Even though the predominant Malvinas/Falklands geopolitical writing is of Argentine origin, as table 9–2 shows, the theme is also present in other countries. From a qualitative perspective, there are interesting differences in the way it appears in the various countries. In Peru and Venezuela (Argentina's closest allies in the war), the writings are very supportive of Argentina. In the Venezuelan case, there are specific and clear parallels drawn to the Essequibo dispute with Guyana.[17] In Brazil and Chile, the two South American nations that were most reluctant to see an Argentine victory, the writing is much more restrained. In fact, in both of these countries, the islands are sometimes referred to as Falklands, using the British name, and there are numerous pointed analyses of Argentina's military shortcomings during the conflict.[18]

The Beagle Channel Islands

This theme was essentially a bilateral problem between Argentina and Chile, although as table 9–2 shows, it received some attention in the geopolitical writings of other nations. The geopolitical literature of both countries was highly jingoistic and provocative in the 1970s and reached a crescendo in 1978, when there was mobilization for war.[19] Intervention by the Vatican managed to lower tensions, and the 1984 signing of a treaty between Argentina and Chile presumably removed this specific issue from future geopolitical consideration. However, an important group of highly nationalistic Argentine geopolitical writers continues to insist that the issue is not dead, that Argentina was cheated, and that the geopolitical implications of the problem for Argentina's Antarctic and South Atlantic interests cannot be set aside. More optimistic assessments stress that the solution of this issue was a major triumph for the new administration of Raul Alfonsín, as it removed a potential conflict situation and thus one justification for higher military budgets and influence. The Beagle Channel case thus also serves as an illustration of the relationships among aggressive geopolitical thinking, the military, and democracy.

The South Pacific

Geopolitical writings focusing on this region are fundamentally a legacy of the 1879–83 War of the Pacific. From the Chilean perspective, Chile's territorial gains at the expense of Peru and Bolivia during that war are a splendid example of several geopolitical "laws" and the successful expansion of Chile in accordance with the organic theory of the state. More recent Chilean geopolitical writings dealing with the Pacific warn of the dangers of Soviet and Cuban naval penetration of the region.[20]

Peruvian geopolitical literature refuses to accept Chilean domination of the South Pacific. Tensions were fairly high among Chile, Peru, and Bolivia at the time of the centennial of the War of the Pacific, and the war was a major theme in Peruvian geopolitical literature of the time. More recently, Peruvian geopolitical writings on the Pacific Basin have stressed that this region is becoming important to all mankind and that Peru must play a leadership role in the area.[21]

Argentine–Brazilian Relations

A somewhat similar situation emerges from an analysis of the geopolitical literature surrounding Argentine–Brazilian relations. This, too, is primarily a bilateral issue, although it spills over into a number of other areas, such as the geopolitics of the buffer states, the South Atlantic, and Antarctica. As table 9–2 shows, most of the geopolitical literature is of Argentine origin; this reflects the quasiobsession of Argentine geopolitical thinkers regarding the relative status of the two countries and a sinking feeling that Argentina is constantly losing ground. Brazilian geopolitical writers pay some attention to the topic but are far more confident of Brazil's status and regard the issue as being of lesser importance. In the late 1960s and 1970s, this was a major theme in Argentine geopolitical writings, especially in the influential journal *Estrategia*, which consistently presented the argument that Brazil was a subimperial surrogate of the United States and that it should not truly be considered Latin American until it broke its unhealthy close ties with the United States.[22] In the eyes of many of these analysts, this happened during the Carter administration and paved the way for the dramatic improvement in Argentine–Brazilian relations in the early 1980s. This is shown in the qualitative change in the geopolitical literature of Argentine–Brazilian relations of the past five years, which has generally abandoned the old theme of rivalry and has adopted themes stressing Brazilian–Argentine cooperation at the service of Latin American integration.

Integration Geopolitics

The geopolitical theme of South American cooperation and integration is an important new addition to the literature. Generally, this current argues that the days of petty border problems between Latin American nations must give way to joint approaches to common problems. The theme includes the argument that democracy is weakened by geopolitically based border conflicts because these conflicts are used by the military to fuel arms races and increase its internal political role.[23] Early versions of geopolitical integration literature frequently were thinly disguised arguments for the hegemony of the larger South American nations, especially Argentina and Brazil, or schemes for buffer-state cooperation in the face of strong and aggressive neighbors.[24] However, in the post-1982 environment, this argument has given way to Latin American solidarity. To some extent, this appears to have been a side effect of the 1982 Malvinas conflict and the international debt crisis. Frequently, this current of the contemporary geopolitical literature of integration is quite critical of the United States and the institutions of the inter-American system that are perceived to serve U.S. interests, not those of Latin America. This current is strongly influenced by Third World ideas, especially the arguments of Peruvian geopolitical writers associated with the Centro de Altos Estudios Militares (CAEM) and the reformist trends within the Peruvian military.[25]

Strains in the Southern Andes (Chile–Argentina)

Bilateral Argentine–Chilean strains are not limited to the Beagle Channel Islands; there are larger issues of subregional rivalry involved. There are still differences over some details of the border along the Andes and the legacy of colonial claims and counterclaims on Patagonia. Demographic geopolitics are also involved, as Argentine Patagonia contains few Argentines, and many Chileans come across the border seeking work. The recent Argentine interest in moving the federal capital from Buenos Aires to a Patagonian city has been presented in the geopolitical literature as a step to correct the historic Argentine neglect of its southern lands.

Bolivia's Outlet to the Sea

As table 9–3 indicates, the geopolitical writings regarding Bolivia's outlet to the sea are essentially a unilateral Bolivian phenomenon and dominate the limited geopolitical output of that nation. Occasionally, Chilean geopolitical writers will criticize these Bolivian ideas, frequently in scathing terms that stress the political, military, and racial inferiority of Bolivians.[26] The Argentine geopolitical literature (indicated in table 9–3) sometimes picks up the Bolivian cause, presumably as an anti-Chilean instrument.

Amazon Basin Geopolitics

Brazilian geopolitical writing has had a strong continental thrust, stressing that the South American heartland of the Amazon Basin is Brazil's *Lebensraum,* which offers vast spaces and resources essential for that nation's march to greatness. Several of Brazil's neighbors fear that the Brazilian thrust into the Amazon will not stop at the international borders. Thus, there is a consistent geopolitical theme and countertheme surrounding Brazil's perceived expansion and the actions that Spanish-speaking South American nations must take to block it. This was one of the elements in the negative geopolitical writing surrounding Argentine–Brazilian relations in the 1960s and 1970s, and it was further fueled by suspicions that Brazil's push for an Amazon Basin pact had a hidden geopolitical agenda, despite the protestations of Brazilian authors.[27] The dramatic improvement in Argentine–Brazilian relations in the past few years has been reflected in the Spanish-language geopolitical literature, which now has generally abandoned the old suspicions of Brazil and supports a closer integration with that nation.

Hydrographic Geopolitics and Hydroelectric Projects

This theme was prevalent during the period when Brazil and Argentina were launching competing hydroelectric projects along the Parana River, which also involves Paraguay and Uruguay. Much of the Uruguayan geopolitical literature of the period focused on this, and there were extensive and highly technical writings in the major Argentine journals on the subject. With the major hydroelectric projects now completed or under way, the topic has dropped in significance, as table 9–3 shows.

Nuclear Concerns

Argentina and Brazil are generally considered "threshold" nuclear countries, with advanced research and energy programs and with the capacity to develop an explosive device in a relatively short period if they chose to do so. As a result, during the period of greatest Argentine–Brazilian strains in the 1970s, an important theme in the geopolitical literature addressed the issue of nuclear rivalry between these two nations. There was considerable suspicion on both sides (especially the Argentine), leading a prominent Argentine geopolitical writer to argue openly that Brazil was building a bomb and that Argentina could not afford to passively accept this.[28] The improvement in Argentine–Brazilian relations has defused this issue, and it no longer receives much attention.

Criticisms of Geopolitical Thinking

Strictly speaking, this theme is out of place in this analysis, as it does not appear in the geopolitical journals or books published by Southern Cone publishers that specialize in this type of literature. It is, in effect, a countertheme that sometimes takes highly negative positions regarding the impact of Southern Cone geopolitical thinking. The criticisms frequently stress the organic concept of the state favored by geopoliticians and the close associations among the national security doctrine, repression, and geopolitical thinking. Geopoliticians are militaristic, violent, and antidemocratic. Given the nature of the Southern Cone's national security states in the past quarter-century, it is understandable that much of this literature is written by critics from the liberal end of the spectrum and is frequently published in exile (often in Mexico). This theme peaked in the later period of the national security states' tenure. With the redemocratization of many Southern Cone nations, there has been a significant current of criticism of geopolitics and warnings that geopolitical thinking (especially within the military) poses threats to these vulnerable democracies.[29] In the late 1980s, an increasingly isolated Chile has been a target of much of this criticism in the journals of other nations: A recent article in the Argentine *Revista de Temas Militares*, titled: "Pinochet: The South American Fuhrer," emphasized the importance of his geopolitical ideas.[30]

Strains between Peru and Ecuador

Ecuador's limited geopolitical output focuses on its territorial mutilations at the hand of Peru during the 1941 war. The Peruvians feel that the issue was settled definitively by the 1942 Rio Protocol, but the Ecuadorans argue that this was signed under duress and is invalid for this reason as well as several technical problems. Like the Bolivian–Chilean dispute over the outlet to the sea, this is essentially a bilateral issue that is strongly upheld by Ecuadoran geopolitical literature and denied by Peruvian geopolitical writings. Periodic border incidents, including a particularly bloody one in 1981, keep the issue alive.[31]   *Kept alive*

The River Plate Basin

River Plate Basin geopolitics concerned Argentine and Uruguayan writers in the late 1960s and 1970s because of a number of unresolved bilateral issues as well as the larger problems of hydroelectric projects along the Parana River. Important bilateral agreements reduced the significance of this theme in the 1970s.

Conclusions: Geopolitical Thinking and Democracy

Geopolitical writings flourished during the years of Nat'l Security States

The data presented in the tables and subsequent analysis show how geopolitical writings flourished in the Southern Cone of South America during the years of the national security states in the 1960s and 1970s. From the beginning, two distinct currents of geopolitical literature were evident: a highly nationalistic and aggressive current, which tended to see neighbors as adversaries, and an integrative current, which tended to downplay excessive chauvinism and portrayed neighbors as allies in cooperative and integrative approaches to common problems. In the 1960s and 1970s, the former current predominated. A shift occurred shortly after the 1982 South Atlantic war, and the predominant current now is the latter.[32]

① Nationalistic & aggressive
② Integrative current ↓ current

It is tempting to postulate the existence of a chain of causal relationships that would establish that aggressive geopolitical thinking (linked to the national security states) increases interstate tensions, which, in turn, serves as the justification for increased military budgets, which, in turn, increases the political role of the military and makes it more difficult for fragile democracies to survive. Conversely, cooperative and integrational geopolitical thinking would lead to lower interstate tensions, smaller military budgets, and a decrease in the political role of the military, thus giving the process of democratization more breathing space. Unfortunately, these causal links are not neatly divided in a Manichaean typology of "evil" jingoistic geopolitics and "good" cooperative and integrative geopolitics. Although further detailed research using content analysis of the geopolitical literature and the background of its authors might cast further light on these possible causal links, in all probability they cannot be satisfactorily proved. In the absence of proved causality, one is left with the strong suggestions sketched out here, to the effect that the Southern Cone national security states and geopolitical thinking started out from the same intellectual foundations (the organic theory of the state) and that they flourished simultaneously in the Southern Cone over the past quarter-century at a time when the prevailing form of government was the nonelected and frequently repressive military regime. These regimes attempted to stimulate the growth of geopolitical institutes and their publications, trying to popularize geopolitical thinking in the media and inserting it into the curricula of the centralized educational systems. In all of this process, geopolitical thinking was associated with patriotism and a generally suspicious perception of presumed hostile neighbors. There are also strong suggestions of links between this form of geopolitical thinking and a series of conflicts between the states of South America. High tension levels were frequently cited in the geopolitical literature as justification for large and strong military establishments.

Most of the articles considered in this analysis were written by retired military officers. The rest of the authors were mostly Active-duty military officers and a small group of civilians who are closely associated with the military. There is little diversity or range of opinion in this group, except for a few military geopoliticians who take Third World positions. To some extent, the body of geopolitical writers represents a small elite, and one might legitimately ask whether their influence is indeed significant. An examination of the number and scope of the geopolitical articles described here and the degree to which these geopolitical ideas have found their way into the media and popular publications suggests that the significance of this mind-set has indeed been felt beyond purely military circles, where these materials are closely linked to strategic thinking and contingency planning. The impact shows up in key decisions taken by the Southern Cone's military rulers of the past twenty-five years, who based many of their programs on geopolitical concepts: Brazil's plans for vast Amazonic road networks, Chile's programs for development of the southern region and colonization of Antarctica, and the Argentine military regime's plans for recovery of the southern islands.

The dangers of mixing the earlier current of aggressive geopolitical thinking with nationalism and irredentism can be seen in several conflict situations that emerged in the late 1970s and early 1980s. The resolution of some of these situations (such as the Beagle Channel problem) tended to reduce the size and budgets of the military and thus presumably tended to strengthen democratic trends in this period. However, many of the old geopolitically inspired conflict situations remain unsolved, and their solution would seem to offer further positive support for the redemocratization process.

The positive current of geopolitical thinking also offers interesting possibilities for supporting the democratization process. The search for joint solutions to problems has lowered tensions and has affected the salience and the role of the military in the political process. In this connection, it would seem useful to explore the assumption that aggressive and chauvinistic geopolitical thinking does, indeed, lead to an increased role for the military and threatens the process of consolidating democracy. If this assumption were validated, then attempts to shift the nature of the military's geopolitical thinking toward cooperative and integrative aspects might have a very positive impact on the transition to democracy.

It seems unlikely that the active and retired military of the Southern Cone will simply cease to think in geopolitical terms or that the considerable flow of geopolitical writings documented in this chapter will stop. By its formation and by its career education, the military tends to stress the relationships among national goals, national power, threats, war hypotheses, and the limitations and possibilities offered by the geographic environment to project that power. However, the civilian political leadership of the Southern Cone can take important steps to encourage the military to move away from the old aggressive and jingoistic tendencies in geopolitical thinking and toward the integrative and cooperative approaches. Joint international military cooperation in maneuvers, education, training programs, and personnel exchanges can do much in this regard, as can the application of confidence-building measures to increase trust between neighboring military establishments.

To stimulate the positive aspects of geopolitical thinking, the civilian political leadership also should encourage a greater diversity of geopolitical views and ensure that independent civilian scholars and strategic analysts are encouraged and have their views considered by the more traditional military geopolitical analysts. Cooperative and integrative projects—such as the development of South American Antarctica, the establishment of a "zone of peace" in the South Atlantic and the Beagle Channel area, and the process of verifying and monitoring a Central American peace process—all offer possibilities for strengthening the positive forms of geopolitical thinking in ways that are supportive of the democratic trend in South America.

Notes

1. See Margaret E. Crahan, *Human Rights and Basic Needs in the Americas* (Washington, D.C.: Georgetown University Press, 1982), especially ch. 3; Jack Child, *Geopolitics and Conflict in South America: Quarrels Among Neighbors* (New York: Praeger, 1985), ch. 4; and Julio J. Chiavenato, *Geopolítica, Arma do Fascismo* (Sao Paulo: Global, 1981).

2. Philip L. Kelly, "Avances Recientes de la Geopolítica del Brasil," *Geopolítica* (Argentina), No. 33 (1986): 63–77; Jack Child, "Geopolitical Thinking in Latin America," *Latin American Research Review* 14, no. 2 (1979): 89–111; and Howard T. Pittman, *Geopolitics in the ABC Countries: A Comparison*, Ph.D. dissertation, The American University, 1981.

3. See Colonel Jorge E. Atencio, *Que es la Geopolítica?* (Buenos Aires: Pleamar, 1965); and General Augusto Pinochet, *Geopolitica* (Santiago: Andres Bello, 1974).

4. Chile, Arzobispado de Santiago, *Dos Ensayos Sobre Seguridad Nacional* (Santiago: Vicaria de la Solidaridad, 1979); Carlos J. Moneta, *La Reforma Militar* (Buenos Aires: Legasa, 1985), pp. 55–69; and Argentina, Comision Nacional Sobre la Desaparicion de Personas, *Nunca Mas* (Buenos Aires: EUDEBA, 1985), pp. 473–76.

5. Eriberto Cortese, "La Argentina: Pais Geopoliticamente Agredido," *Geopolitica* (Argentina), No. 21 (March 1981): 47–50; Carlos Escudee, *La Argentina: Paria Internacional?* (Buenos Aires: Belgrano, 1984); and Manuel Hormazabal, *Chile: Una Patria Mutilada* (Santiago: Pacifico, 1969).

6. See Mario Travassos, *Projecao Continental do Brasil*, 2nd ed. (Sao Paulo: Nacional, 1925); Everardo Backheuser, *A Geopolitica Geral e do Brasil* (Rio de Janeiro: Biblioteca do Exercito, 1975); and Child, *Geopolitics and Conflict*, ch. 3.

7. General Juan E. Guglialmelli, "Islas Malvinas. Exigir Definiciones," *Estrategia*, No. 67–68 (November 1980–February 1981): 5–17; Colonel Luis Alberto Leoni Houssay, "Debemos Continuar la Guerra contra Gran Bretana?" *Revista de Temas Militares*, No. 7 (July–September 1983): 13–25; and "Juego de Simulacion (Islas Malvinas)," *Revista Militar*, No. 704 (April 1981): 46–53.

8. Jack Child, *Antarctica and South American Geopolitics: Frozen Lebensraum* (New York: Praeger, 1988).

9. Pittman, *Geopolitics in the ABC Countries.*

10. General Juan E. Guglialmelli, "Islas Malvinas: Exigir Definiciones," *Estrategia*, No. 67–68 (November 1980): 5–17.

11. Martin Congrains, *Guerra en el Cono Sur* (Lima: Ecoma, 1979); General Juan E. Guglialmelli, ed., *El Conflicto del Beagle* (Buenos Aires: El Cid, 1978); and Admiral Issac Rojas, *La Argentina en el Beagle y Atlantico Sur* (Buenos Aires: Codex, 1978).

12. Theresinha de Castro, "La Crisis de las Malvinas y sus Reflejos," *Geopolítica* 9, no. 26 (1983): 29–34; and Theresinha de Castro, "0 Atlantico Sur: Contexto Regional," *A Defesa Nacional*, No. 714 (July 1984): 91–108.

13. Admiral Guillermo Barros Gonzales, "El Arco de Scotia," *Revista de Marina* (Chile), No. 777 (February 1987): 159–65; Admiral Francisco Ghisolfo Araya, "Chile, Pais Atlantico," *Revista de Marina* (Chile), No. 757 (1982): 712–15; and Pablo Ihl Clericus, "Delimitacion Natural entre el Oceano Pacifico y el Atlantico," *Revista Geográfica de Chile* (Terra Australis), No. 9 (1953): 45–51.

14. Leslie Crawford, "Por un Club Antartico Ibero Americano," *Geosur* (Uruguay), No. 33 (1982): 34–43; General Jorge Leal, "La Antartida Sudamericana y Latinoamericana," *Revista Militar* (Argentina, Circulo Militar), No. 711 (July–December 1983): 14–17; and Carlos J. Moneta, "America Latina y la

Antartida: Posibilidades de Cooperacion Intralatinoamericana," *Opciones*, No. 12 (September–December 1987): 25–33.

15. Child, *Antarctica and South American Geopolitics*, ch. 3.

16. General Osiris Villegas, "Las Razones Aparentes y los Intereses Ocultos Tras la Actitud Britanica," *Geopolítica*, No. 24 (1982): 55.

17. Teniente Coronel Jorge Alvarez Cardier, *La Guerra de las Malvinas: Enseñanzas para Venezuela* (Caracas: Enfoque, 1982).

18. Admiral Joao Carlos Concalves Caminha, "0 Atlantico Sul e a Marinha do Brasil," *Revista Maritima Brasileira* (January–March 1986): 9–20; and Admiral Francisco Ghisolfo Araya, "Conflicto Atlantico Sur: Reflexiones," *Revista de Marina* (Chile), No. 751 (November 1982): 717–21.

19. Hugo G. Gobbi, "Problemas Australes Argentino–Chilenos," *Estrategia*, No. 48 (September–October 1977): 27–36; Andres Ruggeri, "Canal de Beagle: Algunas Reflexiones Sobre el Laudo Arbitral," *Estrategia*, No. 45 (March 1977): 48–61; and Favio Valdivieso "Las Cancillerias y el Nuevo Conflicto Limitrofe Creado por Argentina," *Memorial del Ejército de Chile*, No. 399 (1978): 42–46.

20. Admiral José T. Merino, "Actividades Sovieticas en el Mar de Chile," *Revista de Marina* (Chile), No. 777 (February 1987): 226–27.

21. General Edgardo Mercado Jarrin, "Geopolítica de la Cuenca del Pacifico," in General Edgardo Mercado Jarrin, ed., *El Peru y la Antartida* (Lima: IPEGE, 1984), pp. 195–218.

22. General Juan E. Guglialmelli, "Argentina–Brasil: Enfrentamiento o Alianza para la Liberacion," *Estrategia*, No. 36 (September–October 1975): 1–29.

23. Centro de Investigaciones Economicos y Sociales, Universidad de Lima (CIESUL), *Las Malvinas: Conflicto Americano?* (Lima: CIESUL, 1982); Julian Licastro, "Union Latinoamericana de la Teoria de la Practica," *Estudios Geopolíticos y Estratégicos*, No. 9 (December 1983): 73–77; and General Edgardo Mercado Jarrin, "Coyuntura Geopolitica Latinoamericana," *Estudios Geopolíticos y Estratégicos*, No. 9 (December 1983): 5–20.

24. Jorge Nelson Gualco, *Cono Sur: Eleccion de un Destino* (Buenos Aires: Fabril, 1972); Bernardo Quagliotti de Bellis, "Nacionalismo e Integracion," *Geosur* 4 (December, 1979); and Bernardo Quagliotti de Bellis, *Uruguay y su Espacio* (Montevideo: Geosur, 1979).

25. General Edgardo Mercado Jarrin, "Coyuntura Geopolítica Latinoamericana," *Estudios Geopolíticos y Estratégicos*, No. 9 (December 1983): 5–20; and Tercer Mundo, "Mercado Jarrin: Repensar el Continente," *Tercer Mundo*, No. 95 (March 1987): 90–94.

26. Capitan Luis Bravo Bravo, "Bolivia: Vision Personal de un Enigma Geopolitico," *Seguridad Nacional*, No. 23 (1982): 25–44.

27. Colonel Arthur Cezar Ferreira Reis, "Imperialistas ou Subimperialistas," *A Defesa Nacional*, No. 71 (September 1984): 133–38.

28. General Juan E. Guglialmelli, "Y si Brasil Fabrica la Bomba Atomica?" *Estrategia*, No. 34–35 (May–August 1975): 5–21.

29. Tercer Mundo, "Cambios Geopoliticos en America Latina," *Tercer Mundo*, No. 95 (March 1987): 82–89.

30. Colonel Luis A. Leoni Houssay, "Pinochet: El Fuhrer Sudamericano," *Revista de Temas Militares* (September 1984): 5–20.

31. Francisco Sampedro, *Del Amazonas en 1830 al Condor en 1981* (Quito: Quitoffset, n.d. [1981?]); Gustavo Pons Muzzo, "Ecuador: Pueblo Enganado," *Estudios Geopolíticos y Estraégicos*, No. 6 (April 1981): 34–39.

32. For samples of recent integrative geopolitical thinking published by the Southern Cone military, see Colonel Jose F. Marini, *Geopolítica Latinoamericana de Integracion* (Buenos Aires: Escuela Superior de Guerra Aerea, 1987); Admiral Mario E. Olmos, *La Cooperacion Argentina–Brasil: Nucleo Impulsor de la Integracion Latinoamericana* (Buenos Aires: Instituto de Publicaciones Navales, 1986); and Luiz de Alencar Araripe, "Cooperacao Brasil–Argentina na Area Nuclear," *A Defesa Nacional* (Brasil), No. 734 (November–December 1987).

10
Missions and Strategy: The Argentine Example

Virginia Gamba-Stonehouse

Strategy and the Changing Role of Military Power

In South America, the armed forces have usually taken a leading role in the formation and development of the nation. Revolution and independence have been, on the whole, military experiences. This fact has been greatly exaggerated, so that the military, has perceived its role to have been the foundation of independence and national unity. This has led to the erroneous belief that "the country has been created by the military." As a corollary to this, the military believed that it accelerated progress, particularly in areas such as communications and frontier consolidation, including promotional transportation services, relief of terrain and resources, cartography, and installation of communications.

The military believed that its role was intimately linked to the development and progress of its societies. It proposed to guard and guarantee the development process. Thus, according to its own set of values on order and discipline vis-à-vis civilians, when the military perceives that its nation is being badly managed or administered, it associates the disorder with the republican system per se, rather than with the possibility of a bad administration of the day at governmental levels. This perception among the military has encouraged a paternalistic attitude toward civilians that is not exclusive to Argentina; it encompasses the rest of South America as well.[1]

The military feels it is its duty to interpret the wishes of the "silent majority" in its societies, particularly when internal disorder or governmental immobility on development and economic issues threatens the future of the nation-state. It feels responsible for safekeeping, safeguarding, and guaranteeing a future for the nation that it helped build. Likewise, the military is the natural repository for arms and munitions. An inevitable conclusion is that a military takeover of civilian government is unavoidable. The military justifies its actions because popular acceptance of its intervention seems to be historically mandated. The armed forces seem impatient to demand changes rather than abiding by long-term democratic principles.

This rationale can help explain the historical blind spot that has encouraged the military to play a political role in South American societies. We must understand that the military not only sees itself as the backbone and guardian of its political systems, it simultaneously values its professional roles on defense and security issues. In this second role, it values high skills and modernization of its fighting units.

The basic problem with this dual role of the military is that South American societies (devoid of any significant number of wars in the past 150 years) have come to recognize the military's role solely on a political level. The military views its professional role from within the framework of military institutions, not from the outside. Thus, both public opinion in general and the civilian political leaders in particular tend to ignore the real dimensions of the military's role as defense professionals.

When an upsurge of democratic governments ensues in South America, the political role of the military is diminished or even obliterated. This is reflected in public opinion precisely because the military's professional role and duties in defense are not considered and/or perceived outside the military institutions. On the other hand, there are some very real perceptions in the public opinion relating the military to a "political adversary" image. The historic interference of the military in South American politics has been the source of a negative trend within the institution. The armed forces have become politicized, and this has encouraged the creation of feuds within the internal structure of these institutions. This process of feuding within the highly politicized corps is a real obstacle for the ultimate professionalization of the armed forces today.

For all of the foregoing reasons, it is easy to see why the valid military role is not readily recognized by public opinion. This phenomenon, unless understood and reversed, can lead to the social isolation and frustration of the armed forces in their role as professionals, as was indeed the case in Argentina as of 1983.

The Military Role in Crisis in Argentina: Two Examples

The armed forces in Argentina perceive themselves as passing through a multidimensional crisis in the country's transition to and consolidation of democracy:

> All the Argentine military—whether retired or in service—are confronted by a serious crisis. This is not only with relation to their profession, but

also on their integration back into Argentine society. The indicators of crisis are:

- political and administrative defeat after seven years of military government;
- discussion of the methods to be employed to win an unconventional, sublimited war;
- defeat in a limited, conventional war that demonstrated the flaws in the military doctrine, preparations and operations; and
- the trial of numerous high-ranking officers outside the military institutions.[2]

This crisis has been further exacerbated by the drastic reduction in salaries and benefits received by the officer and noncommissioned officer corps. This, in turn, has often led to officers' having to hold additional jobs in the civilian field in order to support their families. A further problem is the military's loss of prestige and general unpopularity with the public as a whole.

Viewed positively, the existence of a feeling within the armed forces that they are passing through a multidimensional crisis at the time of democratic consolidation can act as a catalyst to propitiate unification, particularly when they are given aims and objectives under a definitive political directive. The negative side of this situation is the lack of reintegration of the armed forces within the social structure of their country on a recognized, valid, and harmonious basis; also lacking are clear directives by the civilian leadership regarding the effective role of the military instrument for the future.

This lack of understanding relating to the military's role in Argentine society, as well as the breakdown in the relationship between the armed forces and public opinion, has been directly responsible for at least three serious internal crises in Buenos Aires, such as that which took place during Easter of 1987:

> The Easter Rebellion was the result of a deadlocked misunderstanding between President Alfonsin's government and the armed forces about what the role of the armed forces in a democracy should be. . . . President Alfonsín came to power knowing only that he did not want the armed forces to have political power or the possibility of recovering it. . . . But President Alfonsín appeared to have little idea of what he did want from the armed forces and nearly four years later government policy is no clearer.
>
> The government had two proposals: to end the autonomy of the three branches of the armed forces and their perpetual infighting, and to end conscription and create a modern, professional army. But this required a concrete programme which could win the respect and cooperation of the military side, and this the government lacked. The government's confusion met an equal confusion within the armed forces.

The junior officers were professionally disillusioned with their high command and the armed forces were weak, humiliated and divided. These officers awaited with some enthusiasm an elaboration of the government's plans. They are still waiting, they say, but now with suspicion and resentment. Instead of a constructive dialogue, they argue, they have suffered three years of social opprobrium and economic hardship and are no nearer understanding what is expected.

The [April rebels] argue that they were forced into the political debate because the government has lowered the prestige of the armed forces and cut the military budget to the bone. "No military professional wants to remain in the armed forces if he cannot fulfill his role as a military man," Major Barreiro said.

Since the government has not assigned them a role, the officers argue that they have been dragged into an analysis of government policies."[3]

Mil. Dragged into analysis of gov't policies b/c gov't has not assigned them a role.

Sincere as these arguments were at the time in Argentina—forcing the government to review its military policies—they fail to take into account that during military regimes, there were also problems in establishing clear dividing lines between the role of the professional armed forces and the political direction of the country. One example of the military's inability to create distinctions between military and political roles in the period prior to 1983 led to serious mistakes in the Malvinas war of 1982 and in the postwar period, as experienced in the armed forces proper and before the democratic transition set in.

In 1982, only a handful of senior officers that managed the state had a clear idea of their foreign policy goal in the intervention in the South Atlantic islands. The system within the armed forces itself was, nevertheless, professionally ill-prepared to fight a conventional war that required active interservice participation and coordination. It also needed the moral backing of the people. When the war ended, the ensuing coup d'etat demonstrated the division between the services and also between those officers who implemented the political decisions (and who saw military intervention as an instrument to force international negotiations) and those officers who thought they were fighting an all-out war for territorial purposes only (for whom the objective of intervention did not include future negotiations). To the latter, defeat was due not to the lack of professionalism in the forces and the breakdown of an ineffective bureaucratic system that would help coordinate policies and strategies, but entirely to the decision to intervene. The net result was blaming the decision to intervene militarily and rescuing a system that does not work.[4]

Geopolitical in nature

The only place where policies were coordinated at both professional and political levels, the military junta, was broken up in 1982 and was not reestablished until the month prior to the elections in 1983. This was the situation that the civilian government inherited. It is interesting to note, here, that the decision-making system in Argentina at the time of the military regime consolidated policies only at the very top. It did not delegate responsibility to lower levels, as it was lacking in strong inter-agency communications as well as in the obvious civil–military linkages.[5] The democratic government has not yet broken away from the previous mode of coordinating at the top. It has not succeeded, so far, in establishing and consolidating strong interagency linkages or in reinforcing civil–military relations. It would seem, therefore, that this trait is a problem of the Argentine governmental system rather than a purely military or a purely civilian mode of behavior.

Toward a New Professional Role: Possibilities and Problems

What has happened and is happening now in Argentina's civil–military relations demonstrates that there is only one way to deal with the problem: Educate on both-fronts—the military and the public. Efforts must be made toward understanding and improving bureaucracies at the institutional level, which, in turn, will lead to cooperation and communication at levels other than merely the very top.

Taking each problem separately, it can be said that the Argentine armed forces cannot be thought of as a special professional corps that is isolated from society in general. There must be a perception within both the military and the civilian body politic regarding the exact professional role of the military is the need for such a role.

The problem for the military (not only in Argentina but in other South American countries as well) is that civilian specialists, as well as the general public, lack experience in attending to military and defense policies and in directing the military instrument as a servant of the state. In this, there is a direct reference to the second problem already described: a lack of interagency communications. Unfortunately, foreign policy has not always recognized the need to consider its relationship to the defense policy of the day, for even in these two arenas, the necessary communication and coordination links are often lacking.

If the valid role of defense policy is to act in support of foreign policy, this has to be recognized by both parties, so as to award a role to the military in both the administration of peace and the promotion of national interests. This does not necessarily imply the use of the threat of force but can be used, for example, in the context of integration, alliances, demonstrations, deterrence, and safeguarding of regional peace. It can also be used in issues that deal with the national economy, such as weapons procurement and the military-industrial complex, as just two examples.[6]

It is vital to reassess and renew the role of the military in order to steer it away from politics. There is a lack of understanding of a professional role for the military in a democratic society. If they are given time and the necessary education and communications structures, civilians can become experts on defense in dialogue with the military and, hence, can consolidate the institutions, thereby improving the situation markedly.

A further problem is that although the military is rightly accused of politicizing its services, the civilians at a public level continue to perceive the military in this role, thus perpetuating it.

This leads to a vicious cycle in which the need for civil–military education is manifest. On the one hand, there is a need to reeducate the military; on the other, there is a need to open up universities to civilians who are interested in defense issues, so that they can manage the defense efforts of the country and, at the same time, be respected by the military as experts in the field. All too often, the only courses open for civilians under democratic systems deal with the political and philosophical aspects of how to keep the military out of politics and "under control," but they do not produce the necessary experts on defense or strategic studies. Civilians need to understand contemporary strategic problems, defense economics, comparative defense policies, the dynamics of the military industrial complex, and the relationship between defense and foreign policies.[7] To complete the picture, given better interagency communications, the structure of defense at civil–military levels should start working for, not against, democracy.

The main problems that are now surfacing in civil–military relations in Argentina during the consolidation of the democratic government are precisely those concerned with the need for professionalism at real and perceptual levels.[8] There is also a need to limit interservice rivalries and to reinforce the Joint Chiefs of Staff, together with the improvement of civil–military relations and the construction of communication and coordination channels at interagency levels.

Ideas for the Promotion of Better Interagency and Civil–Military Relations

In the arena of civil–military relations, it is important to note that public opinion tends to regard this problem only in the light of past perceptions—that is, how to diminish the political role of the military, rather than how to award a valid role to the military instrument in the state today. This is not surprising, because, theoretically, the military worldwide has two relationships with civilians: (1) with the incumbent government and (2) with the public opinion of the respective countries.

The way one area sees the military will reflect on the other; thus, the government's perception of the military will influence public opinion, and the citizens' perception of their military (popular, unpopular, needed, or isolated) will influence the decision makers of a democratic country.

The only real possibility for breaking out of this vicious cycle in civil–military relations in South America is broad-based: Both the public and the military must learn how each party perceives its role is and the validity of its influence within the state. For this purpose, interagency linkages must be built. Communications must be opened between civilians and the military, to discuss not only the elimination of political roles but also the consolidation of the professional role of the military. Reinforcement of democracy can be achieved only through a consolidation of the ministerial and military institutions involved, together with an overall communications network. By reinforcing a professional body of "middlemen" at bureaucratic levels—at both interministerial and interservice levels—the values and language will be common to all.

In this sense, the creation of a joint officers war school and fluid interaction with other schools, such as the diplomatic service and civilian analysts of the Defense Ministry, can help consolidate interagency linkages. This should be accompanied by a governmental campaign to educate the general public regarding the real values of and needs for a professional military role. Part of this project would encourage the establishment of special courses on defense analysis and the modern role of military power for journalists and other interested civilians.

These actions would have an impact on public opinion. Civilians would no longer view the military as an isolated element or even a political adversary of the nation but would view it as an integrated part of the national effort in democracy. This can be achieved by the introduction of courses and seminars, university interests and publications, and war schools, where military personnel would be encouraged to study strategic and defense problems alongside their civilian ministerial counterparts. Thus, the two sectors of society would understand that they can work together and respect each other's point of view.

Political aspirations would be achieved by the recognition of a military role that is clear and legitimate, allowing the civilians to feel respect for the military, with the understanding that it has an important role to play in civilian society.

It is tempting to conclude that the lack of an external threat in South American countries is enough basis for the removal of the armed forces, because they are seen as unnecessary. This is not true, as it is possible to demonstrate that the armed forces can and should take a professional role for deterrence purposes within the region as well as for purposes of regional integration. All countries wish to maintain sovereign status in their defense and foreign policy options. The manner in which this status is upheld varies slightly from region to region and from country to country. In contemporary politics, the first use of force is condemned; wars of conquest are forbidden at the international community level. It follows that conventional deterrence, effective occupation of national territory, and passive and defensive measures to deter through denial, rather than through punishment, should be implemented as a valid role for the South American military.

Because deterrence as a contemporary strategic concept requires recognition of the value systems of deterred and deterrer, it also helps to analyze and understand the needs and perceptions of other parties and to the form communication lines that will make crisis management possible at times of doubt or increased threat perception.[9]

The existence of a professional body of armed forces—modernized and with efficient communication systems as well as the potential to act at all levels of violence in a given situation (proportionality of means vis-à-vis threat perception)—can assist the foreign policy of a country in controlling and managing difficult situations without the need to escalate to an all-or-nothing conflict. Also, in a region where deterrence is applied, a professional military will strive to communicate its intentions and capabilities more clearly with neighboring states. This, in turn, can lead to better relations and linkages at a regional integration level.

The second major area in which military power can be used effectively for both the consolidation of peace and the advancement of national interest is that of military alliances. Through integrated efforts, a whole region can benefit from the reduced perceptions of threat, both internally and externally.[10]

Two examples will suffice to demonstrate the feasibility of these roles for the military in South America. Through strategic studies at both civilian and military levels, an understanding of comparative defense policies will develop. This, in turn, will lead to a recognition of other parties' value systems and will encourage the formation of communication lines between countries that will allow them to recognize each other's signals in moments of crisis, thus permitting the deflation rather than escalation of unexpected incidents. If we take into account the huge frontier borders between South American states, this type of incident is common enough, and mechanisms for the control of escalation, should an incident occur, are vital for the maintenance of regional peace.

The second example can be demonstrated best by citing the recent Argentine–Brazilian integration efforts. Under the umbrella of the Foz de Iguazu agreements between Argentina and Brazil in 1985–86, a framework was created that allows the two countries' militaries to meet and discuss common issues. As a result, it has already been possible for the Joint Chiefs of Staff of the two countries to promote the first series of bilateral seminars on strategic and geopolitical issues. Both militaries took it upon themselves to coordinate meetings of the civilian geopoliticians and the military experts in their countries to discuss common issues, ranging from the theory of deterrence to the ways in which to cooperate in the South Atlantic. The meetings took place during April 1987 in Buenos Aires and were scheduled to continue in Brazil during 1988.

The value of these meetings is that they allow the geopolitical schools of the two countries to understand each other's discourse, respect it, and find points in common, as well as integrating a common language on theoretical issues such as deterrence, military communications and planning problems. As a consequence, it is expected that traditional perceptions of threat will be reduced and a common language will be structured. Taken to its ultimate consequence, these communications lines could eventually serve to analyze common procurement problems and to assure bilateral cooperation in the military-industrial complex, so as not to duplicate effort and to find adequate outlets for military production. On the other hand, this type of integration would also reduce the threat perception resulting from independent capabilities that could be applied by one country against the other. So far, these mechanisms have been successfully applied in the recent technological agreements between Argentina and Brazil concerning the use of nuclear power.

One small and specific example of the sort of mechanism that countries in South America could apply to better civil–military education on defense issues is the creation of a pilot project implemented by the Argentine Joint Chiefs of Staff in a strategy course for both civilian and military individuals. The idea is to gather around a common table two officers of each service and civilian personnel of the Ministry of Foreign Affairs and Defense, as well as academics from the university. After a one-year course on strategic and defense studies, these individuals will have learned how to communicate and manage a common language, which, in their day-to-day activities, will help them sustain the same value systems. The university academics will have learned the academic discipline of strategic studies and will be able to start teaching it at faculty levels, thus multiplying the education effort at other levels in the country. The result of the first years of the project have been excellent, but the difficulty lies in the lack of institutionalization of this type of effort and the lack of understanding of the importance of this type of education within the public opinion of the country.

Conclusions

How could democratic governments help improve civil–military relations in their countries by a change in strategies and missions for the military?

A number of suggestions are possible at this stage, although they are based on the Argentine experience and should be considered in that light.

1. The government must steer the military away from politics and must reinforce professionalism.
2. Professionalism presupposes that the military should be regarded as experts and, thus, should be consulted in areas related to its institutions. The military must be awarded a valid role as adviser and must be allowed to influence issues related to its profession.
3. Professionalism requires high-level skills, which should be rewarded through salaries and benefits of the professional military corps.
4. The resulting increase in skill and pride in professionalism would allow for a reduction of the services, thereby increasing the quality rather than the quantity of the force.
5. Promotions should be carefully monitored so that professional excellence (not character or inter- or intraservice views) will be taken seriously into account.
6. The Joint Chiefs of Staff must be reinforced. A joint war college should be created, where all officers graduating from their own services' war schools should be sent for joint training. In this joint college, integration with diplomats and civilian defense analysts should be encouraged. By the same token, the Ministry of Defense should use the Joint Chiefs of Staff as the valid interlocutor to and from the services.
7. The government must resist the temptation to capitalize, in the short term, on public resentment against the military for its past political actions. Conversely, the government must reflect an attitude toward public opinion regarding the professional usefulness of the military for the administration of peace and the promotion of national interests. This can be achieved only through a campaign to educate public opinion on the role of the military instrument at contemporary universal and national levels.
8. Governments should encourage interagency communications in issues relating to defense and foreign policy. Bureaucracy should be reinforced and upgraded, promoted by recognition of professionalism and high salaries in key posts.
9. Civilian analysts must be educated on defense issues, not only on political philosophy. South American universities are not capable of implementing these studies today because they lack professional civilian experts on defense and strategic studies. Their efforts today center on the adaptation of experts on political science and international relations to fulfill this role.
10. Because of acute economic problems in South America, the relative value of the military profession is downgraded. If the salaries for

these high-risk professionals cannot be upgraded, at least their costs should be lowered (for example, by introducing exemptions and fringe benefits).

11. Governments should encourage the military to use its expertise and services to help in the development of the infrastructure within the community.

12. Confidence-building measures should be structured so that suspicion is removed when interagency and civil–military discourse is analyzed at levels lower than the very top.

13. Foreign governments can help toward this reinforcement of civil–military ties and renewal of military professionalism by (1) offering scholarships to military officers for strategic studies at the university level abroad; (2) formating joint working groups at bilateral and multilateral levels to discuss a program for the optimization of the ministerial civil service levels and their upgrading; (3) promoting an international academic pool to help guide and encourage the formation of strategic studies faculties in South American universities; and (4) educating their own public opinion on issues relating to civil–military relations in South American countries. All too often, foreign analysts and the external news media interpret the news of South America on these issues according to the political image of a military of another era. This only exacerbates distrust, fueling threat perceptions both within and outside the countries in question.

14. At a purely inter-American level, the dialogue should be resumed by the formation of a strategic line of thought that is common to all parties, thus limiting the negative influence of localized geopolitical schools of thought. Bilateral and multilateral training schemes should be promoted.

If these and other suggestions materialize in the near future, two of the most important concepts that consolidate democracy and restore confidence in cooperation will ensue in South America: the formation and consolidation of a valid, recognized professional role for the military instrument; and the upgrading of the "middleman" in national bureaucracies at interagency levels, which would allow for a more stable democratic system.

As a result, democracy will be firmly consolidated at its roots, not merely covered with a temporary varnish that can change perceptions but not substance. In the recognition of new strategies and missions for the military, the consolidation of civil–military relations in South America will be enhanced and the possibilities of stronger international cooperation will be encouraged.

Notes

1. See V. Gamba, "The Role of the Military in the Process of Transition," Paper· presented at the seminar, "Reinforcing Democracy in Latin America," Carter Center of Emory University, Atlanta, Georgia, November 1986.

2. See F. Milia, "La Militaridad Argentina en Crisis," *Boletin del Centro Naval* (Argentina) 102, no. 738 (March 1984).

3. Isabel Hilton and Judith Evans, "Immunity Law Fails to Mollify Young Turks of Argentina," *The Independent* (June 25, 1987): 10.

4. See V. Gamba, *The Falkland/Malvinas War: A Model for North-South Crisis Prevention* (New York: Allen and Unwin, 1987).

5. Ibid.

6. See V. Gamba, *Estrategia: Intervención y Crisis* (Buenos Aires: Sudaméncana, 1965)

7. See R. Borras, "Nueva Politica de Defensa Nacional," *Armas y Geoestrategia* (Argentina) (June 1984): 34.

8. Ibid.

9. See J.C. Garnett, "Deterrence," in J. Bayliss et al., eds., *Contemporary Strategy: Theories and Policies* (New York: Holmes and Meier, 1975), p. 68.

10. See P. Williams, "Alliances," in Baylis et al., eds., *Contemporary Strategy.*

11

The Brazilian Military in the Late 1980s and Early 1990s: Is the Risk of Intervention Gone?

Alexandre Barros

Will Political democracy survive

T he most important political question in Brazil is whether political democracy will survive. Serious political analysts see the ghost of military intervention around the corner. Whether they consider that it will emerge to overthrow the new regime depends on the observer. *econ. prblms* The fear of the return of a military authoritarian regime stems from several factors. First, the new democracies are facing serious problems of economic performance. Whether or not these problems were inherited from the military is a sophisticated question for analysts. It becomes irrelevant when societies face untamable rates of inflation and deep recessions.[1] Ever-growing charges of corruption among public functionaries *perception* further aggravate the problem.[2] People have short memories. Pressed by *of* high and accelerating inflation rates and recurrent public services strikes, a *inefficiency* perception of the inefficiency of democracies develops.

Second, history has shown that people became angry and disoriented *② people become* when they face serious economic problems without hope for a solution. *angry during* If the government is perceived as inefficient, anger and disorientation *econ. prblms* increase.[3]

Optimistic democrats see the solution in direct elections. However, other ghosts show up, the most important of which are populism and leftism. Both carry with them the threat of administrative inefficiency.

Looking at the problem from the angle of the ghost, another reason *Although* to defend the idea that the military will not jump into political adventures *maj. of* again is that it does not want to. However, when the situation begins to *mil. does* be perceived as a "no exit" one, people demand a savior who can put the *not seek pol.* *adventurism* house back in order. It does not matter who that savior may be. This *minority* situation increases the chances of that portion of the armed forces, no *will acquiesce* matter how small it may be, that is always advocating an authoritarian *& called on* regime. *to save country*

Economic problems increase the chances that the radicals may con- *Economic prblm* quer the mass of the officer corps. There is special concern on the part of *improve chance* *of radicals* senior officers regarding the political attitude that prevails among the Brazilian military officers of the late 1980s. Estimates range from the possibility of a highly authoritarian and fascist orientation to a highly authoritarian and socialist orientation.[4]

Furthermore, the armed forces have advantages over other groups aspiring to be potential saviors. They are organized and homogeneous. They also have weapons. The armed forces in Third World countries are the most organized and homogeneous social and professional organizations.[5]

Third, conservative forces panic about the possibility of a populist government. In such a situation, although the military may not be the preferred option, it may be chosen. It is a matter of "sticking to the devil they know."[6]

Finally, there are possibilities of military populism because of the decreasing legitimacy of the civilian government, combined with a lack of support for conservative economic policies. Faced with this, the military and civilian sectors flirt with combining the "organization and regimentation" of a military regime with the "popularity" of a populist one.

What Will Be the Military's New Role?

When Brazilian politicians demand a new role for the military, they think of it in exclusionary terms. They propose that the professional military abdicate the political role they had in the past. However, civilian politicians seldom think of another nonpolitical role for their military.

It is essential to agree consensually on a new role for the military. Otherwise, society will continue to live with a group of professionals who have the same resources for the management of organized violence as their counterparts in developed countries (proportionately, of course) but who do not perform traditional military roles. This is so because of the stage of development of their countries and the necessarily limited international roles such countries can play.[7] The lack of a legitimate function for the military—one that is accepted both by civilians and by the military—is a serious political threat to political stability in Third World countries.

The Brazilian Redemocratization

Brazil's transition has been praised for its lack of political violence and its gradualism. The recent political *abertura* (opening) was gradual and nonviolent. Once the *abertura* had started, the first problem faced by the

Geisel administration was to curb the portions of the intelligence apparatus that were out of control. After this, for the rest of the Geisel administration and during most of the Figueiredo years, the *abertura* was a process of resocializing politically relevant groups. The purpose was to train them for the democratic transition.[8]

Throughout this process, all political groups and actors were testing the limits of their political performance. Unions went on strike and checked how the military reacted. Military officers made political statements and checked how their political competitors reacted.

The first development was the amnesty law, a result of political negotiation. The agreement prevented older cases of deaths on either side—and torture on the side of the military forces—from being raised. Under this law, no military officer has been indicted (although several were denounced in the press) for any crime committed during the days of the military government. The same holds true for civilians: Former exiles and people accused of political crimes (including terrorism) are fully protected *Amnesty* under the amnesty law. After 1982, they stood as candidates for elected *Law* positions; and after 1985, many held government positions by appointment.

On the one hand, this shows the capacity of the Brazilian elite for accommodation and negotiation. On the other, the military establishment emerged from the military regime completely intact. It was touched neither as an institution nor in its human composition.[9]

In terms of composition, no military personnel were purged, expelled, or punished. The military forces on the morning of March 15, 1985, had the same composition as they had during the previous years. The situation has not changed since then.

During the writing of the new Brazilian constitution, from February 1987 to September 1988, the three military services acted politically, as any other lobbying group.[10] This attitude secured all the constitutional provisos that the military wanted and needed.

In spite of all these smooth characteristics of civil–military relations in Brazil, the most important point has not been addressed—namely, what *major* new role for the military will be acceptable both to the military and to the *Questor* political elite? Politicians were not able to offer any alternative that was not exclusionary. No member of the political elite had enough interest or *Pol. elete* knowledge to discuss military matters with the military.[11] *not interested*
or knowledgeable
As noted, the politicians discuss the role of the military only in exclu- *enough to* sionary terms. They always try to define the role of the military casuisti- *discuss* cally. Their focus is on forbidding the military to do what it did in the *m;l. matters* past.[12] There are no attempts to define a role for the military in a con- *w/mil* structive way—that is, spelling out what the military should do and pro- *No attempts* viding it with the resources to carry out this task. *on behalf of*

Politicians to define
role of mil. in a
constructive way.

The flaw in the attitude of the politicians is that by not accepting that the military has to have a specifically military role, the civilian politicians ignore the military problem of institutional unemployment. That is, the society continues to live with a highly homogeneous, strongly professionalized, heavily armed group of professionals that has no defined, legitimate function to perform.[13]

The consequences are easy to imagine. The military remains in the background of politics in the absence of crisis. When a crisis develops, professional soldiers immediately emerge and are called by portions of the political elite to take over political power. As this process has been historically recurrent, and in the absence of an external defense function for the military, these professional soldiers have established themselves in many civilian positions.

Given the nature of the transition agreement, the number of administrative civilian positions the military lost was very small. The continuation of the military in civilian positions was either part of the transition-to-democracy agreement or a result of the fact that the military proved to be efficient in the performance of those tasks. Three years after the civilian administration had been in power, the problem became even more serious. There was a remarkable decay in the quality of Brazilian public administration. This was due partly to a deprofessionalization of public administration after the end of the military regime.[14] The bloating of the administration took place, in many instances, to fulfill a spoils policy. Older civil and military servants remained in civilian administration positions to perform actual administrative tasks. The consequence is that administrative criteria and the purposes of civilian administration end up being de facto military.

For instance, of twenty-eight ministries, six are strictly military. Three of these are the traditional services: the army, navy, and air force. There is also the Estado Maior das Forças Armadas (EMFA), equivalent to the Joint Chiefs of Staff in the United States. And as direct advisers to the president, there are the Chefia da Casa Militar da Presidência da República (Chief of the Military Household) and the head of the Serviço Nacional de Informações (SNI, National Intelligence Service).

The EMFA's functions are not related to the routine operations of the military forces. The three military services have direct operational responsibilities over troops. Military officers run the office of the president. The Chefe da Casa Militar is responsible for liaison with the military ministries. He is also in charge of all administrative functions of the presidency, ranging from the personal security and health of the president to the administration of the presidential and vice-presidential official residences. He also acts as the chief executive of the National Security Council (CSN), which is staffed and operated mostly by military officers.[15]

The SNI is other important branch of the military that has direct influence on the policymaking process. The SNI is in charge of keeping the president informed about what goes on in the country. Advisors and advisory bodies that have an important or quasi-monopolistic role in providing information and intelligence to decision makers become very powerful, because they filter the information received by the decision makers. This limits the options the latter can adopt.

On the positive side, despite the number of years of military regime, Brazilian society was not contaminated by militarism. Ironic as it may sound, this is partly because the Brazilian military always had some constraints about being military *strictu sensu*.[16] The process of military professionalization (as opposed to academic professionalization) of the Brazilian military took place in internal politics. The exceptions were the war of the triple alliance (known in Brazil as the war against Paraguay) and two other international campaigns during the last century. More recently, Brazilian troops participated in World War II on the allied side.[17] These help explain Brazil's lack of militarism.

Despite the public rhetoric, the Brazilian military knows that it has performed very modestly in international affairs. Probably because of this, it feels very uneasy about requesting money for military matters. This was especially true during the years the military was in power.[18] This lack of militarism on the part of the Brazilian military (coupled with Brazilian society's unwillingness to accept more than a given degree of militarization) helped prevent the development of a militaristic regime.[19]

The crucial question being asked is: Are the military going to stay out of politics? Is their degree of professionalization sufficient to keep them in barracks? The answer seems to be a simple no, unless civilians and the military can come to terms about a legitimate and useful function for the military. This question was not addressed by the Brazilian polity during the writing of the new constitution. There are no signs that it will be addressed by the Congress in its regular operations.

Brazil is a country where national defense is not a matter of major concern to the political elite. It is overwhelmingly bigger and certainly more powerful than its immediate neighbors. But so far, it has been somewhat on the fringe of the East–West confrontation. It is virtually impossible to find any member of the Congress (except for retired professional military men occupying elected positions) who is interested in or knowledgeable about military affairs.[20] The reason is simple. Neither international affairs nor military questions bring votes or mobilize people.[21]

Another question pertains to professionalization: Did the professionalization that the military went through help or hinder its chances of getting involved in politics? First, *professionalization* has to be defined. As pointed out earlier, the Brazilian process of military professionalization is

Professionalism

Politicization are intertwined

intertwined with the process of politicization of the military. Virtually any senior military officer is likely to have been through some civilian or quasi-civilian assignment during his career. In addition, the contents of military education stress the role of the military in functions that are not strictly military. Thus, because the military has been involved in politics and in administration for such a long time, professionalization almost necessarily involves some sort of civilian appointment.

In the Brazilian case, then, professionalization, in and of itself, does not diminish the degree of military interventionism. Instead, it makes the military more involved with other civilian affairs.[22] The term for this would be *militarization* (no derogatory meaning). The question, then, would be: Did the Brazilian military go through a process of militarization? The answer is no. During the years of the military regime, the military actually gained more expertise and more ground in civilian arenas of performance. It also took over, more and more, in civilian positions. Whether this is good or bad is a matter of the observer's preference. This is so because although, on the one hand, there was a "militarization" of public administration, the reverse is also true. As the military occupied administrative civilian positions, it were also "civilianized," to an extent, in the process.

Finally, there is the question of military leadership: Is the current military leadership more or less prone to military interventions in politics? Until the 1960s, one of the problems in Brazilian politics was the long tenure of senior military officers on active duty. This gave them the opportunity to develop political leadership above and beyond military institutions. Whether this process was good or bad depended on whose behalf these political generals intervened. Politicians considered that those political generals who intervened favoring their interests were the "good" generals. They were the heirs of the "moderative power" of the emperor. Those who opposed them were the bad guys, the "gorillas," and so forth.[23]

Marshall President Castello Branco put an end to this. He knew the internal military implications of military leadership that had political support outside the military institution. From 1965 on, generals could not remain as generals for more than twelve years, and no general could remain as a general of any one rank for more than four years (there are three ranks of general). Whichever happened first forced a general into retirement. The practical result of this regulation was to prevent generals from developing their own personal leadership, which could be used for political purposes.

Castello Branco's policy was successful, no doubt. Virtually all the generals who retired since this reform went home to private employment or to second careers. All lost their political influence as military officers.[24]

Castello Branco's decision had an unanticipated outcome, however. It is starting to appear now, twenty-three years after the proviso went into force. The consequences are still unclear. The regulation prevented the emergence of personalized leadership among the generals. It turned all the generals into "mutually replaceable parts" in a complex bureaucratic machinery. They can be exchanged to fit the mood of the troops. In the past, leader-generals had political leverage to shift the mood of a portion of the armed forces. Nowadays, a general who does not fulfill the expectations of his peers and subordinates in political terms can be replaced by another general who will be equally effective in leading those troops toward the objectives that are more in line with the corporate mood of the moment.

The fact that there is a democratic regime did not make the process of controlling the military any easier. Now, the solution is not to have control only over the leadership. It involves, instead, a far more complex process of monitoring the mood of the armed forces at several ranks.

Conclusions

It should not be taken for granted that the military will not intervene in Brazilian politics. Assuming that the political system functions normally and that the economic challenges are not unsurmountable, democracy still stands a good chance. However, if these conditions are not met, there is the possibility of another military intervention.

The sources of military instability lie, also, in the realm of the military institution. They have sociological roots that were left untouched in the process of *abertura*.

At this point, political opening continues to take place. The system continues to function. However, unless the question of the legitimate mission of the military is addressed in a creative way, the sources of military instability will remain present. The effort has to be a joint one—civilian and military. Otherwise, the ghost of military intervention will continue to lurk around the corner, ready to overpower democracy at any moment that the economic and political conditions deteriorate severely.

Notes

1. Brazil's inflation rate for 1987 was about 320 percent. For 1988, it was about 920 percent. The lack of confidence in government policy is reaching dangerous levels. Economic policy measures adopted by the government lack credibility. Economic actors do not act accordingly. Between August 1988 and October 1988, the monthly inflation rate jumped from 20 percent to 27 percent. November was an easier month, thanks to talks among labor, business, and the govern-

ment. An inflation rate target was set at 26 percent. It reached 28 percent in December. Projections called for close to 30+ percent in January 1989.

2. In 1987, the then planning minister, Aníbal Teixeira, was indicted for corruption. So far, no legal action has been taken. His successor, João Batista de Abreu, a career civil servant, made all sorts of public statements about the need for austerity. As a civil servant, he was assigned a five-bedroom, government-owned apartment (for which he paid roughly the equivalent of $10 rent). Nothing was wrong with that; as a civil servant, he was entitled to it. However, upon his appointment as planning minister he moved to another government house assigned to the planning minister, maintaining, at the same time, the civil servant apartment, occupied only by a maid. *Correio Braziliense* (December 17, 1988). In another case, General Albérico Barros Alves was appointed director of one of the subsidiaries of Petrobrás. The general was a personal friend of President Sarney. Although the army minister was against his appointment for a civilian position, Sarney appointed him anyway. Shortly after that, private bankers reported that the general's immediate subordinates had been requesting kickbacks from their banks in exchange for maintaining the Petrobrás Distribuidora accounts in their banks. The subject is being investigated by the Financial Administration Committee of the Chamber of Deputies. (Reports about this issue can be found in any Brazilian newspaper from Rio, São Paulo, or Brasília during the period November 20—December 20, 1988.).

3. The Sarney government is facing ever-growing public image problems. Cynicism among the population is increasing dramatically. Tax dodging has become routine. The question in people's minds is: Why pay taxes to a government that gives nothing in return?

4. There are conflicting views about the influence of social origins on the political orientations of officers, especially in a career that socializes its members as intensely as the military does. One thing seems to be clear, however: Those officers who are sons of military personnel have a more continuous socialization than those who are not. Sons of the military receive a coherent set of values throughout their socialization. Thus, their chances of having more coherent values is greater. The social composition of the Brazilian officer corps has been changing rapidly. Traditionally, the army was a stronghold of a "solid middle class." As development increased and new economic opportunities were opened, the armed forces (especially the army) continued to be avenues for social mobility. The social origins of those who traveled along this road, however, changed. Data presented by Barros indicate that cadets whose fathers were of the "lower stratum" increased from 3.8 percent in 1941–43 to 9.1 percent in 1962–66 and to 15 percent in 1970. Furthermore, the number of cadets whose fathers were military increased from 21.2 percent in 1941–43 to 34.9 percent in 1962–66 to 37.3 percent in 1970. The most striking fact is that of this 37.3 percent, only 10.6 percent were son of officers, whereas 26.7 percent were sons of noncommissioned officers and sergeants. See Alexandre de Souza Costa Barros, "The Brazilian Military: Political Socialization, Political Performance and State Building," Ph.D. Dissertation, University of Chicago, 1978. This subject has also been raised in personal discussions with senior military officers.

5. With the changes in social origins, the homogeneity of the military is being

challenged. However, among all elite groups in Brazilian society, the military is the only one that has a systematic and coherent training and socialization system that accompanies its members throughout their professional lives. Thus, although the military may be facing problems of heterogeneity, it is still the only elite group that makes a systematic effort to maintain a certain degree of homogeneity of values among its members.

6. The 1988 municipal elections were surprising to many political analysts. Considering that Brazil is a poor country going through rapid development and modernization, it was expected that popular parties—among them the Partido dos Trabalhadores (PT, the Laborer's party)—would grow steadily. The victory of PT candidates in the 1989 mayoral elections in many cities (including São Paulo, the largest and most important Brazilian industrial city) was surprising to many observers. Part of this victory can be attributed to the lack of viable alternatives in other parties. Part of it is due to the disastrous economic policies of the Sarney administration.

7. On the question of the role of the military, see the brilliant study by William H. McNeill, *The Pursuit of Power* (Chicago: University of Chicago Press, 1982). For a more specific discussion of the South American case, see Alexandre de S.C. Barros and Edmundo Campos Coelho, "The Politics of Military Intervention and Withdrawal in South America", *International Political Science Review* 2, no. 3 (1981). See, also, Alexandre de S.C. Barros, "Back to Barracks: An Option for the Brazilian Military?" *Third World Quarterly* 7, no. 1 (January 1985).

8. See Alexandre Barros and Paulo Kramer, "The Brazilian Military and 'Abertura'," Paper presented at the meeting of the Latin American Studies Association, Mexico City, September 29–October 2, 1983.

9. This situation was completely different from that which took place in Argentina, where at least some military officers who were involved with repression were actually brought to trial by the courts during the Alfonsín administration. The fact that there were no legal proceedings against officers in Brazil should not eclipse the fact that Brazilian military officers have kept their eyes open to what goes on in neighboring countries. As a matter of fact, the concern with the possibility that Brazilian military officers will be brought to trial in a process of *revanchismo* is a central concern of senior military officers in Brazil. This concern will become even more serious in the event of a victory of the Worker's Party (PT), alone or in an alliance, in the 1989 presidential elections.

10. The only privilege the military lobbyists had over their private counterparts was that they had offices in the congress building. Aside from this, they acted competitively with any other lobby. The military lobby was probably the most professional one acting during the meetings of the Constituent Assembly; this is acknowledged by political journalists and observers as well as many members of Congress.

11. The Brazilian political elite's attitude toward the military oscillates between the "Yes, sir" attitude and the "The military doesn't matter" attitude. When the military is in power, professional politicians court it. When the military is out of power, professional politicians simply ignore it and consider that it does not count politically.

12. Aside from the fact that they discuss the role of the military in these

terms, there is also a high degree of cynicism on the part of politicians. They defend the neutrality of the military as long as the military might intervene against their interests. Whenever civilian politicians feel that their own interests are being severely jeopardized, most of them do not hesitate to call in the military to intervene on their behalf. On this issue, see Edmundo Campos Coelho, *Em Busca da Identidade: O Exército e a Política na Sociedade Brasileira* (Rio de Janeiro: Forense Universitária, 1976).

13. See Campos Coelho, *Em Busca da Identidade*, and Barros, "The Brazilian Military."

14. According to press reports, the Sarney administration admitted more than 150,000 new people to the civil service in three years, as opposed to 50,000 during the six years of the preceding administration. These numbers do not include people appointed to jobs in the state and local governments. Under the provisos of the new constitution, civil servants can be admitted only by public examination. In order to circumvent this proviso, President Sarney appointed 2,000 cronies on the eve of the date the new constitution went into effect on October 5, 1988.

15. The National Security Council was "abolished" under the new constitution. The National Defense Council (CDN), which has the same functions and is staffed by the same personnel, was created to replace it. See Brazilian Constitution of October 5, 1988, articles 91 and 84.

16. On this issue, see Barros and Campos Coelho, "The Politics of Military Intervention."

17. I am grateful to Jack Child for pointing out the implications of the professionalization of an armed force in the battlefield (as occurs in countries that face recurrent wars) as opposed to that which takes place in military schools (as is the case with the armed forces of countries that are not exposed to wars).

18. This should not lead to the interpretation that the military did not receive the monies that they wanted. However, on a comparative basis, the Brazilian military received much more money for salaries and upkeep than for military equipment and materiel. For their counterparts in other countries, the tendency has been for the military to request much more for weaponry (aside from the usual professional perquisites).

19. See Barros and Campos Coelho, "The Politics of Military Intervention."

20. The absence of politicians who are interested in or knowledgeable about military affairs should not be confused with an absence of politicians who relate to the military mostly in terms of internal politics. There are many of these.

21. A controversy such as the one over U.S. vice-presidential candidate Quayle's serving in the National Guard to avoid going into the Army would not make sense in Brazil, because military heroism is not a national virtue there outside strictly military circles. Even in these circles, the opportunities for heroism are very limited, given the nonengagement of the country in external wars.

22. Military officers have been discussing this question privately. According to their view, the process the Brazilian military went through was not one of professionalization but, rather, one of bureaucratization. If this is true, then we may be faced with a situation in which the Brazilian armed forces are highly bureaucratized and weakly professionalized *in strictly military terms*. The other

possibility is to consider that the process of professionalization of the Brazilian armed forces is intrinsically different from that of the armed forces of countries that have a significantly different military history, as was pointed out earlier in this chapter (from private conversations with senior military officers).

23. Edmundo Campos Coelho, in *Em busca da Identidade*, dismissed the idea of the military as heirs to the "moderative power" of the emperor. According to him, the idea of the moderative power of the military was a creation of civilian politicians to lure military officers into intervening in politics on behalf of specific political groups.

24. General President Ernesto Geisel is an exception. He still remains an important political figure, who is visited and consulted by civilian politicians as well as military officers. This consultation takes place on a regular basis, as well as when crises seem to be around the corner.

12

The Threat of New Missions: Latin American Militaries and the Drug War

Louis W. Goodman
Johanna S.R. Mendelson

United States presidents have claimed to be involved in a "war on drugs" for more than twenty years.[1] In the 1980s, the issue of the use and control of illegal narcotics has become a major domestic problem for the United States and a pervasive issue in inter-American relations. According to the 1987 National High School Senior Survey, 50 percent of seniors had experimented with illicit drugs.[2] The use of cocaine, which apparently peaked by 1988, is widespread, but sales of particularly virulent forms such as "crack" and "bazuco" continue to surge, as does drug-related violence.[3] Marijuana, by some estimates, has passed corn as the most valuable cash crop in the United States.[4] Although these and other statistics in this field may not be entirely reliable, it has been estimated that "Latin American countries supply about one third of the heroin, perhaps eighty percent of the marijuana and all of the cocaine currently used in the United States, representing three-fourths of a U.S. drug market."[5]

Drug wars are no less an issue in Latin America and the Caribbean. Serious narcotics addiction problems have been reported by the U.S. Department of State in Bolivia, Colombia, Jamaica, Peru, and Mexico, with annual increases since the mid-1980s throughout the hemisphere.[6] The results are both the social damage caused by drug abuse—exacerbation of poverty, crime, poor schools, and the erosion of civil authority—and the ballooning of a huge underground economy and polity fueled by sales of illegal narcotics. In the United States alone, drug sales are estimated at more than $100 billion, more than twice the country's annual oil bill.[7]

When cash generated by this underground economy purchases police, courts, elected officials, and assassins, the foundations of civil authority are shaken. Drug traffickers are said to be buying autonomous spheres of influence in drug-producing countries such as Bolivia, Colombia, Mexico, and Peru and in important transshipment locales such as Honduras and

Panama. Some analysts have argued that narcotics trafficking has created a dynamic "new class," which has displaced traditional oligarchies.[8] Established governments throughout the hemisphere see the drug economy as threatening prospects for democratic politics. The violence and threats to established authority promoted by reported drug cartels have created zones where drug oligarchies set the relations between government and governed. Furthermore, the instability caused by drug-related rivalries and conflicts with civilian authority has increased military concern about the stability of the social and political order. In some cases, this military concern is reported to have been challenged by important military officers with financial ties to narcotics traffickers.[9]

The control of illegal narcotics has been recognized as a serious domestic and inter-American problem for all nations of the hemisphere.[10] It is so severe a problem that the notion of "drug wars" has been transformed from political hyperbole to the question: Should the military, both in the United States and in Latin American nations, be used to interdict and control illegal narcotics?

The proposal to militarize the war on drugs is the latest chapter in a debate chronicled by José Nun, Alfred Stepan, and others about whether military missions should be expanded from the traditional role of external security to a "new professionalism" of internal security.[11] In the 1960s and 1970s, Brazilian, Peruvian, and other Latin American militaries, concerned with domestic threats to social and political order, took the lead in expanding the concept of the core function of the military from preparation for possible foreign wars (external security) to a "preoccupation with subversion and internal security."[12]

Since the early 1970s, virtually every military institution in Latin America has taken it upon itself to examine its role in the larger society. The 1964 Brazilian elaboration of a national security doctrine, which formalized military professional responsibility to respond to internal security threats and to play a role in national development matters, has profoundly influenced debates in other militaries. While military institutions in nations such as Peru, Chile, and Guatemala have developed unique concepts of national security and the role of the military therein, the Brazilian redefinition of the professional military role—to include national security and development activities—has been central to intramilitary debates.

These debates about mission have been influenced by U.S. military policy. Since 1961, the United States has encouraged Latin American militaries to take on primary roles in counterinsurgency, civic action, and other nation-building tasks.[13] These intrainstitutional debates and the focus of U.S. policy changed in the mid-1980s when military presidents were replaced by elected civilians.[14] In Argentina, for example, military missions were scaled back by civilian authorities; and debates within the high officer corps centered on how to maintain professionalism and support democracy.[15] In Guatemala, where the military began a gradual retreat in 1982, culminating in Vinicio Cerezo's assumption of the presidency in 1986, the concept of a national security doctrine was rejected in favor of a "national stability doctrine."[16] This Guatemalan concept sought to define a role for the military in a socially integrated nation, while democratizing the political system. At the same time, U.S. policy was clearly indicating that a primary military role should be the strengthening of democratic political systems. As Assistant Secretary for Inter-American Affairs Elliott Abrams stated at the twenty-fifth commencement of the Inter-American Defense College in 1986:

> Your highest calling must be not to replace failed regimes but to protect successful democracies. You must succeed in the task of forging a new vision of security in which democracy is the cornerstone, not a luxury; where free and open political competition is an ally, not an impediment to peace and development.[17]

Despite such clear statements, the policies of building democratic political systems and eliminating drug traffic have not been easily reconcilable. Within the rubric of military subordination to civilian authority, the dangers of the drug war as a military mission are obvious. As with military counterinsurgency activities of the 1960s, direct Latin American military involvement in the drug war would involve military in police tasks that are technically within the civilian domain; it would also require mastery of a complex combination of political and military skills, likely necessitating the expansion of military intelligence operations; it would blur the line between appropriate and inappropriate domains for military professional actions; it would expand the managerial roles played by the military in society; and it would increase the role military men play in national politics and political decision making.

Involving Latin American armed forces in the drug war threatens traditional concepts of military professionalism in the region. It pushes military men to involve themselves in activities that advocates of democracy would prefer to reserve for civilians.

The preferred solution, of course, would be to treat narcotics trafficking as a police problem; to train special gendarmerie to control it; and to restrict military missions to external security matters. This is, in fact, precisely the strategy that has been adopted by the government of Argentina. Its narcotics police report numerous successful actions against drug smugglers and drug trafficking within its borders. However, the dimension of narcotics trafficking is much smaller in Argentina than it is in the major drug-producing and drug-transporting countries on the west coast of South America.

In Colombia, whose military has sustained a decades-long mission of quelling internal violence, military units have taken up the drug war with mixed results. Until January 1988, when Colombian Attorney General Carlos Mauro Hoyos was assassinated, the military had been reluctant to enter the war on drugs. But this murder tipped the balance for President Virgilio Barco, who declared a state of siege, announced an expansion of the national police force, and convinced the military that it was the only institution capable of eradicating the "narcos" that plagued the nation's social and economic fabric. In an article describing this period in Colombia, journalist Michael Massing wrote:

> The country's generals had long resisted such a course. They regarded the guerrillas, not the "narcos" as their principal enemies and opposed any undertaking that might distract them from the "real" war. In addition, the generals well knew the corrupting power of the drug trade and worried their men might be drawn in. Nevertheless, the growing panic in the country, combined with pressure from the Reagan administration, convinced the military to join the drug war.[18]

The Peruvian military has also taken on this new internal security mission. It has directly confronted the Shining Path revolutionary movement since the early 1980s. Although Shining Path was originally thought to be separate from narcotics trafficking, recent evidence of cooperation among drug trafficking and Shining Path violence have begun to link these problems for the Peruvian military.[19] Since the late 1970s, conflicting reports have identified the Bolivian military as, on the one hand, primary supporter and beneficiary of illegal narcotics activities in the country and, on the other hand, engaged in a campaign to eradicate narcotics production and to prosecute leading drug traffickers.[20]

There is no easy answer to the question of the desirability of military involvement in the drug war. Hemisphere-wide military and civilian officials would prefer that the drug war be handled as a police matter. The dangers of military involvement in the drug war are universally recognized. Debates in the United States on using the U.S. military for drug interdiction are mirrored in the formal and informal argumentation south of the Rio Grande.[21]

The United States has played an important role in shaping military involvement in the drug war in Latin America. Since the late 1970s, through its Department of State's Bureau of International Narcotics Matters (with a 1989 budget of $101 million), the United States has attempted to jointly plan and coordinate antinarcotics programs internationally.[22] In April 1986, President Ronald Reagan signed a National Security Directive that declared narcotics a threat to national security, thereby providing the policy framework for direct U.S. military operations overseas. With this authority, U.S. troops were directly deployed in Bolivia in 1986 in a highly controversial action called "Operation Blast Furnace." This action caused the price of Bolivian coca leaves to fall from $125 to $15 per hundred pounds (approximately $25 less than the cost of production) and caused more than 800 traffickers to flee the country. But as soon as the U.S. troops left Bolivia, the price of coca leaves returned to the $125 level, and the traffickers returned. In addition, Operation Blast Furnace caused both Bolivian nationalists and U.S. critics to complain that Bolivian national sovereignty had been compromised by the presence of U.S. troops, and at a high cost to the U.S. Treasury. A participant in the operation, Colonel Michael H. Abbott, has assessed the possibility of similar future operations:

> [It will] not likely occur: (1) It is very expensive in comparison to the potential return; (2) There is likely to be no real payoff when it is all over; and (3) No country is likely to ask the U.S. military to come and play in its backyard, because the political price is too heavy.[23]

The U.S. Department of Defense's official view of the role of military forces in the war on drugs is "to provide support so that civilian law enforcement agencies can make the necessary searches, seizures, and arrests."[24] In 1989 in Peru, consistent with this guideline, the U.S. Drug Enforcement Agency launched a $24 million program called "Operation Snowcap," in which "more than two dozen armed agents, additional U.S.-flown helicopters and other support personnel were flown to the upper Huallaga Valley, to support Peruvian efforts at the eradication of coca production in that nation's primary production region."[25] This region has been nominally controlled by the Peruvian military since November of 1987, when a state of emergency was declared because of high levels of Shining Path activity in the region.

Such antinarcotics assistance has come under far less scrutiny than many other military aid programs. Questions have been raised about the extent to which the United States is playing a positive role in strengthening civil–military relations, weakened after years of military rule, or whether operations such as Blast Furnace and Snow Cap are encouraging unchecked military action in basically uncontrollable territory.

The trade-off embedded in the question of whether the drug war is a mission for Latin American militaries is obvious. Narcotics trafficking is a huge problem for the welfare of populations in every nation in the Western Hemisphere. Concerted national efforts to reduce both supply of and demand for narcotics have been endorsed by international organizations and by governments from Argentina and Chile to the United States and

Canada. When should the military be involved in the drug wars? When can local police, with enhanced training and resources, handle narcotics trafficking problems without direct involvement of the military? What should be the role of the United States? How can the United States assure that its support for control of narcotics trafficking is supportive of, not antagonistic to, its larger policy objective of strengthening democratic political systems in Latin America?

There are no easy answers to these questions. The long-term solution, of course, includes inducing massive fall-offs in narcotics consumption and finding worthwhile alternative activities for producers of narcotic substances. This is obviously a task for all nations in the hemisphere. In the short term, to the extent possible, the United States and the Latin American nations must strive to support police and border patrol action against drug abuse, production, and transport. Particularly important are bilateral and multilateral agreements permitting hemispheric partners to work together to stem the flow of illegal substances and profits. Finally, civilians and military men are in agreement that the drug war as a mission for the military can be considered only when all other options have failed.[26]

Notes

1. Although President Ronald Reagan's April 11, 1986, National Security Division Directive, "On Narcotics and National Security," may be the most salient recent manifestation of the resolve of the United States, President Richard M. Nixon made a similar pronouncement, which coined the phrase "drug war," on March 24, 1968; and numerous previous U.S. presidents took steps to curtail the use of illicit substances, most notably alcohol during Prohibition, from 1920 to 1933. See James B. Slaughter, "Marijuana Prohibition in the United States: History and Analysis of a Failed Policy," *Columbia Journal of Law and Social Problems* 21 (1988): 417.

2. Reported in the 1988 annual report of the Inter-American Dialogue, *The Americas in 1988* (Washington, D.C.: Aspen Institute, 1988), p.41.

3. Ibid., pp. 42–44.

4. Ibid., p. 43.

5. Rensselaer W. Lee III, "The Latin American Drug Connection," *Foreign Policy*, No. 1 (Winter 1985–86): 142. Estimates for individual countries can be found in U.S. Department of State, Bureau of International Narcotics Matters, *Coordinator of Narcotics Affairs Handbook*, an annual publication.

6. Inter-American Dialogue, *The Americans in 1988*, pp. 44–49.

7. Ibid., p. 41.

8. See Mario Arango, *Impacto del Narcotrafico en Antioquia* (Medellin, Colombia: Arango, 1988), which makes this argument. It has been the focus of much controversy in Colombia.

9. Among the many sources that discuss ties between Latin American armed forces and drug traffickers, see Michael H. Abbott, "The Army and the Drug

War: Politics or National Security?" *Parameters* (U.S. Army War College Quarterly) 8, no. 4 (December 1988): 95–122; and Washington Office on Latin America, "Misguided Policy: The U.S. 'War' Against Narcotics Production in the Andes," *Update* 13, no. 6 (November–December 1988): 1, 5, 6.

10. Inter-American Dialogue, *The Americas in 1988*, and U.S. Department of State, *Narcotics Affairs Handbook*.

11. José Nun, "The Middle-Class Military Coup," in Claudio Veliz, ed., *The Politics of Conformity in Latin America* (London: Oxford University Press, 1967); and Alfred Stepan, "The New Professionalism of Internal Warfare and Military Role Expansion," in Alfred Stepan, ed., *Authoritarian Brazil* (New Haven, Conn.: Yale University Press, 1973), pp. 47–65.

12. Stepan, "The New Professionalism," pp. 53–65.

13. Ibid., p. 52.

14. For a statement outlining U.S. policy, see General Fred F. Woerner, "The United States Southern Command: Shield of Democracy in Latin America," *Defense Magazine* (August 1987).

15. See Carina Perelli's contribution to this volume, "The Legacies of Transitions to Democracy in Argentina and Uruguay" (chapter 3).

16. Succinct statements of the Guatemalan doctrine of national stability can be found in Alfonso Yurrita's contribution to this volume (chapter 5) and in Guatemalan Minister of Defense Hector Gramajo Morales, Address to the Guatemalan Center of Military Studies, November 10, 1988.

17. Elliott Abrams, "A Democratic Vision of Security", speech at the Inter-American Defense College, Washington, D.C. June 13, 1986.

18. Michael Massing, "The War on Cocaine," *New York Review of Books* (December 22, 1988): 62.

19. Abbott, "The Army and the Drug War," p. 98. This subject is discussed in detail in Marcial Rubio Correa's contribution to this volume, "The Perception of the Subversive Threat in Peru" (chapter 7).

20. Abbott, "The Army and the Drug War," pp. 98–99.

21. In the spring of 1988, for example, the U.S. Senate passed and then rescinded legislation authorizing the use of active-duty U.S. troops for the purpose of drug interdiction. See, also, Donald Mabry, "The US Military and the War on Drugs in Latin America," *Journal of Inter-American Affairs* 30 (1988): 53–76.

22. U.S. Department of State, Bureau of International Narcotics Matters, *International Narcotics Control Strategy Report*, March 1989.

23. Abbott, "The Army and the Drug War," p. 106. Abbott describes Operation Blast Furnace on pp. 95–103.

24. Lieutenant General Stephan G. Olmstead, USMC, DOD Task Force on Drug Enforcement, "Statement before Subcommittee on Investigations, House Committee on the Armed Services," July 23, 1987, p. 2.

25. Michael Isikoff, "U.S. Expands Role in Peru's Drug War," *Washington Post* (January 23, 1989): 1, 8.

26. This was the conclusion of a May 1988 conference in Washington, D.C., that involved seventy civilians and high-ranking Latin American military men, as reported in Louis W. Goodman and Johanna S.R. Mendelson, "Whose Drug War Is It, Anyway?" *Christian Science Monitor* (July 22, 1988).

Part IV
Civil–Military Relations and the Future of Democracy in Latin America

13
Civil–Military Relations in a Democratic Framework

Augusto Varas

The use and abuse of the armed forces in the political realm in Latin America has left a negative balance in terms of their stability and institutional development. In turn, the democratic stabilization projects put into place in the region after military interventions have been basically faulty in the sphere of military policy. To the extent that the Latin American democracies fail to perceive clearly the issue of the armed forces' insertion in the democratic process and to identify the national defense in their reform projects, a key problem will remain unresolved; this, in turn, soon becomes a threat to the democratic institutions themselves, through either new autonomous adjustment forms or renewed military interventions.[1]

Theoretical and empirical research of the relations among the armed forces, the society, and the state has thus become a crucial issue for the Latin American democracy. From the findings of such studies, a framework of definitions can be developed, so as to ascertain the role of the armed forces in the internal security and national defense spheres and determine how to insert the armed forces into the state structure and ensure effective civilian control over the armed institutions.[2]

Nowadays, the behavior and interactions among the armed forces, the civilians, and the state occur in the context of three relational systems: *intervention–withdrawal, autonomous adjustment,* and *civilian control.* Each shows specific degrees of underlying state inconsistency, military professionalization, and civil ability to develop a system of linkages among the state bodies in question.

Intervention–Withdrawal

Although there are numerous studies on the causes of military intervention in the Latin American politics, the existence of various viewpoints and the identification of different variables have not led to thorough theoretical presentations.[3] The number of variables, background factors, and explanations of political intervention by the military remains an open question that must be deepened in connection with the major issues of the evolution and consolidation of the region's democratic governmental forms.

In order to get some clues for redefining civil–military relations within a democratic framework, I have chosen to systematize those variables that have been crucial for the armed forces' participation in democratic transition.[4] This will permit us to identify the elements that must be put into place—even though their mere presence may not be sufficient—so that balanced civil–military relations can be established in the future. I will refer to the cases of Argentina (1983), Brazil (1984), Bolivia (1980–82), Ecuador (1979), Peru (1979), and Uruguay (1984) and compare them with those of Chile (1987) and Paraguay (1986).

Delivery of power to the civilians has been contingent on sets of both social and military factors.

Social Factors

The major social factors affecting the military are the transformation of the system of political relations and the local political culture, mass-mobilization capabilities, the status of the civil–military relationship, and the terms of the armed forces' withdrawal. Overall, these factors constitute what could be called opposition *succession capabilities*.

Such social developments challenge the leadership of the armed forces and bring about or increase internal dissent.[5]

A first set of prerequisites for transition, significant for the armed forces, has been the surge of the political system's capability to respond to the issue of *dissident unity*, which creates a new government option. Second, the party system and political-institutional crisis facilitated military intervention in Latin America.[6] However, once such problems were overcome, these forces started to perform a key role in transition toward democracy. Hence, the attempts to develop a new political relationship within the opposition have been effective in creating the prerequisites for transition. This indicates that the greater the transformation of the political system during the authoritarian period, the easier the democratization.[7] Brazil is a case in point.[8] Finally, the isolation of the antiestablishment forces has also helped to deprive the armed forces of political resons to rule. The degree of consensus for such coactive measures tends to be inversely proportional to the breadth of the dissident front.

Some of the changes that propitiated transition took place at the political culture level. The emergence of more pragmatic approaches and the isolation of fundamentalist-type ideologies have helped substitute genuine national will for sector and group interest-led approaches. In this regard, the defeat of "ideologism" and the explicit nationalistic orientation of the democratizing forces have been important factors. A similar situation has been apparent in Argentina, Brazil, Uruguay, and Peru.

Another important factor has been the opposition's capability to create and mobilize national forces for change. Although such mass mobilizations have been common in economic crisis situations, they have also taken place without such a contexts; they have been a means to support basically political targets regarding full civil rights—democracy as a value in itself. Mass mobilizations not only have led to the situation in which the military regimes typically find themselves in their terminal periods—when they lose their capability for crisis management[9]—but also have represented the component of majority will, which is one of the few deterrents the armed forces pay attention to.

In the case of Peru, mass mobilizations attesting general readiness for change strongly influenced the military rulers.[10] In Bolivia, domestic resistance to the García Meza regime was one of the key factors in the ensuing process of unification of the opposition. In Brazil, the mass protests and the campaign for direct elections in 1984 were crucial.[11] In Uruguay, the defeat in the plebiscite, and the inability of the military to legitimate its political project through social consensus, was decisive for the start of negotiations and transition.

When the armed forces face a legitimation crisis in respect to the main forces supporting them, their situation becomes untenable. The inability to set up a stable order—be it legitimate or not—and develop the positive results of the original insurrectional coalition has also been a factor of democratic transition in the region, as shown by the cases of Argentina,[12] Brazil, and Peru.

In Brazil, the arduous relationship between the military government and its supporting business elites was one of the basic reasons for the military's decision to launch an opening process, which admittedly was an almost unilateral initiative of the armed forces.[13] By then, the armed forces were facing several perils.[14] Hence, we can conclude that the ruling armed forces' estrangement from their business elite supporters left them without any chance to manage both the military internecine crisis and the crisis created by the moves of the opposition forces. The mix of mass mobilizations and the estrangement of the business elites created a favorable climate for a military decision to start a transition process.[15] The same situation took place in Peru, although there, mass mobilization and business elite estrangement tended to coincide briefly.[16]

These four sets of factors have made their influence felt within the army barracks. They have challenged the arguments expounded by the military to remain in power: both the negative one—that of fighting the antiestablishment forces—and the positive one—that of legitimizing a new political order through social consensus or by enjoying elite support. The hinge of the institutional self-attributed images is also put in doubt. As the opposition front widens, there is less consensus for repression, and the costs of using force become higher. Hence, the isolation of the armed forces within the state apparatus and the society becomes apparent, thus enhancing the civilians' deterrent capabilities and creating, in the armed forces, a climate that makes them ready to accept a formula for civilian takeover that include low levels of uncertainty regarding the institution's future.

Military Factors

Two sets of military factors can be identified: the crisis of the professional function—resulting from the contradiction between the functions of defense and domestic police tasks; and at the governmental level, the management crisis. These factors coalesce into a single result: erosion of the internal consensus and emergence of a new one, aimed at protecting the collective interests of the armed institutions—their institutional continuity being challenged—through retreat to the barracks.

Regarding the first set of factors, the fact can be established that in all countries analyzed, the professional crisis emerging from the strain between defense and domestic order functions has been detrimental to the armed forces' modernization and professionalization. One of the most evident consequences of this process of the army's becoming a police force has often been the consolidation of an intelligence community that assumes control of the major levers of the military power. This institutional framework tends to freeze professional development and the process of modernization of the armed institutions. The practical effects of this contradiction became apparent in a dramatic manner during the Malvinas conflict. This military defeat can also be explained by the institutional erosion associated with massive violations of human rights.[17]

For these reasons, and because the armed institutions' assumption of police tasks cannot be justified, a political space is created inside the armed forces where the institutionalist groups can demand that the *professional* development be continued. This situation, which was apparent in Argentina, Brazil, and Bolivia, was also noticeable in Ecuador.[18]

The second set of military factors refers to the internal effects of the governmental management crisis of the armed forces. To the extent that the armed forces insert themselves in a different way when they *are* the government, their success or failure ends up affecting their political role.

Thus, the management crisis in Argentina during Videla's term, which was aggravated during Viola's and Galtieri's administrations, paved the way for the military defeat, as the command line was cut off and its verticality was affected by the emergence of internal groups that put the government's management skills into question and brought forth alternative proposals.[19] Such was also the case in Ecuador and Peru.

This type of crisis has compounded the classic problem that the armed forces confront when they take power—namely, becoming as politically split as the society at large. Such new reality transforms the armed forces "into ambiguous political forces,"[20] which necessarily leads them to a process of internecine conflict and threatens their institutional continuity—a key factor if they are to be able to operate in a unified way in a war scenario.

This type of problem could be only provisionally overcome in Uruguay, where the armed forces themselves became a "substitute political party"[21]—a process that was facilitated by a strategic-political context in which the armed institutions have no deterrent capabilities. Only in this context could the military function be denatured, and the police and political responsibilities proper were hypertrophied. The Uruguayan experience, however—unthinkable as it is in other South American countries—shows the limits of the tension between the defense functions and those of a political-police nature.

The other polar case is that of Argentina, where the attempt was made to turn each branch of the defense services into a substitute political party and, simultaneously, to enhance the country's defense capabilities. The end result was the state's becoming divided in three watertight compartments—one for each defense branch— whereby the management crisis deepened[22] and the military deterrence capabilities themselves were eroded.[23]

Crisis Management Capabilities

Because the military institution's political capabilities are determined by its resources, professional ability, and internal coherence,[24] any crack in that coherence affects both the management capabilities and, basically, the crisis management capabilities of the armed forces.

The importance of internal relations management within the armed forces is compounded by the very repression of internal dissent by high-ranking government authorities,[25] which in many cases permits, if not a solution, at least postponement of a solution to the crisis. In the case of Peru, it was not the disagreement within the armed forces that ultimately prevented the military from tackling the crisis. The leading factor was Velasco's inability to orient the process and organize the various internal factions, because of his precarious health condition.[26]

Rewards and Sanctions

Under the circumstances, it becomes particularly relevant to examine the issue of the impact of military rule on the armed forces' development and their relationships with civilians and the state.[27] I am specifically referring to the need to denounce the effects on national unity of the political power monopoly by the armed institutions.

Use of military force within the processes of modernization or political reform has always been catastrophic for national unity. Even though higher levels of economic growth have been attained—through maintenance of the internal order, repression, and wage compression—the net balance is negative in the mid- and long run. Thus, the administrations of Alfonsín, Sanguinetti, Sarney, and even Alan García are still being penalized by the feud between the civilians and the armed forces in Argentina, Uruguay, Brazil, and Peru, respectively. The "full stop" policies in Argentina and Uruguay, "protected democracy" in Brazil, "narco-militarism" in Bolivia, and the Pol Pot–style revolutionary fundamentalism in Peru indirectly stem from the political power monopoly by the armed forces, which failed to produce institutions that served as channels of communication among the elites and among the mass organizations, the social base, and the state's decision-making structure.

Such a historical review of the effects of military rule—through the analysis of specific situations—is a collective "sanction" for those who saw themselves as representing the loftiest concepts of national unity but, in fact, became a factor of national discord. At the same time, it is an institutional "reward" for those armed forces that recognize the fact that national unity can withstand the harshest tests without the need for militarization of the nation's life.

Withdrawal and Democracy

Based on the analysis of the social and military factors that determine the attitude of the armed forces regarding the process of transition to democracy, the following key variables in normalizing civil–military relations can be derived: (1) civil democratic unity, embracing even those elites that, in the beginning, supported the military rule; (2) isolation of the antiestablishment forces that legitimate the armed forces' fulfillment of internal security tasks; (3) effective mass support that does not overflow the institutional framework or generate new crisis; (4) reestablishment of the institutional balance by focusing on professional unity in the armed forces and avoidance of political or ideological fragmentation, as well as governmental and internal security responsibilities that impair appropriate professionalization; (5) moral recovery of the armed forces, which entails recognizing the identity between constitutionalism and democracy; and (6) a change in the sphere of civilian political culture, which makes possible all of the other variables.

Autonomous Adjustment

Between the scenarios of military intervention and civilian control over the armed institutions, there are various midway hypotheses, which I have christened *autonomous adjustment*. Such situations reflect a type of civil–military coexistence whereby the armed forces are not fully in control nor are military decisions a province of civilian jurisdiction. Each accommodation scenario can occur in each and every one of the civil–military relationship dimensions or only in some of them. Such compromise represents the relative balance level that the parties have been able to reach in a specific country and under specific historical circumstances—without, however, being able to make the new arrangement a part of the state's structure.

The contention that it is easier to demilitarize the government than the power is fully relevant in such a context.[28] In a number of countries, the autonomous adjustment scenarios have existed for such a long time that they cannot be depicted as transitional forms—they have become new state forms in Latin America. In some countries, the elites have assumed a leading role in the economic development process. In some others, they have become a key power factor; some governmental programs cannot be executed without them. Thus, autonomous adjustment means the maintenance of veto powers by the armed forces to a lesser extent than in intervention periods but to a greater extent than in periods of civilian control.[29] In such a context, the armed forces as a whole become an active power factor, just as the political parties, the church, the trade unions, and other social institutions and organizations are. Thus, autonomous adjustment entails sustained high levels of state militarization, even in cases where the armed forces do not rule directly.

This new reality—which began to make itself felt in Latin America at the end of the 1970s—reflects a particular set of factors, which will be discussed here. Once these factors have been identified, we will be in a position to specify a second set of tools that may be useful in restoring balanced civil–military relations.

Some structural factors explain why the armed forces have become social conflict arbitrators, social reformers, or modernization agents in various countries.

First, some systems of organization of the armed forces and some civil–military relationship structures are not entirely consistent with constitutional democracy. In Latin America, the most common organizational system is a mix of "cadres and conscripts," which cannot be compared with that of civilian militias and appears in association with nondemocratic government systems.[30]

The existence of permanent professional cadres that train a regular contingent of conscripts—that is, people compulsively recruited under the law—produces interesting sociological dynamics. First, there is the corporative (guild-type), closed situation typical of "professional armies." Second, the compulsory nature of the conscription system reinforces the internal authoritarian attitude of the cadres in respect to the recruits. Third, recruit training focuses on basic military operations. Technical-professional knowledge is reserved for the permanent personnel, whereby their segregation is reinforced. Fourth, this "self-centered" organizational order tends to make the armed forces assume and perform functions progressively differentiated from their military ones, substituting for the civilian institutions in specialized scientific, technological, productive, and even commercial and banking areas. The military world thus secludes itself in an ascending spiral of autarchic self-sufficiency.

Inside the armed forces, the aforementioned factors produce a civil–military relations model that duplicates the military institutional order. Thus, the extension of the organizational categories, and those of internal operation, is projected on the rest of the society, engendering an authoritarian, nondemocratic approach to civil–military relations. The core of this approach is the notion that the civilian element—its categories and values—is irrelevant in terms of the military order and its institutional continuity and, in some cases, us even a threat to the military system itself. Because social change constitutes a more dynamic process in the Latin American countries than in other, northerly regions, social mobilization and demands for participation clash with armed forces that reject conflict, disorder, and sociopolitical diversity or heterogeneity within the state. This structural inconsistency with verticalistic, nondemocratic institutions could well explain some military interventions prompted by social change processes.

Moreover, in most of the region's countries, the integration of the various military branches into one single state organization—the Defense Ministry or the Joint Chiefs of Staff—is an occasional factor. Thus, under the military reforms undertaken in Argentina and Peru, priority has been given to the establishment of a unified command organization for the whole of the armed forces, whereby autonomous bureaucratic dynamics are created that tend to reinforce institutional introspection.

In many cases the relative lack of organic integration in the typical Latin American State[31] prevents the existence of a set of interests that the various social sectors and groups share—a fact that reflects upon the various state organizations. This function has been made even more important by the fact that, historically—from colonial times up to an advanced stage of the independent era—the armed forces have performed a number of political tasks.[32] These conditions facilitate political intervention by the armed forces and simultaneously underpin the military prejudice that civilian politics are "anarchical" and that the military institution should protect itself in their regard.

The military organization is adequate for the performance of functions that are national in scope—that other social organizations or state institutions are unable to undertake, given their fragmentation and basically regional jurisdiction. Within the armed forces as a whole, the army is particularly able to manage adequately defense or any other task of a similar magnitude at a national level because of its structure and the fact that its resources are naturally spread throughout the country. This reality enhances the potential autonomy of the armed forces.

As a result of their permanent interventions in the political realm, the armed forces have been granted a high level of functional autonomy relative to their respective societies and governments. This situation varies from country to country. The degree of autonomy of each Latin American army is the aggregate of a number of simultaneous processes, including a military process of "corporatization" and a civil ability or inability to control the armed forces.

From the military standpoint, the modernization and professionalization processes, together with accompanying situations of sociocultural segregation—some of which I have already mentioned—have unleashed the centripetal forces that "corporatize" (that is, segregate or isolate) the armed forces relative to the civilians. The technological element, specialization in subjects scarcely linked to the civilian life, and the corporative-style accompanying ideologies set barriers and institutional limits between the armed forces and the society. The foregoing would be among the sufficient conditions of the process of autonomous adjustment.

On the other hand, this process has also been affected by the terms of the military ouster from government.[33]

In Argentina, the opposition striving for democracy made military institutional continuity possible through policies that included punishment for massive violations of human rights, but only for the organizers of such actions. The policy of modernization and professionalization of the armed institutions completes a type of civil–military agreement that was not easily reached but set the stage for democratic government—although not for a new civil–military equilibrium.[34]

In Bolivia, the actions against the military narcotics trafficking clique were limited to the most active groups; they received the whole impact of the exemplary measures of the democratic authorities. The implementation of these policies, however, has not been free from problems.

In the Brazilian case,[35] the price of transition has been a remarkable program of enhancement of the country's military capabilities, and no punishment was even considered for those guilty of excesses during the military regime.

A similar case—though a less successful one—has been that in Uruguay, where even though institutional continuity was assured, the approval of a bill of amnesty has encountered serious difficulties.

Withdrawal terms similar to those in Brazil were observed in Peru, where military spending has been dramatically augmented—to the point that the present democratic government has had to take a series of measures designed to set limits to this spending spree.

In Ecuador, however, the civilians striving for democracy were in no position to formulate a consistent initiative. Hence, the armed forces were granted an exceptional statute for institutional insertion into the state, whereby they have reached a level of relative autonomy that can hardly be compared with those of other armed institutions on the American continent.[36]

In sum, although military withdrawal has been the product of a civil and/or military crisis, the terms of withdrawal tend to be highly favorable for the armed institutions, whose institutional continuity has been preserved. However, the greater this protection, the larger their veto power during the transition period and their autonomy during the democratic consolidation period.

In this regard, it is important to stress the need for new conceptual analyses of the phenomenon of autonomous adjustment in Latin America.[37] Such analyses may provide elements for better understanding of the new state forms that are being developed in the region, where the armed forces have an active role. This knowledge would prepare civilians to deal successfully with the task of defining key issues regarding the design of policies of contention—and eventually reduction—of military autonomy.

Civilian Control

As noted before, civilian control over the armed forces should be substantive, rather than formal. Though not exclusively, civilian control capabilities are of a conceptual nature; they have to do with the definition of guidelines and institutional goals[38]—in other words, with the restoration of the professional dimension of the military function.[39] Once the necessary conditions for a new armed forces–society equilibrium and new organic relations between the military institutions and the state have been developed, it becomes necessary to identify the sufficient conditions—the contents, the flesh—of the principle of civil leadership over the armed forces.

The armed forces are an integral part of the defense apparatus; they manage the military deterrent component, whereas the government remains in control of other aspects, such as foreign relations. Thus, the possibility of civilian control over the armed forces to a large extent depends on state and government ability to define the wide variety of subjects connected with national defense in a consistent manner. Consistency exists—as witnessed by civil- and/or military-launched state and government policies—when there is an ability to adopt the programs and measures that will be referred to here. Failure or loss of civil initiative in such spheres results in loss of control over the armed forces. The armed forces need to perceive that clear-cut policies are being implemented and, also, that a lack of civilian control over their processes would represent a big threat for the army—a reality the armed institutions do not clearly recognize. The perception of safety or peril for their institutional position is a very important factor in the study of these organizations.

Gov't must define nat'l defense

why??

Civil control over the armed forces is contingent on the civilians' being aware of all of the relevant (political, economic, technological, and social) variables in the domestic and international realms. To this effect, a governmental, noncorporatized style has to be in place, so as to permit the government to tackle the issues of the state as a whole in pursuance of the interests of the community.[40] This global approach is crucial for the armed forces to "position" themselves as an institution. Each society must face the main military national defense issues and must use a national, democratic approach to solve them.

Professionalization

The fundamental requisite for redefining the role of the armed forces is to professionalize their institution. Contrary to past decades' military-technological innovations and doctrines, those of the present are highly dynamic. The contents of the profession change every year, along with progress in world military knowledge and practice. This generates demands for modernization, which, in turn, changes according to research and development advances and domestic or foreign weapons availability. All of these changes affect the military doctrines on war, its causes, and its linkages with politics and the society.

The new frontier of technological development has already been drawn. Latin America has to assume the approach of the third industrial revolution.[41] These new challenges cannot be faced, however, with the limited resources of individual countries. Regional cooperation and integration are the new concepts that have started to be analyzed. From the military point of view, the progress demands preparation for a new age. For the Latin American armed forces, the only choice is to reinsert themselves, on a cooperative basis, in the regional context and launch a joint research and development effort whereby industrial and/or commercial projects can be put into place. To attain this goal, the institution's energies cannot be wasted in governmental-political projects. Professional commitment is the only chance of "formal" survival after political interregnums.

Regional integration, national coordination, and a new civil–military relationship are the terms of future regional space—as well as naval and land—sovereignty.

New Concepts

To rely on old-fashioned concepts in the attempt to assume new strategic roles in a world with changed dimensions would be nonsense. It is easier to understand the new approach to strategic-military affairs by comparing the various policies emerging from the reality and the needs of the national defense phenomenon.

The traditional approach to internal security, territorial defense, hemispheric security, and conflict between the superpowers has led to accelerated militarization. This trend has been strengthened by a context of short cycles of relative autonomy in the military sphere. Hence, new definitions of those dimensions should reduce and reverse the process of militarization and create self-centered responses that prevent the reappearance of militarization at other levels.

To proceed from the traditional to a modern approach, the strategic target, as well as the means to attain it, would have to be redefined in light of the new international realities. Modern concepts should be developed other than internal repression, intrastate conflict, military balance, and thoughtless alignment on the Western world defense side.

Both civil and military regional leading elites have remained committed to the traditional definitions of the various security and national-regional defense dimensions, despite the change in the strategic context. Such concepts prevent the emergence of a new, self-centered, nonheteronomous definition of national defense. The current national strategic interests are much broader than the military interests. The military dimension itself should not be specific, unless it is conceived among the national defense interests, which in this context have a continental scope. The traditional oligarchic approach of territorial and hemispheric defense being irremediably confined to the territorial perimeter—one that gives priority to the armed forces' police responsibilities—has been detrimental to the performance of military functions and to democracy[42], and has hampered the establishment of a common basis for regional military relations. At present, in order to identify a modern strategic role for the armed forces, the police function has to be revamped and limited to that of curbing the types of behavior that deserve penalties under the law, rather than certain ideologies. And police, rather than the armed forces, have to be relied on for the performance of such functions.

Similarly, regarding intrastate defense, higher, regional levels of military cooperation should be reached, so as to identify common regional strategic interests that are consistent with today's national interests. In the realm of global security, the target should, for the most part, be one of neutrality and self-exclusion from the global conflict, together with voluntary defense of regional interests. Rather than defining itself according to extracontinental interests, Latin America should strive to develop a positive strategic role for itself. Not alien interests but its own interests should be the fundamentals of such a definition. In this context, military cooperation will be instrumental in the protection of the region's common interests.

A new, endogenously created regional security system—aimed at regional cooperation and the nurturing of long-run common interests in the field of defense, rather than assumption of an outstanding role in strategic matters—has become a must in the present circumstances.

The ideological and financial weight of the traditional approach prevents the emergence of national defense formulas other than regional military balance—which, in turn, starts new poverty cycles, followed by heavier repression responsibilities for the armed forces and additional, more acute regional military balance needs. However, the region has become militarily more vulnerable, to the extent that conflicts centered in other areas tend to add the land, sea, and space of Latin America to their original battlefield. In the present circumstances—with armed forces committed to police tasks—little, if anything, can be done to prevent this new form of subordination and submission. To reduce military and economic weakness and to control new poverty cycles, new forms of military cooperation have to evolve in the field of regional security. A new definition of security system defense policies would streamline defense policies and give priority to resource allotment and military spending control, which so far have been relatively incoherent and disorderly.[43]

To settle the controversy regarding Latin America's strategic role, the approach has to switch from privileging geographic aspects to emphasizing conditions that grant Latin America the role of a protagonist, rather than a mere territory, in strategic matters. This new approach would not be necessarily or exclusively referred to close protection of a territory. The nation-state protagonist would thus abandon its territorial approach and adopt the modern one, which takes into account other spheres, such as communications, trade, energy, and finance.

No individual Latin American country is in a position to attain new, self-centered strategic targets, such as hinterland, space, and maritime control. This creates a strong need for integration and cooperation as a means of national sovereignty defense. The state's sovereign power is no longer projected only on a territorial space, as new strategic dimensions have been opened that require new responses. Because this scope of sovereignty necessitates regional cooperation—as a requirement for real autonomy and sovereignty—military ooperation is now the most modern and least costly form of national sovereignty protection.

Military-Industrial Integration

Under long-run developmental policies, new regional military capabilities should be established in order to overcome the area's economic and military weaknesses. Modernization would be ancillary to regional security, but not as in the past, when security and the military were diverted from their military functions in order to attain the targets of the development doctrine through labor training or tool production. Overall, these policies produced military "invasion" of all state sectors. Under a new security approach, each Latin American state should be able to fill and occupy a new, independent, nonhegemonic place in the modern world by integrating the armed forces with other institutions and structures and preventing them from becoming the state coordination and consistency axis.

The new strategic issues are a natural outcome of a different perception of the regional interests. Conceivable goals would be setting up a Latin American space agency; or developing a joint nuclear program with a regional program safeguard system of its own; or integrating regional military industries[44] that are able to make use of the existing resources in the framework of civil development.

Hemispheric Relations

The absence of a self-centered, globally designed and managed Latin American system results from a big void in the civilians' strategic concepts. Such voids are always filled by the armed forces as subsidiary participants. They often do this in an inadequate manner.

The new regional defense system must be seen as the beginning of a process whereby higher peace levels would gradually be reached. Through diminishing internal tensions, mutual confidence-inspiring actions, partial military integration, and reduced arm imports and manufacturing, integration and disarmament projects of a larger scope would be within easier reach.

The diversity of conflict formation structures in the region accounts for the difficulties of integrating them all in a single security system and helps us understand the individualistic, specific position of each Latin American country in the global military field.[45] However, within the issue of regional defense systems, we have identified the issues around which new hemispheric military cooperation forms could be developed. Such regional defense systems should protect the hemispheric collective defense interests through a revision of military relations with the United States and a new design for hemispheric defense that is separated from global confrontation. Because world peace depends on regional defense systems,[46] the need for a U.S. presence in them must be recognized. Moreover, U.S. participation can be turned into an asset and, therefore, into a contribution to global peace.

The United States should abandon the idea of using military means to solve problems such as narcotics trafficking or terrorism. Similarly, the use of techniques for low-intensity conflicts[47] or covert operations should be replaced by economic and social policies aimed at the roots of the social problems from which regional armed tensions, narcotics trafficking, and terrorism stem. The effects of these problems should be controlled by police actions, rather than by military actions, which tend to reproduce the phenomena on a larger scale, rather than checking them. This type of confusion erodes inter-American military relations; confusion is sown at various levels, and the perspective of establishing a common security system of some type is impaired. The military linkages should be democratized through renouncement of the use of force as a means for solving internal conflicts.

This set of policies could turn Latin America into a buffer zone in respect to global conflict. In a way, a special "power void" would be gradually created. However, this void, far from being attractive to the USSR, could generate centrifugal forces, provided that the major external participants remain outside its boundaries. As "one's intrusion attracts that of one's rivals,"[48] the military neutralization of the region and its transformation into a buffer zone would activate the centrifugal forces needed in the area.

In sum, an emphasis on military professionalization; development of new concepts on which a new, modern approach to national defense can be based; integration of the fundamental productive functions of the Latin American armed forces; and a new definition of their professional links with the United States constitute a set of components that could create the sufficient conditions for the restoration of civil–military balance in a democratic framework.

Conclusions

A new formula for civil–military relations in Latin America is a crucial issue in an agenda for democracy. Unless such new links between civilians and the military are established, the viability of the regional democracies would be just another utopian idea in a continent where such ideas are the visible face of a deep inability to articulate interests, negotiations, compromise, and consensus.[49]

To a large extent, these new civil–military relations would depend on the capability of the civil society to develop a theoretical framework consistent with the new realities. It should identify the necessary conditions of restored balance: democratic civilian unity, embracing even those elites that originally supported the military government; isolation of the antiestablishment forces that legitimate the performance of internal security functions; effective mass support within the institutional boundaries that does not engender new crisis; restoration of institutional balance by emphasizing the professional unity of the armed forces; abandonment by the military of governmental and internal security tasks; moral recovery of the armed forces, including a clear perception of the identity between constitutionalism and democracy; and a new civil-political culture.

The possibility of restoring civil–military equilibrium also depends on a number of sufficient conditions: a review of the defense institution organization systems and their organic links with the rest of the state and the society, particularly in the nonmilitary spheres; enhanced organic coherence in the state, which must become a "formal" entity, rather than an anarchic body; definition of the state's subsidiary functions; and civil-political agreement so that this new relationship with the armed forces will be feasible. Consequently, civilian control over the armed forces would be assured through the development of new concepts that can be the basis for a new, modern approach to national defense: professionalization, with strong technological contents; integration of the war materiel productive functions of the Latin American armed forces; and a new formula for the military's professional links with the United States.

Finally, it should be pointed out that the issues of defense and the armed forces have traditionally been dealt with by party and/or sectoral approaches. Each group or party has designed defense policies based on its own political interests. If an effective redefinition of civil–military relations and the capabilities for defense analysis and planning is to be put into place, the defense issues have to be approached from a multiparty, pluralistic perspective. In other words, a national approach is required to tackle the issues of the military reform agenda.

Notes

1. In this regard, see Andrés Fontana, "Notas Sobre la Consolidación Democrática y el Control Civil de las Fuerzas Armadas en Argentina," Paper presented to Consejo para la Consolidación de la Democracia, Buenos Aires, May 13, 1986. See, also, "Will the Brass Return?" *Newsweek* (April 21, 1986).

2. See Riordan Roett, "Argentina's Army Isn't Corralled Yet: Weak Democratic Institutions Leave Civil Authority at Risk," *Los Angeles Times* (April 22, 1987).

3. See Mario Fernández, "La Intervención Militar en la Política en América Latina," *Revista de Estudios Políticos* (November–December 1985). For a theoretical step ahead in this regard, see Fernando Bustamante, "Los Paradigmas en el Etudio del Militarismo en América Latina," *Documento de Trabajo* (FLACSO) (October 1986). Specifically, the variable "civilian political elites' will" has scarcely been developed.

4. For a comparative analysis of the Latin American cases, see Alain Rouquié, "Demilitarization and the Institutionalization of Military-Dominated Politics in Latin America," in Guillermo O'Donnell, Philippe Schmitter, and Laurence Whitehead, eds., *Transition from Authoritarian Rule* (Baltimore: Johns Hopkins University Press, 1986). My analysis, however, will be confined to the South American cases.

5. For a discussion of some social factors, see Ulf Sundhausen, "Military Withdrawal from Government Responsibility," *Armed Forces and Society* (Summer 1984).

6. Alain Rouquié, *El Estado Militar en América Latina* (Buenos Aires: Emecé, 1984), p. 250.

7. For a comparison of several Latin American cases, see Karen L. Remmer, "Redemocratization and the Impact of Authoritarian Rule in Latin America," *Comparative Politics*, 17 no. 3. (April 1985): 253–275.

8. The authoritarian regime thoroughly modified the political divisions, the party organization, the clientele networks, and the electoral loyalties. Ibid., p. 270.

9. Rouquié, "Demilitarization and the Institutionalization of military-Dominated Politics in Latin America."

10. "The July 19 [1977] strike was the first national strike in this century. It showed the extreme isolation of the Morales Bermúdez rule." Henry Pease, "Avances y Retrocesos de la Democratización en Perú," in Augusto Varas, ed., *Transición a la Democracia*: America Latina y Chile (Airavillo, Chile: ACHIP, 1984), p. 60.

11. See Riordan Roett, "The Transition to Democratic Government in Brazil," *World Politics* (January 1986).

12. See Andrés Fontana, "Armed Forces and Neoconservative Ideology: State-Shrinking in Argentina (1976–1981)," Paper presented at the research conference "State Shrinking: A Comparative Inquire into Privatization," University of Texas at Austin, March 1–3, 1984. See, also, Guido Di Tella, "Fuerzas Armadas y democratización en Argentina," in Varas, *Transición a la Democracia*, p. 106.

13. See Saturnino Braga, "La Oposición y la Apertura Política en Brasil," in Varas, *Transición a la Democracia*, p. 99.

14. See Alfred Stepan, *Rethinking Military Politics: Brazil and the Southern Cone* (Princeton, NJ: Princeton University Press, 1988); see, also, William A. Bacchus, "Development Under Military Rule: Factionalism in Brazil," *Armed Forces and Society* (Spring 1986).

15. See Roett, "The Transition to Democratic Government in Brazil."

16. See Pease, "Avances y Retrocesos," pp. 58–59; and the chapters by Peter Cleaves and Henry Pease and those by Cynthia McClintock and Luis Pásara, in Cynthia McClintock and Abraham Lowenthal, eds., *The Peruvian Experiment Reconsidered* (Princeton, N.J.: Princeton University Press, 1983).

17. Report of the Commission Investigating the Crimes of the Argentinian Military Junta, *Nunca Más* (Buenos Aires: Endeba, 1984).

18. See Anita J. Isaacs, "From Military to Civilian Rule: Ecuador, 1972–1979," Ph.D. dissertation, University of Oxford, St. Anthony's College, 1985, p. 364.

19. For an analysis of the cases of Argentina and Brazil in this regard, see Peter Calvert, "Demilitarization in Latin America," *Third World Quarterly* 7, no. 1 (January 1985): 31–43.

20. See Rouquié, *El Estado Militar en América Latina*, p. 337.

21. See Juan Rial, "Los Militares en Cuanto 'Partido Político Sustituto' Frente a la Redemocratización," in Augusto Varas, coordinator, *La Autonomía Militar en América Latina* (Caracas: CLADDE, Nueva Sociedad, 1988).

22. See Andrés Fontana, "Fuerzas Armadas, Partidos Políticos y Transición a la Democracia en la Argentina," in Varas, *Transición a la Democracia*, p. 117.

23. For a military view of the Argentine campaign in the Malvinas, see "Conflicto Malvinas: Informe Oficial del Ejército Argentino," *Armas y Geoestrategia* (December 1983).

24. In this regard, see Abraham Lowenthal, "Ejércitos y Política en América Latina," *Estudios Internacionales*, (July–September 1976): 62. According to Alexandre de S.C. Barros and Edmundo Campos Coelho, the lack of formal succession criteria becomes a genuine threat for the armed forces' discipline, hierarchy, and internal cohesion, as it often leads to confrontations among different military factions. "Military Intervention in South America," *International Political Science Review* 3 (1981): 346.

25. In Chile, there is a high level of intramilitary control. See Genaro Arrigada, *La Política Militar de Pinochet*. (Santiago: ICHEH, 1986).

26. Regarding the Peruvian case, see Liisa North, "Perspectives on Development Policy and Mass Participation in the Peruvian Armed Forces," Working Paper No. 22 (Washington, D.C.: Wilson Center, Latin American Program 1978).

27. "Silence has been and will be the main accomplice of the abuse and outrages by the dictatorial regimes." Juan Goytisolo, *En los Reinos de Taifa*. (Barcelona: Seix Barral, 1986), p. 45.

28. Rouquié, *El Estado Militar en América Latina*, p. 417.

29. For a detailed description of the Latin American cases, see Varas, *La Autonomía Militar en América Latina*.

30. See Samuel Huntington, "Tocqueville's Armies and Ours," Remarks de-

livered to the seminar "Democracy in America Today: A Tocquevillian Perspective," John M. Olin Center for Inquiry into the Theory and Practice of Democracy, University of Chicago, February 15, 1984.

31. In this regard, see Norbert Lechner et al., *Estado y Política en América Latina* (Mexico: Siglo XXI, 1981).

32. See Rouquié, *El Estado Militar en América Latina.*

33. Certainly, these this new forms of autonomous adjustment are, to a very large extent, influenced by the terms of the military withdrawal from government. "The rôle of the terms of the post-militaristic democratization in the democratic development of the Andean South American countries." *Documento de Trabajo,* (FLACSO) (January 1987).

34. In this connection, see Augusto Varas, "Democratización y Reforma Militar en Argentina," *Documento de Trabajo* (FLACSO) (1985). See, also, Carlos Moneta, "Las Fuerzas Armadas y el Conflicto de las Islas Malvinas: Su Importancia en la Política Argentina y en el Marco Regional," *Foro Internacional* (January–March, 1983).

35. Regarding the Brazilian case, see Joao Quartim de Moraes et al., *A Tutela Militar.* (São Paulo: Vértice, 1987); and Eliezzer Rizzo de Oliveira, *Militares: Pensamiento e Acao Politica* (Campinas, Brazil: Papirus, 1987).

36. Formal control by civilians must be distinguished from real autonomy. For a comparative discussion of the constitutional mechanisms for civilian control, see Felipe Agüero, "The Military in the Constitutions of the Southern Cone Countries, Brazil and Spain," in *El Papel de los Partidos Políticos en el Retorno a la Democracia en el Cono Sur* (Washington, D.C.: Wilson Center, n.d.).

37. For a research agenda, see J. Samuel Fitch, "Armies and Politics in Latin America: 1975–1985," in Abraham Lowenthal and J. Samuel Fitch, eds. *Armies and Politics in Latin America* (New York: Holmes and Meier, 1986).

38. Only a few studies conclude with proposals for effective civil control over the armed forces. An outstanding example is Alfred Stepan, *Os Militares: Da Abertura a Nova Republica* (Rio de Janeiro: Paz e Terra, 1986).

39. Such is the approach in General Fred Woerner, "Shield of Democracy in Latin America," *Defense* (November–December 1987); and in J. Samuel Fitch, "The Armed Forces and Democracy in Latin America," Paper prepared for the Inter-American Dialogue, Lima, August 16–17, 1987.

40. At this stage, I would simply like to mention the abundant literature on corporativism in Latin America and its effects. For a comparative analysis, see Fernando Bustamante, "Some Conclusions and Hypotheses on the Issue of Civil Control over the Armed Forces and Democratic Consolidation in the Andean Countries," *Documento de Trabajo* (FLACSO) (April 1987).

41. In this respect, see Carlos Ominami, *La Tercera Revolución Industrial: Impactos Internacionales del Actual Viraje Tecnológico* (Buenos Aires: GEL, 1987).

42. For a similar approach, see Elliot Abrams, Speech at the Inter-American Defense College," Santiago, August 13, 1986.

43. In this regard, see Augusto Varas, "Límites a las Opciones de Desarrollo: Las Políticas de Defensa Nacional," in Enzo Faletto et al., *Repensar el Futuro* (Caracas: Nueva Sociedad, 1986).

44. On the benefits of an integrated arms industry, see Edward A. Kolodziej, *Making and Marketing Arms: The French Experience and Its Implications for the International System* (Princeton, N.J.: Princeton University Press, 1987).

45. By *security system*, I mean a set of express or implicit norms, principles, rules and decision-making procedures around which the participants' expectations converge in a certain area of international relations. *Principles* are beliefs about facts, causes, and rectitude. *Norms* are behavioral measures defined in terms of rights and obligations. *Rules* are action-oriented specific prescriptions or proscriptions. *Decision-making procedures* are prevailing practices for making collective options. See Robert 0. Keohane, *After Hegemony: Cooperation and Discord in World Political Economy* (Princeton, N.J.: Princeton University Press, 1984), p. 57.

46. See United Nations, "Report of the Independent Commission on Disarmament and Security," A/CN.10/38 (New York: United Nations, 1983).

47. See Lilia Bermüdez, *Guerra de Baja Intensidad*, (Mexico: Siglo XXI, 1987).

48. Stanley Hoffman, *Dead Ends*. (Cambridge, Mass.: Ballinger 1983), p. 134.

49. In this context, ideologies and ideologisms could be understood as aborted pragmatism.

14
Civil–Military Relations in Mexico

Adolfo Aguilar Zinser

Most analysts of the Mexican reality maintain that in Mexico, the army stays outside the political sphere. As a result, studies generally assume that it is not in the army barracks that the keys to decipher the riddles of Mexican politics are to be found. Furthermore, those who have attempted to study the armed forces have had to overcome major difficulties in gathering information as well as the resistance of the military, which tries to avoid being scrutinized.

The authoritarian nature of the political system in Mexico is not based on the army's size or its tendency to monitor public affairs. Mexican authoritarianism is channeled through a large array of mechanisms and cooptation and control institutions managed by civilians who, only in extremely serious circumstances, resort to repression or use of force. As a means of muffling or neutralizing protest or dissent, a much larger role is played at the local level by the representatives of the federal or state authorities—including those of the Partido Revolucionario Institutional (PRI)—rather than by the local military and detachment.

During the 1970s, some Mexican and most American analysts began to examine the military issue. Either they foresaw that the military would eventually burst into the political arena in a violent manner or they simply wished to explain, for academic reasons, why the generals have kept their promise not to mix in politics.

Others, however, such as David F. Ronfeldt, uphold the thesis that the processes of growth, professionalization, and modernization of the Mexican armed forces do not, by themselves, tend to promote a significant change in what Ronfeldt calls the "residual" role of the armed forces.[1] According to this view (one that I share), a military coup or simply an expanded role of the military in the governmental decision-making process—if it takes place at all—would not originate in the army itself. In other words, the armed forces would not take the initiative; if they ever do participate in such a process, it would be as associates of civilian sectors that are strong and persuasive enough to convince certain members of the military of the adequacy and timeliness of their assumption of governmental functions.

Although no analysts foresee a military government in Mexico in the near future, some do mention the growing influence and broadening public role of the army. According to this view, new domestic and external circumstances will force the army to perform a more active role in Mexico's public life. A process of "moderate militarization" in certain political areas would bring forth a gradual surge of military activism. This would change the terms of civil–military relations in Mexico.[2]

This chapter takes issue with the view that the Mexican armed forces are demanding increased autonomy. It assumes that the very essence of the relationship between the government's civil and military sectors is based on the principle that the armed forces must be deprived of political weight. To the extent that there is a change in the historic circumstances that explain this relationship, the role of the armed forces may broaden, but this will not happen because the military commanders conclude that the civilians have become unable to fulfill certain tasks or because the military is eager to manage any public affairs that were outside its jurisdiction but, rather, because the civilians themselves would ask the armed forces to become more active players. In this scenario, the military could respond in its own, autonomous way to any clashes or frictions with the civilians. This chapter will review the historical and ideological roots of the civil–military relationship in Mexico and the doctrine of national security. It will also focus on the circumstances behind the view—to me, erroneous—that the Mexican armed forces are prepared to enter more directly into the political arena.

The Historical and Ideological Background of the Pattern of Civil–Military Relations in Mexico

It is not mere coincidence that the Mexican armed forces have been assigned a modest political role from the presidential term of General Lazaro Cardenas (1935–40) to the present. Today's army evolved from an alliance of military chiefs and caudillos in the nation in the context of the revolutionary, political, and social struggle. Since the outburst of the rebellion against the dictatorship of Porfirio Díaz in 1910, armed groups have organized spontaneously to fight for various political and social goals. Thus, the peasant columns of Emiliano Zapata in the south and Francisco Villa in the north were formed, basically to demand land distribution. On the other hand, the constitutionalist army of Venustiano Carranza—the core of today's military structure—was organized to defeat those who formed the stronghold of the old Porfirist structures, who strove to reach power, and also to give the Revolution a centralized command and to neutralize Villa, Zapata, and the regional chieftains and caudillos who challenged the supreme authority of the central government.

During the difficult period of postrevolutionary stabilization and political institutionalization, the army and its commanders played a key role in the struggle for power. For some time, the government's authority was challenged or enhanced through force, rather than through political or ideological mobilization. In the 1920s, arms were also the tools used by the caudillos to consolidate their leadership, thus laying the foundation for today's presidential institution. Between 1920 and 1935, once widespread civil war was over, power was achieved or maintained through a series of rebellions and uprisings organized within the army. In the early 1920s, after the murder of the constitutionalist Venustiano Carranza, General Alvaro Obregon emerged as the leader of the revolution. In 1924, Obregon transferred the presidency to his political ally, General Plutarco Elias Calles. However, in 1927—defying the principles of the Revolution—Obregon had himself reelected for a second term. Shortly before assuming power, he was assassinated, unleashing pent-up political reactions.

The most important event in this context was the establishment, in 1929, of the Partido Nacional Revolucionario, which later, in 1946, was rechristened Partido Revolucionario Institucional (PRI). At the time the PRI was born, most revolutionary caudillos had already been eliminated as a result of military uprisings or subsequent purges within the army. Thus, Calles became the new, unchallenged caudillo and could devote his energies to consolidating the civil institutions and creating political coalitions and negotiation mechanisms. Calles was, to a certain extent, a dam. On the one hand, he was a military leader; on the other hand, he was a politician who ruled and commanded as a party leader, rather than as the head of the army or the government.

General Lazaro Cardenas, who consummated the process of demilitarization of political life and took definitive steps toward government institutionalization, reached power in 1935, still under the patronage of Calles, "the supreme authority." Soon he became estranged from the caudillo and expelled him from the country, an event that concentrated power in the civil jurisdiction. The presidency of the Republic was thus consolidated not only as the formal, legal core of all government institutions—a role explicitly conferred upon it by the 1910 constitution—but also as the most prestigious and legitimate level of public power. Indeed, through a series of reforms and social transformations, President Cardenas made the president the guarantor of the transformation programs of the Revolution, such as agrarian reform and oil nationalization. Thus, the presidential institutions came to be regarded as the cornerstone of national unity and sovereignty.

"Demilitarizing" political life in Mexico was a long process that, to some extent, was initiated during the first years of the revolution and

ended, symbolically, in 1946, when Miguel Aleman Valdez, a law graduate, took power. As early as 1916, after Francisco Villa and Emiliano
Zapata were defeated, the Carranza administration had started a process
of reduction of the size of the army. With Obregon, then the war minister, the number of officers shrank from 50,000 to 20,000 and the number
of troops from 200,000 to 150,000. In addition, Obregon reorganized
military training, reopened the military academy and launched a process
of professionalization of the military cadres through the educational process. In 1921, the officer corps was reduced again to 14,000 and the
troops to 70,000. In the early 1920s alone, military spending in terms of
total government spending diminished from 61 percent (1921) to 35 percent (1923). This trend was made more apparent by General Joaquin
Amaro, General Calles's war minister, who reduced the size of the army
and simultaneously tried to professionalize it, while making sure that
military expenses absorbed a gradually smaller proportion of the resources
available for government spending. From 1932, when Cardenas succeeded
General Amaro as war minister, to the end of the decade, when Cardenas
had become the president, the process of professionalization and reduction
of army size accelerated.

In 1940, a rapid process of national growth and modernization was
initiated. The steady growth of the gross national product, averaging over
6 percent a year for more than three decades, allowed an increase in
social spending and enhanced expectations for progress. Civil–military
relations stabilized, and military capabilities lost importance as an instrument for political control and public authority.

The status of the military in Mexico's political context is still strongly
determined by a number of basic rules of respect for civil power: the
principles that arms are not a suitable instrument to further the goals of
the Revolution and that the organization and maintenance of power are
not contingent on the support of the armed forces.[3]

The process of "politicization" of the Mexican armed forces, then,
implies not their involvement, as such, in government decision making
but, rather, their members' acceptance of the policy that as a requirement
for participating in politics as individuals, they have to formally cease to
perform military functions and abide by the rules of the political game.
Thus, the consolidation of the regime entailed not the growth of its armed
institutions but the development of centralized, strong political institutions
that were endowed with a large amount of powers and, at the same time,
were flexible, prestigious, and legitimate.

Mexico's armed forces maintain that the laws approved and enforced
by the civil power are the source of authority. Contrary to other Latin
American armies, they affirm that the government, to a much larger extent than the private sector, must assume social responsibilities for generating wealth, managing and developing natural resources, and distributing

income fairly. As a rule, the armed forces do not commit themselves, as an institution, to protecting private wealth; however, they do give priority to the task of protecting the nation's economic centers and natural resources. In this respect, they are "civilist" and "statist." Also, in contrast to other Latin American armed forces, which embrace the ideas of reform and social justice only in the context of counterinsurgency strategies, the Mexican armed forces include these very ideas in their security strategy—not as a response to a given subversion scenario but as a type of political commitment on which the overall legitimacy of the government is based.[4]

At all military levels, the president of the Republic is the top authority of the armed forces. As defined in the constitution, he is the "supreme commander" or, as some military call him, the "commander by 'autonomasia'" (per se). That the armed forces are loyal to the president reflects the legal rule, the practice, and the ideological principle that consolidates the respect of the military for the civil government. Subordination to the civil authorities by the military means that the military must abide by the laws, and the highest legal principle is the authority of the president.

The president, with the advice of the defense secretary, is responsible for all appointments and promotions and for the assignment of tasks and functions to the armed forces. The presidential general staff and the presidential guards are commanded by and serve directly the president of the Republic; therefore, service in these units is regarded as the most honorific entry in one's military record.

Unlike in many Latin American countries, where the armed forces do not maintain such an intimate relationship with the president, in Mexico the president is constantly surrounded by the military, which not only protects his security but also accompanies him at all times, even for reasons of protocol. The general staff is responsible for the executive's communication with all places in the national territory and for making available to it the technical and human resources it needs to exercise its authority. For a country that limits the military's functions to such a large extent, it becomes paradoxical, but very revealing, that it is the president's general staff, rather than a civil secretary, that organizes the logistical support for the president.

The Perception of the United States as the Historical and Geopolitical Threat to the Nation's Sovereignty

Mexico's concept of defense includes a very precise identification of its external enemies and how to check them. According to the historiographic school that prevails in Mexico, the United States is the main foreign threat to the national sovereignty of Mexico.[5]

[handwritten margin note: Violence in northern Mexico made U.S. worried about threat to its southern border — U.S. put troops on border]

During the decade of the Revolution (1910–20), U.S. policy for Mexico assumed military undertones to a degree that it had not shown since the last century's confrontation. On the one hand, social unrest and violence in the northern part of Mexico made America uneasy about the threat at its southern border. This led the United States to commission troops to that area immediately. On the other hand, Washington repeatedly attempted to use the argument of force in Mexico to influence the behavior of the revolutionaries.[6]

Relations between the two neighbors so deteriorated that on the eve of World War I, Germany courted Mexico in order to open the United States to a hostile front at its southern border and deprive it of strategic commodities. In February 1917, British spies intercepted the now-famous Zimmermann telegram, whereby the German chancellor promised President Venustiano Carranza German aid to recover the territories Mexico had lost in 1848—in exchange for support. This event contributed to the U.S. decision to declare war on Germany.

World War II altered the picture significantly and promoted a climate of understanding that was reflected—for the first and only time in history—in a military pact whereby Mexico declared war on the Axis powers and committed itself to provide the United States with strategic commodities for the Allied military effort. Indeed, Mexico and Brazil were the only Latin American countries to commission troops to fight on the Allies' side. In February 1942, the Joint U.S.–Mexico Defense Committee was formally created. The Joint Defense Committee developed the so-called Integral Defense Plan, whereby the activities of the U.S. Fourth Army were coordinated with those of the Mexican Pacific Command. This committee managed the lend-lease program with Mexico, under which the United States granted its neighbor $40 million in resources to modernize its army. One of the major legacies of this circumstantial but very close understanding between the two countries was the establishment of the Mexican air base. A special Mexican air squadron was also set up to fight on the U.S. side in the Pacific war front.

During the 1950s, the cold war reopened the gap between Mexican and American foreign policies and the two countries' national security policies. The military alliance Mexico had signed with its northern neighbor vanished. In international forums, Mexico adopted policies quite distant from those of Washington, as far as the U.S. vision of regional security is concerned. American intervention in Guatemala in 1954 and the U.S.-decreed hemispheric quarantine of Cuba in 1962—two moves Mexico condemned—widened the abyss between Mexico's concept of sovereignty, defense and the U.S. national security concept. By rejecting the guidelines and definitions developed by the United States in the context of the East–West confrontation and by stressing the principle of noninterven-

[handwritten note at bottom: Rejected U.S. guidlines concerning East-West conflict.]

tion and self-determination, Mexico made it clear that it was determined not to be considered a military or political ally of the United States.

Mexico's strategic geometry reads that the enemies of the United States are not enemies of Mexico, but under no circumstances are they Mexico's allies or supporters of Mexico's sovereignty in case of U.S. intervention. Consequently, Mexico's armed forces do not consider themselves a part of the U.S.-developed strategic framework of contention of communism in the Hemisphere, nor do they accept the "internal enemy" scenario other Latin American armies have adopted to justify their taking over power with U.S. support.[7]

Historical identification of the United States as the bully—the abusive neighbor whose power, size, and proximity warrant Mexico's continuous watch—has helped Mexico define a national defense of its own wherein no room is left for a military dimension. The military forces of the two countries are so disproportionate—the United States being the biggest military power in the world—that Mexico's national sovereignty cannot be protected by weapons. In the extreme case of a military invasion by the United States, the military contingency plans Mexico could rely on are those of the civil defense forces. Mexico assumes that such an invasion could not be repelled by conventional military resources; the whole population would have to engage in active civil-resistance warfare.

Mexico's National Security Views

There is no such a thing as an explicit political-strategic national security concept in Mexico. However, the state's approach regarding its own protection is, for practical purposes, a doctrine of national security based on a specific interpretation of history, a deep-rooted political culture, and a very strong national identity. The state's foreign policies derive from the international principles of self-determination and nonintervention that are the axis and the compass for Mexico's external profile and the framework of all international pacts the country has ratified.

In the international sphere, Mexico has been very active in multilateral forums, but is has remained very mistrustful and cautious when arranging alliances. Projecting its relations with the United States has led Mexico to see the world as a hostile environment. Consequently, for a long time, the country's main concern has been not widening the scope of its foreign relations and substantially expanding its international presence but, rather, being on guard against alien interests and keeping foreigners out of its international affairs.

In the internal realm, however, Mexico's security policies stem not from the notion of vulnerability but from the belief that even without indiscriminate use of force, the state has access to the resources necessary to make its authority respected at all times and everywhere. It is legitimate enough to defend itself easily against its adversaries. From this feeling of confidence in its internal power stem a number of criteria whereby the civil authorities make distinctions between external threats to the nation's security and internal threats to public peace and the security of the state.

In both internal and external fields of national security, the role of the armed forces is limited and subordinate. In the external sphere, as Mexico does not project deterrent forces abroad and does not recognize a need for responding to any military enemies, the task of the military is limited to coast protection, particularly with regard to the economic resources of the 200-mile-wide so-called territorial sea. Traditionally, the armed forces have not performed any substantial role in monitoring the land borders. Although the border with the United States has always been conceived as an area of foreign penetration, the peril is seen as consisting not of the extreme event of an armed invasion but of the daily economic, political, and cultural influence of the United States through gradual erosion of economic sovereignty and national identity at the border communities. In the south, Guatemala is also seen as a relatively unfriendly neighbor with which there have been some clashes, including a few violent ones. Given the Guatemalans' very strong aversion toward Mexico, and the fact that the army holds a prominent place in the life of Guatemala, Mexico's traditional attitude has been to shun conflict and keep the army at a certain distance from the southern frontier, so as not to give Guatemala a pretext for provocations or militaristic outbursts.

In the domestic sphere, civil institutions are responsible for keeping peace and the security of the state. The army has been assigned ancillary duties in this field—physical protection of strategic value for the operation of the economic and social life, such as hydroelectric complexes, oil fields and petrochemical plants, and ports and airports. The armed forces also manage, on a continuous basis, civic action campaigns (health care, literacy programs, and road-building in isolated communities). They also help enforce certain laws, such as the required registration of and permission to possess firearms and the fight against narcotics production and trafficking. On a limited basis, they also make themselves available to the electoral authorities when there is a need for riot control, and they support the electoral process by monitoring poll stations and the premises where ballots are kept. The army participates in rescue efforts during natural disasters and, at the request of civil authorities and with the consent of the president, helps restore order in cases of social turmoil.

To be in a position to perform their wide range of functions, the armed forces are spread throughout Mexico, distributed in so-called military and naval regions, zones, and sectors. This entails the existence of military barracks in all state capitals, in addition to many small detachments in close contact with the rural civil communities. As a rule, the relations between the populace and the troops are courteous and cordial, although in some cases, clashes occur when the military forces in certain towns participate in police operations or the military personnel abuse their relationship with the local people.[8]

The Armed Forces, the Crisis in Mexico, and Central American Conflict

In recent years, the Mexican armed forces have undergone visible changes that have been closely monitored by political analysts, particularly in the United States. The so-called process of modernization was started in the 1970s, during the administration of President Luis Echeverria.[9] Higher salaries and enhanced resources for technical and professional training of the armed forces reached a peak with the erection of a new, ample, and quite modern military academy. However, it was President José Lopez Portillo who accelerated this process. Since 1981, when Mexico's huge oil revenues permitted a military defense budget source of 54 percent relative to 1980, the ratio of military spending to the gross national product (typically 0.7 percent since 1968) climbed to 1.6 percent. This fresh flow of resources did not significantly increase the army's size; Mexico's armed forces (about 130,000 for a population of 80 million) remain comparatively small, particularly by other Latin American countries' standards.

Together with modernization, researchers' interest in the army was enhanced by the country's political turmoil since 1968 and, from the early 1980s, the serious economic crisis and the war in Central America. These factors are considered the reason for enhancing Mexico's military resources and for the political regime's perceived need to improve its defense and national security strategies to manage new internal and external perils. Based on these factors, many observers believe that the armed forces will soon assume a new, more active role in the life of the country.[10]

The most popular notions circulating in the past few years emphasize the government's added awareness of the threats of external subversion and internal political imbalances. By modernizing the armed forces, the authorities would be expressly recognizing that the economic crisis could spark violent social reactions and create the need for a wholesale use of military force to preserve order and support the institutions. The consolidation, in Nicaragua, of a revolutionary regime able to fully destroy the armed forces and the previous regime in 1979; the civil war in El Salvador, where resilient, bold guerrillas operate; and the armed struggle of

Guatemalan peasants and Indians at the border with Chiapas State turn Mexico into a more or less immediate target of Communist subversion.

The notion of a Central American "domino effect" affecting Mexico is based on the argument that in recent years, Mexico's southern border has become particularly vulnerable and attractive to the rebels. First, the huge social and political problems of the peasant and indigenous populations of the Mexican southeast, who have lost faith in the government, make them natural allies of the Central American forces supporting the guerrillas—so the argument goes. Second, the emigration of over 500,000 Central Americans to Mexico since 1979[11] has led many analysts to infer that the Mexican guerrillas already have bases of operations in Mexico and are able to infiltrate the country's social fabric and promote insurgence. From this, they erroneously conclude that the Mexican army has responded by adopting a counterinsurgency-oriented modernization plan, assuming power in the region adjacent to the southern border.[12]

Mexico's concern for security in the southeast[13] was not prompted either by the Sandinista takeover or the intensification of the conflict in El Salvador but by Guatemalan army raids into Mexican territory, designed to attack refugee camps and, at times, small Mexican communities that were aiding the refugees. The ultimate goal of these attacks was to intimidate Mexico into taking steps against the refugees, such as expelling or relocating them.

Regarding this border problem, the army acted under the law; it let the civil authorities manage the problem, using their own means. The military was well aware that a larger army presence at the border would make it necessary to repel the Guatemalan attacks and escalate the conflict with the neighbor's army. Besides, militarization of the border would strain the relations between the army and the Mexican communities in the area. This cautious attitude proved that the armed forces did not really want to take a political or military initiative at the southern border. Perhaps they did want to exert pressure on the civilians to reach an agreement with the Guatemalan army.

The animosity of Guatemala's military to Mexico is old and deep-rooted. In Mexico's modern history, only one conflict (with Guatemala) brought Mexico to the verge of war. This happened in 1958, when an attack on a Mexican fishing boat by Guatemalan forces led to the severance of diplomatic relations between the two countries, which prepared for war. The conflict, however, was resolved not by use of force but through international mediation.

After a long interval, the government finally decided, in 1984, to transfer the Guatemalan refugees to an area both far from the border and outside Chiapas. This rather unsuccessful and highly criticized operation (only 12,000 a total of 46,000 refugees have been relocated) was effected with direct participation of the Mexican navy, but it did not promote so-called border militarization. It is also widely suspected in Mexican governmental circles that the Guatemalan military could have become a component in a strategy devised by the United States to further objectives contrary to Mexican interests at the Southern border.[14]

Some Considerations on the Future of Civil–Military Relations in Mexico

Neither the thesis that military modernization indicates a more active political role by the armed forces nor the idea that the armed forces perceive counterinsurgency as defense priority can be proved through an analysis of the actual effects of the economic crisis on the government and Mexican society. Lower incomes, unemployment, reduced purchasing power, and the rest of the social effects of the crisis prevailing in the country since 1982 have not been a source of popular rebellion or international communist infiltration. Bureaucratic consensus has deteriorated, and the government structure itself has disintegrated, in part, through the disagreements between the government and the business sector and between the ruling party and its social allies (workers and peasants). There has also been a spontaneous, though not always very apparent, surge of demands for actual participation in political decision making from within the governmental bureaucracy, PRI dissident cadres, union leaders, students, intellectuals, and even businessmen and professionals.

   This sociopolitical struggle has not brought forth a more watchful and energetic attitude by the military, which has demanded a more active decision-making role. On the contrary, the army itself has become affected by internal debate among various ideological groups. However, the conflict of opinions within the officer corps does not revolve around the issue of whether to change substantially the role of the army as an institution that is loyal primarily to the civil authorities. If any such review ever takes hold, it will occur outside the military barracks. It will probably be civilians—both within and outside the government—some business circles, and the conservative middle-class sector that will encourage repressive and authoritarian steps to counter political phenomena that they might perceive as a threat to their interests and privileges.

   The nature of future civil–military relations, therefore, hinges on the military's remaining trustful of and loyal to the civil authorities it recognizes and on no serious frictions or clashes taking place between the two state sectors. In an environment of tension and mistrust, the military could be lured by civilians into meddling in politics. Such civilians will be listened to if the social tensions become serious enough and if a suffi-

[handwritten margin note at top: If a sufficiently large # of officers are prepared to end the traditional role of supporting the Pres. + the civil gov't he heads.]

ciently large number of officers are prepared to run the immense risk of putting an end to the traditional military support for the president and the civil government he heads.

Various factors could strain relations between the civil and military branches of the government. The following is an outline of those factors that, in recent years, have proved to feed such tensions: the struggle against narcotics trafficking, rescue operations in cases of natural calamities, and the participation of the armed forces in civilian elections.

Narcotics Trafficking

[handwritten margin note: Factors which could strain relations btwn Civil + Mili branches.]

During the past few years, the army has broadened its range of activities in the continuous campaign against narcotics trafficking. Presently, 25,000 members of the armed forces are performing activities concerning detection and eradication of crops and interception of drug shipments.[15] Since the first full-scale antidrug efforts during the 1960s, the civilian police—particularly the Federal Judicial Police under the Office of the Attorney General of the Republic—have been formally in charge of the investigations. The army is supposed to rely on information supplied by civilian units regarding its destruction of crops in remote areas. The use of military units in many other areas, however, has tended to become more frequent.

The growth of narcotics trafficking gangs and the availability of huge amounts of cash make the military units participating in the struggle against narcotraffic very vulnerable to bribery. Despite safeguards and continuous personnel rotation, there is a measure of corruption in the army. Corruption compounds civil–military tensions, for some units' efforts can be thwarted by other units' arrangements with the gangs. On the other hand, the military expects civil authorities to take all appropriate steps to defend the prestige of the armed institutions whenever they are accused of bribery, especially when rumors of high-ranking officers' connections with drug gangs are circulated abroad. Hence, the "moralization" drives launched by the civil government to fight corruption have to be managed in a particularly cautious manner with respect to army personnel.

The U.S. demand to participate in a very direct way in Mexico's campaigns against narcotics trafficking has become a source of dangerous civil–military tensions. With the United States requesting information of all types about the army's activities and Mexican cooperation in order to check directly whether the army has, in fact, fulfilled its tasks, the animosity and mistrust of the Mexican military toward the United States have grown, and tensions between Mexican civil and military authorities have

[handwritten margin notes: detection/ eradication of crops, interception; civilian Police formally in charge; issue of bribery; mex. mili distrust U.S. b/c of careful review of its activities]

surfaced. If the military feels that the government is not protecting it or the prestige of the army cadres and chiefs, clashes between the officer corps and the bureaucracy will tend to intensify and produce political effects. The more resources committed by the army, the more visible and risky its participation becomes and the more prone the military commanders will be to fight narcotics trafficking separately from the civilians and even to make the civilians implement the army's criteria and methods.

Participation in the struggle against narcotics trafficking has also put the military in closer touch with the civilian populations in the rural areas and semiurban communities where drugs are manufactured. In such locales, the gangs usually get strong popular support, and traffic eradication efforts require direct, violent, repressive confrontation with the peasants.

Emergency Rescue Operations

Emergency operations related to natural disasters have fallen under the sole jurisdiction of the army for many years, particularly in the rural areas. The emergency plan known as National Defense III (NDIII) provides for the military authorities to supervise the performance of all functions and to coordinate the use of all resources for the duration of the emergency, within an authoritative framework established by the president. In rural areas, the use of these exceptional powers is not politically relevant; in the towns, it is. For this reason, NDIII is generally implemented in the countryside, seldom in urban areas.

During the emergency created by the September 19, 1985, earthquake in the capital, the government made contradictory statements regarding the implementation of NDIII, the army became trapped by ambiguity and confusion, and its rescue activities were paralyzed—a fact that seriously deteriorated its public image. When the earthquake occurred and essentially devastated a downtown area within a circle of some thirty square kilometers, the army mobilized swiftly. During the first hours, the media were advised that the armed institutions were taking care of the aid activities, and so it seemed to be. However, several hours later, the authorities changed their minds and limited the jurisdiction of the army, which was already deploying its resources, to cordoning off wrecked buildings and surveillance of the affected areas. The government seemed afraid to look impotent and subordinate to the military. Under the circumstances, many people, who everywhere saw armed soldiers, rather than army physicians, engineers, and sappers, blamed the army for would-be incompetence, callousness, inefficiency, and disinterest in the face of the tragedy. These charges by the public aroused army resentment against the government, and these feelings are still remembered.[16]

Army Participation in Civilian Elections

Open participation of the army in the notorious local elections in the northern States in 1985 and 1986 led some analysts to contend that the Mexican army also intervenes in a very direct manner in electoral manipulations. And in 1986, Republican Senator Jesse Helms mentioned what he described as secret figures on the 1982 election results, coming, he said, from the presidential general staff. According to these figures, the gap between the votes cast for President Miguel de la Madrid and his rivals was not as large as officially contended. If Helms's documents are genuine, the army has its own vote-counting system; and—even more serious—someone in the president's military general staff itself is ready to disclose such secrets to individuals outside and even hostile to the government.[17]

The army has not always refrained from participating in electoral activities other than those assigned to it by the constitution—that is, monitoring poll stations and protecting poll boxes on election days. During the elections in northern Mexico between 1985 and 1987, it was apparent that the army was absolutely loyal to the regime it was supposed to serve; hence, it tended to help the PRI. It is generally recognized that the troops were sometimes used to fill up certain poll stations with ballots, where the authorities felt that a victory of the PRI was crucial and that was the only way of securing it. The army also intervened, generally in support of the PRI, when the electoral results aroused suspicion.

It has also become customary, during the presidential campaign, for the president's general staff to take care of the security and logistical aspects of the PRI candidate's travel, as happened in 1988 with Carlos Salinas De Gortari. In other words, the general staff's support for the PRI candidate is only one aspect of the loyalty of the armed forces to the presidential institution. Indeed, the incumbent president nominates those officers who are to serve on the PRI nominee's team.

Nevertheless, political manipulation is basically alien to the activities of the army. This does not mean that the armed forces do not decisively influence the outcome of the elections. However, there is a peril that the military could participate more boldly in future electoral contests, particularly if demands for democracy and loss of citizen support for the PRI become widespread and give rise to political intolerance, prompting the government to use all available resources, including military force, to guarantee its continuous rule and the electoral supremacy of the PRI.

U.S.–Mexico Relations

Military relations with the United States are another ingredient of armed forces–government imbalance. Mexico has purchased U.S. weapons that are not needed for the antidrug campaigns, a fact that propitiates closer relations between the two countries. The purchase of F5-E bombers, for instance, has necessitated negotiations and training plans on a scale much larger than anything known since the end of the World War II. Indeed, the U.S. military considers these purchases the first in a series of steps toward closer links with its elusive Mexican counterpart.

However, the defense goals of both countries remain divergent—for example, with respect to the Central American conflict. With the Reagan administration and now the Bush administration giving political preponderance to U.S. national security targets in this area, the aforementioned lack of symmetry has become more significant. In this context, the U.S. military hopes that arm sales will help neutralize these disagreements and foster greater cooperation between the two armies. For one thing, the purchase of the F5 airplanes permitted the Pentagon to open a military liaison office in Mexico that did not exist previously.

Even though, as has been the rule since the postwar period, Mexico refuses to manage its scant military relations with the United States through the Southern Command Administration in Panama, security matters in the coming years conceivably will be assigned higher priority in the context of U.S. management of its relations with Mexico.

The U.S. southern border, which has become the most active frontier in the world, is considered by many Americans to be porous, plagued by threats to the American society—which creates the need for closer monitoring of society in that area. To the extent that the national security debate is focused on military issues related to Mexico, growing expectations for larger complementarity and integration between the Mexican armed forces and the U.S. defense establishment can be foreseen.[18]

A wider range of military common interests between the two countries would necessarily lead to a substantial review of Mexico's security concept and to an internal debate, within the Mexican armed forces, about their role in designing the country's foreign policy. In this case, civil–military relations in Mexico would be crucially affected.

One forecast is that Mexico will eventually be asked to recognize the fact that, in practice, the two countries share security interests and therefore must be consistent with the "friendship" they claim to enjoy and behave as "loyally" and "responsibly" as allies are supposed to act. This could be reflected in various requests, ranging from larger purchases of U.S. military materiel by Mexico to the signing of joint defense agree-

Common Security interest w/ US

ments, even including Mexico's participation in strategic defense programs under NORAD.

Conclusions

Certainly, the future role of the Mexican armed forces cannot be conceived in a context of perpetual civil–military separation or even a split to the extent now apparent. Future civil–military relations might be different, and a number of factors mentioned here could be influential in this respect. However, many of the questions being posed in the United States about the role of the armed forces in Mexico tend to be mere conjectures; some of them are simple rumors being propagated mechanically.

Just as in many other aspects of political life in Mexico, civil–military relations will not be immune forever to tensions and to the impact of a political and economic crisis that is affecting the whole of the society. This chapter has attempted to show how, up to the present, the basic architecture of these relations has not changed. However, the new phenomena outlined here bring forth the need for constant evaluation and monitoring of the political evolution of the military institutions in Mexico as we enter the twenty-first century.

Notes

1. David Ronfeldt's thesis about the armed forces of Mexico is summarized in "The Modern Mexican Military: An Overview," in David Ronfeldt, ed., *The Modern Mexican Military: An Assessment* Monograph Series 15 (San Diego: University of California, Center for U.S.–Mexican Studies, 1984), pp. 1–32. For an update of Ronfeldt's ideas, see David Ronfeldt, "The Modern Mexican Military: Implications for Mexico's Stability and Security," Rand Note N-2288-FF/RC (Santa Monica, Calif.: Rand, February 1985).

2. I have proposed the expression *moderate militarization*; it must not be attributed to others. The description of this phenomenon as a gradual process is also my interpretation of certain ideas being circulated regarding modernization of the Mexican armed forces. Among those in the United States who argue that the Mexican army is assuming an increasingly important role, see Cesar Sereseres, "The Mexican Military Looks South," in Ronfeldt, *The Modern Mexican Military*; and Alden M. Cunningham, "Mexico's National Security," *Parameters* (Journal of the Army War College) 14, no. 4 (Winter 1984).

3. The 1986 PRI basic documents state that the armed forces efficiently protect national security by fulfilling, with exemplary loyalty, their duty of helping to enforce the law and support the institutions created according to the will of the people and by preserving the nations's sovereignty and independence. See Partido Revolucionario Institucional (PRI), *Documentos Basicos* (Mexico: PRI, 1986), pp.

35–36, quoted in José Antonio Hernandez, "La Validez Política y Valor Estrate-gico de la Seguridad Nacional de Mexico," Mimeographed draft, July 1986, p. 21.

4. Numerous statements and declarations have been issued about the social and civilist doctrine of the armed forces. See Rear Admiral Mario Santos Camal, "Mexico Frente a Centro America," Mimeographed, 1984.

5. From the viewpoint of the military, the war between Mexico and the United States in the 1850s was not the only instance in which Mexico had to repel an external invasion to consolidate itself as a nation. Indeed, the wounds left by the 1848 loss of 890,000 square miles of national territory had not yet healed when the country became involved in a fratricidal struggle between conservatives and liberals, which facilitated the landing of European troops at Veracruz in 1861. However, it was not this episode but the war with the United States that impressed on the conscience of Mexico the physiognomy of the external enemy.

6. The U.S. border communities became one of the major sources of weapons and ammunition for the Mexican belligerents. During the Revolution, Washington resorted to arms traffic seizures and tolerance as tools for political pressure in favor of or against the various leaders and groups.

7. For a brief account of the history of Mexican—American relations in the field of security, see Edwin A. Deagle, Jr., "Mexico y la Política de Seguridad Nacional de los Estados Unidos," in Clark Raynolds and Carlos Tello, eds., *US—Mexican Relations: Economic and Social Aspects* (Stanford, Calif.: Stanford University Press, 1983). In the same volume, see, also, Olga Pellicer de Brody, "La Seguridad Nacional en Mexico: Preocupaciones Nuevas y Nociones Tradicionales."

8. The armed forces develop their own contingency and national defense and security plans; however, these plans and programs are not aimed at determining the conduct of other government organizations or (even less) the citizens. The military-designed national security plan is a guideline only for the performance of the functions and responsibilities assigned to the armed forces.

9. Modernization was effected mostly in the sphere of equipment, which, in turn, led to internal restructuring. The army began to manufacture its own armed personnel carriers (DN III) as well as its standard rifle (the German G3). Most mounted units, not long ago conveying an image of rusticity to the Mexican army, have already been fully motorized. The most visible improvement has been the purchase of modern military equipment, including twelve F-5E fighter-bombers bought from the United States in 1981, Forty French Panhard ER-90 vehicles, some fifty Pilatos airplanes, two U.S. destroyers, and six Halcon frigates bought from Spain. These data have been taken from Major Stephen J. Wager, "Basic Characteristics of the Modern Mexican Military," in Ronfeldt, *The Modern Mexican Military*, pp 102–4; and from Guillermo Bolis M., "Los Militares en Mexico (1965–1985)," in *Revista Mexicana de Sociologia* 47, no. 1 (January–March 1985): 173–74.

10. In addition to the studies mentioned in note 7, other representative essays include Delal Baer, "Mexico: Ambivalent Ally," *Washington Quarterly* 10, no. 10 (Summer 1987); and Edward J. Williams, "The Mexican Military and Foreign Policy: The Evolution of Influence," in Ronfeldt, *The Modern Mexican Military*.

11. Between 1981 and 1984, more than 50,000 Guatemalan peasants crossed the border into Chiapas State.

12. For one of the most alarmist assessments of the situation at the southern border, and the contention that the army has militarized this region, see Sereseres, "The Mexican Military Looks South." For an account of the developments at the southern border, see Adolfo Aguilar Zinser, "Mexico and the Guatemalan Crisis," in Richard Fagen and Olga Pellicer, eds., *The Future of Central America* (Stamford, Calif.: Stanford University Press, 1983), pp. 161–86.

13. The Mexican southeast is one of the country's most backward, politically conflictive, and socially lagged regions, but it is also one where the largest energy infrastructe investments have been made in the last few years. The biggest hydroelectric dams and some of the most productive oil fields in operation in Mexico are located in Chiapas, Tabasco, and Campeche. Certainly, the proximity of these vital resource areas to the Central American conflict has created concern among the Mexican authorities and has prompted them to take preventive steps.

14. For a description of the developments at the southern border, the conflict with Guatemala, and the debate at the governmental level on these issues, see Zinser, "Mexico and the Guatemalan Crisis."

15. See Larry Rother, "Mexico Battles Drugs Anew: War Is Far from Over," *New York Times* (June 15, 1987). According to official figures, Conder, Marte, and other joint special programs of the National Defense Secretary and the Office of the Attorney General of the Republic have resulted in the destruction of 33,837 hectares of poppies and 35,993 hectares of marijuana since 1982. See "Resultados Obtenidos en la Campaña Permanente contra el Narcotrafico del Primero de Diciembre de 1982 a la Fecha," *Boletin de Prensa* (Office of the Attorney General of the Republic) (October 14, 1987).

16. For a description of these developments, the measures adopted by the government, and the role of the armed forces, see Adolfo Aguilar Zinser, "El Temblor de la Republica y sus Replicas," in Adolfo Aguilar Zinser, Cesario Morales, and Rodolfo Pena, eds., *Aun Tiembla: Sociedad, Estado y Cambio Social en el Terremoto del 19 de Septiembre* (Mexico: Editorial Grijalbo, 1986).

17. See "The Political Situation in Mexico: Statement of Senator Jesse Helms of North Carolina," Mimeographed paper (Washington, D.C.: Senate Foreign Relations Committee, June 1986).

18. See Georges Fauriol, "Mexico: In a Super Power's Shadow," in Rodney W. Jones and Steven A. Hildreth, eds., *Emerging Power: Defense and Security in the Third World* (New York: Praeger, 1986).

15

Civil–Military Relations in Costa Rica: Militarization or Adaptation to New Circumstances?

Constantino Urcuyo

Costa Rica is known worldwide as a democratic country without an army in an area where dictatorships and militarism are the norm. Since the late 1970s, the confrontation in Central America has brought international notice to Costa Rica. The civil war in Nicaragua between the Sandinistas and their rivals—the former supported by the Soviet Union and Cuba, the latter by the United States—has modified in its entirety the outlook of security in the area, thus changing the context of public security in Costa Rica.

Costa Rican public security institutions have had to change in the new circumstances. Reactions to reforms have ranged from passionate denunciation of a so-called process of militarization to the contention that the creation of an army is the only feasible solution for Costa Rica.

The problem of national security is closely linked with foreign relations. Throughout the administration of Luis Alberto Monge (1982–86), the government's position was isolationism and diplomatic passivity, as reflected in the 1983 declaration of neutrality. This policy engendered criticism from those who thought that neutrality eroded Costa Rica's alliances with its traditional allies. The Arias administration (1986–) represents a new phase in Costa Rican foreign policies, as it actively promoted the Central American Peace Plan. To Costa Rica, promotion of peace has become a shield and the guarantee of its national security in the Central American conflict. The promotion of peace has produced a national consensus in which the idea of militarizing the country is rejected and diplomatic and political instruments to protect national security are emphasized. Also recognized is the need to modernize the police forces to counter terrorism, narcotics trafficking, and other forms of criminal activity.

The main goal of this chapter is to state the principal organizational changes that have taken place in the Costa Rican Public Security Forces (FSP) since the rise of the Sandinistas in Nicaragua and to evaluate their impact on the organization of the FSP and on Costa Rica's political system. Finally, I will discuss whether there is a militarization process in Costa Rica.[1] By *militarization,* I mean the intrusion of the military into areas traditionally reserved to civilians, the penetration of the civilian society by the spirit and the organization of the military—that is, the process of a militaristic society substituting for a civilian one.[2] The perception of this phenomenon presented here is a global one, seen from the point of view of the society and the political system as a whole, not confined to a mere analysis of military organization.

Background: Abolition or Legal Ban?

Since the end of the 1948 civil war, the Costa Rican people have committed themselves to the integrating myth of a country without an army. This myth performs a number of sociopolitical functions. From the external standpoint, it enhances the international legitimacy of a disarmed democracy before potential enemies, thus transforming a source of weakness into one of strength. It also bases external defense on adherence to the hemispheric collective security pacts, thus strengthening political alliance with the United States. From the domestic side:

> The legal ban of an army legitimates the political system by concealing the repressive functions of state power and masking the level of the actual social conflict and the punctual use of force by the State. Electoral democracy in the country with "more teachers than soldiers" is supported by a consensus that can only be maintained through free elections every four years. . . . Antisystem legitimacy is hard to achieve where the State has publicly committed itself to refrain from using military force.[3]

This myth has impaired the analysis and understanding of the phenomenon of the organization and operation of legitimate governmental violence in Costa Rica. Indeed, the lack of a military organization of violence does not necessarily imply that the paramilitary or police organization lacks influence in the sociopolitical realm. Nor does it allow one to forgo analysis of the relationship between these organizations and the political system. On the other hand, the myth has helped enhance the image of Costa Rica as a democratic country, as the absence of an army has been taken as the equivalent of democracy. Apart from myth, the Costa Rican army vanished at the turn of the century; it was outlawed by President José Figueres in 1948. This decision reflected the specific circumstances of Costa Rica's civil war, which ended in 1948.

The Armed Forces Vanish

The Costa Rican armed forces performed an important role during the nineteenth century as participants in the struggle against pirates around

1850, in the 1850–60 palace coups, and in the context of the progressive dictatorship of General Tomas Guardia toward the end of the century. Violence was a constant in the country's political life during much of the nineteenth century.

By the end of the century, however, the specific features of the country facilitated the gradual abolition of the military structure. A comparative analysis of the navy, army, and police budgets clearly shows that the appropriations for national defense started to ebb by the end of the century, whereas those for police began to increase.[4]

The roots of this process are deeper than it appears at first sight. Indeed, others have discussed the specific features of an isolated colonial society, sparsely endowed with economic resources, whose rate of population growth was low, subjected to the leveling influence of widespread poverty.[5] This colonial legacy, together with an independence achieved without serious political shocks or war and the early introduction of coffee production—without the violence of land confiscation that occurred in El Salvador and Guatemala—gave birth to a social structure characterized by low levels of social or political conflict.

In addition, other instruments of social control developed in Costa Rica earlier than in other Isthmian countries because of the rapid organization of an educational system (1869). This made internal repression by military police relatively unnecessary. It was simpler to organize consensus than to repress dissidence.

The external context also posed threats that made it necessary to organize armed forces. Antagonisms with Guatemala were particularly important during the dictatorship of Guardia (1890), who had to face the hegemonistic claims of Justo Rufino Barrios. Border clashes with Nicaragua were equally serious and caused a Costa Rican president at the beginning of the twentieth century to say that there were three seasons in Costa Rica: "the dry one, the rainy one, and that of the war with Nicaragua."

As a matter of fact, by the end of the nineteenth century, the hegemony of the United States in the region became firmly entrenched, leading to international and even domestic conflicts being directly settled by the dominant power. The Central American Treaties signed in Washington in 1907 clearly reflect the role of the United States in Central American relations. The American interventions in Nicaragua also witnessed this fact, as did the American intervention in the 1921 war between Panama and Costa Rica. This tutelary action made it unnecessary to maintain armed forces to perform tasks of external defense.

The convergence of domestic reasons (a low conflict level) and foreign reasons (external defense becoming less important) led to a gradual extinction of the army of the Costa Rican Republic at the turn of the twentieth century and to the simultaneous growth of the role of the police. Indeed, at the outbreak of the 1948 civil war, the total strength of this army was only 300 men.

The Armed Forces Are Proscribed

In 1948, Costa Rica went through a violent political conflict, whose causes can be traced to the early 1920s. At the beginning of the 1940s, the administration of Rafael Angel Calderón Guardia was inaugurated. He promoted important changes (a labor code, a cooperatives act, a welfare system) that brought him the enmity of the traditional oligarchy. The oligarchy then organized itself and, bearing the banner of electoral freedom, launched a civil war in alliance with urban and rural middle-class groups. They overpowered the reformist sector led by Calderón, whose allies were the "progressive" sectors of the Catholic Church and the Communist party.

As an outcome of the war a new caudillo emerged: José Figueres. The newcomer was the leader of the victorious forces. Though he was an ally of the old oligarchy that hoped to put an end to social reforms, the middle-class sectors he represented were not prepared for such an outcome. Figueres had a new plan: diversification of agricultural production, industrialization, bank credit democratization, and maintenance of social reforms. His goals of political and social autonomy estranged him from his former allies. The old coffee growers, however, had never trusted Calderón. They accepted Figueres as a source of leadership and provided him with men and weapons to defeat the alliance of Calderón and the Communist party. However, once the war was over, they tried to restore their past political hegemony.

From the military viewpoint, this became a struggle for the mechanisms of legitimate violence. Figueres's troops had defeated the Communist militias that supported the reformist administration. The old Army of the Republic, commanded by the government of Teodoro Picado (1944–48), who carried on the work of Calderón, remained neutral. Once the war had ended, Figueres disbanded the army.

Organized violence rested in the hands of the victorious leader. The problem of legitimacy, however—how to convert this new force into the legitimate organization of violence—had to be solved. This would have given Figueres an extraordinary amount of power: his political legitimacy as a victorious caudillo, plus the control of the channels of legitimate violence. This alarmed the traditional sectors, which, through political accusations, attempted to subvert Figueres's control of the development and operation of the armed forces. They experimented with a coup (the *Cardonazo* of 1949). Finally, with the support of the constituent assembly, they succeeded in constitutionally forbidding the existence of an army. Figueres had been announcing the abolition of the army since December 1948, with the aim of making political use of the developments he foresaw and preventing the traditional sectors from gaining control of the repressive apparatus anew. He also wanted to enhance his international image to get access to external financing (always difficult for a revolutionary government).

The principal features in the public security context were as follows:

1. Figueres's forces became a new monopoly of the state's legitimate violence. However, they suffered, a *capitis diminutio* through the constitutional ban on their becoming an Army—a factor that, to this day, has prevented the possibility of an autonomous development of the security institutions.[6]

2. The police forces mentioned in the new constitution bear the name Fuerzas de Seguridad Pública (FSP, Public Security Forces), and their leading trait is that they are militarily stronger than the old Army of the Republic. This underscores the symbolic nature of such a constitutional ban.[7]

3. From the legal standpoint, a monopoly of legitimate violence was established. In practice, an oligopoly of organized violence prevailed throughout most of the 1970s. Even though the Liberation Army became the Fuerzas de Seguridad Pública, throughout this period, Figueres and other groups operated private armies parallel to the state's security organization.

4. Mutual mistrust among the groups that had won the civil war led to the systematic firing of members of the FSP after each change of government since 1948.[8]

5. This policy of systematic dismissal has been perceived by some as an intelligent move on the part of the ruling classes, aimed at preventing the formation of an independent military group. Although I have found this to be true to a large extent, the main goal of the political groups was to limit a rapprochement between one another's political foes and the military organizations. Indeed, since 1948, elections have brought about a diffuse bipartisan system with a dominant party, leading, in turn, to a system of alternation in the executive branch of government and the subsequent maintenance of a spoils system.

6. The other major feature of the security organizations during this period was their ambiguous structure. Though the constitution defined them as a police force, from the beginning they have had both police and military responsibilities. They have not confined themselves to safeguarding the domestic public order; they have also defended the country's territorial integrity. They have been trained in the use of weapons that are unnecessary for police functions, they have been organized along military

lines, and they have been trained in military academies. The FSP taken as a whole, then, could best be described as a paramilitary force, even if most of the time they have performed the typical functions of a police force.[9]

7. Between 1948 and 1978, the only instances in which the FSP faced challenges requiring a military-type response were in 1948 and 1955, when groups connected with former president Calderón Guardia invaded Costa Rica from Nicaragua in order to regain the power they had lost in the 1948 war. The country succeeded, however, in attaining national reconciliation, and in 1958, the candidate of the parties opposing Figueres (Mario Echandi), supported by Calderón Guardia, came to power. This restored the mechanism of peaceful transfer of political power, sparing armed confrontations between the political elites.

8. The 1948 and 1955 invasions also illustrate the other major trait of the public security scenario during those years. The Inter-American Reciprocal Assistance Treaty (IARAT) was applied for the first time in 1948 and for the second time in 1955. In both instances, the Organization of American States (OAS) commanded Nicaragua to stop helping the Costa Rican rebels who were trying to overthrow Figueres while simultaneously condemning Somoza for his actions against the Costa Rican government. This incident shows that from 1948 on, Costa Rica entrusted its national defense to the legal mechanisms of the interAmerican system. This explains why, in those years, there was no significant need for a national defense organization, notwithstanding the fact that Costa Rica was surrounded by dictatorial regimes opposed to José Figueres.

9. The political control of the FSP by the civilians is effected through the appointment of civilians as ministers in the departments in charge of security organizations. The present trend is to choose people without any military background. However, up to the early 1980s, an important number of the ministers of security and of the interior were veterans of the victorious faction of the 1948 civil war, though they maintained no links with the security forces. Most of them were civilians involved in other activities at the time of being appointed.

These leading characteristics of the Costa Rican public security model did not vary during its second period of development (1960–78). However, circumstances that were not in place in 1948–60—basically, the Cuban revolution and the process of internal modernization of Costa Rica—underpinned a process of modernization of the FSP. Particularly important was the active participation of the United States (1962–76), targeted at training the weak Costa Rican security organizations in the theory and practice of counterinsurgency.

The Most Recent Past: A Process of Modernization Prompted by a Change in the Geopolitical Context

In the 1960s, the main influence that brought about changes in the structure, training, and ideology of the FSP was the U.S. development of a doctrine of counterinsurgency. In this manner, the FSP was modernized and politicized along counterrevolutionary lines, led by cold war anticommunist ideology.[10]

By the early 1970s, the process of modernization was under way, despite the withdrawal of U.S. military assistance. Two successive National Liberation party administrations (1970–78) reinforced the FSP, as there was no interregime dismissal of police officers. The process of modernization of the FSP raised accusations from the intellectual and leftist sectors that a process of militarization of the country was under way.[11] This conflict became more pronounced during the Figueres administration (1974–78), when the police clashed with students in the streets and with landless peasants in the rural areas.

Almost ten years ago, an analysis of the process of modernization of the FSP (1960–78) led to the conclusion that although the Public Security Forces had been strengthened bureaucratically, the country was not being militarized, as the political intervention capabilities of these forces were not being augmented. However, events surrounding the 1979 Sandinista revolution changed the regional geopolitical context. This prompted major modifications in the structure, operation, and sociopolitical role of the Public Security Forces in Costa Rica.

The Late 1980s: The Traditional Policies Have Become Inefficient

The 1978–79 Sandinista insurrection deeply affected security policies in Costa Rica. The presence of Sandinista forces in Costa Rican territory exposed the country to Somoza's reprisals, and Costa Rica had to organize to face a possible invasion of Somoza forces, aimed at destroying Sandinista bases on Costa Rican soil. Military help from Venezuela and Panama was substantial in those years. However, Costa Rica resorted to traditional mechanisms to face the external threat. The country requested assistance from the OAS and implementation of the IARAT mechanisms, which provided a legal umbrella to maintain the territorial sovereignty and integrity of Costa Rica.

The installation of the Sandinista regime sharply changed this situation. On the one hand, the country was unable to invoke the IARAT as a basis for its national defense against the Managua regime, as the legitimacy of the treaty was challenged by the Sandinistas when they took power and by them and the rest of Latin America after the Falkland/Malvinas episode.

The presence of foci of armed resistance to the Sandinistas on the border posed a problem of control of the national territory in the early 1980s. The military growth of the Sandinistas, their ideological definition as a Marxist-Leninist movement, and their leaning toward the Soviet orbit were a source of concern for the Costa Rican political class. Faced with these new issues, the administration of Louis Alberto Monge (1982–86) attempted to give form to a new doctrine of national security that rested mainly on the Costa Rican policy of neutrality with respect to armed conflicts in the region. This policy was called into question when the cooperation of the Monge administration with the United States in the disclosures of the so-called Irangate affair became exposed.

Costa Rica is still struggling between two contending alternatives: establishing a military force that ensures some resistance capabilities in the event of a Sandinista invasion (until significant external help is in place) or complete disarmament. The latter would entail, on the one hand, helplessness before a potential Nicaraguan attack and, on the other hand, an absolute lack of means to control the anti-Sandinista armed groups that try to use Costa Rican territory as a rearguard in their struggle against the Sandinistas. The Arias administration has effected tougher policies to curb the anti-Sandinista military activities. This notwithstanding, more than 1,500 men (the Northern Battalion) have had to be stationed at the border areas, and the programs of strictly military training initiated during the Monge administration have had to be continued.[12]

Domestically, at least, the intensity of the activities of subversive opposition groups has decreased since the 1970s. This reflects, to some extent, the split of the Costa Rican Left as well as the orientation of their policies of social protest. During the process of Sandinista insurrection, the government of Rodrigo Carazo (1978–82) negotiated with the unions and the Left an exchange of social peace for support to the Sandinistas. However, in the wake of the economic crisis of the early 1980s, Costa Rica was the stage for some terrorist actions by groups that thought the situation was ripe for launching a revolutionary campaign. Though the "official" Left has never acknowledged any connection with these terrorist activities, it is evident that its political interpretation of the situation coincided with that of the terrorists: The wave of revolutionary triumphalism that began to shatter Central America in 1979 was felt intensely in Costa Rica, as the economic crisis of that period seemed to offer excellent opportunities for a revolution. However, as the leftists themselves point out, the economic crisis was not immediately followed by a political crisis, and in 1983, the Costa Rican Left became split over the issue of the best possible way to promote a revolution in Central America starting from Costa Rica.[13] Some spoke of exacerbating class struggle so as to keep imperialism busier. Others suggested just the opposite, to avoid giving an excuse to the northern giant, so as to be in a position to further revolution in Central America through the consolidation of the Sandinista popular revolution and its expansion at a later stage. These different viewpoints, together with a failure to orient labor conflicts, resulted in a loss of intensity of organized social protest in Costa Rica. The effects of economic crisis have been individual social anomie, a widespread surge of crime, new patterns of traditional criminality, more white-collar crime, and a growing awareness by the citizens of the increase in criminality.[14] In addition, the increases in nonpolitical crime and narcotics trafficking present the Costa Rican public security organizations with a fresh, serious challenge. They have responded to it, just as they did when they were faced with the defense of the country's territorial integrity. Let us now examine the major changes that the FSP has undergone in the late 1980s, as well as its relationship to a possible process of militarization of Costa Rica.

Trends

Some processes within the FSP may lead to the conclusion that there exists a militarization of public life. First, the process of differentiation between police and military units at the end of the last decade has been deepened by the creation of new police units, such as the Crime Prevention Unit (1982), the Drug Control Police (1982), the Migration Police (1986), the Metropolitan Police (1983), and the Auxiliary Police (1981). Another step in this direction is the split of operations within the Public Security Ministry—some being assigned to urban commanders, some to border commanders. The men under the border commanders have been trained at the new Murcielago military base.[15]

This operational split could be deemed a sensible step in a process of organizational development aimed at increased police efficiency in the struggle against nonpolitical crime. However, some FSP units have been freed from police tasks and have specialized in the performance of exclusively military functions.

The Nicaraguan issue, the responsibilities for border patrol, the terrorist threat, and the control of the "contras" made it necessary to train some units for military tasks. These included the Northern Battalion, the Special Police Team of the Police Intelligence Section of the Public Security Ministry, Border Patrol Units of the Rural Assistance Guard, the Specialized Police Unit of the Guard, and the creation of the National Emergency

Organization (1982), which became the Public Order Force Reserve in 1985.

The establishment of specific channels for decision-making in the sphere of national security (the creation of the National Security Board in 1982 and the subsequent transformation thereof into the Senior Security and Police Board, as of July 24, 1987) makes it evident that the concern for national security is no longer confined to a police framework—as it was during most of the 1970s, influencing political decisions accordingly—having penetrated, instead, the realm of external defense.

An analysis of the human resources of the security organizations, and of the physical resources assigned to them also indicates a transformation. As early as 1978, I mentioned a trend toward increasing the country's security personnel.[16] More recent data confirm the fact that as an outcome of the issues at the northern border, this trend has become more pronounced. In terms of the physical resources assigned to the security forces, police expenses as a percentage of the national budget have remained flat since 1981, although they have increased by 250 percent in constant-dollar terms.[17] These data have to be supplemented, however, with the amounts of foreign aid to the FSP; only in this way can one get a clear picture of the actual sums assigned to the national defense effort.

The fresh U.S. concern for the security organizations—which manifested itself in growing economic aid, military training in the drug control and intelligence areas, participation of military engineers in civic efforts, and confrontations with the public security minister during the Monge administration—shows the northern power's concern for making Costa Rican security organizations capable of handling the new challenges stemming from the Nicaraguan issue. We have already discussed the goals of this new aid flow; now it is important to give an account of the amounts involved, the specificity of the assistance, and the effects thereof.

Once the legal resistance from the 1974 Foreign Assistance Act was overcome, the U.S. government initiated a liberal flow of aid to the Costa Rican security organizations. In 1982, grants were made to the FSP in the amount of $2.1 million. This was increased to $4.6 million in 1983, $9.1 million in 1984, and $13.2 million in 1985. With the election of Oscar Arias Sanchez in 1986, this amount fell to $2.6 million and then increased to $3.4 million in 1987.[18]

Thirty-five million dollars in six years does not seem to be an excessive amount. However, it has to be measured against the relative importance of this aid. The budgetary expenses for national security totaled some $25 million in 1985 and $27 million in 1986. If we compare these figures with the amount of U.S. aid, we reach the conclusion that in the first of those years (when the most serious incidents took place at the

Nicaraguan border), it represented 50 percent of the budget, and 10 percent in 1986.

Besides grants, the new flow of U.S. assistance consisted of the presence of trainers as well as military engineers who regularly participate in bridge-building efforts in the southern portion of Costa Rica. In addition, three "push and pull" airplanes were bought from the U.S. government.[19] Fourteen members of the U.S. armed forces were available to the Rural Guard as advisors.[20]

This new presence of U.S. military personnel aroused resistance, both from the traditional anti-United States opposition—the leftist parties—and from the security minister of the Monge administration. Indeed, Minister Angel Edmundo Solano Calderón (who performed his functions between 1982 and August 1984) angrily collided with the U.S. ambassador on the issues of the Costa Rican presence in the Central American Defense Council (CONDECA), the training of antiterrorist units in Israel, the training of Costa Rican officers at the Regional Center for Military Training in Honduras, the presence of an antiterrorist unit known as the "babies" (Intelligence and Security Bureau), the ambassador's attitude on strikes at banana plantations on the Atlantic coastline, a visit to the aircraft carrier Ranger off the coast of Nicaragua, and a trip of General Gorman (head of the U.S. Southern Command) to Costa Rica's northern border. According to the former minister, the whole series of clashes was unleashed by the U.S. ambassador's visit to his office in 1984 to request a prompt solution of the banana field strike in the south, and his expulsion of the Ambassador from his office. Solano did not mince words when affirming that the U.S. ambassador promoted the militarization of Costa Rica through the establishment of an army.[21] Solano left the cabinet in August 1984, amid serious political crises.

Some entrepreneurial unions had requested his ouster and that of other members of the cabinet whom they accused of playing the hand of the Sandinistas and Mexico in the Central American crisis. Solano quit, but only after exposing plans for a coup and ordering the security forces to quarters. The press released information about the military readiness actions and a visit of former president José Figueres to the barracks. Finally, however, Solano and other members of the cabinet resigned. The position of Solano was taken by Benjamin Piza, who, according to Costa Rican political circles, is connected with a radical right-wing organization called Movimiento Costa Rica Libre.

The strengthening of the Intelligence and Security Bureau during the Monge administration reflected new national security necessities stemming from the complex regional situation.[22] As a matter of fact, the situation in Nicaragua, and in Central America generally, turned Costa Rica into a focus of arms transfers to the rebel groups operating in the region, which led the intelligence services of their adversaries to launch operations in Costa Rican territory to obtain information about their activities and, in some instances, to organize actions against their foes on Costa Rican soil. This new challenge prompted the development of the new police apparatus. The growing political weight of this organization is witnessed by the fact that its director is a member of the Joint Senior Security and Police Board, at a cabinet level.

In previous studies, the point was stressed that one of the most important grounds for the violence specialists' having remained apolitical is the absence in Costa Rica of military academies for police officers. Apparently, this phenomenon is being changed as a result of the influence of the Academy of Public Force within the FSP training system.[23] This school was established in 1964, but its process of modernization was started by the construction of its own premises in 1981. In 1985, it separated from the Civil Guard under the sole supervision of the public force director. Its autonomy is made evident by the fact that its personnel are considered to be part of the civil service and therefore entitled to protection under the civil service statute.

Countertrends

From the foregoing discussion, it would be relatively easy to conclude, as some observers have, that Costa Rica is going through a rapid process of militarization.[24] I do not agree. The aforementioned facts might point to this conclusion, but such a tendency is countered by adverse trends, some from within the security forces and others from the country's sociopolitical context and the regional situation.

In 1982–87, Costa Rican "policemen-soldiers" were still not granted job security.[25] This was the case even though the same party remained in power. Furthermore, a system of discretionary appointments severely impaired the ability of the FSP to influence the society as a whole. In addition, the high annual rate of resignations (30 percent in 1987) is a symptom of deficient organization, which aggravates the weakness of the FSP.[26]

Another factor limiting militarization in Costa Rica is the low level of social prestige of the policemen-soldiers. A police career is not attractive to educated Costa Ricans. They choose civilian careers, depriving the FSP of a certain amount of talent.

However, the academic level of police personnel has improved steadily since 1983.[27] Their educational background is higher than that of the majority of the population. The acute inflation of the early 1980s led many people with a high school education to seek employment as policemen. Despite this progress, the guard remains academically weak in com-

[handwritten margin note at top: This is not a reason for a mili being weak. This is the case w/ most milis.]

parison to the civilian elites and other branches of the government, which include a large proportion of college graduates and undergraduates. Unlike the military, the security forces do not include so-called *armes savantes*, or technical branches that require specialized personnel.[28] This bureaucratic weakness erodes their capabilities for political-social activism, though it could not be contended that this is a direct factor in the apoliticism of the Costa Rican military-police; rather, it is only one of the ingredients of the environment within which this phenomenon takes place.

Although, in the framework of U.S. policy in Central America, an improvement of the military capabilities of the Costa Rican security organizations would be a positive outcome, there is no evidence that such policy is oriented toward the establishment of an army in Costa Rica. On the contrary, the Sandinistas themselves have sometimes stated that Honduras performs the role of a military avant-garde and Costa Rica that of a political avant-garde in the U.S. regional offensive against the Sandinistas.

From a military point of view, there does not seem to be any reason why a Costa Rican army would enhance U.S. policies, from either the roll-back or the containment viewpoint.[29] The first of these goals—a roll-back—could be attained through the contras or, in an emergency, by U.S. troops stationed in Honduras and Panama. From the point of view of a containment policy, the best way to check Sandinista expansionism would be to maintain a highly legitimate government in Costa Rica, and this can be more easily secured by granting economic support—as has been done so far—to the Costa Rican democracy.[30] An American investigator has been most clear in expounding the importance of Costa Rica for U.S. Central American policy:

> Simply stated, the importance of Costa Rica is almost exclusively political. The country is the most enduring example of democracy in Latin America; a living alternative to the Cuban and Nicaraguan models. The Administration must recognize that the creation of an army would tarnish the democratic image of Costa Rica, thus eroding the country's usefulness to the U.S. political struggle for the hearts and spirits of the Latin American people.[31]

[handwritten margin note: Why would it tarnish its democratic image if army was for the purpose of combating external invasion]

The operation of a regime of competing parties and a deeply rooted democratic political culture also represents an almost unsurmountable obstacle to a would-be militarization process.[32] The sociopolitical conflict can be solved through elections and negotiation. No important sector appears to have lost faith in this conflict-solving system.[33] On the contrary, the specter of the Sandinistas in the north, together with the latent cultural antagonism with Nicaragua, represents, for the government, a further legitimacy ingredient that makes it unnecessary to resort to military control mechanisms in order to preserve public security.[34] All of this is aggravated, in turn, by the presence of a growing refugee population.[35] As long as this situation persists, the development of a military apparatus will be unlikely.

By the same token, since 1948, Costa Rica has been building a "welfare state," characterized by the active intervention of the government in infrastructural development and supply of social services to its citizens. The traditional mechanisms of legitimacy of the political power have been supplemented by a paternalist state.[36]

The model of public security in Costa Rica rests on a social and political structure that generates consensus on the virtues of a political and social system, peacefully solves the issue of the succession of the political elites, satisfies the needs of the parties' clients through a welfare state policy, and operates sophisticated social control mechanisms to prevent conflict from becoming general. The technical and political superiority of the civilian managers and decision makers relative to the chronically weak security subsystem is thus overwhelming. Alain Rouquié was right in affirming:

> On the other hand, the institutions being operative and the parties alternating themselves in power, the creation of a new permanent and stable army has been prevented, which *a contrario* confirms the fact that the autonomy of the armed institutions is one of the sources of their political activism.[37]

A recent government decision clearly illustrates the continual tension between a system that keeps creating instruments for civilian control over the political apparatus and security forces that have always performed a double set of functions (military and civilian) to a certain extent. On July 24, 1987, President Oscar Arias delivered a public address announcing his decision to suppress the military vocabulary being used in the police forces, military uniforms, and quartering of police forces. These measures could be interpreted as an effort on the part of the civilian authorities to suppress militarization of the police.

At the same time, he announced the creation of a new oversight board for FSP matters. The new board includes a police officer (the national security director). The participation of a police officer at a political decision-making level might be a symptom of a growing influence of the security organizations in Costa Rican national security policies.

One of the most often cited signs of militarization was the creation of the Organización para Emergencias Nacionales (OPEN), later transformed into a reserve of the security forces. However, since its inception, all political parties have made it the target of strong criticism, which made it necessary first to modify its name and then to suspend its activities.[38]

The Balance of Trends and Countertrends

My main conclusion regarding the balance of trends for or against militarization is that there is evidence of militarization of a number of police units because of border tensions. However, the development of these military capabilities should not lead one to conclude that there is a process of militarization of the police in their entirety or that a Costa Rican army is being created.

A process of modernization of the police-military forces is evident in Costa Rica. This has not been accompanied, however, by a parallel process of professionalization. It has also not been followed by a process of institutionalization. The path of modernization of the 1960–78 period has been furthered and broadened in recent years, as shown by the new inflow of military aid from 1981–1982. The lack of any formal military education in Costa Rica, the brief (ten weeks) length of the police courses, and the fact that the registration and promotion procedures are based on party or family influence show that these organizations are not concerned with rewarding successful performance; thus, they are not professional in nature. Costa Rican security organizations are not endowed with mechanisms for autonomous renewal and regeneration. These mechanisms occur outside these organizations—in the shift of parties in charge of the executive branch of the government.

Nor are we in a position to conclude that the civilian society is being militarized. There are no symptoms of an exacerbation of social contradictions, and the society's openness grants no opportunities to reduce its legitimacy. Conflict is still solved through persuasion and dialogue. The electoral road remains the one to follow to achieve power. Furthermore, the rejection of militarism remains an outstanding feature of the country's political culture.[39]

It seems the weakness + poor quality of the police force is what makes militarization unlikely.

Is the Costa Rican Pattern Possible Elsewhere?

Many observers wonder whether the social and institutional arrangements of the Costa Rican public security system can be applied in other countries. I believe that they cannot. The so-called Costa Rican model reflects a very specific historical evolution. However, an overview of this background can provide lessons for similar contexts.

The main feature of the Costa Rican model is the subordination of the military elites to their civilian counterparts through systematic erosion of the organizational capabilities of the public security specialists and, therefore, of their opportunities for social and political autonomy. Is this an inherent characteristic of the system or the outcome of a deliberate effort by the decision makers? It is both, though the question appears to

[Handwritten margin note at top: "Don't these police forces have the right to use violence? + This is domestic violence. A mili in theory should only use violence externally against aggressive enemies. A mili used for external threats should not even be used for domestic reasons"]

be irrelevant, as what matters is the effect on Costa Rica of this relationship between civilians and specialists in violence.

From the political standpoint, the effect of noninstitutionalization of legitimate violence has been the estrangement of the security specialists from politics. However, this withdrawal cannot be ascribed only to noninstitutionalization; it is also a result of the relatively nonconflictive development of the society as a whole in the period following the 1948 civil war. The structural determinants, in this context, appear to be more important than the political will of the participants.

From the standpoint of the society, the needs for maintenance of public order, challenged by nonpolitical crime, have not been adequately ministered to because of the scarce professional skills of these organizations for designing a consistent public security policy that can be adapted to the changing needs of a society undergoing a process of modernization.

From the point of view of national external defense and preservation of territorial integrity, these organizations are in no position to respond to the challenges of a new period. This is true both for a potential Sandinista expansion and the activities of the Nicaraguan opposition.

The pattern of apoliticism based on noninstitutionalization of the channels of governmental legitimate violence seemed to be reaching its end in the Costa Rica of the mid-1980s. Institutionalization and professionalization seem to have turned into a necessity, not only on abstract theoretical grounds, but basically in order to further the country's domestic and external sociopolitical processes themselves, which rest on the conditions set by the profound transformations of the most recent years. The strengthening of these organizations during this decade evidences this reality. It surpasses, by far, any political design aimed at maintaining a security structure that arose from a very specific historical background but has proved inadequate in the present circumstances.

In fact, the external threat makes it impossible for the country to entrust its defense exclusively to the collective security mechanisms of the Rio de Janeiro pact (IARAT). The volatility of U.S. Central American foreign policies prevents the country from relying, without reservations, on the unconditional support of the United States in a low-intensity conflict environment, even though, to date, the Reagan and Bush administrations have not rejected any of the Costa Rican government's requests in matters of security.

[Handwritten margin note: "The volatile nature of US Central American policies prevent Costa Rica from reliance on unconditional support on the U.S. in matters of security"]

A long-lasting institutional weakness of the security forces as a whole seems unlikely. This is due to many factors, including greater sophistication of organized crime, a serious narcotics trafficking problem, the high cultural level of the population, the changes in the social mix of the new guard recruits, and the presence of a number of already-institutionalized nuclei within the FSP (for example, the Judicial Investigation Bureau).

New political generations face the challenge of designing security mechanisms that can put into place a process of professionalization while preserving respect for democracy. Within the present structure and operational system of these security bodies, some instruments can be found that, appropriately preserved and developed and supplemented by other elements, make these objectives attainable.

In reality, building a consensus among the democratic majority forces so as to design bipartisan national security policies, supervision of the security bodies by various civilian authorities, a permanent rotation system for the commanders of the security units, civilian political supervision of the promotion system and the military academies, and the development of a national security doctrine based on the country's democratic traditions, not the cold war concerns of larger powers, are the guarantees of a process of democratic professionalization.[40]

Notes

1. There is no need to present an overall analysis of Costa Rica's various national security entities, as this has been done elsewhere. See Constantino Urcuyo, "Les Forces de Securité et la Politique au Costa Rica, 1960–1978," Ph.D. dissertation, University of Paris, 1978.

2. See Norberto Bobbio and Nicola Matteuci, *Diccionario de Política* (Mexico: Siglo XXI, 1982), p. 1000.

3. Constantino Urcuyo, "Les Raisons, les Fonctions, et les Limites de l'Abolition de l'Armee au Costa Rica", Paper presented at the Conference on Military Non-Intervention in Latin America, Aix-en-Provence, October, 1979 p. 7.

4. Urcuyo, "Les Forces de Securité."

5. Samuel Stone, *La Dinastía de los Conquistadores* (San Jose, Costa Rica: EDUCA, 1975).

6. Article 12 of the political constitution states:

The army is proscribed as a permanent institution. For the vigilance and maintenance of public order there will exist the necessary police forces. Only by continental agreement or for national defense will it be possible to organize military forces: the former and the latter will always be subordinate to civil power; they will not be able to deliberate, nor engage in marches or declarations, as individuals or as a collective body.

7. Wayne L. Worthington, "The Costa Rican Public Security Forces: A Model Armed Force for Emerging Nations?" Master's thesis, University of Florida, Gainesville, 1966, pp. 134–35.

8. Ibid., p. 119.

9. Institute of Strategic Studies, *The Military Balance, 1986–1987*, (London: ISS, 1986), p. 9.

10. An analysis of this policy has been presented in Urcuyo, "Les Forces de Securité." See, especially, chapter 2, of "Le Monopole de l'Assistance Militaire."

11. On these accusations of militarization, see FAENA (University Student Organization), *La Militarizacion de Costa Rica* (San Jose, Costa Rica: Colección Realidad Nacional, 1971); and John Saxe-Fernández, "Costa Rica: Estado de Seguridad Nacional?" *Cuadernos Américanos* (May–June 1972).

12. These programs were initiated thanks to the renewal of U.S. military assistance. As Blachman and Hellman have indicated:

In 1981 military assistance was renewed after a lapse of three years. Since then and until mid-1985, the United States provided approximately 26 million dollars to equip and train the Costa Rican forces. The aid program is directed to equip the civil guards with the same equipment used by the U.S. infantryman. Each soldier has an M-16 automatic rifle, and the frontier units have grenade launchers, 80 millimeter mortars, and other combat weapons. Since 1983 five hundred civil guards have been trained in Panama and at Fort Benning, Georgia. In May of 1985 twenty-four advisors of the U.S. Special Forces (Green Berets) started working with four companies of the Guard.

Morris J. Blachman and Ronald Hellman, "Costa Rica," in Morris Blachman and William Leogrande, eds., *Confronting Revolution: Security Through Diplomacy in Central America*, (New York: Pantheon Books, 1986), pp. 178–79.

13. Javier Solís, Alvaro Montero, and Sergio Aragón, "Un Nuevo Camino a Seguir: Una Reflexión Desde la Izquierda," Mimeograph (San Jose, Costa Rica: n.p., 1987), p. 22.

14. In a recent study, it was found that the rate of victimization was 21.3 percent. Of the people interviewed, 202 had been victims of a crime during 1986. ILANUD, AID, and the Center for Justice Administration of the University of Florida (CJAUF), "Estudio Sectorial Sobre la Administración de Justicia en Costa Rica, La Policía en Costa Rica (San Jose, Costa Rica: n.p., 1986), p. 7.

15. In 1985 the Murcielago base, a training school for the Guardia Civil, was created in the north of the country. This school depends on the Academy of Public Force, which is in the center of the country. The Murcielago base has as its objective the training of frontier battalions. During 1985 and the beginning of 1986, 705 civil guardsmen graduated from this school. See ILANUD, AID, and CJAUF,"Estudio Sectorial," pp. 183–184.

16. In Urcuyo, "Les Forces de Securité," p. 242, I indicated that the security forces numbered 200 men in 1963 and 8,500 in 1977, with one policeman for every 668 people in 1963 and one for every 235 in the 1977.

17. In effect, these percentages were 5.6 percent in 1981, 4.2 percent in 1982, 5.7 percent in 1983, 4.9 percent in 1984, 4.5 percent in 1985, and 4.5 percent in 1986. ILANUD, AID, and CJAUF, "Estudio Sectorial," pp. 11–12.

18. See Steve R. Harper, cited in Francisco Rojas Aravena, *Costa Rica: Profundizando la Beligerancia Política y la Neutralidad Militar.* (Miami: Florida International University, n.d.), p. 31.

19. *La Nación* (September 4, 1986).

20. *La Nación* (July 22, 1987).

21. Interview with Angel Edmundo Solano Calderón, ex-minister of public security of the Monge administration, San Jose, Costa Rica, July 15, 1987.

22. Executive decree 16398 (1985) established that the former Agency of National Security would report directly to the president of the Republic. Its functions are undetaking investigations relating to the external security of the country, coordination with international organizations in matters of external security, and maintenance of the security of the state and its physical plant. In this same decree, the activities of the Directorate of Security were made state secrets. From this description, it is apparent that the activities of this organization are those of a political police force. According to the republic's budget, the personnel of this agency increased from 62 in 1982 to 166 in 1986, and its budgetary allocation increased from 1.3 percent of the Ministry of Security budget in the 1982 to 2.6 percent in the 1986. Its activities have been linked to those of OPEN and to the existence in its ranks of an antiterrorist unit trained by Israeli instructors. IL-ANUD, AID, and CJAUF, "Estudio Sectorial," p. 89.

23. The Academy of Public Force functions as a training center but also engages in investigations and assists in the planning and organization of the Ministry of Security. In 1981, its personnel numbered 88 men; in 1987, it was 127. Its budgeted financial resources surpassed 1.5 percent of the budget in 1981 and rose to 2.3 percent in 1986. Ibid., pp. 177–183.

24. Gabriel Aguilera, "La Dimensión Militar en la crisis centroaméricana" *Anvario de Estudios Centroamericanos*, 12, no. 1 (1986), pp. 30, 32; Blachman and Hellman, "Costa Rica," pp. 177–80.

25. "Almost 50 percent of the personnel of the Ministry of Public Security and 77 percent of the Rural Guard are replaced with each change in government." Craig Richardson, "Section 660 of the Foreign Assistance Act of 1974: Implications for the Costa Rican Public Security Forces," paper presented at the 1985 APSA conference, p. 38.

26. ILANUD, AID, and CJAUF, "Estudio Sectorial," p. 109.

27. Pastor Maita, "Caracteristicas y Problemas Institucionales de la Guardia Civil y Rural Costarricense." Bachelor's thesis in Sociology, Universidad Nacional Autoroma, Heredia, Costa Rica, p. 145.

28. An examination of the 1987 budget of the Civil Guard reveals that the personnel include four doctors, one dentist, some computer technicians, one social worker, one social scientist, twelve boat captains, two lawyers, and fourteen pilots. There are no engineers, no economists, no business administrators. The absence of professionals with a university-level education is also reflected in the educational system of the guard; it has been stated:

> There is no formal instruction preparing instructors to teach. . . . The lack of participation by university faculty, especially in the field of law, is notorious in the design and implementation of these instructional programs.

ILANUD, AID, and CJAUF, "Estudio Sectorial," p. 60.

29. The Reagan administration's policy assigns a role to the Public Security Forces in its confrontation with the Sandinistas. The American military appears interested in the Civil Guard's having the capacity to repel an initial Sandinista attack while OAS forces arrive on the scene. This has been confirmed by an official of the Office of Defense Cooperation of the American embassy, who has said: "The United States must help the Costa Rican security forces in such a way as to prevent the direct, frequent, or permanent commitment of the United States." Remarks made by Colonel John Taylor, Director of the U.S. Office of Defense Cooperation, San Jose, Costa Rica, April 10, 1984. Quoted in "Section 660 of the Foreign Assistance Act of 1976," Richardson, p. 25.

30. Pablo Ayón and Jairo Hernandez, "Relaciones Políticas Costa Rica–Estados Unidos: Algunos Aspectos," Graduation thesis, School of Political Science, University of Costa Rica, 1987, p. 131.

31. Richardson, "Section 660 of the Foreign Assistance Act of 1974," p. 35.

32. In the elections of February 2, 1986, abstention was only 18.2 percent, which gives an idea of the internalization of the values associated with political participation.

33. In the elections of 1986, the Communist parties obtained 1.05 percent of the votes for the presidency and 5.13 percent of the votes for deputies. No organized right-wing party exists.

34. In a national survey carried out in November 1986 by the Association for the Defense of Liberty and Democracy in Costa Rica (APRODELI), it was found that 82 percent of those surveyed thought that the Sandinistas constitute or would come to constitute a threat to democracy in Costa Rica, and only 14 percent considered that the Sandinistas did not constitute any threat. To the question of whether the best solution for Nicaragua would be an end to the Sandinista regime, 76.6 percent answered yes and 16.7 percent answered no.

35. In the same survey cited in note 34, it was found that almost 70 percent of the respondents thought that the government should not continue receiving Nicaraguan refugees; 22 percent thought that the asylum policy should continue.

36. The survey conducted by APRODELI (note 34) indicated that there is a strong statist mentality in Costa Rica: 53.3 percent of the responses indicated approval for more state action in society, 55.2 percent desired more state intervention in the economy, and 56.2 percent wanted more state controls.

37. Alain Rouquié, *L'État Militaire en Amerique Latine* (Paris: Editions du Soleil, 1982), p. 238.

38. *La Nación* (July 14, 1984).

39. According to a Gallup Poll conducted in 1984, 83 percent of Costa Ricans were opposed to the creation of an army. Cited in Richardson, "Section 660 of the Foreign Assistance Act of 1974," p. 33.

40. In talks with the highest leaders of the Social Unity Christian party (PUSC) and the National Liberation Party (PLN), I found favorable opinions regarding such policies.

16
The Military and Democracy in Venezuela

Felipe Aguero

The overthrow of dictator Perez Jimenez in 1958 set Venezuela on a sharply different course from the authoritarian turn experienced by most South American countries in the 1960s and 1970s. In stark contrast to this authoritarian trend and to their own militaristic past, Venezuelans successfully overcame the obstacles of the transition and embarked on the construction of a democratic regime. After three decades of uninterrupted democracy, a study of the patterns of civil–military relations that developed in Venezuela should help to illuminate more recent attempts at political democratization in other South American countries.

Democratization in Venezuela was aided by economic and military factors that have not been present in later transitions to democracy. Economic expansion based on oil revenues had created a propitious environment for democratization to take place,[1] and it later helped to satisfy widespread social demands during the consolidation of democracy. In this way, the state and the military were buffered from the kinds of pressures that other, less economically endowed societies have faced while undergoing similar political change. Moreover, the timing of military modernization relative to the strengthening of democratic rule was also important. The military in Venezuela was modernized and strengthened after the construction of democratic institutions. At the time of the transition from authoritarianism, the Venezuelan military had not cohered around well-defined corporate interests to the extent that, for instance, the Brazilian or Argentine military had during similar stages in the transition process in

Admiral Ricardo Alberto de Lima, Defense and Naval Attache at the Venezuelan Embassy in Madrid, and General Miguel Angel Pinto, Director of the Institute for Advanced Studies in National Defense in Caracas, helped the author clarify many aspects of this chapter before it was written. Gabriel Aguilera, Fernando Bustamante, Paulette Higgins, Colonel Jose Machillanda, and Juan Rial made useful comments and suggestions on the manuscript. The author is thankful to them. The views expressed in this essay, however, are exclusively those of the author.

the 1980s. These later transitions therefore faced a more powerful and resilient military.

It is misleading, therefore, to view democratization in Venezuela as a process that developed without major obstacles and friction. This chapter examines the changing patterns of civil–military relations that have developed in Venezuela since the overthrow of Perez Jimenez. Modes of civil–military relations established early in the transition to democracy largely influenced the later, more stable patterns of the military's integration into the democratic regime. I will focus first, therefore, on the dynamics that led to the initiation of democratic construction and the gradual assertion of civilian supremacy during the transition period. I will then look at the patterns that took shape during the consolidation of democracy. The final section will discuss the strains that have developed in civil–military relations over the past few years, with particular attention to military grievances and the challenges they present.

From Dictatorship to Democracy

The Venezuelan transition started with the overthrow of Perez Jimenez in January 1958 and developed through the completion of the first democratic presidential term of Rómulo Betancourt (1959–64). This phase encompassed the period of the Junta de Gobierno, which followed the fall of the dictator, the promulgation of the 1961 constitution, a series of military insurrections, and the illegalization of insurrectionary leftist groups. With the end of the first democratic presidential term in 1964, the transition period—and Venezuela's long history of military interventionism—also came to an end.

The transition coincided with a period of economic crisis. Following the end of the Suez Canal crisis, the demand for petroleum shrank and Venezuela's export earnings declined dramatically. Facing limited fiscal resources, the Junta de Gobierno had to make cuts in public spending, including military spending.[2] At the same time, the government implemented a massive public works program to face soaring unemployment induced by the recession and migration from the countryside.[3] The unpropitious economic conditions during the transition years point to the role of political variables in accounting for the successful regime transition. The factors that facilitated the success achieved in the initial stage of the transition were (1) the decreasing participation of the military in the final phase of the dictatorship; (2) the fragmentation of the armed forces; and (3) the high level of unity reached by civilian forces in pursuing the establishment of a democratic regime.

The Decreasing Participation of the Military in the Final Phase of the Dictatorship

The government that took over in 1948 was anounced as a government of the armed forces.[4] Initially, the government of Perez Jimenez, fraudulently "elected" in 1952, also relied on the institutional support of the armed forces. However, the government soon personalized around the figure of Perez Jimenez, who increasingly relied on the use of repressive agencies alien to the military institution. The National Security—the political police agency—was run by a civilian loyal to the dictator and grew to have more personnel than the smaller of the armed services branches. Large sectors of the officer corps feared and resented the powers of the president and the repressive organizations under his control. Perez Jimenez's reliance on the National Security alienated the officer corps and prevented him from capitalizing on the vast program of modernization of the forces that he conceived and carried out. The purchase of modern combat planes, battleships, and armored vehicles did not translate into military support for the dictator.[5] With the military estranged from the government, the overthrow of the dictatorship would not entail the extrication of the whole military institution; it would entail only the removal of a group of key military personnel from positions of power.

The Fragmentation of the Armed Forces

When Perez Jimenez and his entourage were forcefully ousted, other military officers stepped in and formed the Junta de Gobierno, which included civilians. This junta initiated negotiations with political parties for the adoption of provisional government policies and for the setting of an electoral timetable for the transfer of power. In this context, the problems of a fractured military became apparent.

Conflicting allegiances to old military leaders and generational tensions pitted younger, better-trained officers against senior groups. When the military took over in 1948, it divided along party lines between those who had supported and those who had opposed the previous government of Accion Democratica (AD) in 1945–48. These cleavages persisted through the rule of Perez Jimenez, who repressed officers who had been associated with the AD. During his rule, however, the primary source of military divisions concerned Perez Jimenez's personalistic style and repressive conduct. Several factions opposed his government and staged attempts at overthrowing him.[6] He had always been able to resist these attempts, until his isolation from the Church, business groups, unions, and parties—in the face of manifest popular discontent—substantially reduced his ability to secure military support. The grotesque manipulation of the plebiscite of 1957, which would have perpetuated his power, led to popular revolt and a mutiny that originated in the navy and the air force. The insurrection quickly spread, and Perez Jimenez was forced to leave the country on January 23, 1958.

With the overthrow of the dictator and the formation of a military junta, divisions in the armed forces now centered around the nature of the new government and the role of the military in it. One faction, led by the chief of the general staff, sought to reorganize and continue military rule without Perez Jimenez. This faction had been greatly weakened, however, when Perez Jimenez ousted its leader shortly before the mutiny of January 23. The other faction, interested in preserving unity, sought the complete dismantling of the dictatorship and the retreat of the military to the barracks.[7] This faction, led by Admiral Larrazabal, prevailed in the junta. In its first manifesto, the junta stated the goal of "preserving the unity and institutional commitment of the military" and argued that "the activity of the Armed Forces requires a technical and juridical framework so that they can concentrate on their specific functions."[8] However, tensions and disagreements soon emerged within this new ruling clique, and factions of the military rebelled.

Military insurrections continued even after the first democratic election in 1958. The government of Betancourt had to face at least two major right-wing military rebellions. Former defense minister Castro Leon seized the garrison of San Cristobal in April 1960, in the hope that other garrisons would join. In June 1961, a regiment stationed in Barcelona revolted, with no success. Two additional major rebellions were staged by nationalist, left-leaning military sectors in the bloody insurrections in Carupano and Puerto Cabello in 1963. However, these were the last rebellions against the nascent democratic regime to be initiated by military factions.[9]

The High Level of Civilian Coalescence

In contrast to the fractionalization of the military, leaders of political parties and other civilian organizations reached high levels of coalescence, which, in turn, empowered the military factions that were interested in democratization. Party leaders had come a long way from the divisive experience of the *trienio* (1945–48), the short-lived experience of AD rule under presidents Betancourt and democratically elected Rómulo Gallegos. During this period, the AD had engaged in uncompromising attempts at promoting broad social reforms. The inflexibility of the AD's stance led to its gradual isolation and downfall. During their exile under the Perez Jimenez regime, political leaders came to terms with the need for unity and flexibility in order to defeat the dictatorship and put an end to the cycles of intervention by civil–military factions.[10]

The formation of the underground Patriotic Junta in August 1957, which included all political parties,[11] provided the first concrete indication of civilian unity. This united front mobilized the popular sectors against the dictatorship and continuously called upon the armed forces to disengage from Perez Jimenez and support democracy. Despite the fear of a military veto for including the Communist party and the AD in the Patriotic Junta, civilian leaders deemed broad unity more effective than a restricted front. This assessment proved correct as the civilian alternative gained in credibility and provided encouragement for the expansion of military discontent with the dictator. When the Junta de Gobierno took over upon the overthrow of Perez Jimenez, the civilian front successfully demanded the inclusion of civilians.

Civilian leaders were determined to preserve unity: They agreed on a truce in interparty struggle until democracy was fully established, offered guarantees to the Church, and incorporated representatives of labor and business in the united front. As a way of furthering the credibility of the civilian front, business organizations were granted even larger representation than corresponded to their organizational strength.[12] Political parties then initiated talks aimed at nominating a single presidential candidate. Despite the pervasive interest in unity, however, the AD and the Comite de Organizacion Politica Electoral Independente (COPEI) came with candidates of their own, whereas the Union Republicana Democratica (URD) and the Communist party coalesced behind the candidacy of junta leader Admiral Larrazabal. Nonetheless, the parties did agree to form a committee that would prepare a common platform for all presidential candidates. The committee proposed that the first democratic government include members of all parties in the cabinet, regardless of which candidate was elected.[13]

These agreements were formalized in the Pact of Punto Fijo, and the final documents were signed by all presidential candidates the night before the elections of December 6, 1958. The agreements outlined norms for the collaborative behavior of the electoral contenders as well as substantive guidelines for the future government. All parties committed themselves to eradicate interparty violence, to maintain the political truce beyond the date of the elections, and to prevent competitive electoral dynamics from interfering with the united front. The agreement included a commitment to elaborate a new constitution, to normalize church–state relations, to provide guarantees for private initiative and foreign investment, to revise the relations between the state and the oil companies, and to carry out land reform.[14]

The agreement favored military modernization, technical improvements, and the promotion of norms of discipline and political nondeliberation. The parties also offered to establish a mandatory draft for all eligible persons, following a long-held military claim that sought the conscription of youths of all social backgrounds. Civilian pacts strengthened those sectors within the armed forces that supported democratization and provided the military with specific guarantees that reduced the levels of uncertainty entailed in regime transitions.[15]

Civilian Control under the Betancourt Administration: Organizational Reform and Counterinsurgency

The 1961 constitution incorporated the substantive aspects of the Pact of Punto Fijo while essentially retaining the definition of military roles from the 1947 constitution. The 1961 constitution stated:

> The National Armed Forces comprise an apolitical, obedient and non-deliberative institution, organized by the State to secure national defense, the stability of democratic institutions and respect for the Constitution and Laws, whose compliance will always be beyond any other obligation. The National Armed Forces will be at the service of the Republic and in no case of personal or political persuasions.[16]

To insulate the military from party interference, the constitution provided for exclusive presidential leadership over the armed forces. To insulate the president from party politics, a clause was included that forbids a consecutive second term.

Betancourt moved swiftly to assert his position as commander-in-chief of the armed forces. Without interfering in internal military matters, he did not let the military interfere with government policies. In frequent visits to garrisons around the country, he explained government policies and showed concern for military problems, yet warned that anyone involved in conspiratorial activity would face martial courts.[17] Military uprisings provided the occasion for removals and purges of troubling officers, contributing to the subordination of the military to government control. Despite military opposition, Betancourt also recommissioned army officers who had been dismissed by the dictator on political grounds.

Furthermore, Betancourt made no exceptions for the military in sharing the costs of the economic crisis. Members of the armed forces were subject to the 10 percent reduction in salary levels applied across the board in the public sector.[18] Military spending was also reduced from the highest levels, reached in 1958, and in 1959–60 was cut in a larger proportion than the reductions applied to total government spending.[19]

President Betancourt also weakened military power by initiating significant organizational reforms in the defense sector. The general staff (*estado mayor general*), which integrated the top command structure (*comandancias generales*) of each of the four service branches in the Defense Ministry,[20] was replaced by a joint staff (*estado mayor conjunto*), which performed only advisory functions. The *comandancias generales*, in turn, were detached from the joint structures, except for administrative coordination in the Defense Ministry. In this way, the command structures of the separate services were granted institutional autonomy and were made hierarchically dependent on the president. Another reform led to the dismantling of the joint military school and the creation of separate military academies and general staff schools for each of the services. Betancourt's administration also established mandatory retirement for officers after only thirty years of service, ensuring a faster turnover in the higher ranks. As a consequence, officers at the grade of general or admiral would hold their posts only for very brief periods.

Beyond organizational reforms, civilian control was also enhanced when the government assigned the military a new mission: counterinsurgency. The opportunity was provided by the turn to armed revolutionary strategy by sectors of the Left shortly after Betancourt's inauguration. Groups on the Left initiated guerrilla activities in the cities and, later, in the countryside and attempted to overthrow the government by inciting the insurrection of military units.[21] The connections found between these local insurgent groups and foreign support from Cuba provided the opportunity for the government to assign the armed forces the mission of national territorial defense through counter-subversive warfare. In pursuing this mission, the military, under the political leadership of the civilian government, became involved in the defense of the recently inaugurated democracy.[22]

The outbreak of guerrilla activities signaled the end of the broad consensus among the political forces that had prevailed thus far. This breakdown, however, helped to reinforce military subordination to civilian authorities. The leftist turn to violence did not substantially weaken popular support for the major parties, and the initial support given the insurgency declined significantly following the failed insurrections of Carupano and Puerto Cabello. If the strategy of the Left had introduced divisions in the civilian bloc, a larger and more autonomous military role could have been expected.

Domestic turmoil and counterinsurgency activities did not lead the Venezuelan military to seek an expansion of its political role. When the fighting broke out, the armed forces had not developed the security doctrines that inspired military role expansion, for instance, in Argentina, Brazil, and Peru. The militaries of those countries empowered themselves with national security doctrines that supported their claim to a larger role in facing perceived threats of subversion. In Venezuela, however, strong democratic presidential leadership kept the armed forces engaged exclusively in fighting the guerrilla insurgency.[23] The government's foreign policy of isolating dictatorships on the continent—known as the Betancourt doctrine—was also an integral part of the defense of the nascent democracy.[24] The defense of democracy was thus associated with fighting not only leftist guerrillas, but also resilient military factions supported by foreign right-wing dictatorships.

The internal combat mission of the armed forces declined with the weakening of the guerrillas during the Leoni administration (1964–69) and the pacification proposals issued during the subsequent Caldera administration. Caldera's pacification policy, which allowed for the admission of guerrilla fighters as full citizens if they gave up armed struggle, proceeded despite occasional military opposition. New professional concerns with border disputes and with the assertion of state sovereignty in unpopulated border areas gradually substituted for the military's counterinsurgency mission.

Democratic Consolidation and New Military Roles

Following the end of domestic strife, stable patterns of civil–military relations developed in the context of military modernization and the consolidation of political institutions. Democratic procedures consolidated through peaceful presidential successions and the gradual stabilization of party preferences among the electorate. A predominant two-party system gradually set in, with the AD and the COPEI sharing about 80 percent of the vote toward the beginning of the 1970s. The parties of the Left, formed by groups that had split from the AD and by previously antisystem groups, reinserted themselves into the system and reached representation in the congress.[25] Other short-lived organizations formed during the 1960s elected members to the congress to represent the "protest vote."[26] On the whole, constitutional guarantees to private property, the moderation of the major parties, the strengthening of business and labor organizations, and the extended practice of consensual negotiation around major policy decisions provided possibilities for the representation of all major groups within the existing party structure.

The period of democratic consolidation also coincided with an economic recovery from the earlier downturn of the transition years. Export earnings rose, tax revenues increased as a result of an improved collection system, and import substitution activated local production. Government revenues increased systematically, as did spending in all sectors, including the military. In 1964, military expenditures already approximated the high levels of 1958, and they doubled in real terms in the mid-1970s. Until 1974, military expenditures remained constant relative to the gross national product. With the dramatic upswing in oil prices, however, military spending kept increasing, even though its share of the GNP was reduced.[27] Thus, trade-offs between spending in the military or in the "social" sectors, so critical in other Latin American nations, were avoided in Venezuela during this period. The oil bonanza that resumed after the transition permitted an "expanding-sum game,"[28] in which military modernization was financed without affecting other areas.[29]

A major aspect of this trend of the 1970s was the expansion and diversification of the military education and training system. Following a proposal by the minister of defense, the Institute for Advanced Studies in National Defense (IAEDN) was created in 1972. The institute provides a forum for the integration of upper-level officers and civilian technocrats in the appraisal of the nation's security and defense problems. Attendance at the Institute's seminars and courses is strongly encouraged and may soon become a requirement for promotions to higher military grades. In addition, university-level technical training is provided in the Armed Forces Politechnical Institute, which was created in 1975 and is open to both military and civilian students. The curriculum has expanded to include economics and social sciences. In contrast to the situation in the early years of democracy, when universities were perceived as a breeding ground for revolutionaries, military officers are now generally encouraged to undertake graduate studies in civilian universities. Educational improvements have also made recruitment and promotions highly competitive. [30]

The military has also developed new doctrines and has defined new missions.[31] With the declining emphasis on counterinsurgency activity, the military has concentrated on a reassessment of Venezuela's strategic position in the geopolitical context.[32] The strategic nature of oil production and export and the threats stemming from the unstable and volatile regional context have become a focal point of military concern. This focus has tended to give priority to outward-looking defensive strategies. Yet great emphasis has also been given to the problem of developing "state presence" in unpopulated territories bordering Colombia, Brazil, and Guyana. Along this line, "civic action" operations originally conceived as part of the war against the guerrilla movement turned into broader operations including the construction of roads, canals, schools, hospitals, and airfields, with a view to the integration of bordering areas. This emphasis was formalized in the Organic Law on Defense and Security, passed in 1976, which defined all territories along the border and around strategic production facilities as security zones of public interest and placed them under the supervision of the Defense Ministry.

The military shares with civilian elites a view that the state should play a major role in national development, with an emphasis on technological advances, national autonomy, and equitable distribution. Most officers also believe that the military itself ought to participate in the broadly defined areas of security and development. Some civilian sectors, especially in the moderate Left, have supported this view and have argued for "the full-fledged participation of the military in all aspects of national life" and for the extension of individual political rights to members of the armed forces.[33] This view is opposed by civilians who maintain that "the participation of the security apparatus of the state in the so-called development tasks runs contrary to healthy norms of institutional specialization."[34] In practice, however, military officers do participate in the boards and management of a number of state-owned enterprises, as well as in the administration and protection of several basic industries such as shipbuilding and aeronautics, public utilities, steel, and oil. Military participation in civilian areas has been somewhat expanded by the role of the Armed Forces of Cooperation, which works with other governmental agencies in a number of areas. In addition, upper-level officers have held important positions in the Frontiers Department of the Foreign Affairs Ministry and in committees created for the negotiation of border disputes. The military's domestic role has generally expanded along with the expansion of industry and state bureaucracy.

Modernization and institutional expansion have led the military to strengthen its capacity to assert a larger role in society.[35] This capacity is based partly on national security views that the military has developed in hand with institutional expansion. Although the national security perspectives of the Venezuelan military differ considerably from those held by Southern Cone militaries, they do share an anti-Communist emphasis inherited from the inter-American alliance and from the anti-Castro legacy of the previous counterinsurgency struggle. They also share an expansive view of military security as encompassing all aspects of national life. This view is expressed, for instance, in the Organic Law on Defense and Security, which was passed in 1976 under military auspices. The law created the National Council of Defense and Security (CONSEDE)[36] and established working committees under the coordination of a military-chaired permanent secretariat. The committees were assigned to work on political, economic, social, military, and mobilization affairs. The law expanded military prerogatives in security areas and has been depicted as reminiscent of the Southern Cone type of military security doctrines.[37] The military also urged the passing of the Military Service Law in 1978, which mandates the equitable participation of all social sectors in the military draft. In 1983, the government agreed to revise the Organic Law of the Armed Forces in order to expand active life in the service from thirty to thirty-three years and to empower the president to expand this limit further in specific cases.[38] The growing ability of the military to advance its claims has also hardened institutional boundaries.[39] The military has managed to remain somewhat protected from outside public control by developing, with the compliance of party elites, a buffer zone that deters the prompt investigation of irregularities, excesses in the use of force, or outright corruption.[40]

Improved military capacities have not weakened the existing mechanisms of civilian control, however. These control mechanisms remain centered on the president, who chairs the Council on Defense and Security and oversees the armed services with the help of the minister of defense. The Organic Law of the Armed Forces assigns to the president the command of the forces; empowers him to rule on their organization, administration, and deployment; and authorizes him personally to conduct wartime operations. Even in areas that purportedly have security implications, the government formulates and implements policy with full independence, although the military does make itself heard on policies regarding border disputes.[41] The congress, which has far fewer prerogatives than the executive in the defense and military sector, exerts control through global approval of the defense budget and through authorization of promotions for upper-level officers.[42]

Along with the formal mechanisms of presidential and congressional control, informal mechanisms for influence and control by the major political parties have also developed. Indeed, party influences have created a patronage system that affects decisions about promotions, assignments, appointments to key posts in the military or state agencies, and military contracts and supplies.[43] Although promotions to the grade of colonel and general are usually approved by the congress, the military perceives the decisions of congressional members as based excessively on the purported political inclinations of those up for promotion. This creates an incentive for officers to present themselves as agreeable to politicians and parties. Though this congressional oversight may be regarded as a critical mechanism of civilian control, the military sees it as a distortion of the internal evaluation system based on the assessment of individual personality and performance factors. According to the military's view, external influences distort professional norms, promote internal rivalries, and negatively affect the efficient performance of the military bureaucracy and command.[44] This is one of the major sources of military grievances.

Military Grievances and Party Politics: Strains in Civil–Military Relations

Since the establishment of democracy, civilian elites have encouraged military modernization and participation in state development functions and have agreed to some expansion of military roles. Nevertheless, the development of the military remains truncated at various points. For instance, military agencies in charge of national security planning do not effectively coordinate with state planning agencies. Development plans devised by the military for border areas are deprived of the adequate resources necessary to implement them, and full operational coordination of the forces is hindered by current organizational arrangements. These inconsistencies render formally accepted levels of military participation more symbolic than real.[45] The combination of a lack of joint command and planning structures and external pressures that pull the military in different directions has resulted in the coexistence of separate military spheres: the military operational sphere, itself badly coordinated, and the bureaucratic-administrative or civilianized sphere, subject to politicization and party influences.[46]

The expanding gap between military goals and means, coupled with patronage practices and formal mechanisms of civilian control, has given rise to increasingly outspoken signs of military discontent.[47] The military's criticism is broadly targeted against both the unwillingness or inability of civilians to provide substantive guidelines for the defense sector and military development and the harmful effects of party influences and patronage.

In a carefully written article published in 1984, General Jacobo Yepez Daza, chief of the Operational Planning Group of the Defense Ministry, pointed to the vacuum in existing legislation with regard to the delineation of responsibilities of the top civilian and military authorities in the planning and conduct of defense operations. This vacuum is seen as the result of the organizational measures adopted by President Betancourt in the early 1960s, which aimed at weakening military power but bypassed the need for unified military command structures. The military resents this lasting organizational structure, which has dispersed power among the president, the CONSEDE, the minister of defense, the chiefs of the services, the chiefs of intelligence and the president's advisory military staff.[48] The military would like to see the minister of defense, a military officer, at the top of a single, unified command structure, and it resents the unwillingness of civilians to deal with these issues.[49]

Indeed, military sectors now openly criticize the basic and enduring measures with which the civilians subordinated the military at the outset of democratization. Parties and politicians are perceived as emphasizing measures of formal control without providing substantive answers to military claims. Critics argue that political patronage has taken precedence over professional development, and military "bureaucratism"[50] or "perverse" professionalism[51] has been the result. Parties and politicians are thus blamed not only for containing the development of military potential but also for actively contributing to the destabilization of military structures. In questioning the authority of civilian leaders,[52] military critics have made explicit statements that range from overt threats of military action to more tame, though no less emphatic warnings.[53]

Conclusions

Venezuela's success in establishing and maintaining a democratic regime when most South American countries succumbed to military authoritarian rule is based partially on distinctively Venezuelan factors.[54] The large resources provided by the oil-based economy during the consolidation of democracy allowed for an "expansive-sum game,"[55] in which military demands could be satisfied without significantly affecting other sectors. The Venezuelan political process was thus able to bypass the zero-sum conditions that, in other contexts (for example, Argentina), have exacerbated situations of mass praetorianism and stressed civil–military relations.[56] These situations, however, result not only from a strained economy but also from the absence of institutional mechanisms to channel and accommodate conflicting societal demands. The strength of political parties and the stabilization of the party system now sets Venezuela apart from other cases (such as Brazil) in which an assertive military faces much weaker institutional structures.[57] Finally, the fact that military modernization took place *after* the fall of the dictatorship helped to strengthen civilian control in Venezuela. Under strong presidential guidance, the military was led to defend democratic institutions from foreign right-wing and leftist guerrilla attacks. This mission supported the development of military role-beliefs[58] that were consistent with constitutional democratic orientations. In other countries, such as Brazil,[59] the postauthoritarian definition of new military missions which support more professional roles has been the product of an already strong military that manages to maintain an autonomous position as the guardian of national security.[60]

Despite its role in counterinsurgency in the 1960s, the Venezuelan military did not develop into what Stepan called the "new professionalism of internal warfare and military role expansion," which characterized the path taken by the Brazilian and Argentine military.[61] Neither did the Venezuelan military conform strictly to the "old professionalism" pattern. The armed forces perform functions of external and internal security and have developed highly professional skills, which are employed in both the military and the state administrative spheres under a combined pattern of civilian control and military managerialism. In terms of the models of civilian control proposed by Huntington, the model of "objective civilian control" appears to be consistent with the constitutional definitions and the actual development of military professionalism in Venezuela.[62] However, civil–military relations are also based on a broadly shared developmentalist ethos and on an extended practice of party penetration, influence, and patronage among the military, which make this case also resemble the model of "subjective civilian control." Indeed, the military's dissatisfaction with existing arrangements is driven by this absence of a clear military role and a well-defined pattern of civilian control.

What lies ahead in Venezuelan civil–military relations? How critical are the strains that have recently developed? Experts on Venezuela have long speculated on the conditions and possibilities that would lead to military role expansion and political intervention.[63] Yet these hypothetical trends were discarded in light of the continued preeminence of the factors that have supported democratic stability: economic expansion, the strength of political parties, and the more or less implicit maintenance of the original democratic pact. It is less clear, however, that these factors still maintain their ability to prevent an eventual expansion of military roles. Beyond changing economic conditions, which have lost the dynamism previously driven by the oil sector, and the conditions produced by party competition, a sharp deterioration in civil–military relations would require the development of a perception of threat to the military's corporate identity. Such a perception could result from a praetorianization of the political process, along with the termination of the expanding-sum game, or from serious government mismanagement of an international crisis around border disputes. It could also result from civilian attempts to reduce military autonomy, from a significant increase in internal politicization through party influences, or from expanded dissatisfaction with civilian "negligence" to restructure the existing pattern of civil–military relations. The current situation is far from indicating a serious military threat to the continuation of democracy.[64] Should civil–military relations continue to deteriorate, however, the military would face this situation from a position of high capacity, and one can only hope that civilians display the leadership capacities that led to the founding of democracy in Venezuela three decades ago.

Notes

1. See Terry Lynn Karl, "Petroleum and Political Pacts: The Transition to Democracy in Venezuela," *Latin American Research Review* 22, No.1 (1987), pp. 63–94.

2. See Robert E. Looney, *The Political Economy of Latin American Defense Expenditures* (Lexington, Mass.: Lexington Books, 1986).

3. See Benito Raul Losada, "La Transición Económica," in J.L. Salcedo-Bastardo et al., *Transito de la Dictadura a la Democracia en Venezuela* (Barcelona, Caracas, Mexico: Editorial Ariel, 1978).

4. See Gene E. Bigler, "Venezuela," in Robert Wesson, ed., *The Latin American Military Institution* (New York: Praeger, 1986).

5. See Bigler, "Venezuela"; "Professional Soldiers and Restrained Politics in Venezuela," in Robert Wesson, ed., *New Military Politics in Latin America* (New York: Praeger, 1982); and "The Armed Forces and Patterns of Civil–Military Relations," in John D. Martz and David J. Myers, eds., *Venezuela: The Democratic Experience* (New York: Praeger, 1977). See, also, Winfield J. Burggraaff, *The Venezuelan Armed Forces in Politics: 1935–1959* (Columbia: University of Missouri Press, 1972).

6. See José Ramón Avendano Lugo, *El Militarismo en Venezuela* (Caracas: Ediciones Centauro, 1982).

7. See Andres Stambouli, *Crísis Política: Venezuela 1945–1958* (Caracas: Editorial Ateneo, 1980).

8. See Luis Herrera Campins, "La Transicion Política," in Salcedo-Bastardo et al., *Transito de la Dictadura*.

9. See Robert J. Alexander, *Rómulo Betancourt and the Transformation of Venezuela* (New Brunswick: Transaction Books, 1982); and Avendano Lugo, *El Militarismo*.

10. See Daniel H. Levine, "Venezuela Since 1958: The Consolidation of Democratic Politics," in Juan J. Linz and Alfred Stepan, eds., *The Breakdown of Democratic Regimes: Latin America* (Baltimore: Johns Hopkins University Press, 1978).

11. The Accion Democratica (AD), a party with a social democratic orientation; the Comite de Organizacion Política Electoral Independiente (COPEI), a Christian Democratic party supported by business groups; the Union Republicana Democratica (URD), a populist party; and the Partido Comunista de Venezuela (PCV), the Venezuelan Communist party.

12. See Herrera Campins, "La Transicion Política."

13. Even though the Communists were excluded from these global agreements, they were later included in the committee, chaired by the archbishop of Caracas, that would prepare plans for land reform.

14. See Herrera Campins, "La Transicion Política."

15. The substantive aspects of the future constitution were already defined in the Pact of Punto Fijo. The process of constitution-making, therefore, entailed no major uncertainties and provided no surprises for the military, facilitating the military's acquiescence to democratization. See Felipe Aguero, "Civilian Supremacy and Democracy in Spain," Paper presented to the Workshop on Armed Forces and Democratic Consolidation, Instituto Universitario Ortega y Gasset, Madrid, April 25–28, 1988.

16. This English translation is quoted from E. Bigler, "The Armed Forces." All other translations from original Spanish versions have been made by the author.

17. See Alexander, *Rómulo Betancourt*.

18. See Bigler, "Professional Soldiers."

19. See Looney, *The Political Economy.*

20. See Adrian J. English, *Armed Forces of Latin America* (London: Jane's, 1984).

21. See David Eugene Blank, *Venezuela: Politics in a Petroleum Republic* (New York: Praeger, 1984).

22. A concrete manifestation of the linkage between counterguerrilla warfare and defense of democratic institutions is found in the Plan Republica. The plan operationalizes the role of the military in supervising the electoral process under the general guidance of the Supreme Electoral Council. See Maria Pilar Villabona Blanco, "Politica y Elecciones en Venezuela," *Revista de Estudios Politicos* (Madrid), No. 53 (September–October, 1986).

23. For instance, the president informed the military about his decision to break diplomatic relations with Cuba and to suspend the legality of the Communist party and the Movement of the Revolutionary Left (MIR). He did not ask the military's advice or allow discussion of these decisions. See Alexander, *Rómulo Betancourt*; Rómulo Betancourt, *Respeto y Defensa del Orden Institucional* (Caracas: Divulgacion y Ediciones Palacio Blanco, 1962); and Rómulo Betancourt, *En Defensa del Sistema Democratico* (Caracas: Imprenta Nacional, 1963).

24. On April 22, 1960, during the Second Inter-American Conference for Democracy and Freedom, Betancourt proposed "that around the dictatorial governments be tied a rigorous multilateral prophylactic cordon, for the purpose of asphyxiating them, so that they do not constitute opprobium for the people and permanent menace to the legitimately constituted governments." See Alexander, *Rómulo Betancourt*, p. 526. Venezuela followed this policy by denying diplomatic recognition to the unconstitutional regimes established in El Salvador in 1960, in Peru and Argentina in 1962, in Haiti in 1963, and in Bolivia, Brazil, and Ecuador in 1964. On June 24, 1960, Betancourt escaped, not without injuries, an assassination attempt organized by dictator Rafael Trujillo of the Dominican Republic.

25. See John D. Martz and David J. Myers (eds.), *Venezuela: The Democratic Experience*, rev. ed. (New York: Praeger, 1986).

26. The most important of these organizations was the Nationalist Civic Crusade (CCN), which gathered supporters of former dictator Perez Jimenez. See Avendano Lugo, *El Militarismo*; Judith Ewell, *The Indictment of a Dictator* (College Station: Texas A&M University Press, 1981); and Judith Ewell, *Venezuela: A Century of Change* (Stanford, Calif.: Stanford University Press, 1984).

27. See Looney, *The Political Economy.*

28. See Franklin Tugwell, "Petroleum Policy and the Political Process," in Martz and Myers, *Venezuela.*

29. Salaries for military personnel increased 140 percent in real terms between 1960 and 1974. See Bigler, "Professional Soldiers." Retirement, health, and other social security benefits were reinforced with the passing of the Organic Law of Social Security in 1977.

30. According to Bigler, "Professional Soldiers," the proportion of admissions relative to applications in military academies declined substantially during the 1970s, and only about half of those admitted actually graduated.

31. See General Jacobo Yepez Daza, "El Realismo Militar Venezolano," in

Moises Naim and Ramon Pinango, eds., *El Caso Venezuela: Una Ilusion de Armonia* (Caracas: Ediciones IESA, 1984).

32. See Judith Ewell, "The Development of Venezuelan Geopolitical Analysis Since World War II," *Journal of Interamerican Studies and World Affairs* 24, no. 3 (1982).

33. See Jose Vicente Rangel, "Problemas Fundamentales de Suguridad y Defensa de Venezuela," in Anibal Romero, ed., *Seguridad, Defensa y Democracia* (Caracas: Editorial Equinoccio, 1980).

34. See Luis Enrique Alcala, "La Doctrina de Seguridad en Venezuela," in Romero, *Seguridad.* For contending views in this debate, see Jose Vicente Rangel et al., *Militares y Politica: Une Polemica Inconclusa* (Caracas: Ediciones Centauro, 1976); and General Jacobo Yepez Daza, "El Realismo Militar Venezolano," in Naim and Pinango, *El Caso Venezuela,* p. 347.

35. O'Donnell analyzed the development of the military's capacity in 1955–66 in Argentina in terms of organizational cohesion and doctrinal coherence vis-á-vis the pressures stemming from a praetorianized society. See Guillermo O'Donnell, "Modernization and Military Coups: Theory, Comparisons and the Argentine Case," in Abraham Lowenthal and J. Samuel Fitch, eds., *Armies and Politics in Latin America* (New York: Holmes and Meier, 1986). The development of military capacity in Venezuela does not respond to societal praetorianism. Rather, it supports military insertion in state structures under a modernizing ethos shared with civilian elites.

36. The council is formed by members of the executive cabinet (which includes the minister of defense, an active-duty general), the inspector-general of the armed forces, and the chief of the general staff. The permanent secretary of the council is appointed and removed by the president. His functions are to propose defense and security policies, to propose measures for the adequate employment of national resources, to coordinate national authorities for the purposes established in the law, and to request and gather information on matters deemed important for security.

37. See Ewell, "The Development of Venezuelan Geopolitical Analysis." The Organic Law on Defense and Security empowers the president to employ the armed forces in the control and operation of public services or basic industries and to place their civilian personnel temporarily under military regimentation. The law also allows military courts to resort to "extraordinary" procedures contemplated in the Code of Military Justice when a "state of emergency" or "mobilization" is declared. The law also created the National Intelligence Service. For the law, see *Gaceta Oficial,* No. 1899, August 26, 1976; and "Reglamento Parcial No. 1 de la Ley Organica de Seguridad y Defensa," Decreto No. 2738, *Gaceta Oficial,* No. 31563, September 1, 1978.

38. See Bigler, "Venezuela."

39. For the notion of boundaries between civilian and military institutions, see Robin Luckham, "A Comparative Typology of Civil-Military Relations," *Government and Opposition* 6, no. 1 (1971); and Yoram Peri, *Between Battles and Ballots: Israeli Military in Politics* (Cambridge: Cambridge University Press, 1983).

40. This buffer zone, or "the delicacy norm" (Bigler, "Venezuela") has be-

come visible when journalists, public officials, or others have attempted to denounce irregularities. See *Latin American Weekly Report*, No. 45, (November 17, 1988). The list of questionable events involving the military in the past years has grown; see Coronel (EJ) Jose Machillanda Pinto, *Poder Politico y Poder Militar en Venezuela, 1958–1986* (Caracas: Ediciones Centauro, 1988), p. 175.

41. The armed forces have rejected government proposals for a negotiated settlement of differences with Colombia. A draft border treaty was also rejected in 1982. See Jose Antonio Gil Yepes, "Political Articulation of the Military Sector in Venezuelan Democracy," in Martz and Myers, *Venezuela*. In other areas, however, the government has acted with full independence. The Caldera administration (1969–74) made significant policy shifts without military interference. For instance, Caldera initiated the pacification plan and abandoned the Betancourt doctrine, establishing diplomatic relations with Cuba and other socialist states. Different governments have shifted emphases in the country's approach to the regional context (that is, Nicaragua, Granada), independently of the military's preferences.

42. The congress approves the defense budget without debating specific itemized allocations and cannot control subsequent defense appropriations according to the Organic Law of the Comptroller-General. See Teodoro Petkoff, "Venezuela en el Mundo: Seguridad Nacional desde la Perspectiva del Cambio Social," in Rombero, *Seguridad*. The military's comptroller reports to the president, not to the congress. See Gil Yepes, "Political Articulation."

43. See Machillanda Pinto, *Poder Politico*.

44. Former defense minister, General Luis Enrique Rangel Bourgoin denounced this situation in the following terms:

It is criminal to allow officers with limited qualifications or no merit to bypass the requisites established in the military system, by resorting to outside or hidden favors [using] former presidents, the Church, political leaders, retired generals, their wives or other individuals in order to guarantee their promotion

Luis Enrique Rangel Bourgoin, *Nosotros los Militares* (Caracas: Editorial Sol, 1983), p. 61.

45. See Gil Yepes, "Political Articulation."

46. See Machillanda Pinto, *Poder Politico*; and Yepez Daza, "El Realismo."

47. The defense and public presentation of military views are aided by the existence of several associations of retired officers, as active-duty officers are deprived of individual political rights. Some of these associations are formally integrated in the Defense Ministry and have been instrumental in advancing military claims and in obtaining social and other benefits. See Rangel Bourgoin, *Nosotros los Militares*, pp. 87–89. Some officers join political parties upon retirement, and a few have run for the presidency. Although the views expressed by those who go into politics are not necessarily representative, they do give some indication of the mood that prevails within the military.

48. Rangel Bourgoin, *Nosotros los Militares*, Machillanda Pinto, *Poder Politico*, and Yepez Daza, "El Realismo" make numerous references to the problems

derived from lack of coordination and unified command, which have, indeed, affected the efficacy of decision making in critical areas in the defense sector. The decision to purchase F-16 combat planes from the United States exemplifies the problems inherent in current organizational structures. See Fernando Bustamante y Carlos Portales, "La Venta de Aviones F-16 a Venezuela: Un Caso de Transferencia de Tecnologia Avanzada," *Documento de Trabajo* (FLACSO) (1988).

49. See Yepez Daza, "El Realismo"; Gil Yepes, "Political Articulation"; Rangel Bourgoin, *Nosotros los Militares*; and Machillanda Pinto, *Poder Politico*.

50. Yepez Daza, "El Realismo."

51. Machillanda Pinto, *Poder Politico*.

52. "It is inadmissible for us in the military that none of the members of Congress's Defense Committee, in either of the chambers, has served in the military or has had any training in Defense and Security. And yet they handle military and security legislation!" Rangel Bourgoin, *Nosotros los Militares*, p. 105.

53. Former defense minister General Garcia Villasmil has said that "unless the democratic system is improved, it would become necessary to expand the influence of the Armed Forces so that they can act as referees." Quoted in Rangel Bourgoin, *Nosotros los Militares*. See, also, Yepez Daza, "El Realismo," p. 348.

54. See Augusto Varas, Felipe Aguero, and Fernando Bustamante, *Chile: Democracia y Fuerzas Armadas* (Santiago: FLASCO, 1980).

55. Tugwell, "Petroleum Policy."

56. See O'Donnell, "Modernization and Military Coups."

57. See Martz and Myers, *Venezuela*; and Scott Mainwaring, "Political Parties and Democratization in Brazil and the Southern Cone," *Comparative Politics* (October 1988).

58. See J. Samuel Fitch, "The Theoretical Model Underlying the Analysis of Civil–Military Relations in Contemporary Latin American Democracies: Core Assumptions," Paper prepared for the Inter-American Dialogue, 1987.

59. See Stanley Hilton, "The Brazilian Military: Changing Strategic Perceptions and the Question of Mission," *Armed Forces and Society* 13, no. 3 (1987).

60. See Fitch, "The Theoretical Model."

61. See Alfred Stepan, "The New Professionalism of Internal Warfare and Military Role Expansion," in *Authoritarian Brazil* (New Haven, Conn.: Yale University Press, 1973).

62. See Samuel P. Huntington *The Soldier and the State* (New York: Vintage Books, 1957).

63. See Martz and Myers, *Venezuela*.

64. See Enrique Baloyra, "Public Opinion and Support for the Regime: 1973–1983," in Martz and Myers, *Venezuela*.

17

The Armed Forces and Democracy: The Interests of Latin American Military Corporations in Sustaining Democratic Regimes

Juan Rial

The Armed Forces and Political Elites of Latin America

Arturo Valenzuela has correctly pointed out that the dichotomy "civil military relations" is an idealized projection of relationships of countries such as Great Britain and the United States.[1] It is not very useful for the states of the Third World. There, the armed forces and the political system are highly interconnected, and the subordination of the armed forces is a problem under constant discussion.

Different academic models are proposed to describe the modalities of the relationship between the armed forces and the political system. All of them have a privileged ideal type that accepts the subordination of the military to civilian power, with the two conceived as separate entities. One of the most successful arguments along this line rests on the premise that when political institutions are weak or lack legitimacy, it is possible for the military to intervene actively in politics.[2]

Acceptance of the premise of subordination of the military force as the most desirable model[3] places the key to control in the organizational structure. Only when the armed forces are professionals who, by definition, cannot intervene in politics can a "desirable" civil–military relationship be ensured.

Along the same vein, but taking the relationship between the military and the government as the center of the problem, we have the position of those who take societal development into account. Adam Smith sustained that an army would not be dangerous for freedom (freedom derived from the free play of the forces in the market) if it were placed under the authority of those who are interested in supporting the government.

The current situation in the United States is in line with this position. The U.S. armed forces increasingly tend to be a corporation whose business is security. On the one hand, they constitute an instrument of enforcement; on the other, they are an organization with its own interests. It is in the latter capacity that the armed forces exert pressure on other centers of power—negotiating, imposing their views, or yielding, as the case may be.

In this model, the armed forces take on only part of the global security responsibilities. They lose "military" relevance and form part of the set of security forces that includes the information services, the paramilitary, and police forces.

In the United States, the armed forces, together with the intelligence agencies, constitute the most important part of the security apparatus. The armed forces interact heavily with other economic corporations (from which they buy equipment and services and to which they offer their experience). As a result, the military tends to adopt the management guidelines of business corporations, while businesses tend to incorporate organizational concepts typical of the armed forces. Although there is no spillover of personnel from business to the military, except in upper management, the contrary does occur.

The same objectives guide both the military and the big business elites. There are also no discrepancies with the political class, which has close links to both elites. The assumption of a managerial model by the armed forces eliminates the possibility of intervention by the military in the political system.

As indicated earlier, the situation in Latin America is not compatible with a model of this type. On the contrary, the relationship between leading economic and/or political classes and the armed forces tends to be very difficult. The armed forces are segmented from civilian society and autonomized from the state. Of all the Latin American nations, only three—Mexico, Cuba, and Nicaragua—present the kind of integration that could be assimilable to the model described, although their guidelines differ.

In other Latin American states, there is no integration between the armed forces and the state. During the period of professional construction, the military's separation from society and the state was deepened. This situation made it possible, in many cases, to hide the political role of the armed forces, which, at most, was perceived as subsidiary. The moderating role was cause for factional dispute on the part of the political class.[4]

In general, the military was seen as an annoying but indispensable body—"manageable" by the elites. It was to be kept isolated and used only when necessary. Obviously, the current officer corps can no longer be considered an uncouth organization. Moreover, theoretical positions sustained in the 1960s insisted on a modernized military. Even in advanced countries, there is an acknowledgment of the importance of the cultural levels acquired by the officer corps through a process of ongoing education. Nevertheless, the perception of the military by Latin American civilian society and its political community can be described in Tocqueville's words of 150 years ago: They are perceived as ruder than the rest of the population.

Institutional arrangements provide for the subordination of the armed forces to the government in almost all Latin American countries. In most cases, the president is commander-in-chief (or the equivalent) of the military force, and the parliament establishes the necessary contingent as well as the military budget. The norms for promotion of higher-ranked personnel imply the subordination of the military corporation to civilian power through the intervention of the president and/or the minister of defense and parliament. Although in many cases the armed forces themselves manage the defense ministry (or ministries),[5] in such cases they tend to be considered part of the political power structure, rather than members of the military corporation, even if, in reality, they are representatives of the latter vis-á-vis the state and the government. Vagts believed that the military organization does not permit civilians to exert effective control over it.[6]

Nevertheless, the leading and political classes of Latin America tried to do so. Normally, they "infiltrated" the officer corps, utilizing forms of control that Huntington qualified as "subjective." Appointments based on political loyalties, assignments, or commissions in places far from the centers of power; increases in the number of commanders at the same hierarchical level; and other complementary mechanisms were tried.

But with the growth of professionalism, the members of the armed corps ceased to be as easily controlled. The intellectual capacity of the officer corps increased markedly, even if that fact was not perceived by the members of the political class or, at times, by the members of the military organizations themselves.

Informal or formal methods of control, which go beyond constitutional or legal provisions for the armed forces, have been disappearing. The armed citizen corps (similar to the National Guard), that existed in various Latin American countries during the nineteenth century have vanished. The controls on teaching processes, and on military socialization processes in general, lack validity today.

The creation of parallel paramilitary bodies did not affect the armed forces, except in a very few cases. Moreover, the attempts to do so were successfully resisted, especially when they tended to create "popular militia" forces.[7]

Civil elites lost all possibility of exercising control over military socialization when professionalization processes were left, first, in the hands of European military missions and, later, in those of national officers.[8] More important, with the process of professionalization of the military forces (Europeanization in South American and North Americanization in Central America), civilian elites left the operational definition of the armed forces' objectives in the hands of the military. In the long term, they also ceased formulating doctrines for utilization of those forces. In other cases, they abdicated the responsibility for providing ideology to guide military actions in critical circumstances.

In Central America and the Caribbean, this process led some of the armed corps to their own destruction, as well as to the collapse of the political regimes based on them. In other cases, especially in Brazil and the Southern Cone, a new professionalism was erected,[9] led by a "party," by "military parties,"[10] or by corporative armed factions that attempted to reestablish regimes on the basis of a revised ideology justifying their existence as an armed corps.[11]

In summary, in Latin America (save in the exceptional cases cited—Mexico, Cuba, and Nicaragua), complete subordination of the armed forces to the state occurs rarely. The military constitutes a social body that is segmented from the rest of society and enjoys strong autonomy with regard to the state, despite the fact that it may formally depend on the state. Segmentation has led the armed forces to develop guidelines for socialization, norms, and values that differentiate and isolate them from civilian society. Their autonomy with regard to the state is manifested in their weak control over organizational forms, military education, and management of the budget. In cases where their own decision-making capacity is broader, autonomy is also expressed in the definition of mission and the doctrine of force, as well as in their ideological basis.

Reconstruction of Democracy and the Armed Forces

By the end of the 1980s, the majority of South American countries will probably have democratic regimes. At least that is what the majority of the political communities in those nations hope.[12]

After the surmounting of authoritarianism in Brazil and the Southern Cone, only one dictatorship remains in 1989. Although Pinochet's Chile is based on the new professionalism of the military organization, it is possible that Chile may have a new regime by the end of the year. In the Caribbean, there have been no changes. The recent fall of Duvalier has put the regular military forces in the foreground, although we still do not know where the new regime is going. The Dominican Republic maintains the democratic-liberal pattern; Cuba maintains the socialist pattern;

Puerto Rico continues as a commonwealth of the United States; and the English-speaking Caribbean, after the U.S. intervention in Grenada, presents no significant changes.[13]

Mexico is on the eve of possible political reform, perhaps the reformulation of the corporative pact. In Panama, the Guard—now the Fuerzas de Defensa de Panama (FDP)—continues at the helm. On the other hand, the situation in Central America could change dramatically. Guatemala seems to have entered a process of redemocratization, although the problem of the indigenous population is still present, and its proximity to other countries in conflict could lead to a rapid reversal of the situation.

Political and military considerations have kept the United States from invading Nicaragua. Latin American countries are not willing to do so in the United States' name, as happened in 1965 during the second stage of the invasion of Santo Domingo. If the scenario does not change, the contras can continue to harass, but it is improbable that they can win their war. Nevertheless, the exterior context is not as favorable as it was to Cuba in 1961–62. This last factor creates a high degree of uncertainty regarding Nicaragua's future.

The persistence of the Salvadoran conflict favors Nicaragua, even if, ultimately, it is resolved in favor of the existing regime and its armed forces. Obviously, if the guerrillas triumph, this would not only affirm Nicaragua's role but would also radically alter the balance of power in the region. The war zone includes Honduras (whose political and military fate is tied to the resolution of the conflict), as well as Costa Rica. In the case of Costa Rica, no matter who the winner is, the very existence of the conflict is bound to provoke the militarization of that country, even though it is arguable whether or not this process would imply the creation of a professional armed forces.[14]

The process of reconstruction of democracy (which, in the majority of cases, would be more accurately called construction) seems to be circumscribed to the countries of South America and to only a few in other zones. In the Spanish-speaking Caribbean, the only country involved in this process is the Dominican Republic. In Central America, those that are on that course, such as Costa Rica, are threatened by an international war or are already involved in one.

We shall understand democracy to be, exclusively, the effectiveness of polyarchical rules of the game and of what is called an *estado de derecho*, in line with juridical provisions and even the limitations of those provisions that may be established in accordance with legal resolutions. We do not take into account any definition that attempts to give social content to the word *democracy*. It was not in this sense that the redemocratization process was proposed in the cases where it arose in the 1980s—that is, in the countries that had suffered dictatorial processes.

Within this democratic framework, social inequalities continue to be very marked. A majority of the popular classes continue to live in poverty, and their economic growth will not be sufficient to catch up with the leading countries. Presumably, there will be recurrences of acute social crises, social protest movements, and, perhaps, new attempts by armed groups to gain power.

Keeping this scenario in mind, what are the possible models for the relationship between the armed forces and their governments? Why is democracy the model accepted by the armed forces? To answer this question, we must first try to establish what mission is perceived by the region's armed forces at this point.

For all armed corporations, their raison d'être continues to be to win eventual wars. However, how can one construe a sense of identity with this mission when the possibilities of traditional confrontation among the states have become less and less probable?

In order to establish a clear mission for the armed forces without their segmentation and separation from the rest of society—and without their acquiring unnecessary degrees of autonomy as a social actor—members of both the political class and the military should share a common view of what war and peace mean. This is exactly what does not happen in Latin America, where the actual design of military policy is left entirely in the hands of the armed forces. The only outcome has been constant theorizing about the military mission by military intellectuals, with few relevant practical results.[15]

Much more important is the military discussion of the subject of revolutionary war.[16] This is rarely studied and is often confused with the so-called doctrine of national security, whose origin is erroneously attributed exclusively to U.S. influence.[17]

Neither the academic community nor the political class takes geopolitical thought seriously. However, its importance has been substantial for the destiny of some countries.[18] The definitions of who the enemy is, of the mission of the armed forces, and of the legitimacy of the actions that can be undertaken by armed corporations were the work of "organic intellectuals," many of whom did not belong officially to the military corporation. This elaboration involved the participation neither of the governments nor, of course, of civilian society.

There were various routes for the creation of these doctrines and ideologies and the discourses that express them. Geopolitical conceptions—especially German conceptions, the influence of the French doctrine of *guerre revolutionnaire* (transmitted directly, in Argentina's case, by a technical mission), and the absorption of the elaborations relating to "national security" emanating from the United States—were some of the chief routes. The need for an enemy, any enemy, that could give meaning to military action and reinforce corporate identity was satisfied upon the discovery that wars of a new type could be waged.

Those who elaborated these concepts sustain that current wars differ from the classic interstate confrontation. The new forms of war imply internal confrontations, total mobilization of resources, and manipulation of the population. Identification with the West facilitated identification of the enemy—to wit, communism, Marxism in other formulations, and, more generically, subversion.[19]

The doctrine of the military corporations in many Latin American countries has produced an "operational inversion" with respect to recent positions. The *foquiste* doctrine, originally expressed by Ernesto Che Guevara and subsequently reformulated by Regis Debray, is a key reference point.[20] The new doctrines place the main enemy within the society and the state, responding to the process of militarization of the Left.[21]

Some military intellectuals attempted to elude the formulation of a reactive doctrine, seeking support in the philosophical-religious thought of the Christian Middle Ages and moving toward the integralist position.[22] However, they could not get beyond the basic contradictions between this ideological corpus and the existence of a capitalist society in which a majority of the population is perceived to be located in the middle strata and where there is no space provided for the warriors—a society that adheres to liberal positions and even to post-Enlightenment brands of socialism.[23]

The first point to be considered in a discussion of civil–military relations in democratic countries would have to be the destiny of the armed forces, keeping in mind the following questions:

Why do they exist?
Who is their possible enemy?[24]
What mission do they fulfill?
Who commands, and why?

Lloyd George's aphorism regarding the role of the military in war should be remembered. The political classes of Latin America left the war issue in the hands of the armed forces. The cost has been the political classes' loss of control over the armed corporations and the strong autonomy of the latter. Today, it must be acknowledged that the armed forces not only discuss the subject of war but also make the final decisions. Their autonomy, though not desired, is a fact. And it is only on the basis of the acknowledgment of this point (that is, that the armed forces are a political actor with a voice and doctrine of its own—an actor accustomed to a sphere of decision and autonomy) that the political classes will be able to regain a role in determining the purpose of the military corporation.

The liberal doctrine that shapes the thought of most members of Latin America's political communities tends to be "naturally" antimilitarist. The autonomous armed corporations of the region, on the contrary, only begrudgingly accept liberal principles. Insisting on relationships between the state and the armed forces based on those in advanced countries, and leaving the discussion of new issues in the hands of the armed forces alone, leads to the strengthening of the tendency toward segmentation and autonomization of the armed forces.

Within this framework, the option for democracy begins with this definition of the armed forces' mission. The military corporations, as well as the majority of the political class, perceive an unlimited stock of ideologies, doctrines, institutional arrangements, and modes of political action. In a political culture shaped by the Christian inheritance and the contradictory subsequent jus-naturalist contributions—as well as by the rationalist Enlightenment—the supply of ideologies, institutional arrangements, and modes of political action that are perceived as existent tends to become polarized. The military corporation, through the constant exercise of violence (or threat of violence), has tended toward one extreme of these perceptions.

The majority of the Latin American armed forces reject conceptions regarding class struggle and socialist doctrines. On the other hand, the alternative is not as clear with regard to the predominant socioeconomic form, the forms of the state, the social policies desired, elite or mass politics and the ways to implement them, and the types of institutional arrangements. There are various possible combinations (as indicated in table 17–1), and there are various historical examples of options for nonpolar types.

The preference for democracy or dictatorship appears to be subordinated to a basic ideological option: rejection of class struggle and the doctrines associated with this conception. The democratic regime, on occasion, has been perceived by the military as permissive and, consequently, threatening. Its ability to facilitate development of positions that subvert order constitutes a potential doorway to socialism.

Nevertheless, all dictatorial forms tried must be implemented in the name of a democratic restoration, even if what is advocated is a contradictory form of nonliberal democracy. Attempting to get out of the democratic regime implies reestablishing order while maintaining basic ideological options.[25] The association between democracy and capitalism and the West predominates among the polar options and is the only one, for the moment, that can give legitimacy to military intervention by the armed forces in the political system.

The Legitimacy of Military Intervention and the Option for Democracy

Underlying the problem of military intervention is the problem of its legitimacy. Normally, the armed forces act in the name of something. They cannot justify their actions as a political actor in and of themselves. In Latin America, their segmentation with respect to society and the state is based on the belief that the legitimacy of the armed forces as a political actor is founded on the nation. They exist because of and for the nation. It is to that mythical entity—the nation—that they owe "subordination and obedience."

Operationally, in a democracy, the armed forces should have to fulfill their duties of subordination and obedience to the officials regularly elected to represent the nation. In nondemocratic regimes, subordination is to the existing regime—to a party or to its chiefs, and the like. In the formally democratic regimes of Latin America, however, the armed forces have come to distrust those representatives of the will of the people and the state apparatus as a whole. The armed forces have faith only in themselves and in those they believe to be their immediate allies, both inside and outside the country.

Table 17–1
Alternative Political Cultures

	Type I	*Intermediate Types*	*Type II*
Ideological basis	Contractualism and/or Christianity	Agnosticism	Class Struggle Atheism Christianity
Ideology/doctrine	Liberalism	Anarchism Fascism	Socialism Communism
Political regime	Democracy	Dictatorship	Totalitarianism
Forms of political activity	Elite Mass	Corporatist Clientelist Populist Competitive	Elite Mass
Forms of state and social policies	Welfare state Assistive state of law		Social Authoritarian Assistive Authoritarian
Economic-social form	Market Capitalism		Central planning Socialism

A second substantial point of the discussion on civil–military relations would have to address the following questions:

Does the military have a legitimate right to intervene as a political actor in the political system?

Should this possibility be totally rejected?

If the possibility is accepted, when, how, and with what limitations is it acceptable?

Is it possible to translate it into norms?

If it is considered unacceptable, how can the armed forces be effectively subordinated, in view of their current segmentation with respect to society and their autonomy within the state?

These questions are not easily addressed. Military ideology necessarily has authoritarian contents. Greco-Christian concepts of honor, however, permit attenuation of the effects of those contents. But for this to happen, the single ideological corpus of the military forces can be broken down into many clearly demarcated branches.[26]

The professional image, based on esprit de corps, depends substantially on discipline and hierarchy. Discipline is the "soul" of the military organization; it sustains hierarchy and, with it, subordination. This necessarily leaves little room for dissent and, as in all totalitarian institutions,[27] favors authoritarian tendencies. Diverse forms of punishment are geared to the same end.[28] Discipline, hierarchy, and punishment permit—together with the criteria of technical competence,[29] the normal and normative management of an institution whose ultimate source of authority is the superior commander. In this sense, and in the final analysis, it is the corporative as well as the political ideology of those who may come to exercise such command that will determine the position of the military vis-à-vis the current political regime. Obviously, the basic requirement for this is the unity and verticalism of the military force.

The corporative ideology sought in the advanced countries of the West becomes intertwined with the professional self-image of the military expert. In almost all Latin American countries, however (with the exception of those that do not easily qualify as liberal-democratic—that is, Mexico and Nicaragua), the military does not feel a part of the state or the society as a subordinate entity. The armed forces perceive themselves to be above it—as its founders and guardians of the way of life and the life-styles of society and of the state.

In line with the histories of their countries—in which the creation of the state involved the armed forces in a protagonist role or as the "vertebrate" institution of a society lacking integration[30]—the armed forces cultivated a widely known tradition: supremacy of the warriors.

General von Seeckt, chief of the Reichswehr, considered this force "the pure image of the state," and Juan Domingo Perón sustained that the armed forces were the "synthesis of the nation" and belonged to it exclusively. Nineteenth-century Spain went so far as to legislate the armed forces' capacity as a "moderating power"—a balance between possible forces that could affect national integrity.[31]

As a corporation, the armed forces are an incarnation of legitimate order.[32] Their institutional ideology would have to (1) coincide with that of the political community in which they are erected; (2) represent, in their personnel, the majority of the sectors of civilian society; and (3) include a political culture that would converge with that of the entire political community.

This model describes what happens in the West or in countries where the military force of a dominating or single party predominates. The model is far from what happens in the majority of Latin American nations. In this region, the corporative ideology situates the armed organization above society and the political community, resulting in segmentation and autonomy.

One of the most marked manifestations of segmentation from society is the fact that the military corporation does not represent society either in the social origins of its privates and noncommissioned officers (who are normally from the poorly organized and indigent popular sectors) or in its officer corps (which tends to act as a caste, outside class lines). Perhaps the most visible expression of this phenomenon is the high level of internal recruitment in Latin America, especially in the dominant service, the army.

The political ideology of the armed forces has permitted the creation of "military parties." These military parties duplicate and are superimposed on those parties in the political community whose composition and orientation are basically civilian. Obviously, in speaking of military parties, we are using a metaphor. The armed forces and the services they comprise cannot establish parties, as the very existence of political parties implies negotiation, competition, and political play. If a military force is considered to be of the "ideal" North Atlantic type, those aspects would have to be denied to a great extent. However, as pointed out by Psellus in 1926, in referring to a European-Mediterranean case (Greece), this ideal type does not fit in many cases.[33] The existence of military parties can manifest itself in diverse forms. On the basis of the words of Juan Domingo Perón, Rouquié referred to their existence in the Argentine case and later extended his treatment to other Latin American countries.[34] I myself have worked with the concept in referring to the existence of a single military party in Uruguay.[35]

Military parties can be purely corporative or they can have explicit or tacit allies outside the military sphere. There can be one or more than one. In some cases, the action of a military leader or of a group has resulted in the formation of "classical" parties, such as the Revolutionary Democratic Party (PDR) in Panama, the Christian National Party (PCN) in El Salvador, the Independent Democratic Party (PID) in Guatemala, and National Renewal Alliance (ARENA) in Brazil. In other countries, allied forces have appeared, such as the Partido Nacional of the 1970s in Honduras and the Partido Reformista de República Dominicana of the 1960s and the 1970s. In others still, military actions have mobilized party factions, as in Uruguay from 1973 to 1984. On other occasions, military leaders have controlled traditional parties, and the parties have identified with the preaching of those leaders—as was the case of the Partido Liberal in Nicaragua, controlled by the Somoza family, and the Partido Colorado in Paraguay, under the control of General Stroessner.

Another traditional variant is the formation of parties by military leaders who use their preeminent position in the military corporation—such as the CAN in Guatemala, controlled by General Arena; the National Popular Alliance (ANAPO) of Rojas Pinilla in Colombia; and the phenomenon identified by the name of the leader, such as Peronism in Argentina and Odriism in Peru.

But there is another, more interesting case—that in which the corporation, even if it has civilian allies, reserves for itself a dominant area in political decision making and, though not constituting a classical party organization, acts as if it were one. Diverse opinions and the necessity of negotiating, rather than merely commanding, occur in such a case. When these activities are carried out substantially by active members of the military corporation and the civilian allies take on a subordinate nature, we speak of the appearance of parties or of a military party.

This accentuates the divergence between the political system and the armed forces and the segmentation between society and the military. Constructing or reconstructing democracy requires closing that gap.

The following affirmation may be paradoxical, but I propose it as a route to be explored. The armed forces, which are antidemocratic (given their organizational form and the effects of a historical tradition that reinforced those characteristics) and antiliberal, can come to be partners and trustees of a process of construction or reconstruction of democracies in the countries of Latin America. Keeping in mind our argument with regard to the permanence of capitalism as the predominating socioeconomic form in Latin America, on the one hand, and the identification with the West and its democratic-liberal tradition on the other, the armed forces can ultimately achieve a negative integration. Without abandoning their corporative ideology in the discursive aspects, military organizations can support democratic regimes in practice.

In Latin America, the military organization is unlikely to accept a change in its model of socialization and its internal authoritarian norms. To do so implies a confrontation and a reinforcement of the perceptions of threat to the corporation.

On the other hand, the armed forces can accept that their political ideology tends to converge with that of the majority of society. The countries of the Southern Cone and Brazil do not appear to run the risk of new corporative intervention by the armed forces, as long as the polyarchical game is maintained and each political actor respects the tacit agreement on the current socioeconomic and political system. This implies that opponents must act within clearly visible bounds of loyalty. The emergence of situations in which serious threats are perceived must not be permitted. The armed forces are especially sensitive to what can be perceived as a threat aimed directly at the corporation.[36]

The process can be facilitated if the political actor situated at the other ideological extreme also accepts involvement in a process of negative integration. The basis of the process of integration of social democracy in the political system has been the acceptance of the capitalist system and polyarchical competition.[37]

The social pacts translated into practice the acceptance of capitalism by leftist social movements, complemented by active intervention in the political struggle as competitors for office among the majorities. Social confrontation in Europe has shrunk as the negative integration of the Left has grown. Some of the Latin American Lefts—especially those of the Southern Cone, made up of urban, educated militants—suffered heavy defeats during the revolutionary attempts of the 1960s and 1970s. Many of the movements, including some Communist parties, are now trying forms of negative integration.[38]

A process of this sort can favor the possibilities of negative integration of the armed forces. The idea would be to try to reach a tacit pact of support for the democratic regime. It would also favor those who, within each armed corporation, defend the ideological convergence of the military force and a democratic regime.

At a first stage, this type of agreement could be conceived only with a heavily rational content, in a search for mutual convenience between partners who do not place much trust in one another. But its affirmation would depend on a stronger ethical-political commitment.

Only belief in a myth can ensure a convergence between the armed forces and the political system as a whole. The attempt to reconstruct democracy implies having a myth, and thus far, not much progress has been made along that line. If this does not happen, the swing of the pendulum may lead to the rapid rebirth of military authoritarianism. And it may also lead to polar confrontations that exclude democratic actors from the political community, as happened in Latin America in the 1970s.

This argumentation would seem to reach a somewhat pessimistic point. But unless we are willing to accept (1) that social change is possible only if the current order is destroyed and (2) that this change must be made through a revolution, costly in social terms and bloody, given that it implies the destruction of the existing armed forces—propositions that, at this point, do not seem to be accepted either by the political elites or by the majority of societies in Latin America—then it would seem that the route outlined here could be followed in the region. This applies especially to those countries in which a sizable nucleus of the civilian population has reached a quality of life perceived as acceptable and does not want to risk what has been attained thus far.

Notes

1. Arturo Valenzuela and Pamela Constable, "The Chilean Armed Forces," *Harvard International Review* 8, no. 6 (1986): 25–28.
2. Finer's classic book is the best example of this current. Samuel E. Finer, *The Man on Horseback: The Role of the Military in Politics* (London: Pall Mall Press, 1962).
3. Samuel P. Huntington, *The Soldier and the State: The Theory and Politics of Civil–Military Relations* (Cambridge, Mass.: Harvard University Press, 1957); and *Political Order in Changing Societies* (New Haven, Conn.: Yale University Press, 1968).
4. See Finer, *The Man on Horseback*; Alfred Stepan, *The Military in Politics: Changing Patterns in Brazil* (Princeton, N.J.: Princeton University Press, 1971), and Alfred Stepan, ed., *Authoritarian Brazil: Origins, Policies, Future* (New Haven, Conn.: Yale University Press, 1973).
5. Brazil still does not have a unique ministry of defense but, rather, has three ministries, one for each armed service. Only in 1986 did serious discussion of the creation of a ministry of defense begin in Peru.
6. Alfred Vagts, *History of Militarism: Romance and Realities of a Profession* (New York: Norton, 1959).
7. In Haiti, Duvalier's Ton-ton Macoutes were one of the few cases in which a paramilitary force successfully competed with a "regular" military force, but their degree of professionalization was low. Some countries have gendarmerie or rural or border guards—for example, Argentina (Gendarmeria Nacional) and Peru (Guardia Civil)—or military police (the Policia Militar of the Brazilian states or the Carabineros of Chile). Their position is that of subordinates or auxiliaries of the armed forces, not competitors. Except in the Chilean case, although its representative is an army general, the armed forces do not consider them members of the military corporation, nor do they attribute to them any legitimacy for assuming the role of political actor. The old National Guard, created under the French model of a nation at arms, and the state troopers of the United States, based on

the liberal conceptions of the right to resist oppression, did not survive the modernization of the regular forces at the end of the nineteenth century and the beginning of the twentieth century. The reserves—personnel without permanent military status who may eventually form part of the armed forces—never attained organizational or political relevance in Latin America. The attempts to create or maintain militia forces, based on the perception of belonging to a social class, failed. In Bolivia, after the 1952 revolution, the miner-campesino militia could not maintain itself. In 1955 in Argentina, presumed attempts to create a militia controlled by the Confederación General del Trabajo (CGT) contributed to the erosion of the armed forces' support of Perón. On that occasion, Perón acted like a military man, refusing to arm his supporters against the military rebellion. On the other hand, the Latin American armed forces have already experienced the use of auxiliary forces under their control. In Guatemala and Peru, social control in areas of conflict with guerrilla movements based on agitation and mobilization of the indigenous population is achieved largely through rival Indian groups controlled by the military force.

8. See Genaro Arriagada, *El Pensamiento Político de los Militares: Estudios Sobre Chile, Argentina, Brasil y Uruguay* (Santiago: CISEC, 1981); Jose Murilho de Carvalho, "Armed Forces and Politics in Brazil: 1930–1945," *Hispanic American Historical Review* 62 (1982): 193–223; Frederick M. Nunn, *Yesterday's Soldiers: European Military Professionalism in South America, 1890–1940* (Lincoln: University of Nebraska Press, 1983); Robert A. Potash, *The Army and Politics in Argentina, 1928–1945: Yrigoyen to Perón* (Stanford, Calif.: Stanford University Press, 1969); Carlos Real de Azua, "Ejércto y Política en el Uruguay, *Cuadernos de Marcha* 23 (1969); Victor Villanueva, *100 Años del Ejército Peruano: Frustraciones y Cambios* (Lima: Majia Baca, 1971); Angel Ziems, *El Gomecismo y la Formación del Ejército Nacional* (Caracas: Editorial del Ateneo de Caracas, 1979).

9. See Stepan, *The Military in Politics* and *Authoritarian Brazil*.

10. Michael Psellus, *Chonographia* (Paris: Rene, 1926) Alain Rouquié, *Les Partis Militaires au Brasil* (Paris: Du Soleil, 1980), and *La Politique de Mars: Les Processus Politiques Dans les Partis Militaires* (Paris: La Sycomore, 1981); Juan Rial, *Las FFAA: Soldados Políticos Garantes de la Democracia?* (Montevideo: EBO, 1986).

11. Genaro Arriagada, *Seguridad Nacional y Política* (Santiago: CISEC, 1976), and *El Pensamiento Político*; Joseph Comblin, *Pouvoir Militaire Dans L'Amerique Latine* (Paris: Pierre Delarges, 1977); Eugene K. Keefe, "National Security" in Richard F. Nyrop, ed., *Guatemala: A Country Study* (Washington, D.C.: U.S. Government Printing Office, 1984): Carina Perelli, *Someter o Convencer: El Discurso Militar en el Uruguay de la Transición y la Redemocratización* (Montevideo: EBO, 1987).

12. Guillermo O'Donnell, Philippe Schmitter, and Lawrence Whitehead, eds., *Transitions from Authoritarian Rule: Prospects for Democracy* (Baltimore: Johns Hopkins University Press, 1986).

13. The English-, Dutch-, and French-speaking countries located in Central America, the Caribbean, and northern South America do not have major ties to the other countries of Latin America, but they are neighbors and share a zone of conflict. Some of these new states may find themselves involved in internal wars

or internationalized wars. Their military forces, with their European roots, are closer to the patterns of action of the African nations that are decolonized in the 1960s and 1970s than to those of Latin America. For this reason, I leave them out of the analysis.

14. See the essay by Constantino Urcuyo in this volume (chapter 15).

15. See Arriagada, *El Pensamiento Político*, and Jack Child, *Unequal Alliance: The InterAmerican Military System, 1938–1978* (Boulder, Colo.: Westview Press, 1980), as well as works on geopolitics: Mario Travassos, *Projecao Continental do Brasil* (Sao Paulo: Companhia Editora Nacional, 1935); Jose Carlos Meira Mattos, *Brasil, Geopolitica e Destino* (Rio de Janeiro: Olympio, 1975); Golbery do Couto e Silva, *Geopolitica do Brasil* (Rio de Janeiro: Jose Olimpio, 1967), all in Brazil; and in Argentina, those by Juan E. Gugliamelli, *Geopolitica del Cono Sur* (Buenos Aires: El Cid Editor, 1979); Carlos J. Moneta, *Geopolitica y Politica del Poder en el Atlántico Sur* (Buenos Aires: Pleamar, 1983); and Osiris Villegas, *Tiempo Geopolítico Argentino*, (Buenos Aires: Pleamar, 1975).

16. Buenaventura Caviglia, *PsP. Psicopolítica: Verdadera Dimensión de la Guerra Subversiva* (Montevideo: Ediciones Azules, 1974); Alberto D. Faleroni, *De Rusia a Vietnam: Gran Estrategia Sovética-China* (Buenos Aires: Circulo Militar, 1969) and *La Guerra de la Cuarta Dimensión* (Buenos Aires: Rioplatense, 1976) among others.

17. See Arriagada, *El Pensamiento Político*; and Perelli, *Someter o Convencer.*

18. The transformation of Clausewitz's aphorism on the relationship between war and politics into that of the German, Marshall Ludendorff—who considered politics a form of war and the assumption of the concepts of "total war"—constitutes the strongest indicator of the degree of autonomy reached by the armed forces. See Erich Ludendorff, *La Guerra Total* (Buenos Aires: Pleamar, 1961).

19. See Arriagada, *Seguridad Nacional* and *El Pensamiento Político*, and Perelli, *Someter o Convencer.*

20. Ernesto Che Guevara, *Pasajes de la Guerra Revolucionaria* (Buenos Aires: n.p. 1961); Regis Debray, *Revolución en la Revolución* (Montevideo: Editorial Sandino, 1966).

21. See Arriagada, *El Pensamiento Político.*

22. See Perelli, *Someter o Convencer.*

23. See, for example, Caviglia, *Psicopolítica*, and Faleroni, *De Rusia a Vietnam*, 1969.

24. A review of the problem involving the uses of military force between Latin American states indicates that they almost exclusively relate to persistent border conflicts, such as that of Argentina and Chile over certain islands and canals in Tierra del Fuego, that of Ecuador and Peru in the Amazon, and that of Colombia and Venezuela in the area of Maracaibo. But they do not appear to lead to large-scale confrontations. The inheritance of previous wars maintains latent conflicts, such as that of Chile with Peru and Bolivia over the Atacama desert and northern ports or that of El Salvador with Honduras. Nevertheless, they appear to have been surmounted, as has the one that set Bolivia against Paraguay in the 1930s. Argentina is the only country that maintains an extracon-

tinental conflict and is also the only country that has recently been involved in a military confrontation of a classic type between states, even if it was limited to the scenario of the Malvinas. Nevertheless, for the moment, there does not appear to be a high risk of reinitiating hostilities with Great Britain. Some states, such as Uruguay, have signed very complete treaties that practically eliminate the possibility of border disputes. Others are close to this situation, although border control may create conflicts, even if they can be solved at police levels, such as in Mexico and Brazil. Even in Central America, war has more the character of a civil conflict than of a war between states, in spite of its internationalized nature. In view of these facts, the principal hypothesis of conflict for the military corporations of Latin America refers to an enemy located within their borders.

25. For example the Reichswehr, upon becoming the Wehrmacht, was a founding part of the Nazi regime. The force created to support a democratic regime in a capitalist society opted to support Nazism, upon perceiving that the socialist alternative would lead to anarchy and the dissolution of order as well as eliminating the corporation's monopoly in the use of violence. Subsequently, the relations between the Wehrmacht and the new corporation, the S.S., were also stormy, although this fact was partially concealed by the general situation arising from the great confrontation that began in 1939.

26. Morris Janowitz and Jacques van Doorn, eds., *On Military Ideology* (Rotterdam: Rotterdam University Press, 1971).

27. Erving Goffman, "Characteristics of Total Institutions," in M. R. Stein et al., eds. *Identity and Anxiety: Survival of the Person in Mass Society* (New York: Free Press, 1967) and *Internados* (Buenos Aires: Amorrortu, 1971).

28. Michel Foucault, *Vigilar y Castigar* (Mexico: Siglo XXI, 1983).

29. Alfred Stepan, *Rethinking Military Politics: Brazil and the Southern Cone* (Princeton, N.J.: Princeton University Press, 1987). Stepan insisted on the necessity of improving the professional competence of the armed forces. The inability shown by the Argentines in undertaking joint operations in the Malvinas conflict is an indicator of a loss of efficiency and efficacy. Political disputes among the services made adequate professional action impossible. Stepan also pointed out the interest of the Brazilian armed forces in improving their professional capacity, which had been neglected for the sake of the political administration of society from 1964–1984. In Brazil, the chief armed service, the army, has launched a plan for technological renovation and reorganization of its forces—Forca Terrestre (FT) 90, FT 2000, and FT 2015—following this route. In post-Franco Spain, the "backward" and "politicized" military also face a renovating organizational plan: META. This is part of a broader-reaching agreement between the Spanish political class and the commanders of the armed forces, with a view to a long-term reform, which is, in principle, expected to last some fifteen years. The agreement implies that regardless of who wins the successive elections, the agreement will be fulfilled. To date, I know of no similar proposals in other Latin American countries, particularly in some of the most relevant ones. In Argentina, however, there is a heavy controversy within the corporation itself as to the model of change that should be adopted. In that country, discussion takes place within the military corporation, and we should note the opposition between those who seek an armed force in which the attainment of a high technological level is the center of the

proposal and those who, without discarding the latter proposal, continue to believe that the key is the elaboration of an institutional doctrine based on the maintenance of the traditional values of honor, bravery, selflessness, and so forth, on the part of its members, who must address, at the same time, the hypotheses of external and internal conflict.

30. José Ortega y Gasset, *España Invertebrada* (Madrid: Revista de Occidente, 1952).

31. See Finer, *The Man on Horseback*.

32. See Gwyn Harries-Jenkins and Jacques van Doorn, eds., *The Military and the Problem of Legitimacy* (London: Sage, 1976).

33. Psellus, *Chonographia*, 1926.

34. See Alain Rouquié, *Poder Militar y Sociedad Política en la Argentina*, trans. Arturo Iglesias Echegaray, 2 vols. (Buenos Aires: Emecé, 1982).

35. See Rial, *Las FFAA*.

36. Responsibilities with regard to the past come into play here, especially those related to abuses of the human rights of persons affected by repression during dictatorial regimes. In Argentina, the armed forces accepted the trial of their high commands, the military juntas, with the exception of the last one. That was made possible by the adverse result of the war with Great Britain. There were also other trials, such as that of General Camps and his associates, for the proclaimed intention of Camps to obtain transcendence for his "diabolic banality." But other famous cases (such as that of Captain Astiz) could not be carried out because of the curb imposed by the corporation: the principle of due obedience. In April 1987, a movement within the army—led by the chief of one of the two commando companies that participated in the South Atlantic conflict, Lieutenant Colonel Aldo Rico—proposing the symbolic creation of the "new soldier" for the "new army," resulted in the sanctioning of a new law recognizing the principle of due obedience. This law covered, in fact, almost all those involved in these acts. Subsequently, all the "military parties" and some civilian allies have begun a campaign defending the armed forces' actions against subversives as of 1975. It is very possible that, given the agreement of various forces, this demand may be successful. But the situation is far from clear, and the struggle between the diverse military parties has not been surmounted. In Brazil, it has not been possible even to get this subject on the public agenda. Not much progress has been made in Guatemala, either. In Uruguay, it was the cause of inter- and intraparty confrontations, resolved by a law that prohibits investigation of the past, thereby protecting the entire military corporation. Although the armed forces supported the process of transition toward democracy, they did not accept any responsibility for the legitimacy of the actions undertaken during the 1970s. Behind the issue of human rights the military perceived an attempt by sectors of civilian society and of the political class to condemn them as an institution. The Uruguayan political class unskillfully allowed a subject that constitutes an agreement on fundamentals to become an inter- and intraparty game, which eroded the process of democratic reconstruction. In April 1989, a referendum was rejected to rescind the law approved in December 1986. Although it did not achieve its goals, it attested to a position contrary to the armed forces as an institution among vast sectors or

Uruguayan society, provoking greater segmentation of the armed forces with respect to society. The concept of "fundamentalism," very much in use in Argentina these days—especially after its use by President Alfonsín—is not a very happy one, as it conceals very different processes. In some cases, it refers to the existence of integralist currents; in others, it refers to the existence of integralist currents; in others, it refers to corporative sectors with a radical organic ideology. The Israelis, in condemning Eichmann, showed the importance of certain ethical positions in order to be able to consolidate a regime, even if the practical effects were only symbolic. In Argentina, this was the scope sought for the trials of the juntas, with the understanding that those trials did not put the entire armed coroporation in the defendant's chair. In circumstances where the military corporation was not totally defeated (Malvinas was only a partial episode, materially, and had greater repercussions in the ideological and political sphere of the armed forces) and where it perceives the issue of human rights abuses as an attempt to delegitimize the very existence of the institution, the armed forces expert pressure to prevent all types of trials. The recent processes in Argentina and Uruguay illustrate the errors that can be made as a result of not considering the diverse perceptions of the historical process on the part of the military elites and the political class. The latter consider the military to have been defeated—or at least that is what they transmit to their voters and adherents. On the other hand, the armed forces tend to believe that they have triumphed against internal enemies and that, thanks to these processes, party leaders can once again take up the daily administration of their countries. In the future, the same conflict may arise in Chile, although there, the personal leadership of Pinochet may attenuate the responsibilities to be attributed to the armed forces. On the other hand, the constant activities of the human rights movement have gathered significant evidence against members of the military corporation in that respect. It will depend on the ability of the political class to find an appropriate solution to this issue. Cardinal Silva Enriquez has already outlined a solution based on mutual pardon.

37. Robert A. Dahl, *Polyarchy: Participation and Opposition* (New Haven: Yale University Press, 1971) and Adam Przeworski, *Capitalism and Social Democracy* (London: Cambridge University Press 1985) and *Paper Stones* (Chicago: Chicago University Press, 1986).

38. Regarding the future of "negative integration," Chile and Uruguay are the key countries, given the weight of their Communist parties and allied sectors in the political system. In the other cases, the Left is either almost nonexistent, as in Argentina, or it takes on a nonclassical movementist character, as in Brazil (where there is another form of negative integration). The process of integration in the political system on the part of the Left in Venezuela and the attempts made by the Izquierda Unida in Peru are well known. Nevertheless, the Communist parties run the risk of losing space—in view of the presence of forces that manifestly consider themselves to be Social Democrats—thereby being forced to lose importance as legal parties loyal to the democratic regime. This situation could lead some of their internal currents to opt for radical antisystem postures.

Bibliography

Michael Gold
Juan Rial

General Civil–Military Relations

Abrahamson, Bengt. *Military Professionalism and Political Power.* Beverly Hills, Calif.: Sage, 1972.

Albertoni, Ettore A. *Dottrina della Classe Politica e Teoria delle Elite.* Milano: Giuffr, 1985.

Ambler, John Stewart. *Soldiers Against the State: The French Army in Politics.* Garden City, N.Y.: Doubleday, 1968.

Andreski, Stanislav. *Military Organization and Society.* London: Routledge and Kegan Paul, 1968.

Arriagada, Genaro. *Seguridad Nacional y Política.* Santiago: CISEC, 1976.

———. *El Pensamiento Político de los Militares: Estudios Sobre Chile, Argentina, Brasil y Uruguay.* Santiago: CISEC, 1981.

Aubrey, Crispin. *Who Is Watching You? Britain's Security Services and the Official Secrets Act.* Harmondsworth, England: Penguin, 1981.

Bañon, Rafael, and José Antonio Balmeda, eds. *La Institución Militar y el Estado Contemporáneo.* Madrid: Alianza, 1985.

Basiuk, Victor. "U.S. National Security and Third World Wars: Towards a Strategy for the 21st Century." *SWORD Papers* 4, February 23, 1987.

Bayliss, J, et al. *Contemporary Strategy: Theories and Policies.* New York: Holmes and Meier, 1975.

Baynes, J.C.M. *The Soldier in Modern Society.* London: Eyre Methuen, 1972.

Berghahan, Volker R. *Militarism: The History of an International Debate, 1861–1979.* London: Cambridge University Press, 1984.

Bermudez, Lilia. *Guerra de Baja Intensidad.* Mexico: Siglo XXI, 1987.

Bienen, Henry. "Armed Forces and National Modernization: Continuing the Debate." *Comparative Politics* 16, no. 1 (1983): 1–16.

Binnendijk, Hans, ed. *Authoritarian Regimes in Transition.* Washington, D.C.: U.S. Department of State, Foreign Service Institute, 1987.

Bonnet, Gabriel. *Las Fuerzas Insurreccionales y Revolucionarias.* Madrid: Ediciones Cid, 1967.

Brekinridge, Scott D. *The CIA and the US Intelligence System.* Boulder, Colo.: Westview Press, 1986.

Busquets, Juan. *El Militar de Carrera en España.* Barcelona: Ariel, 1967.

————. *Pronunciamientos y Golpes de Estado en España*. Barcelona: Planeta, 1981

Campbell, Donald T., and Thelma H. McCormack. "Military Experience and Attitudes Toward Authority." *American Journal of Sociology* 62 (1957): 482–90.

Clapham, Christopher, and George Philip. *The Political Dilemmas of Military Regimes*. Totowa, N.J.: Barnes and Noble, 1985.

Clausewitz, Carl von. *On War*. Ed. and trans. Michael Howard and Peter Paret. Princeton, N.J.: Princeton University Press, 1976.

Cochran, Charles L., ed. *Civil–Military Relations: Changing Concepts in the Seventies*. New York: Free Press, 1974.

Cotton, Charles, A. "Institutional and Occupational Values in Canada's Army." *Armed Forces and Society* 8 (1981): 99–110.

Crouch, Harold A. *The Army and Politics in Indonesia*. Ithaca, N.Y.: Cornell University Press, 1978.

De Benedetti, F., ed. *Il Potere Militare in Italia*. Bari, Italy: Laterza, 1971.

Debray, Regis. *Revolución en la Revolución*. Montevideo: Sandino, 1966.

Demeter, Karl. *The German Officer-Corps in Society and State*. New York: Praeger, 1965.

Diaz-Alegria, Manuel. *Ejército y Sociedad*. Madrid: Alianza, 1972.

Downes, Cathy J. "To Be or Not to Be a Profession: The Military Case." *Defense Analysis* 1 (1985): 147–71.

Earle, Edward Mead, ed. *Makers of Modern Strategy: Military Thought from Machiavelli to Hitler*. Princeton, N.J.: Princeton University Press, 1971.

Ellis, Joseph, and Robert Moore. *School for Soldiers: West Point and the Profession of Arms*. London: London University Press, 1974.

Evans, Peter B., Dietrich Rueschemeyer, and Theda Skocpol, eds. *Bringing the State Back In*. Cambridge: Cambridge University Press, 1985.

Faleroni, Alberto D. *La Guerra de la Cuarta Dimensión*. Buenos Aires: Rioplatense, 1976.

Fain, Tyrus G., ed. *The Intelligence Community: History, Organization and Issues*. New York: Bowker, 1977.

Faligot, Roger, and Pascal Krop. *La Piscine: Les Services Secrets Français, 1944–1984*. Paris: Du Soleil, 1985.

Feld, M. *The Structure of Violence: Armed Forces as Social Systems*. Beverly Hills, Calif.: Sage, 1977.

Ferrero, Guglielmo. *Militarism*. London: Ward, Lock, 1902.

Finer, Samuel E. *The Man on Horseback: The Role of the Military in Politics*. London: Pall Mall Press, 1962.

————. "The Retreat to the Barracks: Notes on the Practice and the Theory of Military Withdrawal From Seats of Power." *Third World Quarterly* 7, no. 1 (1985): 16–30.

Foucault, Michel. *Vigilar y Castigar*. Mexico: Siglo XXI, 1983.

Gamba, Virginia. *The Falklands/Malvinas War: A Model for North-South Crisis Prevention*. Boston: Allen and Unwin, 1987.

Garcia, Prudencio. *Ejército, Presente y Futuro: Un Ejército Polémico y Paz Internacional*. Madrid: Alianza, 1975.

Giradet, Raoul, ed. *La Crise Militaire Française, 1945–1962: Aspects Sociologiques et Ideologiques.* Paris: Armand Collin, 1964.

Golman, Nancy L., and David R. Segal, eds. *The Social Psychology of Military Service.* Beverly Hills, Calif.: Sage, 1976.

Goodpaster, Andrew J., et al. *Civil–Military Relations.* Washington, D.C.: American Enterprise Institute, 1977.

Goytisolo, Juan. *En Los Reinos de Taifa.* Barcelona: Seix Barral, 1986.

Granillo Fernandez, Abraham. *La Paz Comunista o la Continuación de la Guerra por Otros Medios.* Buenos Aires: Círculo Militar, 1970.

Harries-Jenkins, Gywn, and Charles Moskos. *Las Fuerzas Armadas y Sociedad.* Madrid: Alianza, 1981

Harries-Jenkins, Gwyn, and Jacques van Doorn, eds. *The Military and the Problem of Legitimacy.* London: Sage, 1976.

———, eds. *Armed Forces and the Welfare State.* London: MacMillan, 1982.

Hastings, Max, and Simon Jenkins. *The Battle for the Falklands.* London: Michael Joseph, 1983.

Heller, Claude, ed. *El Ejército Como Agente de Cambio Social.* Mexico: Fondo de Cultura Económica, 1979.

Herspring, Dale R., and Ivan Volgyes, eds. *Civil–Military Relations in Communist Systems.* Boulder, Colo.: Westview Press, 1978.

Higham, Robin. *The Military Intellectuals in Britain, 1918–1939.* New Brunswick, N.J.: Rutgers University Press, 1966.

Hopple, Gerald W., and Bruce Watson. *The Military Intelligence Community.* Boulder, Colo.: Westview Press, 1985.

Horne, Alistair. *A Savage War of Peace: Algeria, 1954–1962.* New York: Viking, 1977.

Huntington, Samuel P. *The Soldier and the State: The Theory and Politics of Civil–Military Relations.* Cambridge, Mass.: Harvard University Press, 1957.

———, ed. *Changing Patterns of Military Politics.* New York: Free Press, 1962.

———. *Political Order in Changing Societies.* New Haven, Conn.: Yale University Press, 1968.

Janowitz, Morris. *The Professional Soldier: A Social and Political Portrait.* New York: Free Press, 1960.

———. *The Military in the Political Development of New Nations: An Essay in Comparative Analysis.* Chicago: University of Chicago Press, 1964.

———. *Military Conflict: Essays in the International Analysis of War and Peace.* Beverly Hills, Calif.: Sage, 1975.

———. *Military Institutions and Coercion in the Developing Nations.* Chicago: University of Chicago Press, 1977.

———, ed. *Civil–Military Relations: Regional Perspectives.* Beverly Hills, Calif.: Sage, 1981.

Janowitz, Morris, and Jacques van Doorn, eds. *On Military Ideology.* Rotterdam: Rotterdam University Press, 1971.

———, eds. *On Military Intervention.* Rotterdam: Rotterdam University Press, 1971.

Kelleher, Catherine, ed. *Political-Military Systems: Comparative Perspectives.* Beverly Hills, Calif.: Sage, 1974.

Kennedy, Gavin. *The Military in the Third World.* London: Duckworth, 1974.

Klare, Michael T. *American Arms Supermarket.* Austin: University of Texas Press, 1984.

Klare, Michael T., and Peter Kornbluh, eds. *Low-Intensity Warfare: Counterinsurgency, Proinsurgency, and Antiterrorism in the Eighties.* New York: Pantheon, 1988.

Kolkowitz, Roman, and Andrezj Korbonski, eds. *Soldiers, Peasants, and Bureaucrats: Civil–Military Relations in Communist and Modernizing Societies.* London: Allen and Unwin, 1982.

Kolodziej, Edward A. *Making and Marketing Arms: The French Experience and Its Implications for the International System.* Princeton, N.J.: Princeton University Press, 1987.

Kourvetaris, George A., and Betty A. Dobratz, eds. *World Perspectives in the Sociology of the Military.* New Brunswick, N.J.: Transaction Books, 1977.

Lang, Kurt. *Military Institutions and the Sociology War: A Review of the Literature with Annotated Bibliography.* Beverly Hills, Calif.: Sage, 1972.

Lasswell, Harold. "The Garrison State." *American Journal of Sociology* 46 (1941): 455–68.

———. "The Garrison State and the Specialists on Violence." *American Journal of Sociology* 47 (1944): 643–49.

Lernoux, Penny. *Cry of the People: The Struggle for Human Rights in Latin America—The Catholic Church in Conflict with U.S. Policy.* New York: Penguin, 1982.

Liebknecht, Karl. *Militarism.* New York: Huebsch, 1917.

Lijphart, Arend. *Democracies: Patterns of Majoritarian and Consensus Government in Twenty-One Countries.* New Haven, Conn.: Yale University Press, 1988.

Lowenthal, Mark M. *U. S. Intelligence: Evolution and Anatomy.* New York: Praeger, 1984.

Ludendorff, Erich. *La Guerra Total.* Buenos Aires: Pleamar, 1961.

Lyons, Gene, and John Masland. *Education and Military Leadership.* Princeton, N.J.: Princeton University Press, 1959.

Machiavelli, Niccolo. *The Prince and The Discourses.* New York: Modern Library, 1950.

McWilliam, Wilson, C., ed. *Garrisons and Government: Politics and the Military in New States.* San Francisco: Chandler, 1967.

Mandeville, Lucien. "Syndicalism and the French Military System." *Armed Forces and Society* 2 (1976): 539–52.

Maniruzzaman, Talukder. *Military Withdrawal from Politics: A Comparative Study.* Cambridge, Mass.: Ballinger, 1987.

Martin, Michel Louis. *From Warrior to Manager: The French Military Establishment Since 1945.* Chapel Hill: University of North Carolina Press, 1981.

Mosca, Gaetano. *The Ruling Class.* Trans. H.D. Kahn, ed. and rev. A. Livingston. New York: McGraw-Hill, 1939.

Moskos, Charles. *The American Enlisted Man: The Rank and File in Today's Military.* New York: Russell Sage Foundation, 1970.

———. "From Institution to Occupation: Trends in Military Organization." *Armed Forces and Society* 4 (1978): 41–50.

Moskos, Charles, and Frank Wood. *The Military: More Than Just a Job.* Elmsford Park, N.Y.: Pergamon Press, 1987.

Nordlinger, Eric A. *Soldiers in Politics: Military Coups and Governments.* Englewood Cliffs, N.J.: Prentice-Hall, 1977.

Odetola, Theophilus. *Military Regimes and Development: A Comparative Analysis of African States.* London: Allen and Unwin, 1982.

Oseth, John M. *Regulating U.S. Intelligence Operations: A Study in Definition of the National Security Interest.* Lexington: University of Kentucky Press, 1985.

Paret, Peter. *French Revolutionary Warfare from Indochina to Algeria: The Analysis of a Political and Military Doctrine.* New York: Praeger, 1964.

———. *Clausewitz and the State.* New York: Oxford University Press, 1976.

———, ed. *Makers of Modern Strategy: From Machiavelli to the Nuclear Age.* Princeton, N.J.: Princeton University Press, 1986.

Pasquino, Gianfranco. "The Italian Army: Some Notes on Recruitment." *Armed Forces and Society* 2 (1976): 205–17.

Peri, Yoram. *Between Battles and Ballots: Israeli Military in Politics.* Cambridge: Cambridge University Press, 1983.

Perlmutter, Amos. *The Military and Politics in Modern Times.* New Haven, Conn.: Yale University Press, 1977.

———. "The Military in Modern Times: A Decade Later." *Journal of Strategic Studies* 9, no. 1 (1986): 5–15.

Perlmutter, Amos, and Valerie Plave Bennet, eds. *The Political Influence of the Military.* New Haven, Conn.: Yale University Press, 1980.

Richelson, Jeffrey T. *The United States Intelligence Community.* Cambridge, Mass.: Ballinger, 1985.

Rouquié, Alain. *La Politique de Mars: Les Processus Politiques dans les Partis Militaires.* Paris: La Sycomore, 1981.

Rowe, Peter, and Christopher Whelan. *Military Intervention in Democratic Societies.* London: Croom Helm, 1985.

Sarkesian, Sam. *The Professional Army Officer in Changing Society.* Chicago: Nelson-Hall, 1975.

———. *Beyond the Battlefield: The New Military Professionalism.* New York: Pergamon Press, 1981.

Schelling, Thomas C. *Arms and Influence.* New Haven, Conn.: Yale University Press, 1977.

———. *The Strategy of Conflict.* Cambridge, Mass.: Harvard University Press, 1977.

Simon, Sheldon W., ed. *The Military and Security in the Third World: Domestic and International Impacts.* Boulder, Colo.: Westview Press, 1978.

Snyder, G. *Deterrence and Defense: Towards a Theory of National Security.* Princeton, N.J.: Princeton University Press, 1961.

Stouffer, Samuel A., et al. *The American Soldier.* Princeton, N.J.: Princeton University Press, 1949.

Stover, William J. *Military Politics in Finland: The Development of Governmental Control over the Armed Forces.* Washington, D.C.: University Press of America, 1981.

Sun Tzu. *The Art of War.* Trans. Samuel B. Griffith. New York: Oxford University Press, 1971.

Thomas, Jean Pierre Huber, and Christian Rozenzveig. "French NCO's Career

Strategies and Attitudes." *Armed Forces and Society* 8 (1982): 275–301.

Trinquier, Roger. *La Guerra Moderna.* Buenos Aires: Rioplatense, 1973.

——. *Guerra, Subversion, Revolución.* Buenos Aires: Rioplatense, 1975.

Vagts, Alfred. *History of Militarism: Romance and Realities of a Profession.* New York: Norton, 1959.

van Doorn, Jacques, ed. *Armed Forces and Society.* The Hague: Mouton, 1968.

——, ed. *The Military Profession and Military Regimes.* The Hague: Mouton, 1969.

——, ed. *On Military Intervention.* Rotterdam: Rotterdam University Press, 1971.

——. *The Soldier and Social Change.* Beverly Hills, Calif.: Sage, 1975.

Van Gils, M.R., ed. *The Perceived Role of the Military.* Rotterdam: Rotterdam University Press, 1971.

Wayman, Frank Whelon. *Military Involvement in Politics: A Causal Model.* Beverly Hills, Calif.: Sage, 1975.

Welch, Claude E., ed. *Soldier and State in Africa.* Evanston, Ill.: Northwestern University Press, 1970.

Welch, Claude E., and Arthur Smith. *Military Role and Rule: Perspectives on Civil–Military Relations.* North Scituate, Mass.: Duxbury Press, 1974.

Welch, Claude E., Jr., ed. *Civilian Control of the Military: Theory and Cases from Developing Countries.* Albany: State University of New York Press, 1976.

——. "Civil–Military Relations: Perspectives from the Third World." *Armed Forces and Society* 11, no. 2 (1985): 183–98.

Woddis, Jack. *Armies and Politics.* London: Lawrence and Wishart, 1977.

Wolpin, Miles D. "Marx and Radical Militarism in the Developing Nations." *Armed Forces and Society* 4, no. 2 (1978): 245–64.

——. *Militarism and Social Revolution in the Third World.* Totowa, N.J.: Allanheld, Osmun, 1981.

——. *Militarization, Internal Repression and Social Welfare in the Third World.* London: Croom Helm, 1986.

Wright, Quincy. *The Study of War.* Chicago: University of Chicago Press, 1934.

Yarmolinsky, Adam. *The Military Establishment.* New York: Harper and Row, 1971.

General: Latin America

Barreiro, Julio. *Violencia y Política en América Latina.* Mexico: Siglo XXI, 1976.

Beltrán, Virgilio R., ed. *El Papel Político y Social de las FFAA en América Latina.* Caracas: Monte Avila, 1970.

Black, Jan Knippers. *Sentinels of Empire: The United States and Latin American Militarism.* New York: Greenwood Press, 1986.

Briano, Justo P. *Geopolítica y Geoestrategia Americana.* Buenos Aires: Pleamar, 1966.

Calvert, Peter. "Demilitarization in Latin America." *Third World Quarterly* 7, no. 1 (1985): 31–43.

Calvo, Roberto. *La Doctrina Militar de la Seguridad Nacional.* Caracas: Universidad Católica Andrés Bello, 1979.

Cammack, Paul. "Democratization: A Review of the Issues." *Bulletin of Latin American Research* 4, no. 2 (1985): 39–46.

Cammack, Paul, and Philip O'Brien, eds. *Generals in Retreat: The Crisis of Military Rule in Latin America.* Manchester, England: University of Manchester Press, 1985.

Carranza, Mario Esteban. *Fuerzas Armadas y Estado de Excepción en América Latina.* Mexico: Siglo XXI, 1978.

Caviglia, Buenaventura. *PsP. Psicopolitica: Verdadera Dimensión de la Guerra Subversiva.* Montevideo: Azules, 1974.

Chiavenato, Julio J. *Geopolitica, Arma do Fascismo.* Sao Paulo: Global, 1981.

Child, Jack. "La Paz Interamericana y el Sistema de Seguridad Después de la Crisis de las Malvinas/Falklands." *Geopolitica* 26 (1984): 23–34.

————. *Geopolitics and Conflict in South America: Quarrels Among Neighbors.* New York: Praeger, 1985.

————. "Interstate Conflict, Conflict Resolution, and Arms Transfers." *Latin American Research Review* 20, no. 2 (1985): 172–81.

————, ed. *Regional Cooperation for Development and the Peaceful Settlement of Disputes in Latin America.* Boston: Martinus Nijhoff, 1987.

————. *Antarctica and South American Geopolitics: Frozen Lebensraum.* New York: Praeger, 1988.

Child, John. *Unequal Alliance: The Interamerican Military System, 1938–1978.* Boulder, Colo.: Westview Press, 1980.

Coll, Alberto R., and Anthony C. Arend. *The Falklands War: Lessons for Strategy, Diplomacy and International Law.* Boston: Allen and Unwin, 1985.

Collier, David, ed. *The New Authoritarianism in Latin America.* Princeton, N.J.: Princeton University Press, 1979.

Comblin, Joseph. *Pouvoir Militaire dans l'Amerique Latine.* Paris: Pierre Delarges, 1977.

————. *La Doctrina de la Seguridad Nacional.* Santiago: Vicaria de la Solidaridad, 1979.

Crahan, Margaret E. *Human Rights and Politics in the Americas.* Washington, D.C.: Georgetown University Press, 1982.

Cuellar, Oscar. "Notes on Political Participation of the Military in Latin America." *International Journal of Politics* 1, no. 2–3 (1971): 110–58.

de Castro, Theresinha. "La Crisis de las Malvinas y sus Reflejos." *Geolitica* 9, no. 26 (1983): 29–34.

————. "O Atlántico Sur: Contexto Regional." *A Defesa Nacional* 714 (July 1984): 91–108.

Dominguez, Jorge I. "Los Conflictos Internacionales en América Latina y la Amenaza de Guerra." *Foro Internacional* 25, no. 1 (July–September 1984): 1–13.

Echeverri U., Alvaro. *El Poder y los Militares: Un Análisis de los Ejércitos del*

Continente y Colombia. Bogota: Fondo Editorial Suramerica, 1978.

El Control Político en el Cono Sur, 2nd ed. Mexico: Siglo XXI, 1980

Feit, Edward. *The Armed Bureaucrats: Military-Administrative Regimes and Political Development.* Boston: Houghton Mifflin, 1973.

Fishel, John T., and Edmund S. Cowan. "Civil–Military Operations and the War for Moral Legitimacy in Latin America." *SWORD Papers* 8, n.d.

Fishel, John T., and Courtney E. Prisk. "A Strategy for Legitimacy." *SWORD Papers,* 3, February 20, 1987.

Fitch, John Samuel. "The Political Impact of U.S. Military Aid to Latin America." *Armed Forces and Society* 5, no. 3 (1979): 360–86.

———. "Integrating the Military." *Harvard International Review* 8, no. 6 (1986): 18–19, 23–24, 28.

Fruhling, Hugo, Carlos Portales, and Augusto Varas. *Estado y Fuerzas Armadas.* Santiago: FLACSO, 1982.

Gallon Girardo, Gustavo. *La República de las Armas.* Bogota: Centro de Investigación y Educación Popular, 1981.

Gamba, Virginia."The Role of the Military in the Process of Transition." Paper presented at the seminar "Reinforcing Democracy in Latin America," Carter Center, Emory University, Atlanta, Georgia, November 1986.

Gonzalez Casanova, Pablo, ed. *No Intervención, Autodeterminación y Democracia en América Latina.* Mexico: Siglo XXI, 1983.

———. *Los Militares y la Política en América Latina.* Mexico: Océano, 1988.

Goodman, Louis W. "Civil–Military Relations." *Harvard International Review* 6 (1986): 13–16.

Grindel, Merilee S. "Civil–Military Relations and Budgetary Politics in Latin America." *Armed Forces and Society* 13, no. 2 (1987): 255–75.

Guevara, Ernesto. *Pasajes de la Guerra Revolucionaria.* Buenos Aires: n.p. 1961.

Hartlyn, Jonathan. "Military Governments and the Transition to Civilian Rule." *Journal of Interamerican Studies and World Affairs* 26, no. 2 (1984): 245–81.

Herrera Lasso, Luis. "Crecimiento Económico, Gasto Militar, Industria Armamentista y Transferencia de Armas en América Latina." *Foro Internacional* 23, no. 3 (January–March 1983): 242–65.

Herrick, Robert M., John T. Fishel, and Max Manwaring. "Operational Excellence (The Essence of Counterinsurgency)." *SWORD Papers* 7, July 22, 1987.

Herrick, Robert M., M.G. Manwaring, L. Duryea, J.T. Fishel, and S.C. Donehoo. "What Is to Be Done: Counterinsurgency." *SWORD Papers* 1, July 15, 1986.

Licastro, Julián. "Unión Latinoamericana de la Teoría a la Práctica." *Estudios Geopolíticos y Estratégicos* 9 (December 1983): 73–77.

Lipset, S.M., and A. Solari, eds. *Desarrollo en América Latina.* Buenos Aires: Paidós, 1967.

Johnson, John J. *The Military and Society in Latin America.* Stanford, Calif.: Stanford University Press, 1964.

Lagos, Humberto, and Arturo Chacón. *La Religión y las FFAA y de Orden.* Santiago: Rehue, 1986.

Lechner, Norbert, ed. *Estado y Política en América Latina.* Mexico: Siglo XXI, 1980.

Levy, Daniel. "Comparing Authoritarian Regimes in Latin America: Insights from Higher Education Policy." *Comparative Politics* 14, no. 1 (1981): 31–52.

Lieuwen, Robert. *Arms and Politics in Latin America.* New York: Council on Foreign Relations, 1961.

Linz, Juan J., and Alfred Stepan, eds. *The Breakdown of Democratic Regimes.* Baltimore: Johns Hopkins University Press, 1978.

Looney, Robert E. *The Political Economy of Latin American Defense Expenditures.* Lexington, Mass.: Lexington Books, 1986.

López, Jaime Pinzón, and Reynaldo Muñoz Cabrera. *América Latina: Militarismo, 1940–1975.* Bogota: Oveja Negra, 1983.

Loveman, Brian, and Thomas J. Davies, Jr. *The Politics of Antipolitics: The Military in Latin America.* Lincoln: University of Nebraska Press, 1978.

Lowenthal, Abraham F., and J. Samuel Fitch, eds. *Armies and Politics in Latin America.* New York: Holmes and Meier, 1986.

Lowy, Michael, and Eder Sader. "The Militarization of the State in Latin America." *Latin American Perspectives* 12, no. 4 (1985): 7–40.

Malloy, James M., ed. *Authoritarianism and Corporatism in Latin America.* London: Feffer and Simons, 1977.

Malloy, James M., and Mitchell A. Seligson, eds. *Authoritarians and Democrats: Regime Transition in Latin America.* Pittsburgh: University of Pittsburgh Press, 1987.

Manwaring, Max G., and Robert M. Herrick. "A Threat-Oriented Strategy for Conflict Control." *SWORD Papers* 2, November 6, 1986.

Marini, Alberto. *De Clausewitz a Mao Tse-Tung: La Guerra Subversiva y Revolucionaria.* Buenos Aires: Círculo Militar, 1968.

———. *Estrategia sin Tiempo: La Guerra Subversiva y Revolucionaria.* Buenos Aires: Círculo Militar, 1971.

Marini, José F. *Geopolítica Latinoamericana de Integración.* Buenos Aires: Escuela Superior de Guerra Aérea, 1987.

Markof, John, and Silvio R. Duncan Baretta. "What We Don't Know About Coups: Observations on Recent South American Politics." *Armed Forces and Society* 12, no. 2 (1986): 207–35.

Martin del Campo, Julio Labastida, ed. *Dictaduras y Dictadores.* Mexico: Siglo XXI, 1986.

Martz, John, ed. *U.S. Policy in Latin America.* Lincoln: University of Nebraska Press, 1988.

McAlister, Lylen, Anthony Maingot, and Robert A. Potash, eds. *The Military in Latin American Sociopolitical Evolution: Four Case Studies.* Washington, D.C.: Center for Research in Social Systems, 1970.

Mercado Jarrin, Edgardo. "Coyuntura Geopolítica Latinoamericana." *Estudios Geopolíticos y Estratégicos* 9 (December 1983): 5–20.

Mouzelis, Nicos. "On the Rise of Postwar Military Dictatorships: Argentina, Chile, Greece." *Comparative Studies in Society and History* 28, no. 1 (1986): 55–80.

Needler, Martin C. "The Military Withdrawal from Power in South America." *Armed Forces and Society* 6, no. 4 (1980): 614–24.

———. "Why the Military Leaves Power." *Harvard International Review* 8, no. 6

(1986): 10–12, 17.

Nordlinger, Eric A. *Soldiers in Politics: Military Coups and Governments.* Englewood Cliffs, N.J.: Prentice-Hall, 1977.

North, Lisa, "Civil–Military Relations in Argentina, Chile and Peru." Politics of Modernization Series No. 2. Berkeley, Calif.: Institute of International Studies, 1966.

Nunn, Frederick M. *Yesterday's Soldiers: European Military Professionalism in South America, 1890–1940.* Lincoln: University of Nebraska Press, 1983.

Nyrop, Richard F. *Guatemala: A Country Study.* Washington, D.C.: U.S. Government Printing Office, 1984.

O'Donnell, Guillermo. "Modernization and Bureaucratic-Authoritarianism: Studies in South American Politics." Berkeley, Calif.: Institute of International Studies, 1973.

O'Donnell, Guillermo, Philippe Schmitter, and Lawrence Whitehead, eds. *Transitions From Authoritarian Rule: Prospects for Democracy.* Baltimore: Johns Hopkins University Press, 1986.

Olmos, Mario E. *La Cooperación Argentina–Brazil: Núcleo Impulsor de la Integración Latinoamericana.* Buenos Aires: Instituto de Publicaciones Navales, 1986.

Pena, Alfredo. *Democracia y Golpe Militar.* Bogota: Carlos Valencia, 1979.

Pérez Llañez, María Angélica, ed. *Las Fuerzas Armadas en la Sociedad Civil.* Santiago: CISEC, 1978.

———. ed. *Subversión y Contrasubversión.* Santiago: CISEC, 1978.

Philip, George. "Autoritarismo Militar en América del Sur: Brasil, Chile, Uruguay y Argentina." *Foro Internacional* 25 (1984): 57–76.

———. *The Military in South American Politics.* London: Croom Helm, 1985.

Pittman, Howard T. *Geopolitics in the ABC Countries: A Comparison.* Ph.D. Dissertation, The American University, 1981.

Procesos de Reconciliación Nacional en América Latina. Bogota: Instituto de Estudios Liberales, 1986.

Quagliotti de Bellis, Bernardo. "Nacionalismo e Integración." *Geosur* 4 (December 1979).

Rattenbach, Benjamín. *El Sistema Social-Militar en la Sociedad Moderna.* Buenos Aires: Pleamar, 1972.

Reif, Linda L. "Seizing Control: Latin American Military Motives, Capabilities, and Risks." *Armed Forces and Society* 10, no. 4 (1984): 563–82.

Remmer, Karen L. "Redemocratization and the Impact of Authoritarian Rule in Latin America." *Comparative Politics* 17, no. 3 (1985): 253–75.

Richards, Gordon. "Stabilization Crises and the Breakdown of Military Authoritarianism in Latin America." *Comparative Political Studies* 18, no. 4 (1986): 449–85.

Ropp, Steve C. *Panamerican Politics: From Guarded Nation to National Guard.* New York: Praeger, 1982.

Rouquié, Alain. *El Estado Militar en América Latina.* Trans. Daniel Zadunaisky. Mexico: Siglo XXI, 1984.

Rouquié, Alain, and Jorge Schvarzer, eds. *Cómo Renacen las Democracias?* Buenos Aires: Emecé, 1985.

Sandoval, Isaac. *Las Crisis Políticas Latinoamericanas y el Militarismo.* Mexico: Siglo XXI, 1979.

Santos, Juan Manuel et al. *Seguridad Nacional y Bien Común.* Santiago: CISEC, 1978.

Schmitter, Philippe, ed. *Military Rule in Latin America.* Beverly Hills, Calif.: Sage, 1973.

Schoultz, Lars. *National Security and United States Policy Toward Latin America.* Princeton, N.J.: Princeton University Press, 1987.

Tiano, Susan. "Authoritarianism and Political Culture in Argentina and Chile in the Mid-1960's." *Latin American Research Review* 21, no. 1 (1986): 73–98.

Varas, Augusto, ed. *Transición a la Democracia: América Latina y Chile.* Ainavillo, Chile: ACHIP, 1984.

———. *Militarization and the International Arms Race in Latin America.* Boulder, Colo.: Westview Press, 1985.

———. ed. *La Autonomía Militar en América Latina.* Caracas: Nueva Sociedad, 1988.

———. *La Política de las Armas en América Latina.* Santiago: FLACSO, 1988.

Vasconi, Tomás Amadeo. *Gran Capital y Militarización en América Latina.* Mexico: Era, 1978.

Veliz, Claudio, ed. *The Politics of Conformity in Latin America.* Oxford: Oxford University Press, 1967.

Villegas, Osiris. *Guerra Revolucionaria Comunista.* Buenos Aires: Círculo Militar, 1962.

Wesson, Robert, ed. *New Military Politics in Latin America.* New York: Praeger, 1982.

———, ed. *The Latin American Military Institution.* New York: Praeger, 1986.

Wiarda, Howard J. "The Military and Democracy." *Harvard International Review* 8, no. 6 (1986), 18–19, 23–24, 28.

Wolpin, Miles. "Military Radicalism in Latin America." *Journal of Latin American Studies and World Affairs* 23, no. 4 (1981), 395–428.

Mexico

Boils, Guillermo. *Los Militares y la Política en Mexico: 1915–1974.* Mexico: El Caballito, 1975.

Gutierrez Santos, Daniel. *Historia Militar de Mexico, 1325–1810.* Mexico: Ateneo, 1961.

León Turán, Jesús de. *El Ejército Mexicano.* Mexico: Secretaria de la Defensa Nacional, 1979.

Lozola, Jorge Alberto. *El Ejército Mexicano (1911–1965).* Mexico: El Colegio de Mexico, 1970.

Central America and the Caribbean

Aguilera Peralta, Gabriel. *La Integración Militar en Centro América.* San Jose, Costa Rica: INCEP, n.d.

Atkins, G. Pope. *Arms and Politics in the Dominican Republic.* Boulder, Colo.: Westview Press, 1981.

Chinchilla Aguilar, Ernesto. *Formación y Desarrollo del Ejército de Guatemala.* Guatemala: Editorial del Ejército, 1964.

Etchison, Don L. *The United States and Militarism in Central America.* New York: Praeger, 1975.

Jenkins, Brian, and Cesar Sereseres. "U.S. Military Assistance and the Guatemalan Armed Forces." *Armed Forces and Society* 3 (1977): 575–94.

Pereira, Renato. *Panamá: Fuerzas Armadas y Política.* Panama: Nueva Universidad, 1979.

Argentina

Aguiar, F.R., et al. *Operaciones Terrestres en las Islas Malvinas.* Buenos Aires: Círculo Militar, 1985.

Andrada, B.H. *Guerra Aérea en las Malvinas.* Buenos Aires: Emecé, 1983.

Atencio, Jorge. *Que es Geopolítica?* Buenos Aires: Pleamar, 1965.

Beltran, Virgilio R. "Political Transition in Argentina: 1982 to 1985." *Armed Forces and Society* 13, no. 2 (1987): 215–33.

Canton, Dario. *Military Interventions in Argentina: 1900–1966.* Buenos Aires: Instituto Torcuato di Tella, 1967.

———. *La Política de los Militares Argentinos.* Buenos Aires: Del Instituto, 1971.

Cardoso, Oscar Raul, Ricardo Kirschbaum, and Eduardo van der Kooy. *Malvinas: La Trama Secreta.* Buenos Aires: Sudamericana/Planeta, 1983.

Ceresole, Norberto. *1988: Crisis Militar Argentina.* Buenos Aires: Instituto Latinoamericano de Cooperación Technológica y Relaciones Internacionales, 1988.

Comisión Nacional Sobre la Desaparición de Personas. *Nunca Más: Informe de la Comisión Nacional Sobre la Desaparición de Personas.* Buenos Aires: Eudeba, 1984.

Congrains, Martin. *Guerra en el Cono Sur.* Lima: Ecoma, 1979.

Cortese, Eriberto. "La Argentina: País Geopolíticamente Agredido." *Geopolitica* 21 (May 1981): 47–50.

Díaz Bessone, Ramón Genaro. *Guerra Revolucionaria en la Argentina (1959–1978).* Buenos Aires: Fraterna, 1986.

Díaz Loza, Florentino. *Doctrina Militar del Ejército.* Buenos Aires: Peña Lillo, 1975.

Escudé, Carlos. *La Argentina: Paria Internacional?* Buenos Aires: Belgrano, 1984.

Fink, Andrés. *Los Gobiernos de Facto ante el Derecho y ante la Circunstancia Política.* Buenos Aires: Depalma, 1984.

Fontana, Andrés. *Fuerzas Armadas, Partidos Políticos y Transición a la Democracia en Argentina.* Buenos Aires: Estudios CEDES, 1984.

———. "Fuerzas Armadas, Partidos Políticos y Transición a la Democracia en Argentina: 1981–1982." Kellogg Institute Working Paper No. 28. South Bend, Ind.: University of Notre Dame, 1984.

Fraga, Rosendo Maria. *Ejército:Del Escarnio al Poder (1973–1976)*. Buenos Aires: Sudamericana/Planeta, 1988.

Gamba, Virginia. *Estrategia, Intervención y Crísis*. Buenos Aires: Sudamericana, 1985.

Gobbi, Hugo G. "Problemas Australes Argentino–Chilenos." *Estrategia* 48 (September–October 1977): 27–36.

Goldwert, Merwin. *Democracy, Militarism, and Nationalism in Argentina, 1930–1966*. Austin: University of Texas Press, 1972.

Graham-Yooll, Andrew. "Argentina: The State of Transition, 1983–85." *Third World Quarterly* 7, no. 3 (1985): 573–93.

Gualco, Jorge Nelson. *Cono Sur: Elección de un Destino*. Buenos Aires: Fabril, 1972.

Gugliamelli, Juan E. "Y Si Brasil Fabrica la Bomba Atómica?" *Estrategia* 34–35 (May–August 1975): 5–21.

———. "Argentina–Brasil: Enfrentaminento o Alianza para la Liberación?" *Estrategia* 36 (September–October 1975): 1–29.

———, ed. *El Conflicto del Beagle*. Buenos Aires: El Cid, 1978.

———. "Islas Malvinas. Exigir Definiciones." *Estrategia* 67–68 (November 1980–February 1981): 5–17.

Hodges, Donald C. *Argentina, 1943–1987: The National Revolution and Resistance*, rev. ed. Albuquerque: University of New Mexico Press, 1988.

Imaz, José Luis. *Los Que Mandan*. Buenos Aires: Eudeba, 1964.

Leal, Jorge. "La Antártida Sudamericana y Latinoamericana." *Revista Militar* 711 (July–December 1983): 14–17.

Leoni Houssay, Luis Alberto. "Debemos Continuar la Guerra contra Gran Bretaña?" *Revista de Temas Militares* 7 (July–September 1983): 13–25.

———. "Pinochet: El Fuhrer Sudamericano." *Revista de Temas Militares* (September 1984): 5–20.

Luna, Félix. *De Perón a Lanusse*. Buenos Aires: Planeta, 1972.

Milenky, Edward S. *Argentina's Foreign Policies*. Boulder, Colo.: Westview Press, 1978.

———. "Arms Production and National Security in Argentina." *Journal of Interamerican Studies and World Affairs* 22, no. 3 (August 1980): 267–88.

Moneta, Carlos. "Las Fuerzas Armadas y el Conflicto del las Islas Malvinas: Su Importancia en la Política Argentina y Su Marco Regional." *Foro Internacional* 23, no. 3 (January–March 1983): 266–86.

———. "Armed Forces and Democratic Government in Argentina: Towards a New Civilian–Military Relationship." Paper presented at a conference on the transition from military to civilian rule in South America, Columbia, South Carolina, March 22–27, 1987.

———. "América Latina y la Antártida: Posibilidades de Cooperación Intralatinoamericana." *Opciones* 12 (September–December 1987): 25–33.

Moneta, Carlos J., Ernesto López, and Aníbal Romero. *La Reforma Militar*. Buenos Aires: Legasa, 1985.

Moro, Rubén O. *La Guerra Inaudita: Historia del Conflicto del Atlántico Sur*. Buenos Aires: Pleamar, 1985.

Most, Benjamin A. "Authoritarianism and the Growth of the State in Latin America: An Assessment of Their Impacts on Argentine Public Policy, 1930–1970." *Comparative Political Studies* 13, no. 2 (July 1980): 173–203.

Munck, Ronaldo. "Democratization and Demilitarization in Argentina, 1982–1985." *Bulletin of Latin American Research* 4, no. 2 (1985): 85–93.

———. "The 'Modern' Military Dictatorship in Latin America: The Case of Argentina (1976–1982)." *Latin American Perspectives* 47, no. 4 (1985): 41–74.

O'Donnell, Guillermo. *El Estado Burocrático-Autoritario, 1966–1973: Triunfos, Derrotas y Crísis.* Buenos Aires: Belgrano, 1982.

Orsolini, Mario Horacio. *La Crísis del Ejército.* Buenos Aires: Arayú.

Perina, Rubén M. *Onganía, Levingston, Lanusse: Los Militares en la Política Argentina.* Buenos Aires: Belgrano, 1983.

Pétric, Antonio. *Así Sangraba la Argentina: Salustre, Quijada, Larrabure.* Buenos Aires: Depalma, 1980.

Philip, George. "The Fall of the Argentine Military." *Third World Quarterly* 6, no. 3 (1984): 624–37.

Pion-Berlin, David. "The Fall of Military Rule in Argentina: 1976–1983." *Journal of Interamerican Studies and World Affairs* 27 (1985): 55–76.

Poneman, Daniel. *Argentina: Democracy on Trial.* New York: Paragon House, 1987.

Potash, Robert A. *The Army and Politics in Argentina, 1928–1945: Yrigoyen to Perón.* Stanford, Calif.: Stanford University Press, 1969.

———. *The Army and Politics in Argentina, 1945–1962: Perón to Frondizi.* Stanford, Calif.: Stanford University Press, 1980.

Quinterno, Carlos Alberto. *Militares y Populismo (La Crísis Argentina Desde 1966 Hasta 1976).* Buenos Aires: Temas Contemporáneos, 1978.

Ramos, Jorge Abelardo. *Historia Política del Ejército Argentino.* Buenos Aires: Roncagua, 1973.

Ranis, Peter, "Deadly Tango: Populism and Military Authoritarianism in Argentina." *Latin American Research Review* 21, no. 1 (1986): 149–65.

Rodriguez, Leopoldo F. "Fuerzas Armadas en Argentina." *Geosur* 7, no. 75–76 (July–August 1986): 2–48.

Rojas, Isaac. *La Argentina en el Beagle y Atlántico Sur.* Buenos Aires: Codex, 1978.

Roth, Roberto. *Los Años de Onganía.* Buenos Aires: La Campana, 1980.

Rouquié, Alain. "Military Allegiance and Political Control of the Army During the Peronist Regime (1946–1955)." *International Journal of Politics* 1, no. 2–3 (1971): 164–95.

———, ed. *Argentina, Hoy.* Buenos Aires: Emecé, 1982.

———. *Poder Militar y Sociedad Política en la Argentina*, 2 vols., trans. Arturo Iglesias Echegaray. Buenos Aires: Emecé, 1982.

Ruggeri, Andrés. "Canal de Beagle: Algunas Reflexiones Sobre el Laudo Arbitral." *Estrategia* 45 (March 1977): 48–61.

Ruiz Moreno, Isidoro J. *Comandos en Acción: El Ejército en Malvinas.* Buenos Aires: Emecé, 1986.

Salduna, Horacio. *La Reforma Militar.* Buenos Aires: El Cid, 1983.

San Martín, Salvador. *El Poder Militar y la Nación.* Buenos Aires: Troquel, 1983.

Saravia, José Manuel. *Hacia la Salida*. Buenos Aires: Emecé, 1968.

Scenna, Miguel Angel. *Los Militares*. Buenos Aires: Belgrano, 1980.

Snow, Peter. *Political Forces in Argentina*, rev. ed. New York: Praeger, 1979.

Uriburu, Eduardo J. "El Plan Europa, el Ejército y Su Contribución a la Estrategia del Desarrollo." *Estrategia* 2 (July–August 1969): 15–22.

Vacs, Aldo Cesar. *Discreet Partners: Argentina and the USSR Since 1917*, Trans. Michael Joyce. Pittsburgh: University of Pittsburgh Press, 1984.

Varas, Augusto. "Democratización y Reforma Militar en la Argentina." *Documento de Trabajo* (FLACSO), 1986.

Villegas, Osiris. *Políticas y Estrategias para el Desarrollo Nacional*. Buenos Aires: Pleamar, 1969.

——. *Triunfo Geopolítico Argentino*. Buenos Aires, Pleamar, 1975.

——. *El Conflícto con Chile en la Región Austral*. Buenos Aires: Pleamar, 1978.

——. "Las Razones Aparentes y los Intereses Ocultos Tras la Actitud Británica." *Geopolítica* 24 (1982): 55.

Wynia, Gary. *Argentina; Illusions and Realities*. New York: Holmes and Meier, 1986.

Bolivia

Bravo Bravo, Luis. "Bolivia: Visión Personal de un Enigma Geopolítico." *Seguridad Nacional* 23 (1982): 25–44.

Prado Salmon, Gary. *Poder y FFAA, 1949–1982*. La Paz: Los Amigos del Libro, 1984.

Brazil

Arruda, Antonio de. *ESG: Historia de Sua Doutrina*. Rio de Janeiro: GRD, 1980.

Backheuser, Everardo. *A Geopolítica Geral e do Brasil*. Rio de Janeiro: Biblioteca do Exército, 1952.

Barros, Alexandre de Souza Costa. "The Brazilian Military: Professional Socialization, Political Performance and State Building." Ph.D. dissertation, University of Chicago, 1978.

——. "Back to the Barracks: An Option for the Brazilian Military?" *Third World Quarterly* 7, no. 1 (1985): 63–77.

Bruneau, Thomas C. "Consolidating Civilian Brazil." *Third World Quarterly* 7, no. 4 (1985): 973–87.

Campos Coelho, Edmundo. *Em Busca de Identidade: O Exército e a Política na Sociedade Brasileira*. Rio de Janeiro: Forense Universitaria, 1976.

Carvalho, Jose Murilho de. "Armed Forces and Politics in Brazil: 1930–1945." *Hispanic American Historical Review* 62 (1982): 193–223.

Castro Martinez, Pedro Fernando. *Fronteras Abiertas: Expansionismo y Geopolíti-*

ca en el Brasil Contemporáneo. Mexico: Siglo XXI, 1980.

Coelho, Edmundo Campos. *Em Busca de Identidade: O Ejercito e a Política na Sociedade Brasileira.* Rio de Janeiro: Forense-Universitaria, 1976.

Golbery do Couto e Silva, *Geopolítica do Brasil.* Rio de Janeiro: Editorial José Olympio, 1967.

Escola Superior de Guerra (ESG). *Doutrina Básica.* Rio de Janeiro: ESG, 1979.

———. *Complementos da Doutrina.* Rio de Janeiro: ESG, 1981.

———. *Fundamentos da Doutrina.* Rio de Janeiro: ESG, 1981.

Faoro, Raymundo. *Os Donos do Poder.* Porto Alegre, Brazil: Globo, 1976.

Ferreira Reis, Arthur Cezar. "Imperialistas ou Subimperialistas." *A Defesa Nacional* 71 (September 1984): 133–38.

Goncalves Caminha, Joao Carlos. "O Atlántico Sul e a Marinha do Brasil." *Revista Maritima Brasileira* (January–March 1986): 9–20.

Gurgel, Alfredo Amaral. *Seguranca e Democracia.* Rio de Janeiro: Olympio, 1975.

Hilton, Stanley. "The Brazilian Military: Changing Strategic Perceptions and the Question of Mission." *Armed Forces and Society* 13 (1987): 329–51.

Kelly, Philip L. "Avances Recientes de la Geopolítica del Brasil." *Geopolítica* 33 (1986): 63–77.

Lagda, Ana. *SNI: Como Nasceu, Como Fonciona.* Sao Paulo: Brasiliense, 1983.

Mainwaring, Scott. *The Catholic Church and Politics in Brazil, 1916–1985.* Stanford, Calif.: Stanford University Press, 1986.

Meira Mattos, Jose Carlos. *Brasil, Geopolítica e Destino.* Rio de Janeiro: Olympio, 1975.

Oliveira, Eliezer Rizzo de. *As Forcas Armadas: Política e Ideologia no Brasil (1964–69).* Petropolis, Brazil: Vozes, 1976.

———, ed. *Militares, Pensamento e Acao Política.* Campinas, Brazil: Papirus, 1987.

Quartim de Moraes, Joao, Wilma Peres Costa, and Eliezer Rizzo de Oliveira. *A Tutela Militar.* Sao Paulo: Vértice, 1987.

Rouquié, Alain. *Les Partis Militaires au Brasil.* Paris: Du Soleil, 1980.

Silva, Golbery do Couto e. *Geopolitica do Brasil.* Rio de Janeiro: Olympio, 1967.

———. *Conjuntura Política Nacional o Poder Executivo e Geopolitica do Brasil.* Rio de Janeiro: Olympio, 1981.

Skidmore, Thomas E. *De Getúlio a Castelo.* Rio de Janeiro: Artenova, 1975.

———. *The Politics of Military Rule in Brazil, 1964–1985.* Oxford: Oxford University Press, 1988.

Stepan, Alfred. *The Military in Politics: Changing Patterns in Brazil.* Princeton, N.J.: Princeton University Press, 1971.

———, ed. *Authoritarian Brazil: Origins, Policies, Future.* New Haven, Conn.: Yale University Press, 1973.

———. *Rethinking Military Politics: Brazil and the Southern Cone.* Princeton, N.J.: Princeton University Press, 1988.

Travassos, Mario. *Projecao Continental do Brasil.* Sao Paulo: Companhia Editora Nacional, 1935.

———. *Introducao e Geografia das Comunicaaes Brasileiras.* Rio de Janeiro: Olympio, 1942.

Werneck Sodré, Nelson. *Historia Militar do Brasil.* Rio de Janeiro: Editora Civilizacao Brasileira, 1968.

Chile

Arriagada, Genaro. *La Política Militar de Pinochet: 1973–1985.* Santiago: Salesianos, 1985.

Arzobispado de Santiago. *Dos Ensayos Sobre Seguridad Nacional.* Santiago: Vicaría de la Solidaridad, 1979.

Barros González, Guillermo. "El Arco de Scotia." *Revista de Marina* (Chile) 777 (1987): 159–65.

Blakemore, Harold. "Back to the Barracks: The Chilean Case." *Third World Quarterly* 7, no. 1 (1985): 44–62.

Buzeta, Oscar. *Chile Geopolítico: Presente y Futuro.* Santiago: CISEC, 1979.

Ghisolfo Araya, Francisco. "Conflicto Atlántico Sur: Reflexiones." *Revista de Marina* (Chile) 751 (1982): 717–721.

———. "Chile: Pais Atlántico." *Revista de Marina* (Chile) 757 (1982): 712–15.

Grugel, Jean. "Nationalist Movements and Fascist Ideology in Chile." *Bulletin of Latin American Research* 4, no. 2 (1985): 109–22.

Hormazábal, Manuel. *Chile: Una Patria Mutilada.* Santiago: Pacífico, 1969.

Ihl Clericus, Pablo. "Delimitación Natural entre el Océano Pacífico y el Atlántico." *Revista Geográfica de Chile* (Terra Australis) 9 (1953): 45–51.

Joxe, Alain. *Las Fuerzas Armadas en el Sistema Político Chileno.* Santiago: Universitaria, 1970.

Lagos, Humberto, and Arturo Chacón. *La Religión y las Fuerzas Armadas y de Orden.* Santiago: Rehue, 1986.

Merino, José T. "Actividades Soviéticas en el Mar de Chile." *Revista de Marina* (Chile) 777 (February 1987): 226–27.

Nunn, Frederick. *The Military in Chilean Politics: Essays on Civil–Military Relations, 1810–1973.* Albuquerque: University of New Mexico Press, 1976.

Pinochet, Augusto. *Geopolítica.* Santiago: Andrés Bello, 1974.

Smith, Brian H. *The Church and Politics in Chile.* Princeton, N.J. Princeton University Press, 1982.

Valdivieso, Favio. "Las Cancillerias y el Nuevo Conflícto Limítrofe Creado por Argentina." *Memorial del Ejército de Chile* 399 (1978): 42–46.

Valenzuela, Arturo, and Pamela Constable. "The Chilean Armed Forces." *Harvard International Review* 8, no. 6 (1986): 25–28.

Valenzuela, Samuel, and Arturo Valenzuela, eds. *Military Rule in Chile: Dictatorship and Opposition.* Baltimore: Johns Hopkins University Press, 1986.

Varas, Augusto and Felipe Aguero. *El Proyecto Político Militar.* Santiago: FLACSO, 1984.

Colombia

Behar, Olga. *Las Guerras de la Paz.* Bogota: Planeta Colombiana, 1985.

Bermúdez Rossi, Gonzalo. *El Poder Militar en Colombia: De la Colonia al Frente Nacional.* Bogota: Expresión, 1982.

Deas, Malcolm. "The Troubled Course of Colombian Peacemaking." *Third World Quarterly* 8, no. 2 (1986): 639–57.

Landazábal Reyes, Fernando. *Conflícto Social.* Medellín: Bedout, 1982.
——. *Páginas de Controversia.* Bogota: Bedout, 1983.
——. *El Precio de la Paz.* Bogota: Planeta, 1985.
——. *La Integración Nacional.* Bogota: Planeta, 1987.
Maullin, Richard. *Soldiers, Guerrillas, and Politics in Colombia.* Lexington, Mass.: Lexington Books, 1973.
Pinzón de Lewin, Patricia, ed. *La Oposición en Colombia: Algunas Bases para Su Discusión.* Bogota: Centro de Estudios Internacionales, 1986.
Ruhl, Mark J. *Colombia: Armed Forces and Society.* Syracuse, N.Y.: Syracuse University Prss, 1980.
——. "Civil–Military Rlations in Colombia." *Journal of Interamerican Studies and World Affairs* 23, no. 2 (1981): 123–46.

Ecuador

Corkill, David. "Democratic Politics in Ecuador, 1979–1984." *Bulletin of Latin American Research* 4, no. 2 (1985): 63–74.
Fitch, J. Samuel. *The Military Coup d'Etat as a Political Process: Ecuador, 1948–1966.* Baltimore: Johns Hopkins University Press, 1977.
——. "Class Structure, Populism, and the Armed Forces in Contemporary Ecuador." *Latin American Research Review* 19, no. 1 (1984): 270–74.
Isaacs, Anita. "From Military to Civilian Rule: Ecuador, 1972–1979." Ph.D. dissertation, University of Oxford, St. Anthony's College, 1985.
Pons Muzo, Gustavo. "Ecuador: Pueblo Engañado." *Estudios Geopoliticos y Estratégicos* 6 (April 1981): 34–39.
Sampedro, Francisco. *Del Amazonas en 1830 al Condor en 1981.* Quito: Quitoffset, n.d.
Varas, Augusto, and Fernanado Bustamante. *Fuerzas Armadas y Política en Ecuador.* Quito: Universidad Central del Ecuador, 1978.

Paraguay

Lezcano, Carlos Maria. "Fuerzas Armadas en Paraguay: Situación Actual y Perspectivas." Paper presented to the Congreso Latinoamericano de Sociologı;acutea, Rio de Janeiro, March 1986.

Peru

Angell, Allan. "El Gobierno Militar Peruano de 1968 a 1980: El Frascaso de la Revolucion Desde Arriba." *Foro Internacional* 25 (1984): 33–56.
Centro de Altos Estudios Militares. *Planteamientos Doctrinarios y Metodológicos de la Defensa Nacional.* Lima: CAEM, 1985.
Centro de Investigaciones Económicas y Sociales. *Las Malvinas: Conflícto Americano?* Lima: CIESUL, 1982.

Crabtree, John. "Peru: From Belaunde to Alan García." *Bulletin of Latin American Research* 4, no. 2 (1985): 75–83.

Einaudi Luigi. *The Peruvian Military: A Summary Political Analysis.* Santa Monica, Calif.: Rand, 1969.

Jaquette, Jane S., and Abraham F. Lowenthal. "The Peruvian Experiment in Retrospect." *World Politics* 39, no. 2 (1987): 280–96.

Lowenthal, Abraham F., ed. *The Peruvian Experiment: Continuity and Change Under Military Rule.* Princeton, N.J.: Princeton University Press, 1975.

McClintock, Cynthia, and Abraham Lowenthal, eds. *The Peruvian Experiment Reconsidered.* Princeton, N.J.: Princeton University Press, 1983.

Mercado Jarrín, Edgardo. *El Perú y la Antártida.* Lima: IPEGE, 1984.

Moncloa, Francisco. *Perú: Qué Pasó? (1968–1976).* Lima: Horizonte, 1977.

Nunn, Frderick. "Professional Militarism in Twentieth Century Peru: Historical and Theoretical Background to the Golpe de Estado of 1968." *Hispanic American Historical Review* 59 no. 3 (1979): 391–417.

Rodriguez Beruff, Jorge. *Los Militares y el Poder: Un Ensayo Sobre la Doctrina Militar en el Perú, 1948–1968.* Lima: Mosca Azul, 1983.

Scurrah, Martin J. "Military Reformism in Peru: Opening Pandora's Box." *Latin American Research Review* 21, no. 1 (1986): 244–57.

Solar, Francisco José del. *El Militarismo en el Perú.* Caracas: Solartre Libros, 1976.

Stepan, Alfred. *The State and Society: Peru in Comparative Perspective.* Princeton, N.J.: Princeton University Press, 1978.

Tuesta Soldevilla, Fernando. *Perú 1985: El Derrotero de Una Nueva Elección.* Lima: Centro de Investigación de la Universidad del Pacifico y Fundación Friedrich Ebert, 1986.

Villanueva, Victor. *El Militarismo en el Perú.* Lima: Scheuch, 1962.

———. *100 Años del Ejército Peruano: Frustraciones y Cambios.* Lima: Mejía Baca, 1971.

———. *El CAEM y la Revolución de la Fuerza Armada.* Lima: IEP, 1972.

Uruguay

Burgueño, Regino, and Juan José Pomoli. *La Experiencia Uruguaya.* Montevideo: Centro Militar, 1984.

Crawford, Leslie. "Por un Club Antártico Ibero Americano." *Geosur* 33 (1982): 34–43.

Finch, Henry. "Democratization in Uruguay." *Third World Quarterly* 7, no. 3 (1985): 594–609.

Junta de Comandantes en Jefe de las FFAA (JCJ). *Las FFAA al Pueblo Oriental.* Montevideo: JCJ, 1977.

———. *Testimonio de una Nación Agredida.* Montevideo: JCJ, 1978.

Methol Ferre, Alberto. *Geopolítica de la Cuenca del Plata: El Uruguay Como Problema.* Montevideo: Diálogo, 1967.

Perelli, Carina. *Someter o Convencer: El Discurso Militar en el Uruguay de la Transición y la Redemocratización.* Montevideo: EBO, 1987.

Perelli, Carina, and Juan Rial. *De Mitos y Memorias Políticas: La Represión, El*

Miedo y Después . . . Montevideo: EBO, 1986.

Quagliotti de Bellis, Bernardo. *Uruguay y su Espacio.* Montevideo: Geosur, 1979.

Ramirez, Gabriel. *Las FFAA Uruguayas y la Crísis Continental.* Montevideo: Tierra Nueva, 1972.

Rial, Juan. *Las FFAA: Soldados Políticos Garantes de la Democracia?* Montevideo: EBO, 1986.

Venezuela

Alvarez Cardier, Jorge. *La Guerra de las Malvinas: Enseñanzas para Venezuela.* Caracas: Enfoque, 1982.

Betancourt, Rómulo. *Respeto y Defensa del Orden Institucional.* Caracas: Divulgación y Ediciones Palacio Blanco, 1962.

———. *En Defensa del Sistema Democrático.* Caracas: Imprenta Nacional, 1963.

Bigler, Gene E. "Armed Forces' Professionalization and the Emergence of Civilian Control over the Military in Venezuela." Caracas: Instituto de Estudios Superiores de Administración, 1975 (mimeographed).

Blank, David Eugene. *Venezuela: Politics in a Petroleum Republic.* New York: Praeger, 1984.

Burggraaff, Winfield J. *The Venezuelan Armed Forces in Politics, 1935–1959.* Columbia: University of Missouri Press, 1972.

Bustamante, Fernando, and Carlos Portales. "La Venta de Aviones F-16 a Venezuela: Un Caso de Transferencia de Tecnología." Documento de Trabajo FLACSO 1988.

Ewell, Judith. *The Indictment of a Dictator.* College Station: Texas A&M University Press, 1981.

———. "The Development of a Venezuelan Geopolitical Analysis Since World War II." *Journal of Interamerican Studies and World Affairs* 24, no. 3 (August 1982): 295–316.

———. *Venezuela: A Century of Change.* Stanford, Calif.: Stanford University Press, 1984.

Karl, Terry Lynn. "Petroleum and Political Pacts: The Transition to Democracy in Venezuela." *Latin American Research Review* 22, no. 1 (1987): 63–94.

Levine, David H. "Transitions to Democracy: Are There Lessons from Venezuela?" *Bulletin of Latin American Research* 4, no. 2 (1985): 47–61.

Martz, John D., and D.J. Myers, eds. *Venezuela: The Democratic Experience.* New York: Praeger, 1977.

Rangel, José Vicente, et al. *Militares y Política (Una Polémica Inconclusa).* Caracas: Centauro, 1976.

Rangel Bourgoin, Luís Enrique. *Nosotros los Militares.* Caracas: Sol, 1983.

Romero, Aníbal, ed. *Seguridad, Defensa y Democracia.* Caracas: Equinoccio, 1980.

Salcedo-Bastardo, J.L., et al. *Tránsito de la Dictadura a la Democracia en Venezuela.* Caracas: Ariel, 1978.

Villabona Blanco, María Pilar. "Política y Elecciones en Venezuela." *Revista de*

Estudios Políticos (Spain) 53 (September–October 1986): 215–37.

Ziems, Angel. *El Gomecismo y la Formación del Ejército Nacional*. Caracas: Ateneo de Caracas, 1979.

Index

About the Contributors

Felipe Agüero, trained at the Catholic University of Chile and Duke University, has written on the role of the military in politics in Chile, Spain, and Venezuela.

Adolfo Aguilar Zinser is associate professor in the School of International Service at The American University. Mr. Aguilar served in the administration of Mexican president José Echeverria, directed the Institute for Advanced Study, CESTEEM, and headed the program on Central America for the Center for Research and Teaching in Economics in Mexico City. In 1987 and 1988 Mr. Aguilar was a senior associate of The Carnegie Endowment for International Peace in Washington, D.C.

Gabriel Aguilera is director of the Latin American Faculty of the Social Sciences Center in Guatemala City, Guatemala. Through 1988 Mr. Aguilera served as senior researcher in FLACSO's San Jose, Costa Rica headquarters.

Alexandre Barros, trained at the Catholic University of Rio de Janeiro and the University of Chicago and formerly a professor and senior researcher at the Instituto Universitario des Pesquisas de Rio de Janeiro, is a consultant in political risk analysis who has written widely on the Brazilian military.

Jack Child is professor in the department of language and foreign studies at The American University. The author of numerous books and articles on geopolitics in the western hemisphere, Dr. Child retired from the United States Army with the rank of colonel and currently conducts research on Antarctica.

John Samuel Fitch, professor of political science at the University of Colorado and director of its Center for Public Policy Research, has written widely on armies and politics in Latin America, focusing his field research on the military in Ecuador and in Argentina.

Virginia Gamba-Stonehouse, trained in strategic studies at the University of Strathclyde, Wales, has taught strategy at the high commands of the Army, Air Force, Navy, and Chancery in Argentina. Ms. Gamba-Stonehouse is currently carrying out research under the auspices of a MacArthur Foundation International Security Fellowship.

Richard Millett is Professor of History at the University of Southern Illinois, Edwardsville. Dr. Millett has published widely on politics and society in Central America including his *Guardians of the Dynasty: A History of the Nicaraguan Civil Guard.*

Carina Perelli is senior researcher at PEITHO Montevideo, Uruguay. Trained at the University of Grenoble, France, and at the University of Notre Dame, USA, Ms. Perelli is a political scientist focusing on ideology, the military, and society.

Maria Susana Ricci died in 1988. At the time of her death she was senior consultant and editor of the military magazine *Circulo Militar,* published by the army of Argentina.

Marcial Rubio Correa is professor of law at the Catholic University, Lima, Peru. Dr. Rubio is widely known for his expertise on the military and human rights in Peru.

Constantino Urcuyo is senior researcher at CIAPA in San Jose, Costa Rica. Trained in France, Dr. Urcuyo has written widely on Costa Rican and Central American politics and society.

Augusto Varas is a senior researcher at the Latin American Faculty of the Social Sciences in Santiago, Chile. Trained in the sociology department at Washington University in St. Louis, Dr. Varas has written widely on issues of war and peace and political society in Latin America.

Alfonso Yurrita, trained as an architect, has served on the faculty of Landivar University in Guatemala City, Guatemala, and is currently advisor of institutional development to the Minister of Defense of Guatemala.

About the Editors

Louis W. Goodman is dean of the School of International Service at the American University. Dr. Goodman has written widely on the impact of policies in developed nations on prospects for development in Latin America.

Johanna S. R. Mendelson, trained in history at Washington University in St. Louis and in law at The American University, is on the research faculty of the School of International Service at The American University and is an honors fellow in the Executive Office of Immigration Review at the United States Department of Justice.

Juan Rial, trained in history in Uruguay, senior researcher at PEITHO, serves as professor of political science in the School of Law and Social Sciences at the University of Uruguay. Dr. Rial has written widely on the military and politics focusing on Uruguay and the Southern Cone.

Senate Arms service Committee

Praetorium